Separate *and* Unequal

Separate *and* Unequal

PUBLIC SCHOOL CAMPAIGNS AND RACISM IN
THE SOUTHERN SEABOARD STATES 1901-1915

by Louis R. Harlan

Chapel Hill

THE UNIVERSITY OF NORTH CAROLINA PRESS

Copyright, 1958, by
The University of North Carolina Press

Manufactured in the United States of America

To my two children of school age,
Nat and Benny

Preface

PUBLIC EDUCATION always had many champions in the South from the time of Thomas Jefferson's forceful support of the idea in the eighteenth century. Later the state school systems established by Reconstruction governments persisted through the ensuing decades in spite of severe agricultural depression. In the early years of the twentieth century the slow growth of public schools was strongly affected by two significant factors. One of these was the southward flow of surplus capital from the industrial development in the Northeast along channels of philanthropy and business development. Also of great importance was the White Supremacy movement within the South, started in the nineties and beginning to solidify by the turn of the century into a system of laws and customs discriminating against Negroes. The impact of these two factors—Northern philanthropy and Southern racial views—on public education in the Southern seaboard states during the decade and a half after 1900 forms the central theme of the present study.

The Southern Education Board, a philanthropic and propaganda agency with which the study is much concerned, organized public school campaigns from Virginia to Texas, but its main energies were centered in the states examined here—four Southern states on the Atlantic seaboard, Virginia, North Carolina, South Carolina, and Georgia.

These states shared the features which made for unity in the South's diversity and set it apart from other regions: the hereditary curse of Negro slavery, the history of defeat and frustration, the colonial economy and attendant poverty, the fertility of its people and their continuous emigration, the color line hedged about by law and custom, the segregated school systems. Yet these Southern seaboard states did have a certain unity of their own. They were the oldest-settled Southern commonwealths, their denuded soil had borne more crops, been washed by more rains. Out of the eternal surplus of their population, more of their healthy adults had been drained off westward and northward for a longer time than in the newer Southern states. Geographically as well, these Southern seaboard states were homogeneous in a way that was important to their school systems. Each had all of the main elements of the "valley section": the tidewater or coastal plain, or simply low country in the South Carolina idiom, with swamps, cotton plantations, and Negro majorities; the Piedmont, full of small hills, small farms, small towns, small industries, cotton and tobacco; the eastern Appalachians, with marginal land, outside of a few valleys, and marginal whites. Public schools in each of these regions, transcending state boundaries, followed a distinctive pattern reflecting its economy and race relations. Florida has been excluded; although a seaboard state, it is not one of the older states and does not have this valley-section pattern. Alabama in many ways fits the seaboard pattern, as Horace M. Bond has shown, except for its late settlement and the Birmingham steel industry. Northward on the seaboard, Maryland differs from regions south of the Potomac in many obvious ways.

While the schools of lowland "black counties" differed markedly from those of the mountains and Piedmont, the states were the political units. Public schools were institutions of the states, and the educational reformers organized their campaigns within states. The state is, therefore, the unit of organization of this study. The delimitation in time to the period from 1901 to 1915 is not entirely arbitrary. These are the years when the Southern Education Board flourished. By 1915 the pattern of racial discrimination in public schools was rather complete. By that time Southern public support of white education was on a quite different basis from that in 1900. The terminal date of the study does not meet the full flood of wartime prosperity after 1915, nor the great migration of Negroes out of the South, nor the efforts of such agencies as the Rosenwald Foundation to modify the dismal design of the Southern Negro school. The dual significance of the period studied here is that the first vigorous, large-scale efforts were made by native Southerners to improve their schools according to standards prevailing among their Northern neighbors, and that at the same time the gap of discrimination widened between white and Negro, town and rural schools.

A rather long essay on sources has been supplied, but the reader should be forewarned about the unreliability of one source—educational statistics. The figures of the crusading educational propagandists have been used only rarely and with special caution. Wherever possible, the statistics of federal and state governments were used. Those of the United States Commissioner of Education, whose budget was too small for his task, were, in the period of this study, largely second-hand figures taken from the state educational reports. The federal commissioner's reports, though containing some incomplete, out-of-date, and interpolated statistics, have been used in cases where the published state reports lacked significant data on school population or Negro schools. Records from the United States Census Office on the ethnic composition of population and on wealth, debt, and taxation are subject to the inevitable minor errors of poorly trained census-takers. The state school reports have been used primarily for educational statistics. Often submitted by harassed teachers or careless local school officers, and compiled by an untrained clerk or two in the capital, these reports include manifest errors and omissions. The best that can be said is that they are usually more accurate than the federal reports based upon them. Using with caution what seemed to be the best educational statistics available, the author believes that the picture these statistics present of the Southern seaboard schools would not be changed substantially by more precise data.

The subject of this study is only indirectly related to the issues and problems involved in the federal Supreme Court decisions in the School Segregation Cases in 1954 and the desegregation movement of which they are a part. This is true for several reasons. Quantitative measurement of Negro and white educational opportunity has been used almost exclusively. What Theodore Brameld calls the "qualitative and immaterial" costs of racial discrimination are important to society and the courts, but their measurement is beyond the competence of the historian and the range of his material. Social psychologists and others are more competent than the writer for research in that area. This study rather thoroughly demonstrates that in the years following the *Plessy v. Ferguson* decision in 1896 the "thin disguise of 'equal accommodations'" did not deceive anyone. But the decision of 1954 was based upon evidence that "Separate educational facilities are inherently unequal" because of detrimental effects on colored children, and upon the principle that "in the field of public education the doctrine of separate but equal has no place." The present study elaborates upon the growth of inequality rather than separation, which had existed since Reconstruction years, and the relationship of inequality to the regional public school movement. This regional movement, which made spectacular improvements in white educational facilities through higher taxes and the fiscal savings of racial discrimination, is also a matter of importance to everybody in the region and the nation.

The Negro was certainly the central, though not the exclusive, theme in the history of Southern public education between 1900 and 1915. Perhaps the reader should, at the risk of tedium, have a statement of the assumptions which underlie the present treatment of the Negro theme. They seem to be five: (1) While the Negro child deserved no more consideration than the white child in public education, he had a right to expect just as much. (2) Scientific research indicates that group differences in innate intelligence and educability, if they exist at all, are insignificant as compared with individual differences and environmental influences. (3) Economic and institutional factors were of primary importance in the development of Southern public schools and the racial practices connected with them. (4) Despite the racial inequalities and the limitations of separate schooling as a means of "solving the race problem," improvement of white education in the South has been one of the means by which Negroes of the region may expect eventually to secure their heritage of human rights. (5) Education by itself, without other forms of action, including

Preface

intelligent protest, would never solve the major race problems; on the contrary public schools might inculcate orthodox racism, and sometimes have. The leaders of the Southern Education movement accepted three of these assumptions, had the doubts of their age about the second, and rejected the fifth. In substance, they argued that public education would increase the productivity and income of white Southerners and destroy the economic basis of racial discrimination. While this argument had some validity, it put too heavy a burden on one social institution. Social change depends on information, to be sure, but also on will and action.

I wish to acknowledge my indebtedness to the Ford Foundation for a grant under its program for assisting American university presses in the publication of works in the humanities and the social sciences.

I am in debt to a number of persons for the better points of this study:

Professor C. Vann Woodward of The Johns Hopkins University suggested the general topic, gave helpful advice on sources, and read some chapters as many as three times. Professor Nannie M. Tilley of East Texas State College gave me advice on three chapters at an early stage, arranged for my leaves of absence necessary for research, and made twenty pages of detailed criticism of the manuscript just before it went to the printer. I am indebted also to Professor Charles A. Barker and Professor Sidney Painter of The Johns Hopkins University, who read the manuscript and helped me to bring the subject into focus. Miss Catherine Neal drew the map in Chapter VI. Dr. David Campbell Butler, Miss Betsy McCampbell and my wife read the proof. Librarians and custodians of manuscripts at The Johns Hopkins University, East Texas State College, the University of North Carolina, and the Library of Congress gave indispensable technical assistance. Mrs. Martha Dodd Stern permitted my perusal of the William E. Dodd Papers in the Library of Congress. Personal encouragement from Dr. Philip G. Davidson, the late Dr. Frank L. Owsley, Allen Dorset Harlan, and particularly my wife sustained my efforts during critical times. Finally, this study would have been impossible without the late Charles W. Dabney, author of *Universal Education in the South* (2 vols., Chapel Hill, 1936), who deposited in the Southern Historical Collection of the University of North Carolina his voluminous collection of manuscripts on the Southern Education Board.

Louis R. Harlan

Contents

	Preface	vii
I.	The Uses of Adversity: An Introduction	3
II.	Seedtime: North Carolina in the Nineties	45
III.	The Southern Education Board: A Regional Approach to Public Education	75
IV.	North Carolina: A Schoolhouse a Day—for Whites	102
V.	Virginia: The Machine and the Schools	135
VI.	South Carolina: Inequality as a Higher Law	170
VII.	Georgia: Public Schools and the Urban-Rural Conflict	210
VIII.	Educational Expansion and the Context of Racism	248
	Essay on Sources	270
	Index	282

Separate *and* Unequal

CHAPTER I

The Uses of Adversity: An Introduction

INTRODUCTION of the Northeastern public school into the South was an important war aim of the North in the Civil War and found its place in the postwar Reconstruction program. The public school was to have a dual purpose—to stand *in loco parentis* for the freed Negro and to act as an entering wedge of the New Order, a means of bringing the conquered white people into ideological harmony with the victors. At the end of the tragic internecine conflict, the humanitarians sought to justify the breakdown of democracy and the resort to violence by a radical reconstruction of Southern society on the ruins of the slave-plantation economy. At the same time, during the war and the Reconstruction period, men moved by considerations of political and economic power were interested in harnessing the Industrial Revolution to reward their section and themselves. The Schoolma'am and the Carpetbagger rode into the South together, Yankees both, one to uplift, the other to exploit. Though the Carpetbagger often spoke of developing the country, he was primarily concerned with the opportunities available in a colonial area. The Northern teacher in the South, on the other hand, modeled her program after that of the Massachusetts town public school, which had developed in an area of high population density and expanding industry. The Schoolma'am's ideal, though not impossible, was difficult of attainment in the South.

It was clear by 1900, thirty years after the state school systems were created in the South, that the Massachusetts school existed nowhere in the region, except for white children in a handful of cities. Not even the American school system, a Southern Negro teacher told a federal investigating commission in 1901, existed in his county. "What is the American school system?" he asked. "When you have no schoolhouse, and when you have no teacher, why call it a school system? If you must take a little old, tumble-down log hut, with no desks or blackboard or map or text-books, except a blue-back speller here and there, and the man who teaches can hardly count his cotton weights, and school only lasts three months a year, can you say that is an American school system? Even if exceptions for the better exist, this condition of things bears as heavily on the poor whites as on the negro. We live in a land of one-room cabins, mere crop-mortgaged cotton peasants."[1] This condition certainly did not bear as heavily on whites as on Negroes, but only that equivocation before a white gathering mars the candor of the description. Such a school had little relation to "the American system." By 1900 the Southern public school had proved a hardy perennial, surviving as a democratic institution in such incongruous places as poverty-stricken rural areas of states ruled by oligarchies. Anchored in the sod, in the needs and aspirations of common white and Negro, it was stunted and starved.

Though there were Southern schools before the Civil War, some supported by local taxation or by state Literary Funds, universal education was not accepted as a state obligation through state taxation until the Reconstruction era.[2] The Southern states led in the establishment of state universities, but on the eve of the war there was about one elementary school per forty square miles in South Carolina, and Draconic laws forbade the education of Southern Negroes. The typical ante-bellum educational institution

---

1. Rev. Pitt Dillingham, principal of Calhoun Colored School, Lowndes County, Alabama, in *Report of the Industrial Commission* (19 vols., Washington, 1900-02), X, 164-65. Though his school was outside of the Southern seaboard, his description fits the rural schools of that region.

2. Edgar W. Knight (ed.), *A Documentary History of Education in the South Before 1860* (5 vols., Chapel Hill, 1949-53), contains abundant evidence of ante-bellum schools. *Idem*, "Education in the South," letter to the editor, in *Nation*, C (March 18, 1915), 304, and rejoinder by Samuel J. Fisher in *ibid.*, C (June 17, 1915), 682-83, are early evidence of sectional debate on the history of Southern education. Fletcher H. Swift, *A History of Public Permanent Common School Funds in the United States, 1795-1905* (New York, 1911), is a useful reference on its subject.

The Uses of Adversity: An Introduction   5

was the pauper school, rather than the common or free school, and illiteracy was symbolic of an ethical failure of the Old Order, as it was in the same period a cardinal indictment of English aristocratic rule.

Southern state-supported common schools, then, were revolutionary institutions, cut by aliens from the alien pattern of New England education. In framing new school laws, Carpetbaggers were assisted by emancipated Negroes and, in Virginia and Georgia at least, by native whites. Between 1868 and 1870 the new plans were developed on paper in constitutional conventions and legislatures from Virginia to Georgia, as elsewhere in the South. Provision for Negro education in this region antedated that in some border states: Delaware, for instance, limited public schooling to whites until 1875. The schools themselves materialized more slowly, under special handicaps. In Georgia, for example, corrupt legislators diverted school funds into improper channels. Local resentment of the new institutions by some whites was aggravated by the bankruptcy which followed the Confederate collapse. Coeducation of Negroes and whites does not seem to have been a major focus of the hostility of native whites; segregation was legalized in Virginia and Georgia from the start and was practiced in the other states.

Though the schools themselves were poorly maintained at the end of Reconstruction, the public school idea was successful in the long view. It was more than a mere fad among freedmen. The state system of public education in the "conquered territories" ranks as one of the few constructive and permanently popular achievements of Radical Reconstruction.[3] Native white Redeemers who restored Home Rule in the South, politically if not economical-

---

3. This view is strongly presented in W. E. Burghardt Du Bois, "Reconstruction and Its Benefits," in *American Historical Review*, XV (July, 1910), 781-99; and *idem*, *Black Reconstruction* (New York, 1935). Dissenting views are expressed by Henry L. Swint, *The Northern Teacher in the South, 1862-1870* (Nashville, 1941), and E. Merton Coulter, *The South During Reconstruction*, Vol. VIII of *A History of the South* (Baton Rouge, 1947), pp. 70-91, 315-30. A balance in favor of this phase of Reconstruction is struck by recent research, John and La Wanda Cox, "General O. O. Howard and the 'Misrepresented Bureau'," in *Journal of Southern History*, XIX (November, 1953), 427-56; George R. Bentley, *A History of the Freedmen's Bureau* (Philadelphia, 1955); Henderson H. Donald, *The Negro Freedman* (New York, 1952), pp. 93-109.

ly, in the mid-seventies usually promised to retain the public schools. "Free men! Free ballots!! Free Schools!!!" was the title of a Wade Hampton pamphlet in 1876 in the campaign by which South Carolina's oligarchy returned to power. Such exclamations indicate, if they do not measure, a phase of reconstruction which had gone beyond sudden counter-revolution.

Attitudes in the dominant Northeast were also changing. In the Gilded Age educational philanthropy for the freedmen waned as industrial corporations expanded. With rare exceptions the humanitarian Radicals retreated from the South along with the political agencies of Reconstruction, and many of them also retreated from their earlier philanthropic position into a mood of cynicism. Considerations of power gained ascendancy over considerations of reform. Black Reconstruction had failed. Its economic measures were not sufficiently radical to give the freedmen land on which to defend their freedom, in an agrarian society in which land was the basis of security. Its educational measures were not so much too little as too brief. The wards of the nation, left to shift for themselves, were especially vulnerable, for it was as true as in Jefferson's day that to expect men to be ignorant and free in a state of civilization was to expect what never was and never would be.

There was a final effort at national responsibility in the eighties. Amid the ruminations of the Great Barbecue was heard the voice of Senator Henry W. Blair of New Hampshire urging the passage of his bill for federal aid to states for public common schools in amounts proportionate to the extent of illiteracy. This bill circumvented most of the objections raised against the earlier Hoar bill of 1870 and would disburse the embarrassing surplus built up by high-tariff collections. Southern opinion, though divided, was predominantly in favor of the bill, and it aroused enthusiasm among educators. But the Northern press, led by the New York *Evening Post* and the *Nation,* set upon Blair and his bill like snarling dogs. The Senator was a "crank." His "Humbug Bill" was "quixotic," "preposterous," and a "nuisance." Republicans and Alliancemen, for different reasons, opposed the measure, nor was Grover Cleveland's celebrated courage enlisted

The Uses of Adversity: An Introduction 7

in its behalf.[4] The bill passed the Senate three times, each time failing in the House, until finally the Senate defeat of 1890 ended the movement. Southern whites and Negroes, their hopes dashed, blamed the failure on New England votes. Gordon C. Lee has concluded that "with a Godkin favoring the bill the results might have been quite different." Equally significant, as Lee notes, is the fact that Edwin L. Godkin of the *Evening Post* and the *Nation*, plumed knight of nineteenth-century liberalism, did oppose the bill.[5]

The residue of Northern interest in Southern education was some philanthropic foundations, notably the Peabody Education Fund for both races and the Slater Fund for Negroes, and a number of missionary organizations of diminished membership and scope of activity. "Ministering now and then, in obscure localities, to individuals and families, brings no permanent relief to the race," observed J. L. M. Curry on the basis of wide experience. Society could not be essentially "improved by tinkering at it in spots; and no uplift that amounts to anything" could be

4. Gordon C. Lee, *The Struggle for Federal Aid, First Phase: A History of the Attempts to Obtain Federal Aid for the Common Schools 1870-1890:* Teachers College, Columbia University, Contributions to Education, No. 957 (New York, 1949), fills the need for a careful monograph on the history of efforts for federal aid to public schools, and carefully reviews the public debate. Quotations are from Rayford W. Logan, *The Negro in American Life and Thought: The Nadir 1877-1901* (New York, 1954), pp. 192-93. For an account based on the Jabez L. M. Curry Papers, see Merle Curti, *Social Ideas of American Educators* (New York, 1935), pp. 270-73. A sample of New-South opinion is Robert Bingham, *The New South: An Address in the Interest of National Aid to Education Delivered February 15, 1884* . . . (2nd ed., n.p., 1899); on Northern opinion, see [Carl Schurz], "National Aid to Common Schools," editorial in *Nation*, XXXVI (February 1, 1883), 96, and also editorials in *ibid.*, XLII (January 21, 1886), 51-52, XLII (February 18, 1886), 142-43, XLII (March 4, 1886), 184, XLVI (January 5, 1888), 5-6. Southern views are treated in detail in Allen J. Going, "The South and the Blair Education Bill," in *Mississippi Valley Historical Review*, XLIV (September, 1957), 267-90.

5. Lee, *The Struggle for Federal Aid, First Phase*, p. 139. See Amory D. Mayo, *The Government of the South by the Plain People* . . . (Berea, Kentucky, 1905?), for a jeremiad against New England by a persistent humanitarian; in *Proceedings of the Department of Superintendence of the National Educational Association at Its Meeting in Washington, February 14-16, 1888*: Bureau of Education, Circular of Information No. 6, 1888 (Washington, 1888), pp. 146-65, cf. addresses by Superintendents Alexander Hogg of Fort Worth, Texas, and J. A. B. Lovett of Huntsville, Alabama, with that by Superintendent A. P. Marble of Worcester, Massachusetts. In fairness to Godkin and some Southern opponents, their opposition to the Blair bill stemmed from opposition to the protective tariff.

secured "except through the class, as a whole, that requires it."[6] The Peabody and Slater Funds appropriated money for Negro education only to schools which conformed to Southern white insistence on "industrial education" for the subject race. The missionary associations stood more firmly for Negro human rights. The curriculum in both industrial schools and missionary colleges was "antediluvian," as Myrdal has pointed out. The colleges, however, did maintain the ideal of aspiration, a *sine qua non* for the development of Negro leadership.[7]

In the Redeemed South, meanwhile, upper-class oligarchies honored the letter of their pledges to retain the state school systems, though freely expressing doubt and disinclination. The whites never quite brought themselves to complete repudiation of democracy or the destruction of Negro schools. Negroes never quite renounced citizenship and equality of rights. And the Negro schools occupied the zone between, being kept deliberately poor but not destroyed. All of the Southern schools, like the economy of the New South, remained in an unwholesome condition.[8]

Negro children were generally segregated during Reconstruction, and laws requiring the practice were passed as soon as native whites controlled the state governments. Besides the inequality inherent in the segregation of a lower-caste minority, there was also a widening discrepancy in financial support between Negro and white schools administered by whites. White schools were so poorly maintained that this gap was not as wide as it later became. The landlord and creditor cared little for the schools of the masses, regardless of race. The fact that the Negro schools were not

6. Curry's report as agent and chairman of education committee, in *Proceedings of the Trustees of the John F. Slater Fund for the Education of Freedmen, 1897* (Baltimore, 1897), p. 11.

7. Gunnar Myrdal and assistants, *An American Dilemma: The Negro Problem and Modern Democracy* (2 vols., New York and London, 1944), II, 906; August Meier, "The Vogue of Industrial Education," in *Midwest Journal*, VII (Fall, 1955), 241-66.

8. Charles W. Dabney, *Universal Education in the South* (2 vols., Chapel Hill, 1936), I, 162-63; Edgar W. Knight, *Public Education in the South* (Boston, 1922), pp. 415-23. See the disenchanted view of George Washington Cable, "Education for the Common People of the South," *Cosmopolitan*, XIV (November, 1892), 65, quoted in Philip Butcher, "George W. Cable and Negro Education," in *Journal of Negro History*, XXXIV (April, 1949), 128; Arlin Turner, *George W. Cable: A Biography* (Durham, 1956), pp. 194-226.

The Uses of Adversity: An Introduction 9

completely abandoned may be explained by the Fifteenth Amendment, under which Negroes retained a potential suffrage, and by white fear of illiteracy among freedmen.[9] Though the schools of neglected men survived, they too were neglected by the conservative regimes of the seventies and eighties. Most of the school funds were county funds. The states did furnish some money from licenses and convict lease, for "the southern Bourbon Democrats saw no incongruity in taking convict blood money and earmarking it for public education."[10] In the nineties white small farmers who gained control of Southern seaboard state governments increased expenditures and built new schools, mostly for whites. In 1900 the schools were little better than in their infancy in the seventies, and in some ways they were worse.

There are limits to what statistics will reveal; the federal reports on education were based on inaccurate reports from the states. But the contrast is clear between Southern and other American school systems. The average term in the Southern seaboard was less than 100 days, about half that of New England.[11] Even for these short terms, only three-fifths of the children in the Southern seaboard were enrolled, and less than three-fifths of those enrolled were included in average daily attendance. Thus barely over one-third of the children of school age in these states were normally in school.[12] The average North Carolina child

---

9. W. E. Burghardt Du Bois, *The Negro Common School*: Atlanta University Publications, No. 6 (Atlanta, 1901), p. 38.

10. Fletcher M. Green, "Some Aspects of the Convict Lease System in the Southern States," in Green (ed.), *Essays in Southern History Presented to Joseph Gregoire de Roulhac Hamilton. . . :* The James Sprunt Studies in History and Political Science, XXXI (Chapel Hill, 1949), 122; Sidney M. Finger, in *North Carolina School Report, 1886-1888*, p. xxiv.

11. The schools of Virginia were open in 1900 only 119 days, in Georgia 112 days, in South Carolina 88.4 days, and in North Carolina only 70.8 days out of 365, while in the North Atlantic states the school term was 177.1 and in Massachusetts 189 days. *Report of the Commissioner of Education for the Year 1899-1900* (2 vols., Washington, 1901), I, lxix. The Virginia figure is for the year 1898-99. Some state reports give different estimates of the school terms. The federal commissioner's method of determining length of term, however, as explained in his report for 1900, I, lxx-lxxi, seems the most accurate of several customary methods.

12. Over a million children of school age were not enrolled, and another half-million were absent on the average day. *Report of the Commissioner of Education, 1900*, I, lxvi-lxviii.

attended school 21.9 days a year, or one-fifth as long as the Massachusetts child.[13]

In school finance the contrast was equally striking. The average daily expenditure per pupil in attendance in 1900 ranged from 8.2 cents in Virginia to 5 cents in South Carolina, while it was 20 cents in Massachusetts. The difference in school terms made annual expenditures more divergent, ranging in the Southern seaboard from $9.70 in Virginia to $4.34 in North Carolina, whereas the national average was $20.29 and the Massachusetts total was $37.76 per pupil. On a basis of school population regional discrepancies were wider yet. For each child of school age in South Carolina $1.80 was expended, and in North Carolina $1.65; the amount in Massachusetts was $21.55, over twelve times as large.[14]

There was far less to attract young Southerners to schools. The value of school property for every child of school age ranged from $5.33 in Virginia to $1.64 in North Carolina. In the nation as a whole it was $24.20 and in Massachusetts $60.92. Children of the Northern state were given nearly forty times better facilities than young North Carolinians. Of course the Southerners had the advantage of a milder winter—small comfort for broken panes or drafts through the cracks of a rough-hewn schoolhouse.[15]

Salaries of teachers in the Southern seaboard were also lower. As nearly as they can be computed, the average annual salary was $168.19 in Virginia, $82.87 in North Carolina. Such salaries hardly compared with the $566.09 average in Massachusetts, and the agricultural state of Kansas paid its teachers $236.26 a year.[16]

---

13. *Ibid.*, I, lxix. The Massachusetts figure was 107.4 days per school-age child. "The teachers of public schools always make out averages above the actual," reported J. G. Fulton, Goodwill, Forsyth County, North Carolina, in *Tenth Annual Report of the North Carolina Bureau of Labor Statistics, 1896* (Winston, 1897), p. 193.

14. *Report of the Commissioner of Education, 1900*, I, lxiii, lxviii, lxxvii, lxxix; *North Carolina School Report, 1898-1900*, pp. 154-56.

15. *Report of the Commissioner of Education, 1900*, I, lxiii, lxxiii.

16. The yearly salary was $122.98 in Georgia, $122.28 in South Carolina. *Georgia School Report, 1900*, pp. 32-33; *South Carolina School Report, 1899*, pp. 77, 117; *Report of the Commissioner of Education, 1900*, I, lxix, lxxii, lxxiii. South Carolina and Virginia figures are for the school year 1898-99. For convenience, titles of state school reports will be cited in shortened form as above, with appropriate calendar or school years. Figures above were computed by multiplying average monthly salary of male teachers by the number of male teachers, and the same for female teachers, adding these totals, then dividing by the total number of teachers, and multiplying by the number of

The Uses of Adversity: An Introduction

By any quantitative measurement, Southern seaboard schools were unlike non-Southern schools. They were not faithful replicas, even in miniature, of the Massachusetts pattern. Southern school facilities in fact represented one of the extremes of which the mean was a misleading national average. In view of their educational facilities, it is not surprising that in the four Southern seaboard states there were 1,517,450 illiterates ten years of age or over in 1900, of whom more than one-fourth were native whites. With less than one-tenth of the nation's population, these states were burdened with over one-fourth of the nation's illiterates.[17] A less formal measure, the number of library books, shows a similar disparity. Virginia had 20 books for every hundred inhabitants, North Carolina 13. It is true that Kansas, Nebraska, and the Dakotas were even more bookless, but rural Maine had 81 books and Massachusetts 204 for every 100 people.[18]

Besides these regional discrepancies which set Southern schools apart from the rest of the country, there were gaps within the region between the educational offerings of one school and another. An institutional fault line separated the Negro school from the white school in the same community. In South Carolina in 1915 the average white child of school age received twelve times as much from the school fund as the average Negro child.[19] Moreover, each community by maintaining two schools made districts too large, except in urban areas, and schools too small. A second discrepancy which baffled educational reformers was that between rural and urban areas.[20] Cities and small towns raised walls about

---

months of the school term, the latter being on the basis of twenty days in each school month. The contrast with Northern states is more striking when it is considered that 42 per cent of the teachers in the Southern seaboard were men and therefore more often heads of families, whereas only 9 per cent in Massachusetts and 33 per cent in Kansas were men.

17. United States Census Office, *Abstract of the Twelfth Census of the United States, 1900* (Washington, 1902), pp. 74-75. Illiteracy in South Carolina was 35.9 per cent, a proportion greater than in Hawaii and topped only by Louisiana. North Carolina had a larger proportion of white illiterates, 19.4 per cent, than any other state except New Mexico. In South Carolina and Georgia a majority of Negroes ten or over were illiterate, and for the four states 49.9 per cent were illiterate.

18. *Report of the Commissioner of Education, 1900*, I, 944.

19. See below, Chapter VI. On enrollment rather than school population, the discrimination was eight to one. *South Carolina School Report, 1915*, p. 20.

20. The city of Richmond, for example, expended $29.98 per child of school

their taxable property and maintained good schools, while rural children struggled along in one-room schools with rudimentary equipment. Rural Negroes under the dual system suffered not merely a double, but a compound handicap. And nearly all Negroes were rural.

By its sanction of "separate but equal" facilities for whites and Negroes in the *Plessy v. Ferguson* case in 1895, the federal Supreme Court not only recognized a Southern *fait accompli* as to separation, but also ignored the real condition of inequality of facilities.[21] The over-all extent of racial inequality in education can only be estimated, for the pertinent statistics are incomplete and inaccurate. The federal commissioner's guess in 1900 was that in sixteen former slave states and the District of Columbia the average Negro child received half as much school money as the average white child, that Negroes, with 32.8 per cent of the school population, received about 20 per cent of the school funds.[22] This proportion was only an estimate, and seems to be too high. By the commissioner's records for 1899-1900 in his next report, Negroes in North Carolina received 28.3 per cent of the school funds for 34.7 per cent of the school population. But federal records for South Carolina indicate that Negroes, who were 61.0 per cent of the school population, received only 22.6 per cent of the school fund.[23] And the South Carolina state report shows Negroes getting only 20.8 per cent, or barely one-sixth as much per child.[24]

---

age in 1914-15, and had $89.07 in school property per child, while rural Prince Edward County, Virginia, expended $9.22 per child and had $11.25 in school property per child, and mountainous Bland County, Virginia, expended $7.27 and had $8.44 in school property per child. *Virginia School Report, 1914-1916,* pp. 217, 233, 239, 258, 269, 275, 340, 353, 359. The balance at the end of the year has been subtracted from the figures for expenditures.

21. The legal implications and effects of this decision are ably discussed in Harry E. Groves, "Separate But Equal—The Doctrine of *Plessy v. Ferguson,*" in *Phylon,* XII (First Quarter, 1951), 66-72.

22. *Report of the Commissioner of Education, 1900,* II, 2501. The estimate was based on records of North Carolina, Kentucky, Florida, Maryland, and the District of Columbia. These were not all typical Southern states.

23. *Reports of the Commissioner of Education, 1900,* II, 2503; *1901,* I, xcix-c. There was no accounting of school funds for Negroes in Virginia and Georgia.

24. *South Carolina School Report, 1900,* p. 253. According to the federal commissioner's estimate of Negro school population in South Carolina, Negro children of school age in South Carolina received 55.13 cents each, one-seventeenth of the national average, and one-thirty-ninth of the Massachusetts average.

The Uses of Adversity: An Introduction 13

In Georgia the average Negro child received at most one-fourth as much as the average white child,[25] and in Virginia about one-third as much.[26]

Negro children suffered other disadvantages also. Terms were shorter, by as much as thirty days in South Carolina. Negro attendance was less by about 40 per cent, with about one-fourth of the Negro children attending. Their schools were fewer and therefore more distant, an important factor in a rural region with poor roads and bridges. There were fewer teachers in small schools. In Georgia there were 110 Negro children per school and 108 per teacher, while the average white school had 68 and the white teacher only 61. The average Georgia Negro teacher's salary was $95.83 a year, about half that of whites; in North Carolina white teachers received less than $100 a year, but Negro women only $64.42 a year.[27] Negro public school property in Georgia amounted to $23.79 per school, less than 25 cents per Negro child, less than one-fifth as much as for white children. In Virginia in 1908 there were seats for 50 per cent of Negro children and for 83 per cent of white children.[28] Negro schools were open about four months in the year.

Considerable evidence supports the charge of W. E. B. Du Bois that "enforced ignorance" was "one of the inevitable expedients for fastening serfdom on the country Negro." By "determined

---

25. Georgia's Negro children, who were 44.32 per cent of the school-age population in 1899, received 21.55 per cent of payments to teachers. Since these payments were about 90 per cent of the school fund, and Negroes certainly received less supervision and far less for school buildings and equipment, the estimate above seems conservative. Du Bois, *The Negro Common School*, pp. 68-69.

26. By the same measure as in Georgia, Virginia Negroes in 1899 were about 42 per cent of the school population; their teachers received 21.16 per cent of salary payments, which represented about 90 per cent of total school expenditure. *Ibid.*, p. 52; *Report of the Commissioner of Education*, 1900, II, 2503.

27. *North Carolina School Report, 1898-1900*, pp. 155-56; Du Bois, *The Negro Common School*, pp. 68-69; United States Census Office, *Abstract of the Twelfth Census of the United States, 1900*, p. 73; *Report of the Commissioner of Education*, 1900, I, lxiii, lxxii; Frank A. De Costa, "The Relative Enrollment of Negroes in the Common Schools in the United States," in *Journal of Negro Education*, XII (Summer, 1953), 420-22. Figures above are computed on the basis of population of school age. Only 25.6 per cent of the Negro children of Georgia and 25.2 per cent of those in South Carolina attended school daily.

28. Du Bois, *The Negro Common School*, pp. 68-69; *Virginia School Report, 1907-1909*, pp. 152, 258.

effort," he declared in 1907, Negro schools had been made less efficient than twenty years earlier; "the nominal term is longer and the enrolment larger, but the salaries are so small that only the poorest local talent can teach. There is little supervision, there are few appliances, few schoolhouses and no inspiration."[29] Though Negro schools in Southern cities were generally better off because of their proximity to white wealth, some were like those of Augusta, whose superintendent reported in 1904 that 2,100 pupils of the 6,500 in the Negro school population were accommodated only by having two sessions a day in the lower grades, giving the teacher as many as 100 pupils to teach in the two sessions.[30] Jabez L. M. Curry, the elderly agent of the Peabody Fund and the John F. Slater Fund, found the Negro occupying "an incongruous position in our country," and all of the work in the Negro's behalf seemed hedged about with "discouragements and difficulties," "complications and limitations."[31]

Southerners never knew quite what to expect of federal investigations, nor quite what to say on the Negro question. Most witnesses before the Industrial Commission in 1901 swore that school funds were distributed "equally per capita, absolutely." Harry Hammond, cotton grower of Beach Island, South Carolina, was more frank:

"Q. Is that distribution fairly equitable?"

"A. I suppose it is; the money does the most good in the white schools. The wording of the law is that it shall be distributed according to the best uses that can be made of it."[32]

The differences between white and Negro schools continued to widen. In 1900 the South Carolina Negro child received about

29. Du Bois, "The Economic Revolution," in Du Bois and Booker T. Washington, *The Negro in the South: His Economic Progress in Relation to His Moral and Religious Development, Being the William Levi Bull Lectures for the Year 1907* (Philadelphia, 1907), pp. 102-03.

30. Thomas Jesse Jones and associates, *Negro Education: A Study of the Private and Higher Schools for Colored People in the United States:* United States Bureau of Education, Bulletins, 1916, Nos. 38 and 39 (2 vols., Washington, 1917), I, 32.

31. Jabez L. M. Curry, *Difficulties, Complications, and Limitations Connected with the Education of the Negro:* The Trustees of the John F. Slater Fund, Occasional Papers, No. 5 (Baltimore, 1895), 14-15, 20.

32. Testimony in *Report of the Industrial Commission*, X, 826. Cf. Governor Allen D. Candler of Georgia in *ibid.*, VIII, 537.

The Uses of Adversity: An Introduction　　　15

one-sixth as much as the white child for education. By 1915 the disparity had doubled and the Negro child received only one-twelfth as much. The system of segregation, far from being a burden, was a convenient means of economizing at the expense of Negro children.[33]

The schools of the Reconstruction period were largely in the towns, and as the urban schools advanced, a differential grew between them and rural schools. Yet the Southern people were overwhelmingly rural. "The thought of the North is of cities. Ought it to be the same in the South?" asked George S. Dickerman in 1901. Crowded communities anywhere might copy the Massachusetts schools, but would they fit a people whose cabins and country homes were a mile apart? "New England has not yet answered in her own domain the question of education for her rural people. But in the South this is the main question. . . . The neglected few in Massachusetts or Maine multiply into millions."[34] And it was in the country districts that both the financial and social costs of the dual school system were heaviest. In the cities Negro and white school districts were coterminous with areas of residential segregation, whereas in rural areas children of the two races were scattered out side by side. "Usually we separate the races in our thought and discussion," Dickerman noticed. "It is not so easy to separate them actually."

In Virginia, which seems fairly typical of the Southern seaboard states in the matter of urban-rural disparity, there were nineteen

33. In 1915 Negro children represented 61.02 per cent of the school population and received 11.24 per cent of the school fund. This estimate is computed from *South Carolina School Report, 1915*, p. 310; *Report of the Commissioner of Education, 1917* (2 vols., Washington, 1917), II, 17, estimating school population in 1915. Valuable studies of racial inequalities of school opportunity in this period include Du Bois, *The Negro Common School;* Du Bois and Augustus G. Dill (eds.), *The Common School and the Negro American:* Atlanta University Publications, No. 16 (Atlanta, 1911); Charles L. Coon, "Public Taxation and Negro Schools," in *Twelfth Conference for Education in the South, Proceedings* (Atlanta, 1909), pp. 157-67. Indispensable to the study of the general problem are two works by Horace M. Bond, *Social and Economic Influences on the Public Education of Negroes in Alabama 1865-1930* (Washington, 1939), which also appeared under the title: *Negro Education in Alabama: A Study in Cotton and Steel;* and *The Education of the Negro in the American Social Order* (New York, 1934).

34. George S. Dickerman, "The South Compared with the North in Educational Requirements," in *Fourth Conference for Education in the South, Proceedings* (Winston-Salem, North Carolina, 1901), pp. 15-16.

independent city school systems, which in 1907-08 expended for education over twice as much per child as the rural schools, and had four times as much school property per child. Three-fourths of city school buildings and only one-fiftieth of rural school buildings were of brick; all of the 596 log schools were in rural districts. There was a school library book for every third white city child, one for every six white rural children, with few for any Negroes anywhere. Richmond, which may be compared with Charleston or Atlanta in other seaboard states, expended $14.19 per child of school age, nearly three times as much as in rural schools. It had about one-seventh of the state's school property, over five times as much in value per child as in rural areas. There was a book for almost every white child in the Richmond school libraries.[35]

Pitifully meager as it was, "the State 'average,' and even the County 'average,' charitably covers, as with a blanket, the nakedness of the backwoods country schools."[36] This was true of all of them, though not equally so. Within the rural areas the schools were operated at different levels. Weak support of Negro schools gave rise to a difference between white schools. School money derived from state taxation flowed from the state capitals to the counties in proportions based upon total enrollment, and, *mirabile dictu*, without regard to race or color. The "black counties," usually located on the coastal plain or lower Piedmont of each state and having a large Negro proportion of population, received money from the state for Negro children, gave Negro schools the usual pittance, and used the considerable remainder for the support of white schools. In "white counties," usually in the mountains and upper Piedmont and having few if any Negroes, school authorities received a negligible sum for Negro children, gave Negroes usually even less for their scattered little schools, but even so had but an infinitesimal residue to apply to white schools. The motive, method, and procedure were the same in white and black counties, but the results were not at all similar.

There were variations of this practice in the several states, but

35. Computed from *Virginia School Report, 1907-1909*, pp. 113, 152, 218, 244, 258.
36. *South Carolina School Report, 1902*, p. 13.

The Uses of Adversity: An Introduction

only minor ones. An example from each state will perhaps illuminate the pattern. In five Virginia black counties in 1907-08, Negro children were 69.83 per cent of the school population, but salaries of Negro teachers were less than one-third of the counties' total salary payments. Assuming that other school payments were divided in the same proportion as salaries, though almost certainly they were lower, white schools in these five counties received as a bonus about $10,000. The White Man's Burden rested lightly indeed. In the same year in five populous white counties, the Negro 6.08 per cent of the school population received only 2.6 per cent of salary payments. But here little blood could be wrung from a stone. Only about $500 went to white schools by virtue of the presence of Negro children.[37]

Eight rural counties in North Carolina in which the Negro proportion of the school population was about 60 per cent or higher paid annual salaries to white teachers about twice as high as in the nineteen counties where 90 per cent were white.[38] In South Carolina nearly all counties had Negro majorities, and there nearly all of the school funds were derived from taxation within the counties. Within each county the white schools in districts with Negro majorities were especially favored by the system of

---

37. The five black counties in Virginia—Amelia, Charles City, James City, King William, and New Kent—received from the state $26,617.50. Since Negro children were 69.83 per cent of their aggregate school population, the Negroes' share of the state fund was $18,587.00. Negro teachers in the five counties received salaries amounting to $10,867.88. The five white counties—Bath, Craig, Giles, Highland, and Shenandoah—received from the state $34,622.32, of which only $2,105.04 accrued to them by virtue of the Negro 6.08 per cent of the school population. Negro teachers received $1,655.59 in salaries. Computed from *Virginia School Report, 1907-1909*, pp. 67-79, 128-50, 194-214. Figures for school revenue do not include balance.

38. The annual salaries of white teachers in black counties were: Edgecombe, $250.02; Halifax, $249.59; Vance, $248.48; Craven, $219.26; Robeson, $214.69; Warren, $165.53; Hertford, $148.39; Bertie, $136.26. In the white counties annual salaries of white teachers were: Ashe, $77.72; Alexander, $91.36; Alleghany, $93.62; Yancey, $97.18; Mitchell, $100.16; Yadkin, $104.84; Graham, $105.55; Clay, $106.15; Watauga, $107.87; Cherokee, $108.08; Swain, $113.42; Wilkes, $116.90; Madison, $118.30; Macon, $119.79; Stanly, $125.29; Surry, $128.88; Jackson, $149.04; McDowell, $163.01; Haywood, $203.51. Negro salaries in the black counties were also slightly higher, by about 30 per cent. And part of the differences in salary resulted from greater taxable wealth in the black counties. But there were few local taxes in either area, and consequently there was a great dependence on county taxation and state appropriations in both. *North Carolina School Report, 1906-1908*, Part II, pp. 184-91, 193-200. Figures are for the school year 1907-08.

apportionment, and had long terms, good houses, and high salaries. Georgia had so large a state school fund that counties with a large Negro population needed no local taxation to maintain comparatively good white schools. They simply gathered up and enrolled as many Negro children as possible. Thus the twenty-one Georgia counties with Negro names on two-thirds or more of their school rolls reported monthly expenditures per Negro pupil ranging from 25 cents to 79 cents and, with four exceptions, from $1.50 to $4.00 per white pupil. In thirteen counties less than one-tenth Negro, the monthly expenditures for whites ranged from 75 cents to $1.14, on the whole less than half of the amounts for whites in black counties.[39]

Thus the white people of black counties—or black districts in South Carolina—received special advantages from state and county funds by virtue of their Negro children. Their educational and political leaders were the chief defenders of the existing system of apportionment, and sometimes even appeared to be paternalistic champions of a dependent race. A glance at the Negro schools of black counties would put that claim to rest. In Greene County, Georgia, for example, three-fourths of the Negro schools in 1910 convened in churches and private homes, and at least three Negro schoolhouses were built by closing down the schools for three months and using the teachers' salaries to buy materials.[40] W. E. B. Du Bois spent several months in 1898 taking his own census of Negroes in Dougherty County, Georgia, where whites were outnumbered by five to one. He found that only 27 per cent of the Negroes could read and write. Of the Negro schoolhouses there he reported: "I saw only one schoolhouse there that would compare in any way with the worst schoolhouses I ever saw in New England. . . . Most of the schoolhouses were either old log huts or were churches—colored churches—used as schoolhouses."[41]

39. *Georgia School Report, 1906*, pp. 364-67. The black counties were Burke, Chattahoochee, Clay, Clinch, Columbia, Dougherty, Greene, Harris, Jasper, Jones, Macon, McIntosh, Putnam, Quitman, Stewart, Sumter, Talbot, Taliaferro, Terrell, Troup, and Warren, in the coastal plain and lower Piedmont. The white counties, all but one of which were in the northern corner of the state, were Catoosa, Dawson, Echols, Fannin, Forsyth, Habersham, Murray, Paulding, Pickens, Rabun, Towns, Union, and White.

40. Arthur F. Raper, *Tenants of the Almighty* (New York, 1943), p. 138.

41. Testimony of Du Bois in *Report of the Industrial Commission*, XV, Part II, 159-61; *Georgia School Report, 1896*, p. ccccxvii.

The Uses of Adversity: An Introduction

The leading opponents of Negro education came from the mountains and Piedmont of every Southern seaboard state. Probably their primary motive was to hold down the Negroes, but they were not unaware of the use made of Negro school funds in the black counties.[42] Their redundant theme, louder in the wake of disfranchisement campaigns around the turn of the century, was that white men's taxes should not be used to educate Negro children. In a sense, the battle between hill and plain over Negro education was a sham battle. If indirect taxes be included, Negro schools under the existing system were receiving little, if any, more than the share of tax funds paid by Negroes.[43] This was pointed out when up-country legislators proposed to give Negroes only the receipts from their taxes, and usually sufficed to still the clamor. As George Washington Cable said in the nineties, "The Negro, so far from being the educational pauper he is commonly reputed to be, comes, in these states, nearer to paying entirely for his children's schooling, such as it is, than any similarly poor man in any other part of the enlightened world."[44] But within each state there was a sectional impasse among whites about the direction of educational policy that, while it revolved about the Negro school, was really a question of which white schools got the available funds. One result was the retardation of all rural schools, while the relatively unvexed cities and towns, largely in the Piedmont, developed much more adequate schools for their own children. The Southern rural white was hoist by his own petard.

42. Key points out that, in their actual voting, the whites of black counties, rather than those of the uplands, have been the most ardent supporters of White Supremacy. V. O. Key, *Southern Politics in State and Nation* (New York, 1949), pp. 5, 9.

43. Du Bois, in *The Negro Common School*, pp. 90-91, concluded that in seven states in 1899 Negroes paid as much as they received, in four others whites paid less than 25 per cent of the cost of Negro schools, and in four others the whites paid between 25 and 50 per cent of the cost of Negro schools. Coon, in "Public Taxation and Negro Schools," *Twelfth Conference for Education in the South, Proceedings*, pp. 160-65, concluded after a careful analysis of taxation and educational expenditures in Virginia, North Carolina, and Georgia, that Negro schools in 1906-1907 were "not a burden on white taxpayers." Both argued that Negroes as legal residents were entitled to their share of corporation taxes, that they paid their share of liquor taxes and fines, and that in a unique way they contributed to Georgia's revenue from convict hire. See also Du Bois and Dill, *The Common School and the Negro American, passim*.

44. Quoted in Richard R. Wright, Jr., *Self Help in Negro Education* (Cheyney, Pennsylvania, 1909?), p. 18.

Just as the national "average" obscured sharp regional differentials in educational facilities, so similar inequalities existed within the Southern region. Negro schools were almost everywhere in the South at the base of the educational pyramid. The levels among white schools, in ascending order, were those of mountain rural areas, Piedmont rural areas, rural black counties, towns, and cities. The rural Southerner was poorly armed for his twentieth-century plunge into a capitalistic economy and world upheaval. The poor schools limited rural whites as well as Negroes, but in every Southern community the inferiority of Negro schools had a special significance as a symbol of inferior personal status.[45]

Despite the variations in schools between Negro and white and between geographical areas, the main outlines of the Southern seaboard rural school were similar enough to be described in general. The local literature early in the century reveals the rural schoolhouse and the small farmer's or tenant's dwelling house as products of the same culture.

The North Carolina rural schoolhouse, described with restraint by Charles L. Coon, may be taken as the type for white schools of the Southern seaboard, with some diminutions and deprivations for the rural Negro school.

The school-house is a shabbily built board structure, one story high. The overhead ceiling is not more than nine feet from the floor. There is one door at the end of the house; there are six small windows, three on either side. There are no blinds and no curtains. The desks are home-made, with perpendicular backs and seats, all the same size. There is a dilapidated wood stove, but no wood-box, the wood for the fire being piled on the floor about the stove. The stove is red with rust and dirt, never having been polished and cleaned since it was placed in position for use. The floor of the house is covered with red dirt and litter from the wood. . . . There is no teacher's desk or table. There is one chair. The walls and windows are covered with dust and seem never to have been washed. The children's hats and coats are hung on nails around the room. All their books are soiled and look very

[45]. See Abram Kardiner and Lionel Ovesey, *The Mark of Oppression* (New York, 1951), a psycho-social study of the effect of discrimination on Negro personality. Unfortunately, the sample was too small and localized. The general conclusion is that traumatic Negro personalities cannot be obviated merely by Negro education. "It is the white man who requires the education."

much like their surroundings. There are no steps to this school-house. An inclined plane of dirt serves that purpose. The yard is very muddy during the winter, and the general appearance of the place anything but attractive.[46]

The school's outhouse and well were apparently beneath comment. Many rural schools were far worse. Stumps, briars, or honeysuckle covered many a school yard, and the public road was the playground. At a Pamlico, North Carolina, school the house which belonged to the children in winter was turned over to goats for the other eight months. A county superintendent of the Albemarle area of North Carolina described the school of that area as "something like an old Virginia rail fence grown up with weeds."[47]

The rural schoolhouse seemed to one Southern editor "the very mudsill" of the educational problem. When the North Carolina schoolhouse loan fund was organized in 1903, county superintendents got their schoolhouses on the waiting list by describing them as "log houses," "shanties," or "tenant houses."[48] In one of the richer counties there were fifteen houses valued at less than $50 each in 1902; forty-five of the ninety-six schoolhouses of Richmond County in the black belt were log houses in 1900, and all ninety-six were valued at $70 apiece. Swain County's two Negro houses were valued at $20 each. If these were extreme examples, the average was little better; white schoolhouses in North Carolina were valued at $175 on the average, and Negro houses at $122.[49] In rural South Carolina the schoolhouse was in "the style of a one-room negro cabin," often "a log hut with a swayback roof and a 'stick-and-clay' chimney." When the state normal school sent a student to Marion County to organize school improvement clubs, she found some of the "submerged tenth" of schools without schoolhouses, and reported:

> These schools are often held in what serves as a church also. The remote situation and accompanying graveyard must have anything but

46. Quoted in Robert D. W. Connor, "The Women's Association for the Betterment of Public School Houses in North Carolina," Bulletin of the Department of Public Instruction (Raleigh, 1906), p. 12.
47. *Ibid.*, pp. 37-42; H. B. Ansell, Superintendent of Currituck County, in *North Carolina School Report, 1898-1900*, pp. 120-21.
48. *North Carolina School Report, 1902-1904*, p. 19.
49. *North Carolina School Report, 1898-1900*, pp. 340-43.

a cheerful influence. Once when I was observing the utter desolation of such a place I asked a passing youth why all the doors and windows were left open. "Yes'm," he said, "they ain't nothin' in there to git hurt." And when I went in, I realized what he meant. There was literally nothing in the way of equipment except one table and a few benches fastened at one end to the wall. No association could be organized here.[50]

"How niggardly, how cruel," complained a Virginia teacher, "to locate a schoolhouse on a cliff, or on a bank, or over a gulley, which is worthless for farming! Such a place might do for a stable, or a pig-sty, or a prison, but not for the children. . . ."[51]

"O, *equipment*," came the cry from Moncks Corner, South Carolina, "—tools for our teachers to work with—(it's like digging potatoes with one's hands)." Funds for such physical improvements must come from the taxation of a semiliterate and impoverished people. But the teachers could complain. "How can you teach drawing with a two-by-four blackboard?" was a topic for discussion at a Virginia teachers' institute.[52] At Jamison, South Carolina, in what its principal described as "a fit specimen of the old-time country school," "The blackboards were inadequate; scraps of sheepskin served for erasers; no maps; no charts or globes; windows without shutters and with numerous panes lacking; the desks, while patented, were unable to seat the pupils. . . ."[53]

The experience of a Negro teachers' institute in the eighties, conducted by a New England teacher returning briefly to the scene of his Reconstruction labors, illuminates the problem facing most rural teachers of this period. A spirited virtue was made of necessity.

We strove, too, to avoid another mischievous mistake: the mistake of supposing that expensive apparatus, or, indeed, furniture of any kind

---

50. L. T. Baker, "Richland's Rural Schools," in Columbia *State*, August 12, 1906; Penelope McDuffie, in *South Carolina School Report*, *1903*, p. 63.

51. B. W. Cronk, Pembroke, Virginia, in Richmond *Times-Dispatch*, January 27, 1907.

52. A. H. DeHay, Superintendent of Berkeley County, in *South Carolina School Report*, *1914*, p. 65; *Virginia Journal of Education*, II, No. 3 (December, 1908), 7.

53. John W. Inabinet to Mary T. Nance, September 5, 1907, quoted in *South Carolina School Report*, *1907*, p. 37.

The Uses of Adversity: An Introduction 23

(blackboards excepted), are necessary to the illustration of most of the teaching of our common schools. A base ball did duty in explaining the motions of the earth; . . . sand spread on the floor did duty as relief maps; pebbles picked up on the school grounds furnished the basis of a talk on common sense. . . .[54]

Such materials taxed the ingenuity of the most artful teacher. In the hands of one teacher in the "Dark Corner" of a mountain county, they limited instruction to something less than elementary, or even rudimentary. The teaching of geography without a map consisted largely of gestures with the index finger.[55]

One thing that retarded the elementary school and prevented the existence of public high schools was a multiplicity of private schools, sometimes distinguishable from the public schools only by their pretensions. It seemed to Colonel Stringweather that in his town "every old lady and every second young lady has a select school for chillern, and I hear of three more that will start in the fall. . . . There's a school under the auspices of every church in town."[56] There are many sentimental recollections of these schools, but perhaps the genre description by Ludwig Lewisohn is more realistic:

The village possessed one other school which charged a somewhat higher fee—two dollars a month, I think—and boasted an aristocratic flavor. It was kept by a broken-down gentleman of Huguenot extraction who was said to have been immensely wealthy and to have lived in barbaric splendor before the Civil War. Major Maury was a man prematurely old, slightly deaf and shaken by palsy. His features were almost hidden by harsh bunches of beard, and hair grew in long strands out of his ears and nostrils. He sat by the window, smoking a pipe and chewing tobacco at the same time. There, in a weary, mechanical way, he heard the lessons which we were supposed to have prepared in the other bare rooms or on the porch of the windy and abandoned cottage. The ten or twelve pupils played and studied around that sunken-eyed old man in a half-hearted kind of way; the manner

---

54. Mortimer A. Warren of Litchfield, Connecticut, principal of State Normal School for Colored Teachers, report of session from July 6 through July 30, 1886, in *South Carolina School Report, 1886*, p. 31.
55. W. Zachariah McGhee, *The Dark Corner* (New York, 1908), pp. 123-30.
56. [Walter Hines Page], *The Southerner, a Novel: Being the Autobiography of Nicholas Worth* (New York, 1906, new ed., 1909), p. 132.

and the mood of the place float to me across the years in images of cold discouragement and mouldering desolation.[57]

At a place such as Charleston in this period, public-school training was thorough and authoritarian. "They were young enough to be grounded in the necessities of a liberal education without having their callow judgment consulted, and to be caned when they were lazy or rowdy." A century-old mansion in Charleston served as a boys' high school; an elderly, one-legged athlete taught physical culture.[58]

In the back country, however, such amenities were utterly lacking. Charles H. Otken found, in a typical rural school:

a young lady teacher having from twenty-five to thirty-five pupils, attempted to teach the six common-school studies [spelling, reading, geography, arithmetic, English grammar, and American history] . . . and eight advanced studies besides, pursued by three pupils. She worried through the four months, attended one or two teachers' institutes, closed with a general examination and a concert, and she was paid for her work from $120 to $140. The best pupil in the school . . . was perplexed to know to what the product of a half of a half referred.[59]

The old maxim: "As is the teacher, so is the school" was proved in the Southern seaboard by the custom of appropriating money to schools only for teachers' salaries, leaving building and grounds to the care of local patrons. Even so, teachers were so poorly paid that they were objects of charity, in rural districts usually riding a circuit of patrons' farmhouses in the tradition of the maiden aunt. Many communities set teachers apart under a rigid special code of behavior. In a country of violence and raw corn whiskey they had to set standards fit for a Bible Commonwealth. Certainly the incomes of teachers encouraged the more abstemious virtues, unless pushed down to the level of desperation. As a Southern editor expressed it, a harassed teacher must "by her precept and example mold 50 or more young pagans into models of virtue and propriety" when "scarcely able to keep honest herself on the wages

---

57. Ludwig Lewisohn, *Up Stream: An American Chronicle* (New York, 1922), pp. 46-48.

58. *Ibid.*, pp. 64-65; Robert Molloy, *Charleston: A Gracious Heritage* (New York and London, 1947), pp. 158-59.

59. Charles H. Otken, *The Ills of the South* (New York, 1894), pp. 194-95.

The Uses of Adversity: An Introduction 25

she gets."[60] Only the general poverty of the region could explain the attraction of a rural teaching position.

But it was astonishingly easy to become a teacher. Until well after the turn of the century, applicants were examined for certification by a county superintendent, who asked his own questions, graded the papers, and was not bound to dismiss or reject a teacher who failed. Outsiders found "tremendous" nepotism and favoritism in appointing teachers.[61] "Any eighth-grade pupil" could pass the examinations sent out from his office, said a South Carolina state superintendent. One county in that state was "so notorious that . . . in this Mecca failure is reputed to be only a remote possibility," and other counties "issue certificates on almost any pretext," declared an indignant superintendent, "ignoring the law (a condition to be bitterly condemned)."[62] Charles S. Barrett of Georgia, president of the Farmers' Union, perhaps exaggerated a little in his story of one such examination: "The applicant was asked if he taught that the world was round or flat, and he replied that if his patrons wanted the round system he taught that, and if they wanted the flat system, he taught that. While this story may be a little overdrawn, it is an illustration of the lack of training of many teachers who taught in the country sections."[63]

It is not surprising, then, that there was at least one instance of "a girl, not 'sweet sixteen,' but only thirteen years of age being employed to teach a public school."[64] By 1900 Southern men were

60. Richmond *Times-Dispatch*, quoted without date in Columbia *State*, January 1, 1913.

61. Hollis B. Frissell to Edwin A. Alderman, January 10, 1902, copy in Charles W. Dabney Papers, Southern Historical Collection (hereafter cited as S.H.C.), University of North Carolina; Dabney, *Universal Education in the South*, II, 320. This affected Negro teachers as well as white. W. Scott Copeland, in Richmond *Times*, February 1, 1902.

62. *South Carolina School Reports, 1908*, p. 30; *1909*, pp. 27, 30; *1910*, p. 56. "Ponies" were widely used, and in 1913 the state teachers' association lobbied for a reform of examinations; but two business firms, one of which seems to have advertised the ponies, hired a lawyer to go before the committees on education of the legislature and defeat the bill. *South Carolina School Report, 1915*, p. 153.

63. Charles S. Barrett, *The Mission, History and Times of the Farmers' Union* (Nashville, 1909), p. 88. In a similar story, an Alabama superintendent swapping horses with a constituent at a county fair, threw in a first class teacher's certificate "to boot." Isaac W. Hill, state superintendent of Alabama, in *Ninth Conference for Education in the South, Proceedings* (Lexington, Kentucky, 1906), p. 47.

64. *North Carolina School Report, 1898-1900*, p. 71. Sometimes a large or bright pupil was given charge for a day or more during a teacher's absence. *The Patron and Gleaner* (weekly, Lasker, North Carolina), July 21, 1892.

just beginning to be replaced by women as teachers, for during the long agricultural depression, "If a man could not quite go the church, he set up as a teacher, and even to this day, if you scratch a Southern teacher, a preacher will wince." Perhaps the rural teacher described by John A. Rice was reasonably typical of the period in the Southern seaboard: "a country boy, himself just out of school, as touchy as a rattlesnake in spring, and scared. He had no imagination, his ignorance was profound, he needed the money to go to college . . . these were his qualifications."[65]

"A large per cent. of these instructors of the youth work in the fields eight months in the year and teach four," reported one "Corn Cracker" from the Carolina Piedmont. "Many of them have but a vague, undefined idea of what a summer resort is, and many of them were never as far away from home as Charlotte." It was a rare treat for them to go to a county teachers' institute for a week, "to get among refined, scholarly people, hear good music, and get an inkling of the spirit of progress in the air."[66] At these institutes teachers drilled themselves in the contents of elementary textbooks, because their examinations for certificates were drawn largely from this juvenile material.

But the teachers needed more than occupational therapy. "Reason as we may," said a state superintendent, ". . . about the nobility of the work and the glorious rewards of it hereafter, back of this question of better teachers must still lie the cold business question of better pay."[67] This question was especially aggravated in Georgia, where the pay was over a year late and teachers were "discounting their claims to curbstone brokers at ruinous rates."[68] But everywhere salaries were so low that, as a rural weekly expressed it, only Negroes and women would work for such "scanty wages."[69] When prices began to rise after the depression of the

---

65. John A. Rice, *I Came Out of the Eighteenth Century* (New York, 1942), pp. 146, 199. "I learned nothing from my teacher," he added, "except that I could learn algebra, which neither of us had ever seen before, faster than he; but I learned a lot from my friend the bully."—*Ibid.*, p. 147.

66. "Corn Cracker" [M. L. White, Lattimore, North Carolina], letter to the editor, in Charlotte *Observer*, August 1, 1905.

67. James Y. Joyner, in *North Carolina School Report, 1902-1904*, Part I, p. 56.

68. Message of Governor Allen D. Candler, in Atlanta *Journal*, October 24, 1900.

69. New Bern (North Carolina) *Daily Journal*, August 7, 1904. "It is

nineties, the real wages of teachers actually declined.[70] On the whole, teachers accepted their situation stoically. "We are betrayed by politicians whom we exalt to office," remarked a teacher; "we are reviled by ignorant sectarians who know nothing but a beaten path of ignorance and superstition; we are son[s] of our poverty, but we thank God and take courage that we are promoters of civilization...."[71] And so many of them were indeed.[72]

The "old law of supply and demand,"[73] with the farm wage as a measurement, worked particular hardship on Negro teachers, though lack of other suitable jobs drove the better-educated Negroes into teaching. In Georgia in 1900, for example, five of the fifteen Negro teachers of Telfair County and seventeen of the thirty-seven in Newton County received monthly salaries of $10, while seven white teachers of Telfair County received $15 a month, each for a term of five months. Four white teachers in Milton County received $6.81 a month or $40.86 a year, and two Negroes in the same county $5.80 a month or $34.80 a year. "Teaching seems to be the meanest of trades," said William H. Hand of South Carolina.[74]

---

simply iniquity," said Justice Walter Clark of North Carolina. "There is no other word for it."—Speech at Greensboro, North Carolina, July 30, 1912, in "Cyrus B. Watson for Judge Clark" (pamphlet, n.p., 1912?), p. 13.

70. *North Carolina School Report, 1902-1904*, Part I, p. 38.

71. "Corn Cracker" [M. L. White], in Charlotte *Observer*, August 13, 1905. On the patience of Southern teachers, cf. Rosa Pendleton Chiles, *Down Among the Crackers* (Cincinnati, 1900), p. 30.

72. "We get a large number of students from the country who have been taught *at* by some 18 year old girl no more fit to *teach* than a pig is to count potatoes," wrote an exasperated Virginia professor. A. W. Drinkard, Department of English and Economics, Virginia Polytechnic Institute, Blacksburg, Virginia, to William E. Dodd, Randolph-Macon College, Ashland, Virginia, October 17, 1904, in William E. Dodd Papers, Library of Congress.

73. Marion L. Brittain, "The Work of the Normal Schools as the County Commissioner Sees It," in Southern Educational Association, *Proceedings, 1900* (Richmond, 1901), p. 309. "The main trouble with our rural school," said a low-country South Carolina superintendent, "is, that trustees and patrons are so slow in realizing the value of a high-priced teacher. It seems that as the only salaried people with whom they have to deal is [*sic*] the farm laborer, they, in all their comparisons, use this as a standard, and thereby form the opinion that teachers are paid too much salary already."—Joe P. Lane, Superintendent of Marion County, in *South Carolina School Report, 1909*, p. 61.

74. *Georgia School Report, 1900*, pp. cclv, cclxxv, ccxciv, cccxlviii (Roman numerals were used in pagination throughout the report, apparently to train the teachers); William H. Hand, "Report of State High School Inspector, 1915-1916," *Bulletin* of the University of South Carolina, No. 51 (December, 1916), p. 8.

But it was not simply that education was one of the South's low-wage industries. The Southern educational structure tapered sharply at the top. "If all the high school graduates in Georgia were immediately and violently seized and put in the normal schools, they would constitute only a small part of the teachers required in the common schools of the state and a large per cent. of these common school teachers could scarcely be said to have a high school education."[75] In 1903 Georgia had only seven four-year public high schools graduating ninety-four students; South Carolina in 1900 claimed thirty, Virginia twenty-eight, and North Carolina four. But careful inspection revealed that such lists were "largely worthless," some schools being nonexistent and other "so called high schools" unable to meet the standard of the rest of the country.[76] Many a "college" was really a high school, many a high school in reality a poorly organized elementary school. Of course the woods were full of private academies; then there were "fitting schools," fiefs of some college or other, often on the same campus, taught by the professors, and verging imperceptibly into the college. The "village school of thirty-five pupils," South Carolinians had to be told, "ranging from beginners to first lessons in Algebra and Latin, is miscalled a high school. Often it has not a full high school course of even a year; often it has no regular course at all." A single teacher, by teaching two classes at the same time, might "prepare" pupils in all of the various subjects required for college entrance.[77]

A subsidiary problem of Southern seaboard schools was poor supervision. "I suppose that the most hopeless places in the world a decade ago were the offices of the superintendents of public

75. Brittain, "The Work of the Normal Schools as the County Commissioner Sees It," Southern Educational Association, *Proceedings, 1900*, p. 309.

76. Dorothy Orr, *A History of Education in Georgia* (Chapel Hill, 1950), pp. 263-64; *Report of the Commissioner of Education, 1900*, II, 2289-90, 2323-26, 2339-41; Bruce R. Payne, "A Cursory Review of High School Conditions in Virginia, Sept. 15th, 1905," report of the Professor of Secondary Education of the University of Virginia to the General Education Board, enclosed in letter to Edwin A. Alderman, October 18, 1905, in files of the president, University of Virginia. A good analysis of the Southern high schools is in [Abraham Flexner and Frank P. Bachman], *The General Education Board: An Account of Its Activities 1902-1914* (New York, 1915), pp. 71-76.

77. Report of William H. Hand as state high school inspector, in *South Carolina School Report, 1906*, pp. 62-84.

The Uses of Adversity: An Introduction 29

instruction in most of these commonwealths," wrote Walter Hines Page in the more optimistic year, 1907. "In some of them, you would find men without hope, without plans, without any adequate knowledge of an educational system, who lazily compiled lists of inaccurate figures, drew pitiful salaries, and published dull reports that had no particular meaning."[78] The South Carolina state superintendent was paid much less than the principal city superintendents in the state. It seemed to one South Carolina legislator that the "huge giant using his strength to crush out ignorance" was "a giant without a head."[79]

The county superintendent was often a pensioner of the local political machine, "nothing under the sun but a political ringster, a ballot stuffer, or the head of the regime that does it," as an angry Virginia Republican complained; he explained that the local ring had cut old copies of the Congressional Record to ballot size, stuffed them into the box, and counted in the winning candidates at a recent election.[80] From Virginia to Georgia and beyond, reformers complained that the office was a pension for "good soldiers" or "a cheap reward to some well-meaning but incompetent man for some party service—past, present or future."[81]

But more important than the means of selection was the fact that it was a part-time job. Superintendents were usually the poorest paid of all county officials, and " 'poor pay' means 'poor

78. Walter H. Page, "A Journey Through the Southern States: The Changes of Ten Years," in *World's Work*, XIV (June, 1907), 9006-07; Joseph D. Eggleston and Robert W. Bruère, *The Work of the Rural School* (New York and London, 1913), pp. 262-70.

79. Charleston *News and Courier*, January 26, 1901. The superintendent could not even force county superintendents to report, and much clerical work was inaccurate. For years the length of the school term was computed by adding the averages of city schools and of rural schools, and dividing the sum by two, although city schools represented only about 13 per cent of the total enrollment. *South Carolina School Reports, 1906*, p. 7; *1914*, p. 27; South Carolina Department of Agriculture, Commerce, and Immigration, *Handbook of South Carolina, 1907* (Columbia, 1907), pp. 170-71.

80. Albert O. Porter, *County Government in Virginia, A Legislative History, 1607-1904*: Columbia University Studies in History, Economics and Public Law, No. 526 (New York, 1947), pp. 336-37; J. H. Lindsay (comp. and ed.), *Report of the Proceedings and Debates of the Constitutional Convention, State of Virginia, Held in the City of Richmond, June 12, 1901, to June 26, 1902* (2 vols., Richmond, 1906), I, 1059, 1184.

81. Letter of William H. Hand to the editor, in Columbia *State*, January 1, 1914; *North Carolina School Report, 1896-1898*, p. 10.

preach.' "[82] Spare-time superintendents often "know nothing whatever as to whether or not the school is being properly managed and taught."[83] A number of them openly sided with property owners opposing increased taxation for public education.[84] That was sometimes a reason for their being selected.

By 1900 every state save two outside of the South compelled attendance, but no Southern state except Kentucky did so. And the Kentucky law was flagrantly ignored in the rural areas.[85] All through the back country rural children were out "behind the plow handles, milking the cows and playing in red gullies." Their minds seemed to one farmer like "the rays of the diamond which are forbidden by the rough to send forth their lustre."[86] Malthusian pessimism rolled from the mouths even of some educators as they watched cotton—the crop, the thread, the cloth—absorb the energies of old and young. "It is 'King Cotton' that has been our tyrant," declared a county superintendent, "keeping the boys and girls out of school, fettering them in ignorance, poverty and tenantry." It seemed that if farmers would change to grain crops, "to be gathered by the fathers," there would be a harvest of golden children in nine-month schools.[87]

But Southern cities did not escape the cultural poverty of a colonial region. Nosing about a Richmond museum at the turn

---

82. Frank A. Magruder, *Recent Administration in Virginia:* Johns Hopkins University Studies in Historical and Political Science, Series XXX, No. 1 (Baltimore, 1912), 29-30; Charleston *News and Courier*, January 17, 1900.

83. J. M. Quarles, delegate from Augusta County, in *Virginia Constitutional Convention, 1901-1902*, I, 1059. "How can he determine whether the children have been properly taught, if he knows nothing about the subject except what he may read, text-book in hand, as children recite?" asked the future bishop James Cannon. Editorial in Richmond *Christian Advocate*, April 22, 1909, quoted in *Virginia Journal of Education*, I, No. 9 (June, 1909), 22.

84. A Georgia county superintendent declared at an educational meeting: "I am not opposed to local taxation, but I am opposed to any further appropriation for public schools."—W. H. Wooding, quoted in *Georgia School Report, 1901*, p. 90.

85. C. Vann Woodward, *Origins of the New South*, Vol. IX of *A History of the South* (Baton Rouge, 1951), p. 399; resolutions of Kentucky Educational Association, 1913, in *Kentucky School Report, 1913-1915*, pp. x-xi.

86. W. Carl Wharton, Waterloo, South Carolina, letter to the editor, in Columbia *State*, August 10, 1909.

87. A. V. Roesel, Superintendent of Marlboro County, in *South Carolina School Report, 1914*, p. 91. William Knox Tate, the state high school inspector, hoped for rural emancipation through the mechanical cotton picker. *South Carolina School Report, 1911*, p. 124.

The Uses of Adversity: An Introduction 31

of the century—a museum which should have been "rich with the spoils of time"—Henry James sensed that "the illiteracy seemed to hover like a queer smell; the social revolution had begotten neither song nor story—only, for literature, two or three biographies of soldiers, written in other countries, and only, for music, the weird chants of the emancipated blacks."[88] If this impression did less than justice to Southern literature, it was true to its milieu.

But apathy was not the explanation of Southern educational backwardness. "The country people longed for something better," recalled Charles S. Barrett of the Farmers' Union. Just as they wanted to pay off their mortgages, "They wanted better schools and better teachers, but did not know how to secure them."[89] There were many Southerners, following a pattern common in subordinate regions, who were ready to "turn Yankee" in one respect or another if it promised better schools or the other rewards of a dominant people.

Colonel Robert Bingham, of Bingham School in Asheville, North Carolina, described on several occasions his visits to Northern public schools:

After some weeks spent looking at the working of the public schools in Massachusetts, I was called upon at our University Normal School to tell about what I had seen. I said, ". . . The country produces nothing but granite and ice, and yet I was told that the average per capita wealth of Boston is over $1,700, and of the whole State over $1,000; . . . and they pay the highest per capita school tax in the world; and that it becomes us to find where the secret of this Samsonian strength lies."

And when some one said I was "turning Yankee," I went on to say "that I had seen some other things. I saw a free-school house built with tax money which cost $750,000; I saw the names of 100 free school teachers, head masters of the Boston schools, who got nearly four-thousand-dollar salaries; I saw women (there are about 100 of them in Boston, free-school teachers) who get two-thousand-eight-hundred-dollar salaries. Now there are," I said, "three hundred and

---

88. Henry James, *The American Scene* (New York and London, 1907), pp. 386-87. On the other hand, after a view of the old city, "a patient who has been freely bled," the city library "struck me as flushing with colour and resource, with confidence and temperament."—*Ibid.*, p. 390.

89. Barrett, *The Mission, History and Times of the Farmers' Union*, p. 181.

fifty teachers present, and you know that you do not get more than an average of $25 per month, and you don't get that for more than four months in a year; and you know further that if you could superinduce a set of conditions under which . . . the best man among you would have a chance at a four-thousand-dollar salary, as a free-school teacher, $1,000 more than our Governor gets, and the best woman among you a chance at a two-thousand-eight-hundred-dollar salary as a free-school teacher, $300 more than our Chief Justice gets, if you could do this, you know very well that you would all 'turn Yankees,' unless you have lost your senses."[90]

The superinducement—there was the rub!

In black and white, only the skeleton of the Massachusetts school could be found in the Southern seaboard. Descendants of Puritans might attribute Southern conditions to original sin, and some Southerners might blame Carpetbaggers of the more recent past. But Southerners had more measurable handicaps to their efforts to match the Northern schools which accompanied the Industrial Revolution.

In the first place, the average Southerner had over twice as many children to support and educate as the adult elsewhere in the country. For every 100 children of school age in New York in 1900 there were 125 male adults, in Massachusetts 135, in Nevada 196. But in Virginia there were only 76, in Georgia 68, in North Carolina 66, and in South Carolina 61. This meant that for each dollar provided per school child, the average adult in Massachusetts had to provide 74 cents, the adult in Virginia had to provide $1.31, and in South Carolina $1.64.[91] This predicament can be explained by the high birth rate and emigration rate of the Southern seaboard, and in the case of Negroes partly by the high death rate.

In its higher birth rate the Southern seaboard simply intensified the rural trend everywhere.[92] Even on the incomplete basis of

90. Bingham, *The New South: An Address*, pp. 7-8.
91. In 1903, the average adult male in North Carolina contributed $3.18 to provide $2.11 for each child of school age, while in Massachusetts the contribution of $16.97 provided $22.98. To equal Massachusetts' expenditure, the North Carolinian would have needed to contribute $34.70. *Report of the Commissioner of Education, 1903*, I, lxxvii, lciv.
92. The credit and "furnish" economy, lower cost of childbirth, lack of cost accounting, lower standard of obligation to children, rural ignorance of contraceptives, and lower standard of creature comfort reduced incentives to limit

registered births, more children were born in Georgia in 1900 than in Massachusetts, though the population was only 79 per cent as large.[93] Mortality records, even less accurate, indicate that Negroes had a higher mortality rate for both infants and adults, making even more children per adult than for the whites.[94]

But the high proportion of children in the Southern seaboard was also caused by emigration, a phenomenon so important to the nation that the South is sometimes called the "seedbed" or human reservoir. In 1900, of the living persons born in the Southern seaboard states, one-eighth were living in other states, whereas only one out of 200 residents of these states was born elsewhere. This trend had been going on since the Cumberland Gap was discovered, but by 1900 the stream was turning northward.[95] Emigration on such a scale, taking one-eighth of a generation, must have stemmed from a stronger motive than the desire of the moth for the star. The Southern seaboard was overwhelmingly rural,[96] and its population density was high as rural areas went. The pressure of population upon land was excessive, creating a surplus of agricultural labor.[97] When people pushed one another

---

family size. Rupert B. Vance, *All These People: The Nation's Human Resources in the South* (Chapel Hill, 1945), pp. 95, 105-06; *Abstract of the Twelfth Census of the United States, 1900*, p. 90.

93. United States Census Office, *Twelfth Census of the United States*, Vol. III: Vital Statistics, Part I: Analysis and Ratio Tables (Washington, 1902), 320, 356. In the four Southern seaboard states there were 32 births for every 1000 of population, whereas for the nation there were 27. *Ibid.*, pp. 286, 320, 494, 532; *Abstract of the Twelfth Census of the United States, 1900*, p. 32.

94. *Ibid.*, pp. 178-85; Vance, *All These People*, pp. 347-50, 364; Myrdal, *An American Dilemma*, I, 157-81; Louis I. Dublin, "The Health of the Negro," in Donald Young (ed.), *The American Negro: Annals* of the American Academy of Political and Social Science, CXL (November, 1928), 77-85; E. Franklin Frazier, *The Negro in the United States* (New York, 1949), pp. 171-96.

95. *Abstract of the Twelfth Census of the United States, 1900*, pp. 48-53.

96. The proportion living in rural areas or in hamlets of less than 2,500 persons in 1900 ranged from 81.7 per cent in Virginia to 90.0 per cent in North Carolina, in contrast to 59.8 per cent in the nation and 31.8 per cent in the North Atlantic states. *Ibid.*, p. 38.

97. Virginia had 46.2 persons per square mile, South Carolina 44.4, North Carolina 39.0, Georgia 37.6, whereas the United States average was 25.6. Partly this was a reflection of the intensive agriculture as well as of birth rate. But it does indicate a crowded agriculture and an explosive Negro rural population. *Ibid.*, p. 32. On causes of Negro migration, see particularly Frank A. Ross and Louise V. Kennedy (comps.), *A Bibliography of Negro Migration* (New York, 1934). An intensive analysis of causes of Southern migration is Wilson Gee and John J. Corson, 3rd, *Rural Depopulation in Certain Tidewater*

out of rural backwashes, what little industry and other occupations the Southern seaboard had were insufficient to absorb the continuous increments to the labor force. Industrial wages were lowered and the remaining surplus spilled over into other states. This was by no means an adequate solution of the problem of surplus population, because more young adults left than old people or children, more men than women, more able-bodied than halt or blind, more with energy than with lassitude. Moreover, the emigration was not balanced as in the Northern seaboard by the predominantly adult-male immigration from Europe.[98] The "youngness" of the Southern seaboard population, besides making more schoolchildren per adult male, made more consumers for each producer, more mouths to be fed. Less would remain above subsistence for less tangible services such as education.[99]

With more children to educate, the resident of the Southern seaboard, in common with other Southerners, had less wealth and income with which to support education. In 1900 the true value of property per capita was estimated at $594 in Virginia, $422 in Georgia, $362 in South Carolina, and $360 in North Carolina, whereas in New York, despite its indigent immigrants, there was $1,720, in Nevada $4,503. The national average, the "equator" between these poles, was $1,165. It was not that the Southern seaboard was poor in resources, of course. The money value of all property rose during the next decade, and in 1912 the true value per capita ranged from $1,086 in Virginia to $794 in North Carolina; meanwhile in New York the amount had risen to $2,626, in Nevada to $5,038. While the value of Southern seaboard property had doubled, Southern and non-Southern states remained at corresponding distances from the national "equator."[100] Cur-

---

and Piedmont Areas of Virginia (Charlottesville, 1929). Also useful are Dorothy Swaine Thomas *et al., Research Memorandum on Migration Differentials:* Social Science Research Council, Bulletin 43 (New York, 1938), pp. 141-59; and Myrdal, *An American Dilemma,* I, 182-201.

98. Vance, *All These People,* pp. 45-47, 124-39, 153; *Twelfth Census of the United States: Statistical Atlas of the United States, 1900* (Washington, 1903), Plate No. 29.

99. Vance, *All These People,* Table 16, on p. 60.

100. United States Census Office, *Wealth, Debt, and Taxation* (Washington, 1907), p. 44; United States Bureau of the Census, *Wealth, Debt, and Taxation, 1913* (2 vols., Washington, 1915), I, 26.

rency inflation represented some of the increase, while another considerable portion represented increased Northern ownership of Southern property.

This disparity in wealth between regions was not new, and began to narrow somewhat after 1900. But the optimistic Southern leader Josephus Daniels was reminded in 1903 that a million people in Georgia still lived in log houses. "I know it is not popular to say that the South is poor," he commented, "but . . . while grinding proverty has passed, the bulk of the people have succeeded as yet in making but small accumulations."[101] The average Southeastern farm in 1900 was 97.6 acres and valued at only $1,008; in the country as a whole the size was 146.2 acres, the value $2,896. The Southeastern farm was thrice removed in value from the national "equator."[102]

In income also, the Southerner failed the first grade while his Northern neighbor was promoted. In the first federal income-tax returns, for the last ten months of 1913, the Southern seaboard states with nine per cent of the national population reported only three per cent of the incomes above $2,500, only seven of the 1,598 incomes above $100,000, and none of the 179 incomes over $400,000.[103] The earliest reliable estimates of per capita income in 1919 show the Southern seaboard states at the bottom again. South Carolina was 30 per cent below the national average, Virginia 37 per cent below, Georgia and North Carolina 39 per cent below. Most non-Southern states were proportionately above the average.[104]

The adult male of the Southern seaboard thus had twice as many children as his Northern counterpart, to be educated in two

101. *Sixth Conference for Education in the South, Proceedings* (Richmond, 1903), p. 148.
102. Vance, *All These People*, Table 37, on p. 164. The value included land and buildings. In 1910 and 1920 the Southeastern farm remained about one-third of the national average.
103. United States Bureau of Foreign and Domestic Commerce, *Statistical Abstract of the United States, 1914* (Washington, 1915), pp. 26-27, 603-04. The population proportion is based upon the estimate for July 1, 1914.
104. Maurice Leven in collaboration with Williford I. King, *Income in the Various States: Its Distribution 1919, 1920, and 1921* (New York, 1925), p. 256. Since 1919 was an unusual year, perhaps a clearer view of the trend is revealed by the averages for the three years 1919, 1920, and 1921, which show Virginia 37 per cent, North Carolina 47 per cent, Georgia 52 per cent, and South Carolina 54 per cent below the national average.

separate school systems, with less than half as much property and barely half as great an income with which to do it. It is not surprising that the South did not have the American system of education, much less the Massachusetts type of school. Diagnosis of Southern economic "illth" is beyond the range of this monograph, but its bearing on the educational history of the Southern seaboard warrants a brief note of the symptoms.

In an economy that was national in scope by 1900, Southerners generally, of both ethnic groups, were the hewers of wood and drawers of water. In 1910, 61.1 per cent of the gainfully employed were in extractive occupations and 17.1 per cent in manufacturing and mechanical industries, whereas in the nation as a whole 35.7 per cent were in the extractive and 27.9 per cent in manufacturing and mechanical occupations. New England had only 10.7 per cent and the Middle Atlantic states only 14.2 per cent in extractive occupations. Thus four to six times as large a proportion of Southern seaboard workers were in the least remunerative class of occupations.[105]

In agriculture, the chief extractive occupation in the Southern seaboard, two cash crops—cotton and tobacco—predominated. Their grooves ran deep and closely linked the region with industrial capitalism. Just as the South was crowded down in the lower general category of occupations, so within this category Southerners were at the bottom. When non-Southern commodity prices generally rose in the two decades after 1896, these leading Southern crops lagged behind the general price rise. Cotton market prices hovered between seven and fourteen cents and averaged about ten cents during the period.[106]

The Southern tenant farmer was a weak foundation on which to build any social institution, and tenancy was more widespread in the South than elsewhere in the nation. In the cotton and to-

---

[105]. United States Bureau of the Census, *Thirteenth Census of the United States*, Vol. IV: Population, 1910, Occupation Statistics (Washington, 1914), 44-45.

[106]. Nannie M. Tilley, *The Bright-Tobacco Industry 1860-1929* (Chapel Hill, 1948), table on p. 354. On economic and climatic reasons for concentration on these crops, see Vance, *All These People*, pp. 177-78, 188; Rupert B. Vance, *Human Geography of the South* (Chapel Hill, 1932), pp. 93-105, 229-30; Calvin B. Hoover and B. U. Ratchford, *Economic Resources and Policies of the South* (New York, 1951), pp. 3-5.

The Uses of Adversity: An Introduction 37

bacco counties of the North Carolina coastal plain, for example, the percentage of farm tenancy in 1909 ranged from 54.2 per cent in Robeson County to 72.8 per cent in Edgecombe County, and was on the increase.[107] Tenancy was particularly prevalent among Negroes.[108] Yet it was the farmers who began first among native Southerners to wrestle with the problem of universal public education. Rising up during the long depression in the late eighties and nineties, members of the Farmers' Alliance and Populist Party seized control of state governments and made the first substantial gains in public education since Reconstruction. Educational advancement was not, however, a primary objective of the organized farmers. Though they did not shy away from social legislation, their political existence was so precarious and their poverty so pinching that they were able neither to pin their hopes on the slow processes of formal education nor to charge up their troubles to illiteracy or ignorance.

The farmers' movement came too late to control national policies without urban votes, and after 1896 the rank and file of Southern Populists straggled leaderless back into the Democratic fold, where they were subjected to party discipline, voted for machine candidates, and joined in the disfranchisement campaigns. But they brought their radical principles with them; they had not spelled out *Progress and Poverty* and *Wealth against Commonwealth* to no purpose. And they gave support to the nearest equivalent, a Southern progressivism which "sprouted in the soil that had nourished Populism but . . . lacked the agrarian cast and the radical edge that had frightened the middle class away from the earlier movement."[109]

---

107. Tilley, *Bright-Tobacco Industry 1860-1929*, pp. 94-95, tables showing census figures on tenancy in tobacco counties.

108. On the plight of the Negro tenant farmer, see George B. Tindall, *South Carolina Negroes 1877-1900* (Columbia, S. C., 1952), pp. 121-22; William Garrott Brown, "The White Peril: The Immediate Danger of the Negro," in *North American Review*, CLXXIX (December, 1904), 838. In 1910 over three-fifths of Virginia Negro farm operators were owners, but the proportion was only one-third in North Carolina, one-fifth in South Carolina, and one-eighth in Georgia. United States Bureau of the Census, *Negroes in the United States*, Bulletin 129, 1915 (Washington, 1915), p. 160.

109. Woodward, *Origins of the New South*, p. 371. See his chapter "Progressivism—For Whites Only," *ibid.*, pp. 369-95, for an account of the movement.

Almost all Southerners in the 1900's professed friendship for the public school, but progressive factions gave educational reformers the most effective support. They were more ready to tax the capitalist and property-owner to provide the funds. On the other hand, the new progressivism was "For Whites Only," and hunger for opportunity conflicted with the doctrine of equality of opportunity. Here was the dilemma. "Note our chains binding us fast to the Negro question," wrote William E. Dodd early in the century. "I fear the South would defeat Govt. ownership of railways in order to save the 'Jim Crow' laws!"[110] By the same talisman many a white Southerner would oppose better schools in order to prevent a Negro child from sharing in the benefits.

The alternative to Southern agrarianism and progressivism was leadership by Southern businessmen who were strengthening their bonds with outside capitalists. But the Southern businessmen had little to offer the educational reformers. Their economic policy for the South was less realistic than that of the "hayseed Socialists," for all that they shaved off their beards. And their desire for low taxes and low wages ranged them against educational reformers. The agrarian rebels, understanding the implications of national centralization of economic power, were the first large group in the nation who sought to harness this power, by federal intervention, to the public good. Southern businessmen, on the other hand, appealed to the Northern investor with cheap resources and cheap labor.[111] And the spokesmen of the farmers took a more enlightened view of public education than those who hungered for cotton mills.

Southern industry was too limited in extent and type to be a major factor in the life of these rural states; in 1900 only 3.8 per cent of the population were industrial wage-earners. And Southern industries generally were of the low-wage and low-value-creating type, processing the region's resources for distant markets. Southern seaboard cotton mills, lumber mills, and tobacco factories, representing the bulk of the region's industry, employed 134,857

---

110. William E. Dodd to Walter Clark, September 7, 1906, in Hugh T. Lefler (ed.), "Selected William E. Dodd–Walter Clark Letters," in *North Carolina Historical Review*, XXV (January, 1948), 91.
111. Woodward, *Origins of the New South*, pp. 114-20, 309-11.

The Uses of Adversity: An Introduction

workers, at average annual wages ranging from $281.75 in Virginia lumber mills to $136.27 in North Carolina tobacco factories.[112]

While the 29,434 workers under sixteen in Southern seaboard industries represented a jealously protected interest of their employers, these were only 3 per cent of the number of children of school age not enrolled. Child labor was more important as a factor in depressing Southern wages, which were about 53.2 per cent of the New England level in the cotton textile industry and 69.5 per cent of the Northern wage in the lumber industry.[113]

Though there were personal exceptions, neither the Northern investor nor the Southern manager in these Southern cheap-labor industries had an economic concern for a trained labor or an educated citizenry. Of course "A boy in the printing business that can not read and write is of very little practical value,"[114] and Southern railway telegraphers who misspelled in Morse code presented a baffling problem.[115] In the main industries of the little "one-crop" factory towns of the Southern Piedmont, however, education was a thing to be reserved for the children of mill officials, bankers who handled their local deposits, merchants who found a market in the new numbers.

The Negro child's share in Southern education was related to the Southern economy, but is not entirely explained by it. He was a marginal child in school opportunities as his parent was the marginal man in agriculture. But the inferior opportunities were also part of the pattern of Southern racial customs. Education went deeper than dwellings, eating, riding, and spectator amusement in setting the races apart. It wove the tapestry of habit that was draped over the hard walls of caste. And where whites

112. *Twelfth Census of the United States, 1900*, Vol. VIII, Manufactures, Part II: States and Territories (Washington, 1902), 136-43, 666-69, 832-35, 905-06, 910-17. For trends in the major Southern industries until 1910, see *Thirteenth Census of the United States, 1910*, Vol. IX, Manufactures 1909: Reports by States, with Statistics for Principal Cities (Washington, 1912), 230-31, 912-13, 1152, 1280-81.

113. Richard A. Lester, "Trends in Southern Wage Differentials since 1890," in *Southern Economic Journal*, XI (April, 1945), 339.

114. George L. Dooley, printer, Charlotte, North Carolina, in *Fourteenth Annual Report of the North Carolina Bureau of Labor and Printing, 1900* (Raleigh, 1901), p. 297.

115. W. B. Swindell, Order of Railway Telegraphers, Charlotte, North Carolina, in *Eighth Annual Report of the North Carolina Bureau of Labor Statistics, 1894* (Raleigh, 1894), pp. 272-74.

had all the power and controlled the Negro school funds, the Negro schools conformed within their cramped limits with values of the whites. The white landowner and employer of Negroes had little use for Negro literacy; the poorer white feared the power that literacy would give the Negro. Inferior education for Negroes seems to have been one of the few things upon which most whites agreed. Despite its poor facilities, there was magic in the Southern public school, which Southern whites were reluctant to share.[116]

Negro disfranchisement in the South near the turn of the century affected the school systems in several ways. In the first place, disfranchisement made the Negro vote negligible and stripped Negro school funds of what meager protection they had earlier enjoyed. In states where the change was made by constitutional convention, educational law was altered at the same time to make easier the diversion of Negro school funds to white schools at county or district levels. In the two states which disfranchised by constitutional amendments, North Carolina in 1900 and Georgia in 1908, racial prejudice was fanned to get whites to vote for measures they feared might disfranchise them too. Under the spell of White Supremacy orators, poor whites voted for poll taxes and illiterate whites for literacy tests. The social cost of this sort of propaganda is indicated by the rise in lynchings and the drop in voting participation.

Secondly, the literacy test for suffrage in several states, particularly North Carolina, created some demand among poor rural whites for enough education to qualify their children to vote, even though illiterate whites were often allowed to vote by arrangement with election judges and by other means. The South Carolina and Virginia constitutional conventions, on the other hand, were dominated by political leaders who did not stir the white electorate on education. By the time of the Georgia amendment, it was clear that literacy clauses could be evaded by whites, and besides there were alternatives such as "good character," "understanding," pos-

---

116. On the role of the Negro school in the pattern of segregation, see Myrdal, *An American Dilemma*, I, 337-44, 632-33, II, 879-907; William E. Burghardt Du Bois, *The Souls of Black Folk* (Chicago, 1903, 13th ed., 1922), pp. 60-74.

The Uses of Adversity: An Introduction   41

session of forty acres or $500. But North Carolina educators, who capitalized on the momentary excitement to launch a public school crusade, eventually stimulated similar movements in other Southern states.[117]

Thirdly, while disfranchisement registered the ebb of Populism and hopes for political action, many agrarians, rather than surrender hope as their leaders were doing, hitched their hopes to other stars such as education. The educational orator offered a Promised Land not open to the adult farmer himself. But the very failure of his own high hopes in the agrarian movement inured the farm parent to this shortcoming of the educational movement. As for Negroes, they took to the same educational faith for very similar reasons. It was one of the few avenues of aspiration open to a frustrated and depressed people.

Disfranchisement, however, was only the legal aspect of the political phase of White Supremacy, which was itself the simplified propaganda slogan of a more complex movement. Whites had been supreme all along, of course. And the public attitudes of extreme racism and public policies of racial aggression beginning in the nineties simply intensified earlier trends. Woodward argues convincingly that extreme racism rose to dominate Southern affairs not by conversion, but by a weakening and discrediting of various forces which had earlier held it in check. The chief restraining forces he describes were Southern conservatism, Southern Populist radicalism, and Northern liberalism.[118]

Southern conservatives, who found Negroes useful, regarded Negrophobia as a mark of lower-class status and protected some of the Negro's elemental rights until the nineties. As they lost popularity largely because of their economic policies and were challenged by Populism, conservatives themselves raised the cry of "Negro domination." At the same time they used controlled Negro ballots in the black counties to defeat Populist whites and achieve what they called White Supremacy. To say the least, this

---

117. Key, *Southern Politics in State and Nation*, pp. 556-69. North Carolina disfranchisement and its effect on education are discussed in the next chapter.
118. C. Vann Woodward, *The Strange Career of Jim Crow* (New York, 1955), pp. 51-52 *et passim*. This brief account and fresh interpretation of racial segregation will be used without further citation on the next few pages.

weakened their moral authority as opponents of extreme racism.

Radical Populism pursued a racial policy consistent with its equalitarian principles, but both policy and movement collapsed under the pressure of conservative White Supremacy tactics. Its heritage was frustration and bitterness, and many disappointed ex-Populists made the Negro the scapegoat of their disappointment. Turning from a hopelessly stronger foe to a helplessly weak one, they convinced themselves that the Negro was an author rather than a fellow victim of their defeat. This mood offered a stimulus rather than a check to racism.

Most Negroes were silent during the White Supremacy movement because of fear or apathy. Booker T. Washington of Tuskegee Institute, the universally recognized leader of the Negroes, sought for his people a "social adjustment," to borrow a term from recent sociologists, an adjustment based on accommodation to the demands of the dominant whites. He established rapport with the dwindling group of upper-class Southerners of paternalistic humor. Through lectures and fund-raising tours in the North he built alliances with philanthropic capitalists and won powerful friends for his conservative race leadership. To the businessman of the New South persuasion, busily humming the tune of progress in a period of depression and race conflict, Washington offered a Negro labor force which would avoid unions and radicalism. The Negro Moses was significantly an educator, taking the long road through the wilderness of Southern race relations. Even his protest against racial disfranchisement was qualified. "In the degree that you close the ballot box against the ignorant," he told the Louisiana disfranchisement convention, "you open the school house."[119] And even in education there had to be accommodation to the ideas of whites on school boards as to what was suitable for

---

119. Quoted in Logan, *The Negro in American Life and Thought*, p. 210. On Washington's leadership, the best biographical study so far is Samuel R. Spencer, Jr., *Booker T. Washington and the Negro's Place in American Life* (Boston, 1955), pp. 87-143. Also see Oliver C. Cox, "The Leadership of Booker T. Washington," in *Social Forces*, XXX (October, 1951), 91-97; Bond, *Negro Education in Alabama*, pp. 195-225. But August Meier, "Toward a Reinterpretation of Booker T. Washington," in *Journal of Southern History*, XXIII (May, 1957), 220-27, presents impressive evidence of Washington's surreptitious but "direct attack upon disfranchisement and segregation."

The Uses of Adversity: An Introduction 43

members of a subordinate race. These school board members, usually of the class which Washington sought as allies, provided a Negro education inferior in quantity and quality. Nor did endowed industrial schools for Negroes escape the racial handicap. Hampton and Tuskegee led many of their graduates up blind alleys of manual skill at a time when skills were being displaced by new machinery and techniques of mass production.

The failure of Northern emancipators and their sons to resist effectively the Southern wave of racism may be explained by many changes in Northern attitudes since Reconstruction. The Northeast and West wooed the South politically. Northern liberals conciliated Southern whites in the hope of reciprocal support for reform measures. Others had long since laid down the burden of the freedmen to turn without restraint to the pursuit of economic gain, which proved more exciting and rewarding. A less direct, but pervasive influence on Northern attitudes was the climate of Social Darwinism in which the progressive movement flourished. One of its offshoots was racism, which applied the metaphor of the "struggle for existence" uncritically to racial groups. Used in Europe and America to condone imperialism, racism became a vogue in America in time to coincide with the Southern White Supremacy movement. The white North for a whole generation was ethically disarmed for the task of lecturing Southerners about aggression against American Negroes.[120] And some Northerners were ready to draw on Southern white experience for the management of "new-caught, sullen peoples" in American colonies.[121]

Around 1900 came "the end of the Negro's resistance to the determination on the part of the white South to reduce him to a subordinate status,"[122] and a nation-wide "peculiar institution" for the freed Negro had been developed. The incidental violence

---

120. Robert Bingham, "Sectional Misunderstandings," in *North American Review*, CLXXIX (September, 1904), 363.

121. Richard Hofstadter, *Social Darwinism in American Thought, 1860-1915* (Philadelphia, 1944), pp. 69-70, 154, 174-76. On Darwinism as a common element in reform movements and imperialism, see William E. Leuchtenburg, "Progressivism and Imperialism: The Progressive Movement and American Foreign Policy, 1898-1916," in *Mississippi Valley Historical Review*, XXXIX (December, 1952), 483-504.

122. Frazier, *The Negro in the United States*, pp. 161-62. Rayford W. Logan suggests that "the nadir" was reached about 1901.

began to taper off before the end of the nineties, as Negroes bowed in submission to the ten-to-one odds.[123] The new stratification was a Color Line, compounded of segregation, discrimination, and the imminent threat of violence.

123. See, for example, the diagram of lynchings from 1882 to 1936, in Frazier, *The Negro in the United States*, p. 160. The peak of lynchings was in 1892, when there were 163, and they tapered off as Negroes accepted, outwardly at least, the status accorded them by whites.

CHAPTER II

Seedtime: North Carolina in the Nineties

"RAILROADS AND SCHOOLS would change the state of affairs," the young educator Edwin A. Alderman noted in his journal in 1889 as he traveled from school to school in an educational investigation of the whole state of North Carolina. "The negro is the main trouble here," he observed in the eastern part of the state, "though that is merely an excuse." "I am convinced that the demand for better schools must come from the *West*." A convert to the secular religion of the New South, Alderman believed that railroads would bring industry, which in turn would increase the rewards of economic life, quicken intellectual life, and stimulate public education as an internal improvement. But he sadly noted at an industrialized town farther west: "Concord has the largest factory in the state, street cars, electric lights, & water works. Improvement in schools generally comes last." At Kinston, which had recently abandoned its public graded school, "The Property men as usual run things and kill off all school aspirations."[1]

Alderman's reflections were usually those typical of a member of the South's small middle class; yet he had a sharp eye. At one "typical, rickety, cheerless public school house," he counted thirteen panes of glass out of the windows and noted down the number in

---

1. Edwin A. Alderman, "Institute Statistics," two MS notebooks kept during an educational tour as Institute Conductor in 1889 and 1890, with weekly entries, Edwin A. Alderman Papers, Alderman Library, University of Virginia, quoted in Clement Eaton, "Edwin A. Alderman—Liberal of the New South," in *North Carolina Historical Review*, XXIII (April, 1946), 212-13.

his journal. Watching the pupils, he commented: "The solemn-faced little children of this county haven't much showing in life. A mortal lethargy seems settled over all, what changes a *good* school in every district would bring, Blair's bill would give it. These people know the public schools only to sneer at them so far as I can see and this is not to be marvelled at if a tree shall be judged by its fruits."[2] Alderman's journalist friend, Walter Hines Page, already on the ladder of success in New York though "dead broke" upon migration from North Carolina three years earlier, blamed the "mummies" for most Southern difficulties, including lack of education, and swore that the same stones rolled in the country roads that had slowed the march of troops to Bull Run. But Alderman in his travels found ignorance in its natural setting—rural poverty, isolation, racial tension, the opposition of landlords and mill barons to schools that might "spoil a field hand" or a low-wage worker, and a "ragged individualism" which resisted taxation. While the Dividing Line had moved northward since William Byrd's day, like a good many things Southern, Lubberland was still there. The Tar Heel stood in the same need of the democratic opportunity for enlightenment as when the Whig Calvin Wiley used the Literary Fund to float two state banks and internal improvement ventures. Alderman and his colleague Charles Duncan McIver, who saw the regional problem in the large and yet familiarly, refused to allow its enormity and complexity to discourage them from efforts to cope with it. In this respect they were forerunners of the Southern regionalists of the school of Howard W. Odum and Rupert B. Vance, though their methods were less scientific.

North Carolina's state tax-supported system of public schools, begun in its complete form during Reconstruction, had survived Redemption.[3] But conservative legislatures and state courts in the eighties manned the lines against increases in state funds. The Barksdale case[4] in 1886 is a gauge of the temper of the times.

2. *Ibid.*, p. 210.
3. Daniel J. Whitener, "Public Education in North Carolina during Reconstruction, 1865-1876," in Fletcher M. Green (ed.), *Essays in Southern History Presented to Joseph Gregoire de Roulhac Hamilton, Ph.D., LL.D., by His Former Students at the University of North Carolina:* The James Sprunt Studies in History and Political Science (Chapel Hill, 1900—), XXXI (1949), 67-90.
4. *S. Barksdale et al. v. Commissioners of Sampson County*, in *North Carolina*

The state constitution, requiring a minimum school term of four months, also provided a maximum for property taxation, 66-2/3 cents per $100 assessed value, which was insufficient to maintain all schools for four months. In the Barksdale case, the majority of the state supreme court maintained that since education was not "a necessary expense," the state was obligated only to "do what can be done within the prescribed limits" of taxation. In spite of the escape clause in the constitution which allowed extraordinary taxation for any necessary expense of government, the court gave precedence to property rights over human rights and declared that the duty of the county commissioners was "performed when all the resources open to them are employed and exhausted in an effort to maintain them for the designated period." For the next twenty-two years, until the reversal of the Barksdale decision, efforts at educational improvement were channeled largely into local tax campaigns and pressure for legislative appropriations.

Meanwhile the town graded schools for whites, appearing most thickly in the Piedmont in the seventies and eighties, were reinforced in 1883 by the passage of a state-wide "local assessment" act sponsored by Senator William T. Dortch of Goldsboro. Because it allowed taxes disguised as assessments to be divided by race and applied to the schools of the race voting for the assessment, the act violated two clauses of the constitution, one which required uniform taxation and another prohibiting discrimination in the distribution of school funds. A temporary boom in white graded schools was halted when wealthy real-estate owners, resentful of taxation, and Negro leaders, hoping for equal school opportunities, joined forces to challenge the act. When the state supreme court enjoined collection of such segregated taxes, town graded schools dropped like rotten fruit. Some towns, notably Wilson, openly defied the supreme court ruling for years. Durham began to supplement the state fund by private subscription, and some smaller towns such as Kinston converted their public schools to private schools rather than support Negro education. Others

---

Reports, XCIII: *Cases Argued and Determined by the Supreme Court of North Carolina, October Term, 1885, Reported by Theodore F. Davidson, Annotated by Walter Clark* (Raleigh, 1908, original pagination used), pp. 472-88.

manfully took up the White Man's Burden when they saw no other choice.[5]

A fruitful collaboration began in 1889 between Alderman, then superintendent of Goldsboro schools, and Charles D. McIver, a teacher at Peace Institute in Raleigh after a brief career at Winston and Durham in the Dortch Act days. They were appointed state conductors of weekly teachers' institutes in all of the hundred counties. Pedagogically the assignment was absurd, but the two young men interpreted their charge broadly and turned Saturday of each weekly session into a public school rally. And "on that day one theme only was discussed, the Gospel of Popular Education in all its relations." After three years of full-time campaigning, assisted by a half-dozen other school officials, the two men went to the newly organized state Normal and Industrial School for white women in 1892, McIver as president and Alderman as professor, and used it as a base for a continuing campaign.[6]

Finding no encouragement among the propertied men of the towns, the educational reformers glanced at the white farmers, who formed the bulk of the voting population. Hard-bitten, discontented, they certainly did not run things, but they did have aspirations and were busy organizing the Farmers' Alliance to give expression to both discontent and hope. About 700 people, mostly

---

5. Marcus C. S. Noble, *A History of the Public Schools of North Carolina* (Chapel Hill, 1930), pp. 407-08; Charles L. Coon, "School Support and Our North Carolina Courts, 1886-1926," in *North Carolina Historical Review*, III (July, 1926), 416-18; Charles L. Lewis, *Philander Priestley Claxton: Crusader for Public Education* (Knoxville, 1948), pp. 35-39; William K. Boyd, *The Story of Durham: City of the New South* (Durham, 1925), pp. 178-84; J. Kelly Turner and John L. Bridgers, Jr., *History of Edgecombe County, North Carolina* (Raleigh, 1920), pp. 380-81. A recent article by Frenise A. Logan, "The Legal Status of Public School Education for Negroes in North Carolina, 1877-1894," in *North Carolina Historical Review*, XXXII (July, 1955), 346-57, is a definitive study of this subject.

6. Noble, *A History of the Public Schools of North Carolina*, pp. 428-39; Eaton, "Edwin A. Alderman—Liberal of the New South," pp. 208-13; Dumas Malone, *Edwin A. Alderman: A Biography* (New York, 1940), pp. 23-47. The atmosphere of the Institutes shows through the formalities in the reports of Alderman and McIver, in the *Biennial Reports of the Superintendent of Public Instruction of North Carolina for the Scholastic Years 1889-1890 and 1891-1892* (Raleigh, 1891, 1893), hereafter referred to as *North Carolina School Report*, with appropriate years. Rose Howell Holder, *McIver of North Carolina* (Chapel Hill, 1957), based on the McIver Papers, was published when the present work was in press; on the Institutes, see *ibid.*, pp. 80-113.

farmers, heard Alderman speak on education at the Union County courthouse in 1889. There were similar large crowds in Lincoln and Alexander counties, and a delegate to the state Alliance convention told Alderman that Alliancemen were "hot for an increase of 50%" in public school appropriations. The relation of the voting masses of farmers to the public schools became clearer in the educator's mind, and on the hustings the agrarian dust settled as a mantle on the city-bred man. The organized farmers, for their part, though certainly not primarily concerned with education, incidentally allied themselves with the school men, sponsored the white state agricultural and mechanical college[7] and the college for women, and the state Negro college, and above all endorsed the improvement of the common schools. The state Alliance program in 1890 included a "Demand" for better schools, by means of a 50 per cent increase in state taxation. And when the Alliancemen spoke of universal education, they really meant it. "We want it understood that we embrace in this appeal to our General Assembly the negro children of the State," wrote Leonidas L. Polk in the *Progressive Farmer*.[8]

Harassed by depression conditions and angry over the *laissez faire* views of the local conservative Democratic leaders, the farmers disrupted for a decade the oligarchy which had held power since the end of Reconstruction. Men pledged to the farmers' program, still largely within the Democratic party, captured the legislature in 1891 and passed laws raising school taxes 25 per cent and creating state higher schools for white women and for Negroes. But on other counts they proved a disappointment to both farmers and educators,[9] and were swept out at the next

7. On the role of farm leaders in founding the college, see David Lockmiller, *History of the North Carolina State College of Agriculture and Engineering of the University of North Carolina* (Raleigh, 1939), pp. 21-49; Stuart Noblin, *Leonidas LaFayette Polk: Agrarian Crusader* (Chapel Hill, 1949), pp. 163-82. The new college had an agrarian cast, and the first president conscientiously forced into agriculture many country boys who wanted to get rich by way of the engineering course.

8. *Ibid.*, p. 253, quoting from an editorial on January 13, 1891.

9. Their school tax was declared unconstitutional. In *Board of Education of Bladen County v. Board of Commissioners of Bladen County*, in *North Carolina Reports*, CXI (September Term, 1892), 578-92, Justice James C. MacRae for the majority cited the Barksdale precedent and declared that "we are constrained by the principle involved in the maxim *stare decisis*, in which is bound up the

election. The session of 1893 cleared the statute books of most of the changes.[10]

After 1893 many farmers broke completely with the Democratic party, became Populists, and by joining with Republicans in state elections acquired the name of Fusionists. They captured control of the state, and their brief experiment in coalition government in a Southern state in the late nineties, after the sun had set on agrarian radicalism in the rest of the country, thrust public education to the front as a real public question. A constructive task was set for the long Southern "era of good feeling" which ensued.

Most Democrats responded to the challenge of Fusionism by even more complete economic and social conservatism. But some of them realized that it was the coupling of Democratic names with Whig measures that had caused their overthrow. George Howard, after talking with one of the conservative North Carolina judges, thought "of the times when he was a bitter Whig and I a Democrat of the old style. I must tell him this and tell him that men without faith in democracy, like himself, assuming the name have brought us to this."[11]

"If the 'shroud and pall' shall ever come to their order," the state Alliance president said prophetically to the convention in 1894 in reference to the pledge of a 25 per cent increase in the school tax, "this and other noble legislation shall be a monument.... More of your money ought to go direct to the children's education." Five-cent cotton and ten-cent tobacco, the crop lien system, and the necessity of working children for the family's support had, in the past, made many a farmer a more stubborn opponent of legislative support of education than were the railroads, the textile manufacturers, and the tobacco industrialists, though the latter could more easily escape taxation than could the landowner. But the farmer's children must go to the public schools or not at all.[12]

---

stability of judicial decision, on which depends not only respect for law, but knowledge of law. . . ."

10. John D. Hicks, "The Farmers' Alliance in North Carolina," in *North Carolina Historical Review*, II (April, 1925), 162-87.

11. George Howard to Henry G. Connor, November 6, 1895, in Henry G. Connor Papers, S.H.C., University of North Carolina.

12. Raleigh *News and Observer*, August 24, 1894.

Seedtime: North Carolina in the Nineties   51

Fusionist capture of the legislature in 1895 brought little change in the schools. In the election of 1896, however, Populists and Republicans between them gained control of not only the legislature but a complete slate of state offices, including a Republican governor and a Populist school superintendent. Debates on public school policy became heated; all three parties endorsed improvement of schools and denounced their opponents' policy as retrogression. Undoubtedly some Populists used the issue to divert attention from their association with the heirs of the Carpetbaggers. Conservative Democrats used education as evidence that they were opposed not to reform, but to radical agrarianism and Negro domination; but their educational record was against them. Whatever their motives, politicians in the late nineties ripped a few seams in the strait jacket imposed by the conservatives to stunt the public school. The role of the Fusion political leaders was important, and not merely because they forced the Democrats to modernize their conceptions of the role of government in society. It was over the protest of leading Democrats that the Fusion superintendent and legislature framed a democratic educational program.

Contrary to local tradition, it was Fusion that placed a teacher in the office of state superintendent. Convening before the Populists in 1896, the Republicans left three blanks in their slate as a come-on to the Populists. Ignoring the Republicans, the Populists nominated a complete ticket of their own. The Republicans won the election and carried with them Populists for the offices they had not contested, and thus it was that Charles H. Mebane became state superintendent of public instruction. His role in the Fusion regime has been generally misunderstood.[13] Mebane was a Populist—apparently not connected with the Republican textile

13. Helen G. Edmonds, *The Negro and Fusion Politics in North Carolina, 1894-1901* (Chapel Hill, 1951), pp. 51-53. Born in 1862 in Guilford County, Mebane had taught at Catawba College for about ten years before his election. Later he was president of Catawba College, 1901-04; superintendent of Catawba County, 1904-09; state school loan fund agent, 1909-13; Judge of Catawba County Recorder's Court, 1914-15; from 1903 until his death, owner and editor of the *Catawba County News* and *Catawba News-Enterprise*. *Catawba News-Enterprise*, December 17, 1926; *State School Facts* (Raleigh, monthly), XIX (April, 1947). An example of the misunderstanding of Mebane is Henry M. Wagstaff, *Impressions of Men and Movements at the University of North Carolina* (ed. by Louis R. Wilson, Chapel Hill, 1950), p. 61.

manufacturer B. Frank Mebane—and a member of the Reformed Church, which took no part in the contests between denominational colleges and state colleges in the nineties. He voted for William Jennings Bryan and for the Populist rather than the Republican nominee for governor in 1896. While in office, Mebane worked to give professional dignity to a department of the state government which had been a cat's-paw of patronage politicians, and insisted that he was a partisan only of the children, who had no votes.[14]

The Fusionists in 1895 passed a state tax law to bring all terms up to four months, but the supreme court invalidated it. So in 1897 the school reformers centered on a local taxation law which would allow a willing district to tax itself beyond the state and county maximum limit.

As the legislature convened, Edwin A. Alderman became president of the University of North Carolina, which he was determined to make "the chief public school." Alderman's championship of schools for the masses was based on conviction, and was not merely a political coat. He arrived at the legislature to join McIver and devote his rare histrionic talents to the cause of popular education. As his friend Tom Dunston, the Uncle Tom of Chapel Hill, said of Alderman, he could "designate, expostulate, and prevaricate like the vast writers of antiquity." Scorning the fulsome periods of the old-fashioned Southern orator, Alderman yet had the Southern genius for manipulating words. "Nobody but a deaf man could have ever walked out on him."[15]

Agents of the denominational colleges, at this juncture in their long contest with the state university and colleges, adopted new tactics and championed larger appropriations "sorely needed for the lower education of the children of the great masses of the people." Fresh funds for the "lower education," a Baptist editor

14. Letter of George A. Grimsley (city superintendent, Greensboro) to the editor, in Raleigh *News and Observer*, April 10, 1900; *State School Facts*, XIX (April, 1947); open letter by Mebane, in Raleigh *News and Observer*, April 10, 1900; *Biblical Recorder* (Baptist weekly, Raleigh), July 9, 1902. Cf., however, Luther L. Gobbel, *Church-State Relationships in Education in North Carolina since 1776* (Durham, 1938), pp. 149, 169, 171; J. G. de Roulhac Hamilton, *North Carolina since 1860*, Vol. III of *History of North Carolina* (Chicago and New York, 1919), p. 365.

15. Malone, *Edwin A. Alderman*, p. 80.

pointedly observed, might be obtained from the annual appropriations to the state university and colleges.[16]

North Carolina denominational educators, led by President James B. Shearer of Presbyterian Davidson College, the Southern Baptist editor Josiah W. Bailey, and the Southern Methodist John Carlisle Kilgo, president of Trinity College, had invited legislators for years to investigate infidel teaching, unfair competition, and "godless" goings-on at the state university and colleges, and demanded an end to all state aid to the state institutions. "The Battle for Christ in Education" was now temporarily halted by a truce in the mid-nineties.[17]

In the jaundiced view of one opponent of taxation, there was a seamy side to the friendly rivalry of lobbyists Alderman and McIver with Kilgo and Bailey. Thomas D. Boone wrote to the Raleigh *News and Observer* that these "two very antagonistic elements" had "different ends in view." He said:

The advocates of State aid [to higher education], and they are found everywhere, hope to distract the attention of the people from the battle royal that has been, much against their will, forced upon them, and thereby postpone if not entirely relieve themselves of the opposition that will not down at their bidding. The anti-State aiders, and their number is increasing daily [,] expect so to burden the people with increased taxation for public schools—that the people will openly revolt against an increase of their burden and demand a cessation of the horse leech cries of "give"—"give." A truce has been on for some time, but . . . a day of reckoning between these two discordant elements will come and then look out to see the fur fly.[18]

16. *Biblical Recorder*, December 2, 1896, quoted in Herbert L. Swain, "Editorial Views of the Religious Press in North Carolina" (unpublished M.A. thesis, University of North Carolina, 1942), p. 62.

17. Wagstaff, *Impressions of Men and Movements at the University of North Carolina*, p. 61; Gobbel, *Church-State Relationships in Education in North Carolina since 1776*, pp. 169, 192-95, and for the private thoughts of these embattled Christians, p. 171. Kilgo, as a friend of the Washington Duke family and a Republican, denounced Thomas Jefferson from the pulpit as a "monster" and infidel. He was reported to have said that the centers of vice and immorality were in the towns "where the Graded Schools and other Christless institutions have gotten in their work." Paul N. Garber, *John Carlisle Kilgo, President of Trinity College, 1894-1910* (Durham, 1937), pp. 58-83; *Webster's Weekly* (Reidsville, North Carolina), July 28, 1898; John C. Kilgo, "Some Phases of Southern Education," in *South Atlantic Quarterly*, II (April, 1903), 137-51; Kemp P. Battle, *History of the University of North Carolina* (2 vols., Raleigh, 1907-1912), II, 307-12, 478-93.

18. Raleigh *News and Observer*, August 4, 1897.

To provide enough money to operate all schools in the state for four months, or at least to test again the Barksdale decision, a law of 1897 increased the general property tax beyond the constitutional limit of property taxes per $100 at one-third of the poll tax.[19] The supreme court promptly declared the act unconstitutional, basing its decision on the Barksdale precedent and principle. This action reinstated the school tax at the level of 1895, insufficient to provide a four-month term.[20]

The Fusion legislature of 1897 also passed "An act to encourage local taxation for schools" which *required* an election every two years in each township until a majority of qualified voters of the township should vote in favor of a local tax. There was no loophole for tax-dodgers; the rate of tax to be voted on was to be fixed by the county commissioners, but the law specified a minimum rate. As a further encouragement, $50,000 was appropriated to match any local tax funds or private subscriptions. To repeal a local tax, one-third of the qualified voters would have to petition for a special election and then muster a majority of the qualified voters. This act was precisely what the school men had asked for. Opponents of the law failed in efforts to get the attorney general to annul it.

These two acts, increasing state taxation and providing for local tax elections, were the most important changes since the school system was organized, and represented, as the educational historian Amory D. Mayo remarked, "a decided revolt against the spirit of reaction."[21] Yet the first act was soon nullified by the state's highest judges, and the second was frustrated by public confusion, apathy, and the active opposition of partisan Democrats.

Local tax elections were scheduled in August, a few months

---

19. In 1895, for example, the poll tax was $1.29, the property tax 43 cents per $100, or $1.29 on $300. By the terms of the law of 1897, the poll tax remained $1.29, and the property tax rate became 46 cents on $100, or $1.38 on $300.

20. Samuel H. Thompson, "The Legislative Development of Public School Support in North Carolina" (unpublished doctoral dissertation, University of North Carolina, 1936), pp. 325-27; Edgar W. Knight, *Public School Education in North Carolina* (Boston, 1916), p. 325.

21. Amory D. Mayo, "The Final Establishment of the American Common School System in North Carolina, South Carolina, and Georgia, 1863-1900," in *Report of the Commissioner of Education for the Year Ending June 30, 1904* (2 vols., Washington, 1906), I, 1017.

after the passage of the act. A local tax committee was hastily organized by the school men, and included such Democratic politicians as future governor Charles B. Aycock and ex-governor Thomas J. Jarvis, the Southern Railway lawyer Fabius H. Busbee, Daniel A. Tompkins, a Charlotte cotton-mill owner, and Julian S. Carr, a Durham tobacco manufacturer soon to be a candidate for the United States Senate in opposition to the Democratic machine. Carr promised $500 to the county with the highest percentage of votes in favor of local taxation.[22]

Down from the "place of grim struggle and plain living," as he described his university, came Edwin A. Alderman to weave his spell among the folk, to help in "arousing the intellect of a whole people." Charles D. McIver was equally effective; he challenged the mind and the heart while Alderman charmed the ear.[23] Barnyard humor enlivened McIver's more or less conversational style. Another educational crusader was Philander P. Claxton, later federal commissioner of education, a rather heavy but convincing speaker. In the *Biblical Recorder*, Josiah W. Bailey eased the fears of white Baptists that the funds raised by local taxation would be divided between whites and Negroes in proportion to their numbers. He stated categorically that "this is not so. The money so raised will be divided according to the judgment of the township school committee. For instance, we have Local Taxation now in Raleigh; but the money is not divided between the races according to school population."[24] Alderman and McIver, on the other hand, shrugged off such inquiries about the division of local tax funds by charging that anybody who opposed the education of Negroes opposed also the education of whites. The campaign even brought forth from Wake Forest a voice defending Negroes' right to public education. The main argument against Negro education, said Charles H. Utley, was that Negroes paid no taxes, which made "a class distinction and not a race distinction," and might also exclude the children of the poor white man. "Once en-

22. Raleigh *News and Observer*, July 14, 28, 31, 1897.
23. Malone, *Edwin A. Alderman*, pp. 77, 91; Holder, *McIver of North Carolina*, pp. 71-72, 95-97, 175-77.
24. Raleigh *News and Observer*, July 10, 1897; *Biblical Recorder*, August 4, 1897.

forced, where would it end? The wealthier would again protest against being taxed for the poor."[25]

The Populist architect of Fusion, United States Senator Marion Butler, stated for his party that "No ignorant people were ever prosperous or progressive," that the farmers' legislature had pushed state support as far as impoverished farmers could stand, further than the state courts would support, and that local taxation was the road now open to better schools. The Populist Superintendent Mebane appealed to county superintendents to have the *"pluck, push and power"* to *"pound"* into people a sense of responsibility for their children. Certainly the Populist element in Fusion was steadfast in support of the local tax movement.[26]

The denominational press at first seemed equally staunch. The editor of the *Biblical Recorder*, surveying thirty years of education through state taxation, found that terms were growing shorter instead of longer, that 200,000 illiterates were "living but silent" witnesses of its failure. Only local taxation could banish the ignorance which stood "like a monster—all powerful" in the doors of 50,000 homes. Local tax, said Bailey, was "the poor man's tax, the poor child's hope." But on the same page the editor equivocated: "We have not advocated the tax in any township where incompetent men have charge. We don't want the money of the people squandered." The competent men, it turned out, were White Supremacy Democrats in control of townships "west of Raleigh." Bailey had stated the main argument by which local taxation was defeated.[27]

About a month before the local tax election, the Raleigh *News and Observer* suddenly stopped writing editorials in favor of local taxation, and began to feature letters opposing it. Editor Josephus Daniels decided that the local tax ought to fail wherever the schools were made "the football of politics, by little politicians." The appointment of an occasional Negro as one of three township committeemen to represent the Negro schools was to be an issue in

---

25. Letter to the editor, in Raleigh *News and Observer*, August 6, 1897.
26. Raleigh *News and Observer*, August 8, 1897; *North Carolina School Report, 1896-1898*, pp. 44, 81.
27. *Biblical Recorder*, July 28, 1897. For Bailey's account of the campaign, see Joseph [Josiah] W. Bailey, "Popular Education and the Race Problem in North Carolina," in *Outlook*, LXVIII (May 11, 1901), 114-16.

Seedtime: North Carolina in the Nineties 57

the approaching election of 1898. On the eve of the local tax election, therefore, the *News and Observer* kept studiedly neutral; it gave perfunctory reports of opposition to the tax here and there, and published occasional wild charges against Negro school committeemen. Eventually emotions reached such a pitch that it was hard to find a Negro willing to serve on a school committee. The *News and Observer* informed readers that voters need only absent themselves from the polls to defeat local taxation.[28]

The school men knew in advance what arguments their opponents would present, and McIver even supplied his campaigners with a list of them: "I don't believe in the principle of taxing one man to educate another man's children"; "the poverty of the people"; "the negro argument"; the "friendly attitude toward education" of those opposing a tax for education; "the unconstitutionality of the act"; "the fear that those who are quietly trusted to manage the revenues derived from the regular state tax may not have sufficient sense or honesty to manage the educational revenue from a local tax"; and "the general omnibus objection that any additional tax, however small and for any purpose whatever, will be oppressive to the people." All of these objections, said McIver, were "as familiar as the words of any old song" to those who had won local tax elections in the towns. He called on his campaign workers to answer them with logic and facts.[29]

These "old songs" were indeed sung in the campaign. Said William D. Pruden of Edenton: "The little good, which the efforts [taxation for public education] seem to do those who get the lion's share of the appropriations for schools in the East, sometimes greatly shakes my faith and tempers my zeal."[30] Here the "friendly attitude toward education" argument was combined with the Negro argument. "Come out from the shadows cast by brick and granite walls," called Thomas D. Boone, "—eat with the common people their corn pone and middling meat and learn some practical common sense ideas on the school question." Dur-

28. Raleigh *News and Observer*, July 11, 23, 27, 28, August 3, 4, 7, 8, 10, 11, 1897; *North Carolina School Report, 1896-1898*, pp. 11-13. Superintendent Mebane, fearful of violence against Negro committeemen, suggested that Negroes choose white men to represent their schools and thereby "avoid race prejudice."
29. Quoted from his speech as reported in Raleigh *News and Observer*, July 10, 1897.
30. Raleigh *News and Observer*, July 11, 1897.

ing the educational agitation, he said, he had "time and again . . . been told by both white and black that they were not in a position to dispense with the labor of their children even as much as four months. So a longer school period, if it means an advantage to any class of men, must only mean the betterment of incompetent teachers to doze in the shade of ill ventilated school rooms and blink at a baker's dozen of lazy boys and girls." The next impractical scheme, he warned, would include free textbooks, food, and raiment. Boone ran the whole gamut of McIver's list.[31]

"I do not believe in much law as regards education or labor," said a manufacturer. Similar sentiments prevailed among employers of Negroes in the East.[32] The Honorable L. L. Smith denounced the compulsory character of the act. He was "a friend of education and of the public schools," he said, but "It is the spirit of state socialism, which fully developed means state despotism. I could as conscientiously vote for an empire as a tax under that statute." It was unwise to increase the school tax "at the expense of the county tax." Besides, illiteracy could surely be wiped out by the present system, "providing" four months of schooling to each child for fifteen years.[33] Josiah Bailey warned that to send a child to a public high school or college would make "a jellyfish Baptist of him or her,"[34] but did not openly oppose local taxation for public elementary schools.

"Can the white people of a district take advantage of the special taxation act and exclude the negroes?" J. L. Cornwell, principal of Spring Hope High School, asked Mebane. "I don't mean to prevent them but to go ahead and levy a special tax among themselves without saying any thing to the negro."[35] Apparently the answer was negative, because Spring Hope was not among those which voted for the tax.

To answer these critics, McIver decided to call on Walter Hines Page, whose "very name is exclamatory." They were

31. Letter to the editor, in Raleigh *News and Observer*, August 4, 1897.
32. W. S. Parker, president of Roanoke Mills, in *Tenth Annual Report of the North Carolina Bureau of Labor Statistics for the Year 1896* (Winston, 1897), p. 140.
33. Letter to the editor, in Raleigh *News and Observer*, August 7, 1897.
34. *Biblical Recorder*, August 11, 1897.
35. Letter of April 5, 1897, in records of the superintendent of public instruction, Department of Education, Raleigh.

"just going into a great educational campaign," he wrote to the editor of the *Atlantic Monthly* urging him to come home again and nail the theses of the educational movement on the door of the Normal and Industrial College at Greensboro. "As a rule we have a local tax for educational purposes only in the towns," McIver wrote, urging Page to speak about the rural people and to emphasize "the equality of human rights in the matter of intellectual culture."[36] With a genius for titles, Page called his speech "The Forgotten Man." He spoke more eloquently of the neglected women: "thin and wrinkled in youth from ill prepared food, clad without warmth or grace, living in untidy houses, working from daylight till bed-time at the dull round of weary duties, the slaves of men of equal slovenliness, the mothers of joyless children—all uneducated if not illiterate.... Our civilization, so far as they are concerned, has been a failure," Page concluded. "Since both the politician and the preacher have failed to lift this life after a century of unobstructed opportunities, it is time for a wiser statesmanship and a more certain means of grace." The means of grace and the "only effective means to develop the forgotten man" was "a public school system ... generously maintained by both State and local taxation."[37] But the wiser statesmanship was apparently no more plentiful in the New Order than in the day of politician and preacher. Some North Carolinians still seemed to prefer that the Forgotten Man remain forgotten. As Page retreated to Boston, Josephus Daniels threw an editorial after him: "Mr. Page owes his present position to the fact that he has made himself a leader among leaders.... It took him fifteen years to write the speech. It was the result of more than that many years of reflection.... He believes so firmly that the doctrine he expounded is based on eternal truth that, having sown the seed, he will await with confidence the day of harvesting."[38]

When the returns on the local tax elections were tallied they were a slim harvest; only twelve of the 1,300 districts voted in

36. McIver to Page, April 15, 1897, Walter Hines Page Papers, Houghton Library, Harvard University; Peter M. Wilson, *Southern Exposure* (Chapel Hill, 1927), p. 171. The normal school became a college in 1897.
37. "The Forgotten Man," in Walter H. Page, *The Rebuilding of Old Commonwealths: Being Essays Towards the Training of the Forgotten Man in the Southern States* (New York, 1902), pp. 24, 26, 31.
38. Raleigh *News and Observer*, May 19, 1897.

favor of increased taxation. The cause of this abject failure, said McIver, was that the teachers had no campaign fund and the question did not get a fair presentation to the people. Josephus Daniels put the blame on the Negro question, and Superintendent Mebane blamed Democrats like Daniels who used the local tax election as a springboard for the 1898 legislative election.

Public education played only a small part in the White Supremacy election of 1898 by which the Democrats recaptured the legislature. Though they had a perfunctory plank endorsing improvement of the schools, the Democrats were primarily concerned with power. In the black counties they stripped down to their red undershirts—a peculiarly Southern symbol of terrorism—and stalked about frightening Negroes and other Fusionists away from public meetings and the polls. Whatever latent liberalism the party contained was submerged under the leadership of Furnifold M. Simmons, who subsequently occupied what William E. Dodd called "the Lumber trust's seat" in the United States Senate.[39] Simmons later wrote with remarkable frankness, "During the campaign I secured the services of former Governor T. J. Jarvis to visit the bankers, the railroad officials, and the manufacturers of the State, to represent to them the intolerable conditions prevailing under the Fusion domination." "From these economic leaders," and from men of lesser means, he said, "I obtained all the campaign funds I needed."[40] Simmons and Jarvis also held a secret meeting with Josiah W. Bailey, President John C. Kilgo, and the influential Methodist, the Reverend John E. White. Both Simmons and Jarvis were alumni of Trinity College, and the latter was also a trustee. Kilgo was as Republican as the Washington Duke family, but he and Bailey agreed to swing behind White Supremacy if Simmons would see that the legislature held down appropriations to the state university and colleges. This bargain put the very life of these institutions in jeopardy.[41]

39. William E. Dodd to Walter Clark, June 4, 1911, in Aubrey L. Brooks and Hugh T. Lefler (eds.), *The Papers of Walter Clark* (2 vols., Chapel Hill, 1948-50), II, 116.
40. J. Fred Rippy (ed.), *F. M. Simmons, Statesman of the New South: Memoirs and Addresses* (Durham, 1936), p. 23.
41. *Ibid.*, p. 29; Josephus Daniels, *Editor in Politics* (Chapel Hill, 1941), pp.

The tactics of the campaign, the intimidation and the bargains, were "in many ways distasteful" to such respectable conservatives as Henry G. Connor, who became speaker of the house in the next session, but his friend George Howard said "I suppose anything must be justifiable to preserve a woman's virtue, a man's honor, and our Christian civilization."[42] Such men were disturbed when their Christian soldiers used rather violent language about "choking the Cape Fear River with the bodies of negroes" and killed several Negroes in the Wilmington race riot, at the conclusion of which the leader of the mob was elected mayor.[43] "When Democratic rallies were held, mills and shops were shut down so that the operatives could attend the speakings."[44] And the Democratic party in its desire for a return to power gave the railroads and industrialists "the bridle by which to check progressive legislation."[45]

Mixed with the very cries of jubilation of the Supreme Whites were heard insistent demands that school taxes be divided by race. The old Redeemers who already had been through this, at the end of Reconstruction, were irritated. As Jarvis wrote to Connor, soon to be chairman of the joint committee on education, on November 16, 1898: "While I am in favor of making it impossible for the negro to govern, I am not in favor of making a heathen of him to live in our midst. To say that no money shall be appropriated to negro schools except what the negro pays is practically to say that he shall have no schools, and that the negro children are to grow up as heathen in a so-called Christian land. I am

---

318-24; Aubrey L. Brooks, *A Southern Lawyer: Fifty Years at the Bar* (Chapel Hill, 1950), pp. 51-52.

42. Connor to George Howard, November 11, 1898, Howard to Connor, November 14, 1898, Aycock to Connor, November 10, 1898, Connor Papers, S.H.C., University of North Carolina.

43. Connor to George Howard, November 11, 1898, Howard to Connor, November 14, 1898, [George Rountree], "Memorandum of My Personal Recollection of the Election of 1898," Connor Papers; Daniels, *Editor in Politics*, pp. 283-312; testimony of George Henry White, Negro Congressman from the second district of North Carolina, in *Report of the* [United States] *Industrial Commission*, X, 426.

44. Charlotte *Observer*, November 17, 1898, quoted in Edmonds, *The Negro and Fusion Politics in North Carolina*, p. 153.

45. *Loc. cit.*

opposed to any such policy. . . . The matter is giving me no little concern."[46]

In compliance with the bargains made by Simmons and Jarvis, the legislature of 1899 cut down almost all of the Populist-inspired legislation of 1897. The railroad commission was abolished; needed increases in the appropriations to the state higher schools were withheld. McIver and Alderman, arriving as usual to petition the legislature, were led aside by Simmons and given their first knowledge of the bargain with Kilgo and Bailey. McIver's face flushed with rage. "You have sold us out," he charged.[47] A Baptist legislator from Iredell was delighted. He exclaimed, "By heavens, Simmons, hold them to the promise!" And Simmons did. Alderman became "very sick of the legislature" and "hurt of mind and heart." Soon he was packing his bags, having resigned to become president of the privately endowed Tulane University in New Orleans. He felt he had done as much as he could in North Carolina.[48]

The victorious Democrats also repealed the local tax law of 1897 and kept piously within the constitutional maximum of taxation. The educational campaigners held their ranks and put up a struggle, however, and Alderman stayed long enough to take part. But the school forces carried less weight than in the previous session. It was not merely that the state superintendent was of another party than that which controlled the legislature. The campaign support of the Democrats by the capitalists was *quid pro quo*. "Through Jarvis, I also promised the large corporations that their taxes would not be increased during the biennium," Simmons wrote in his memoirs.[49] Under a new local tax law

46. Quoted in Henry G. Connor, "Thomas Jordan Jarvis and the Rebuilding of North Carolina," in *Proceedings of the Sixteenth Annual Session of the State Literary and Historical Association of North Carolina, Raleigh, November 8-9, 1915*: Publications of the North Carolina Historical Commission, No. 20 (Raleigh, 1916), p. 91.
47. Rippy (ed.), *F. M. Simmons*, p. 29.
48. Alderman to Henry G. Connor, May 16, 1899, Howard A. Foushee (lawyer and legislator, Durham) to Connor, May 16, 1899, Connor Papers, S.H.C., University of North Carolina; Malone, *Edwin A. Alderman*, pp. 95-102; Raleigh *News and Observer*, May 3, 1900. Josephus Daniels thought it was the higher salary that induced him to leave. *Ibid.*, April 8, 1900; Daniels, *Editor in Politics*, pp. 322-24.
49. Rippy (ed.), *F. M. Simmons*, p. 29.

Seedtime: North Carolina in the Nineties 63

written by the Democrats, elections were to be held not automatically or recurrently, but only if one-third of the qualified voters petitioned the county commissioners. An upper limit of 30 cents per $100 of property was designed to hold in check any possible local enthusiasm.

But this was only part of the omnibus education act, hailed in some quarters as the greatest educational advance of the decade. A sum afterwards termed "The First Hundred Thousand" was appropriated to the counties from the general state tax fund. The apportionment, however, was not to be on the basis of need to help counties poor in taxable property, but per capita on the basis of the school census. The sum amounted to only about $1,000 for the average county, far less than might have been secured by a local tax.[50]

If there were shortcomings and jokers in the omnibus education act, the legislature tried to make up for them by the creation of incentive. A constitutional amendment requiring voters to read and write was passed for ratification in the election of 1900. Its clearly explained purpose was disfranchisement of Negroes; but in order to placate suspicious western counties where white illiteracy approached 40 per cent, a Grandfather Clause which would terminate in 1908 was appended. By the amendment, adult white illiterates would be protected by permanent registration because their grandfathers could vote in 1866, before the advent of Negro suffrage. But any illiterate white boy who reached voting age after 1908 was liable, according to its terms, to lose his privilege of voting. As Charles Brantley Aycock of Goldsboro explained the situation to mountain whites: "We recognize and provide for the God-given and hereditary superiority of the white man and of all white children now thirteen years of age, but for the future as to all under thirteen we call on them to assert that superiority of which we boast by learning to read and write."[51]

50. Thompson, "The Legislative Development of Public School Support in North Carolina" (unpublished doctoral dissertation, University of North Carolina), pp. 344-54; *North Carolina School Report, 1898-1900*, p. 89.
51. Quoted in Robert D. W. Connor and Clarence H. Poe, *The Life and Speeches of Charles Brantley Aycock* (New York, 1912), p. 84. The Lily White mountain Republicans were carried for the amendment by such appeals. Edmonds, *The Negro and Fusion Politics in North Carolina*, pp. 198-204, improves upon William A. Mabry, *The Negro in North Carolina Politics since Reconstruction*:

The Democratic convention of 1900, "standing and cheering like Apache Indians," chose Aycock by acclamation as candidate for governor. He would popularize the amendment, and Furnifold M. Simmons would direct his campaign. The candidate was a stalwart from just below the fall line, a goldbug conservative who had formerly been a railroad lawyer; in 1898, when the Populists under Marion Butler sent the olive branch to the Democratic convention, Aycock pitched it into the wastebasket. He had no trouble working with Simmons and "White Supremacy." In fact, he had been a leading Red Shirt in 1898. Aycock's record also included support for public education, an important factor in view of the literacy clause of the suffrage amendment the Democrats were sponsoring. Born into a moderately prosperous family of foot-washing Baptists in Wayne County, Aycock had watched his own mother put her mark on a deed. A lingering memory of this occasion might have affected his attitude as a conservative politician. A fellow student of educational campaigners Alderman, McIver, and James Y. Joyner at the state university, he had served as county superintendent for two years in his youth, while waiting for his law practice to develop, and had been a school trustee of Goldsboro for a decade. Though William T. Dortch had been his first political tutor, Aycock had also absorbed some of the more universal ideas about education from Alderman, who taught in Goldsboro in the eighties. Aycock alone among leading Democrats had supported the local tax campaign of 1897 to the bitter end.[52]

It is unlikely, however, that Aycock was intensely friendly to education until about the time of his gubernatorial campaign. Alderman recalled years later that the conversion was slow:

Papers of the Trinity College Historical Society, Series XXIII (Durham, 1940), pp. 57-72. See also Mabry, "'White Supremacy' and the North Carolina Suffrage Amendment," in *North Carolina Historical Review*, XIII (January, 1936), 1-24.

52. See the most complete account of Aycock's career, Connor and Poe, *Charles Brantley Aycock*, pp. 77-78. Rupert B. Vance has written with more insight and perspective in "Aycock of North Carolina," in *Southwest Review* (Dallas, Texas, quarterly), XVIII (Spring, 1933), 288-306. Robert W. Winston, *It's a Far Cry* (New York, 1937), pp. 253-54, gives some interesting sidelights on Aycock as a corporation lawyer. See also Raleigh *News and Observer*, April 29, 1900.

I lived in the town with Aycock, of course, during all those days from '82 to '89. At that time Aycock was not particularly interested in public education. He was a young lawyer, entirely consumed with the law, and I do not think terribly eager about the whole idea of compulsory education. In fact, I would imagine he would be against compulsory education. He was an intense individualist at that time. I do not remember any opposition, particularly, but I do not recall that, those years, he was giving much thought to that problem. I used to talk . . . with him about my job, and what I was trying to do. He was interested but not fiercely so. I think it is fair to say that his wonderful interest in public education and his enormous and unforgettable service to it, came to him later, and I have always cherished the hope that some things I said to him about the situation may have been seed well sown, and no man can deny that he made a brave and devoted contribution to the whole idea.[53]

Opportunism was clearly a factor of some weight in Aycock's stand upon the two planks of disfranchisement and universal education. And surely it was opportunism for his party leaders to select this obscure county-seat lawyer as a gubernatorial candidate. If he was sincere about his plank of universal education, he was, as Rupert B. Vance says, more honest than his political associates believed him to be.[54]

The same Democratic convention which selected Aycock for "Educational Governor" nominated for state superintendent one Thomas F. Toon. "Of all the names brought out by the political convention last week," said an observer, "his was the least known."[55] The leading party newspaper even misprinted his name in reporting the convention.[56] Toon was one of the state's three surviving Confederate Brigadiers, a Baptist deacon from the Eastern black belt, and head of a small private academy. For

53. Alderman to Charles W. Dabney, December 31, 1929, copy in Dumas Malone MS notes for his biography of Alderman, Alderman Library, University of Virginia; Edmonds, *The Negro and Fusion Politics in North Carolina*, p. 216, n. 49.

54. Vance, "Aycock of North Carolina," *Southwest Review*, XVIII, 295.

55. Quoted in Raleigh *News and Observer*, April 18, 1900. The *News and Observer* discovered, however, that "he is a noble Christian man" and that "All the book companies in the world could not buy him—though we do not intimate that they desire to do anything of the kind."

56. He was listed as William S. Toon in Raleigh *News and Observer*, April 12, 1900. The error may have been malicious; editor Daniels favored Mebane's continuance in office.

sixteen years he had been agent for the Atlantic Coast Line Railway, and had served in the state senate and house. Toon's elevation to high office was "an example of the office seeking the man."[57] In this case, conservative Democrats needed him to head off the renomination of Mebane for superintendent on the Democratic ticket.

Fusion superintendent Mebane, like many Populists, was unhappy in tandem with Republicans such as Governor Daniel L. Russell and the high-tariff, gold-standard United States Senator Jeter C. Pritchard. As early as 1899 he indicated dissatisfaction with Republican school policies, and perhaps he was also infected by the White Supremacy contagion. On the eve of the Democratic state convention Mebane announced that he was once more a Democrat and wanted another term in office. He was reported to have the impressive backing of Democratic Congressman John H. Small, Josephus Daniels, the Charlotte *Observer*, and "College professors, high school men, graded school men, public and private school teachers in all sections of the State, State aid and anti-State aid advocates, many of the leading newspapers of the State, political and religious, nearly every officer of the North Carolina Teachers' Assembly, and the leading educational journal of North Carolina and the South."[58]

Though Mebane's friends testified that he had voted for William Jennings Bryan and William A. Guthrie rather than William McKinley or Daniel L. Russell in 1896 and for Democrats in 1898, he was out of the running on the first ballot. Colonel Paul B. Means, a prominent Democrat, tried to make a seconding speech for Mebane and was obstructed by "hisses, cat-calls, jeers and an uproar that lasted as long as Means occupied the rostrum—nearly half an hour." The Colonel was trying to say: "I'm Democrat enough to nominate a man in whose Democracy I have faith" amid shouts from his audience like "let him go in the rear ranks awhile," and "Name a Democrat." Toon won the nomination from equally obscure favorite sons on the fourth ballot and was

57. Raleigh *News and Observer*, April 12, 1900, January 15, 1901, February 20, 1902.
58. George A. Grimsley, letter to the editor, in Raleigh *News and Observer*, April 10, 1900. See also *ibid.*, March 28, 1900.

elected with Aycock over a Populist dark horse on the Fusion ticket.[59]

If Toon's nomination casts doubt on the contention that the Democrats sincerely planned to improve the school system, Aycock himself sometimes gave cause for skepticism. Helen G. Edmonds' careful analysis of Aycock's campaign speeches reveals that in the early speeches in the eastern part of the state, where there were Negro majorities, he devoted his attention to Negro officeholders, the unfitness of the Negro to govern, and the need of good government. Later, when he was speaking to the white majorities in the western counties, repercussions against the literacy clause of the constitutional amendment caused him to give sudden emphasis to education. In that section he began to promise "a school house on every hill-top," open four months in the year, so that the white boy who could not qualify to vote by 1908 would have no excuse. It was expedient for the Democratic machine to couple education with suffrage restriction in its bid for power.[60]

The Democratic campaign promise of four-month schools, Josiah W. Bailey later recalled, "was made with especial regard to white children. Without this the amendment would have been defeated." Constitutionally the pledge necessarily included schools for Negro children, "though little was said of that," and when Aycock chose the term universal education, "His adjective was peculiarly fortunate."[61]

Whatever the various reasons, Aycock from "a hundred platforms, to half the voters of the State," traveling 5,000 miles by

---

59. Raleigh *News and Observer*, March 28, April 4, 5, 7, 8, 10, 12, 17, 19, May 3, 1900; Kemp P. Battle, "Paul Barringer Means" (leaflet, n.p., n.d.), in Stephen B. Weeks Collection of Caroliniana, North Carolina Room, Wilson Library, University of North Carolina.

60. Edmonds, *The Negro and Fusion Politics in North Carolina*, pp. 204-05. Miss Edmonds believes that the turning point was when Aycock began his second western tour. "The issues we are discussing this year amount to but one thing, the negro question," said Aycock at Burlington. Raleigh *News and Observer*, April 17, 1900. Two days later at Greensboro he promised a four-month school which would "next to revolutionize" the Old North State, and a suffrage amendment that would act as a spur to the illiterate. Raleigh *News and Observer*, April 22, 1900, quoting from Greensboro *Telegram*. Miss Edmonds finds that other White Supremacy orators, Locke Craig, Furnifold M. Simmons, and Alfred M. Waddell, omitted education from their speeches. They too were party spokesmen.

61. Bailey, "Popular Education and the Race Problem in North Carolina," *Outlook*, LXVIII, 115.

rail and 1,000 miles by buggy, "pledged the State, its strength, its heart, its wealth, to universal education." Aycock is reported to have said in his home county before his nomination that the phrase "universal education" included schools for Negroes. Later, at the Democratic state convention, what he actually did say was that "universal education of the white children of North Carolina will send us forward with a bound in the race with the world." In Asheville during the campaign he spoke to an audience embittered by the recent refusal of city property-owners to give support to the county schools. "It is a fact," he stated, looking the guilty ones in the eye, "that many people of wealth and education have been indifferent to the education of the masses. But the present campaign compels even this small class to become advocates of universal education. In this way the campaign is accomplishing great good." In one section the shout was "nigger, nigger," and in another it was "white man, white man, white man." As far as the campaign was concerned the educational slogans were largely a sweetening to the bitter incitement of race hate in which Aycock participated, whether or not he intended later to enlarge educational opportunity.[62]

Aycock won the governorship overwhelmingly against the Republican candidate Spencer B. Adams, partly by the use of terrorism against Negro and white voters. Adams was opposed to public educational improvements that would raise taxes, and Aycock is said to have told the Republicans that "the women, the preachers, and the teachers are with us, and you cannot defeat . . . that combination." Governor Aycock was, in William E. Dodd's opinion, "too timid for the times, afraid of the interests where . . . not in one way or another tied up with them." In his speeches on the amendment and education, however, he convinced most people that somehow the two were inseparably linked. "The spirit is abroad in the land," he told an applauding audience at Waynesville in the west, "and if there is any man going around opposing the amendment and yet claiming to favor public education put him down as a liar."[63]

62. Winston, *It's a Far Cry*, p. 252; Connor and Poe, *Charles Brantley Aycock*, pp. 117-18; Raleigh *News and Observer*, April 20, 1900.
63. "The North Carolina Election," editorial in *Outlook*, LXV (August 11,

The amendment which disfranchised Negroes was also ratified in the same election. Negroes had already been eliminated from all school committees and educational administration. And when James Y. Eaton, one of the last Negro legislators, presented a petition of Negro citizens in 1899 for a guarantee of equal length of term for white and Negro schools, it was buried by the education committee.[64] After 1900 the Negroes could no longer bargain votes for schools in the legitimate manner of political man. In the Southern tradition of the Negro story, the Raleigh *News and Observer* quoted a Negro politician at the Republican convention of 1900: "Heretofore 'Publicans been beggin' us an' Democrats been buying us, now seems dat nobody wants us." The Republicans became as Lily White as the Democrats, and the Negro was helpless to protect the public schools of his children. Henry G. Connor, who had been speaker of the house when the suffrage amendment was framed, and who became chairman of its education committee in 1901, found that Democrats intended to use suffrage restriction not against illiterate Negroes only, but against all Negroes. As he privately expressed his qualms: "I fear that the shrinkage in the number will make the Negro absolutely indifferent to his political interests and welfare and the whites will be emboldened to oppress him in his material and educational interests. It is a serious question whether 100,000 freemen can maintain any satisfactory status in North Carolina without any political power."[65] John C. Kilgo, also ruminating on the educational values involved in Negro disfranchisement, concluded that "the withdrawal of the right of franchise from those unable to read

---

1900), 841-43; Jeter C. Pritchard, quoted in Raleigh *News and Observer*, April 29, 1900; Aycock, quoted in *ibid*., April 25, 1900; Spencer B. Adams' speech at Mocksville, quoted in Greensboro *Daily Industrial News*, September 23, 1906; Dodd to Walter Clark, June 4, 1911, in Brooks and Lefler (eds.), *The Papers of Walter Clark*, II, 117.
64. Edmonds, *The Negro and Fusion Politics in North Carolina*, p. 108.
65. Raleigh *News and Observer*, May 2, 1900; Connor to George Howard, November 3, 1902, quoted from Mabry, "'White Supremacy' and the North Carolina Suffrage Amendment," *North Carolina Historical Review*, XIII, 23. Connor's friend Howard favored an electorate for the state senate consisting of those owning at least $500 assessed value of real estate. "This would vary the two houses and add much to the conservatism of the Government." Howard to Connor, February 3, 1899, Connor Papers, S.H.C., University of North Carolina.

is a motive, but whether it is sufficient to stir a worthy spirit of education, some sincere men justly doubt."[66]

Kilgo's partner in Christian education and White Supremacy, Josiah W. Bailey, hoped to find some way to by-pass Negro education to promote education for whites. "It were futile to deny that there are political leaders in the South with no mean following who would keep the negroes in ignorance in order to keep them out of politics," he thought, and these leaders were "ready to debar them by some other means when the present barriers shall have been overcome." Furthermore, white opposition to Negro suffrage was only one of the reasons for white opposition to education of Negroes from the common tax funds. There was also the "old attitude of master and slave" which bolstered the large landowner's conviction that to educate a Negro was to "ruin a good farm hand"; the antipathy of poor whites who competed somewhat with the Negro in the labor market; "the fear in some quarters that the negro children, not being deterred by poor clothes, etc., will go to school in larger numbers than the white children"; and the widely held feeling that "it is folly to spend . . . on colored children when the opportunities of the white children are so limited." These considerations led Bailey to support publicly the limitation of local tax funds to white education.[67]

Geographical maldistribution of educational opportunity could be alleviated by state "equalization" funds to the poorer counties. But the constitution and supreme court limited state taxation of property and held back all of the schools. Justice Walter Clark of the state supreme court saw hitherto untapped tax resources that might be used for public education. Aycock's pledge of a four-month term in every county could be redeemed, said Clark, if the legislature placed a 5 per cent tax on railroad gross receipts, which, following the example of many states outside of the South, would yield more than $800,000 and still allow the railroads to siphon some $5,200,000 net profit from the state. Not a dollar of this profit had ever before paid "one cent of tribute to God nor Caesar."

66. Kilgo, "Some Phases of Southern Education," *South Atlantic Quarterly*, II, 149.
67. Bailey, "Popular Education and the Race Problem in North Carolina," *Outlook*, LXVIII, 114-16.

What tax could be more equitable? Where else could the state raise the money which was needed if the schools were to be improved? The teachers, who had stirred up the sentiment for better schools, must now indicate the source of justly and easily raised funds. "Declamation is cheap," Clark lectured the state teachers' association. "Words butter no parsnips." "Think what $1,000,000, added to your school fund annually in North Carolina can do! What a real impetus it would give to the cause of education!"[68]

Perhaps the new president of the state university no longer carried a free pass on all the railroads of the state, as had been true a few years earlier.[69] But apparently faculty appointments were still cleared with Colonel Alexander B. Andrews, vice president and general manager of the Southern Railway.[70] And the Democrats who had received crucial support from the railroads were unlikely to increase railroad taxes for the sake of the schools. As the legislature of 1901 convened and Aycock entered office, "There was an evident and determined purpose, on the part of the [railroad] Presidents to get Aycock to enter into 'agreements' 'stipulations' &c. &c." Soon Walter Clark and Josephus Daniels were accusing Aycock and the legislature of surrender to "corporate influences" and "tax dodging corporations."[71] Daniels continued to follow the Aycock camp rather closely, but privately wondered at what had been wrought. "The same influences that put North Carolina in the whig column after [Nathaniel] Macon had passed

---

68. Walter Clark, "How Can Interest Be Aroused in the Study of the History of North Carolina?" address at Wrightsville, June 12, 1901, in Brooks and Lefler (eds.), *The Papers of Walter Clark*, II, 523-25. For other expositions of these ideas, see a speech by Clark reported in Raleigh *News and Observer*, May 25, 1899; *North Carolina School Report, 1898-1900*, p. 35; Charles D. McIver, "The Teacher as a Citizen," in Raleigh *News and Observer*, August 13, 1905, p. 17.

69. William J. Battle (ed.), *Memories of an Old-Time Tar Heel* (Chapel Hill, 1945), p. 271 (the memoirs of Kemp P. Battle).

70. Dodd to Clark, May 9, 1919, in Lefler (ed.), "Selected William E. Dodd–Walter Clark Letters," *North Carolina Historical Review*, XXV, 95; "When I was a youngster and briefless, the University of North Carolina needed a man in history. I was informed by an ex-President then influential that if A. B. Andrews recommended me I would be appointed." Andrews was a member of the board of trustees. Dodd applied in 1900, when Francis P. Venable was president. Presumably Kemp P. Battle was the ex-president then influential.

71. Connor to Howard, February 9, 1901, Connor Papers, S.H.C., University of North Carolina.

away, are working now to make the democratic party a virtual whig party," he wrote William E. Dodd.[72]

The agrarian decade of the nineties in North Carolina had proved a school for educational campaigners. They had learned to "sow the seed" of educational enthusiasm among the masses, to temper their own zeal to resilient strength, and to seek fulfillment in concrete achievements rather than vague promises. The campaigns seem to have had only a negligible effect on the schools themselves. In 1900 the term was only about 70 days out of 365; one-third of the children attended; and the expenditure was only two cents per child per day.[73]

Yet school men had made considerable progress. The day had passed when a school teacher who claimed to have any rights that "a partisan politician, a sectarian preacher, or a local editor was bound to respect, was regarded as a pestilent fellow and a mover of sedition," concluded "Corn Cracker," a Cleveland County teacher. But the millennium had not arrived. His own county superintendent selected all of the 125 or 150 teachers, white and Negro, from Baptist and Methodist Sunday schools.

But many guns have been silenced, and now the politicians who let Dr. E. A. Alderman, Prof. C. H. Mebane, Dr. J. W. Bailey, and others, fight the battle, while they winked and smirked in derision, have now captured the band-wagon, and swear that they have been there all the time.

Governor Aycock, Prof. J. Y. Joyner, are loyal, and perhaps, a corporal's guard of others may be exempt, but at present their names are not on my old list. . . .

So, while much is being done (and I rejoice thereat) the educational millenium [sic] has not set up here just yet.

. . . So far it is all left to merchants and preachers.[74]

"Railroads and corporations will have their hired lobbyists to instruct and persuade you," Mebane warned the incoming legisla-

---

72. Daniels to Dodd, April 4, 1901, Dodd Papers, Library of Congress.

73. *North Carolina School Report, 1898-1900*, pp. 327, 334-35. The term was reported as 70 days in the federal commissioner's report.

74. Letter of "Corn Cracker" [M. L. White, Lattimore, North Carolina?] to the editor, in *Progressive Farmer* (Raleigh weekly), June 29, 1902, clipping in Charles D. McIver clipping books, Woman's College of the University of North Carolina, Greensboro. See also the highly literate "Clodhopper" of Beaufort County, *ibid.*, July 16, 1902.

ture as he left office, "but the little whiteheaded boys and girls, the ragged boys and girls, and all the boys and girls whose only hope for preparation for life and its stern realities is in the public schools, these little ones will have no one to plead with you personally day after day."[75] Conservative leaders such as Henry G. Connor, men who were responsible for the resort to force, the institutionalization of Negro subjection, and the one-race, one-party oligarchy wedded to outside corporations, knew what they had done and were troubled in conscience. "I shall try to do my duty to the State and the Roads," Henry G. Connor wrote privately, "but between the demagogue and the R. Rd. Lobbyist I shall go down. I know that the incoming Govr. is anxious to avert this fight. We are all anxious to inaugurate an era of good feeling between the people and those who represent and control the industrial movement in the State. We intend to keep our pledges in regard to educating the children—but we wish to do no injustice to any class of our people or property."[76]

In the "era of good feeling," this solicitude for the fortunes of corporations was matched by the sentiment of William A. Graham, farmer of Machpelah, for the children of tenants and farm laborers of both races, people without any class of property. He testified before a federal commission in 1901: "I have lived among these people and my daughters have taught in the schools. If he gets the books, he can not get the shoes, and he must have both to go to school. Our schools begin in December and run through the winter. There should be a term in the summer time."[77]

The educational problem was not a single one, but rather a complex of social problems. Antiquated and poorly furnished one-room schools in two separate systems were taught by poorly trained and poorly paid teachers. Funds must come from the self-taxation of a poor people hampered by the inertia of a political machine linked with propertied interests hostile to taxation. Antagonism between the white and the Negro masses could be utilized

---

75. *North Carolina School Report, 1898-1900*, p. 71.
76. Connor to Howard, December 26, 1900, Connor Papers, S.H.C., University of North Carolina.
77. *Report of the Industrial Commission*, X, 439. Machpelah was in Lincoln County. *Ibid.*, X, 433.

by opponents of increased expenditure for universal education. And the desire of whites for education increased the temptation to deprive Negro schools of funds at a time when Negroes could not even make articulate complaint. Educational reformers in North Carolina obviously needed firm support from some quarter.

CHAPTER III

The Southern Education Board: A Regional Approach to Public Education

"I AM GROWING very intense upon the negro question," Robert C. Ogden of New York wrote to his fellow philanthropist George Foster Peabody in 1896. Ogden predicted that the ensuing ten years would cover the Negro's crisis, "and within that period it will be determined whether as a mass his race is to rise or fall in this country. I very much fear the fall."[1] The cause of this pessimistic concern was, of course, the White Supremacy movement which was accumulating force all through the nineties. And out of this concern grew the Southern Education Board, in which Northern philanthropists and Southern educators joined to direct a region-wide public school crusade for fourteen years after 1901.

As Ogden explained the attitude of the philanthropists at a Southern gathering, "While we were originally interested in the South through negro education, our impulses have risen from negro education to the question of the entire burden of educational responsibility that you have throughout this entire section of the country."[2] The Southern Education Board was an intersectional partnership of moderate progressives, moderate in the North on the delicate racial and sectional issues, and progressive in the South in the limited sense that it offered education as a key to regional progress. In challenging racism by good will, tact, and hard work, the Board's efforts were a test of the efficacy of moderate progres-

1. Ogden to Peabody, June 11, 1896, Robert C. Ogden Papers, Library of Congress.
2. *Fourth Conference for Education in the South, Proceedings* (Winston-Salem, 1901), p. 6.

sivism in a field where the radicals of Reconstruction had signally failed. But it found itself plunged into the stream of a more powerful movement which had been accumulating force for a decade. This current of extreme racism enveloped all other movements in the region within its context, tingeing them with its attitudes and deflecting them from their original directions into its own stream. "These new antipathies are not defensive, but assertive and combative," Edgar Gardner Murphy noted at the time; "this popular temper is . . . frankly and ruthlessly destructive."[3] Southern progressivism could not avoid or evade the White Supremacy movement, nor could the Southern Education movement.

The Northerners of the Board were from New York rather than Boston. Robert C. Ogden was manager of John Wanamaker's New York department store. George Foster Peabody,[4] a Wall Street banker, and the young railroad president William H. Baldwin, Jr.,[5] had long been associated with Ogden as trustees of Negro industrial schools. These men, with help from Andrew Carnegie and the General Education Board, financed the Board's modest budget.[6] Walter Hines Page and J. L. M. Curry,

3. Edgar Gardner Murphy, *The Basis of Ascendancy* (New York, 1909), p. 27.
4. Born at Columbus, Georgia, Peabody had a deep, sentimental interest in his native region and was a trustee of Hampton Institute and other Southern schools. He, like Ogden, apparently had no investments in Southern enterprises comparable to his extensive holdings elsewhere. Robert C. Ogden to Peabody, January 10, 1895, Robert C. Ogden Papers, Library of Congress; Louise Ware, *George Foster Peabody: Banker, Philanthropist, Publicist* (Athens, Georgia, 1951), pp. 17-29, 47-56, 70-85.
5. The son of abolitionists, Baldwin became an active trustee of Tuskegee Institute while vice president and general manager of the Southern Railway and an employer of black labor. By 1901 his business life was apparently divorced from the South and he was president of the Long Island Railroad. He retained his influence on Booker T. Washington and was president of the General Education Board. His memorial biography is John Graham Brooks, *An American Citizen: The Life of William H. Baldwin, Jr.* (Boston and New York, 1910).
6. Expenditures from 1901 to 1914 were slightly over $400,000, or about $30,000 annually. Treasurer's reports, of which those for the year 1904, the latter half of 1906, and the first half of 1912 have not been located, indicate that Peabody gave in the thirteen years $84,279.90; Carnegie, $100,000; the General Education Board, $79,000.00; Frank R. Chambers of New York, $50,000; the Russell Sage Foundation (after 1908), $52,500; Robert C. Ogden, $33,719.88; and Lillian W. Johnson, $5.10. This was a total of $399,504.88, not including interest or contributions in the missing reports. Expenditures for the Southern seaboard states were $41,181.84 in Virginia, $26,553.71 in North

The Southern Education Board: A Regional Approach 77

Southerners transplanted in the North, served as intersectional diplomats.[7] Most of the Southern members were college presidents. The veteran campaigners Charles D. McIver, Edwin A. Alderman, and Charles W. Dabney[8] had been partners in the earlier North Carolina school crusade. Edgar Gardner Murphy, on the other hand, had attracted the philanthropists' attention by his Southern race conference at Montgomery, Alabama, in 1900.[9] These were the chief policy-makers, though other Southerners were later added.

The new philanthropists were not as concerned about Negro civil rights as had been the humanitarian radicals of an earlier generation.[10] William H. Baldwin's hard-boiled philanthropy as-

---

Carolina, $17,286.41 in Georgia, and $16,791.12 in South Carolina. The above figures, which are only approximate, are based on the annual and biennial reports of the treasurer (George Foster Peabody) to the Southern Education Board, that Board's report to the Russell Sage Foundation in October, 1913, and September, 1914, in Charles W. Dabney Papers, S.H.C., University of North Carolina; Hollis B. Frissell to Henry St. George Tucker, November 27, 1903, in Hollis B. Frissell Papers, Hampton Institute, Virginia; L. G. Myers (an employee of Peabody) to George S. Dickerman, January 10, 1907, in George S. Dickerman Papers, S.H.C., University of North Carolina; Edward W. Dodd to Ogden, July 14, 1911, Ogden Papers, Library of Congress; George S. Dickerman, "The Conference for Education in the South and the Southern Education Board," in *Report of the Commissioner of Education, 1907*, I, 327.

7. Then in his eighties, Curry had been for over twenty years the agent for the Peabody Education Fund and John F. Slater Fund. He was glad to be able to shift his burden to younger shoulders before his death in 1903. "These movements are very encouraging to one, who (weary and hopeless) has been laboring along these lines for twenty years," he wrote his old friend **Daniel Coit Gilman**, August 30, 1901. Daniel Coit Gilman Papers, The Johns Hopkins University.

8. Dabney, president of the University of Tennessee, explained in his MS memoirs, written about 1940, how his interest in the movement was aroused. Dabney Papers, S.H.C., University of North Carolina.

9. An Episcopal clergyman of Montgomery, Alabama, Murphy got help from Ogden, Page, and Peabody in organizing his conference. Ogden to Page, April 5, 1900, Page Papers, Houghton Library, Harvard University; series of letters during 1900 in Ogden Papers, Library of Congress; Booker T. Washington to Emmett J. Scott, March 11, 1900, Murphy to Washington, January 11, 1901, Booker T. Washington Papers, Library of Congress; Isabel C. Barrows, "The Montgomery Conference," in *Outlook*, LXV (May 19, 1900), 160-62; Montgomery *Advertiser*, January 11, 1900; "The Montgomery Conference," in *American Monthly Review of Reviews*, XXI (June, 1900), 655-56. Scattered sources on Murphy's career in Southern social reform are brought together in Allen J. Going, "The Reverend Edgar Gardner Murphy: His Ideas and Influence," in *Historical Magazine of the Protestant Episcopal Church*, XXV (December, 1956), 391-402.

10. Ogden could say "Amen" to several stanzas of Rudyard Kipling's "The

sumed that the Negro "will willingly fill the more menial positions, and do the heavy work, at less wages," leaving to whites "the more expert labor." Baldwin's advice to the Negro was quite specific: "Avoid social questions; leave politics alone; continue to be patient; live moral lives; live simply; learn to work ... know that it is a crime for any teacher, white or black, to educate the negro for positions which are not open to him. ..."[11]

Though the philanthropists may have been complacent about an inferior status for Negroes, they were perturbed by the social and economic hindrances placed on Negroes by the sovereign whites. After several experiments with self-help schemes within the Negro community, they concluded that the key to Negro problems lay within the white community. There had to be a working compromise between the "best North" and the "best South,"[12] a Get Together Club like that which was solving New York City's most baffling social problems. The "best North," in Ogden's scale of values, was composed of men like himself, conservative business and professional people; the "best South" included educators and a remnant of upper-class paternalists, "a minority powerful to restrain if not always powerful to accomplish."[13] And if there were objections to "social equality," it was not necessary for Negroes to attend the meeting.[14] After all,

---

White Man's Burden," even in the presence of Negroes. Clipping from Philadelphia *North American*, June 21, 1901, in George S. Dickerman clipping books, S.H.C., University of North Carolina. Page, Albert Shaw, and Lyman Abbott, spokesmen for the movement, accepted Negro disfranchisement without protest. *Capon Springs Conference for Christian Education in the South, 1899* (Washington, n. d.), pp. 28-29.

11. *Ibid.*, pp. 72, 74.

12. Ogden to Richard Watson Gilder (editor of *The Century*), February 25, 1903, Ogden Papers, Library of Congress—University of North Carolina. This collection, used by the writer at both repositories and for a time claimed by both, is now in the Library of Congress with the main body of Ogden Papers.

13. The phrase was Edgar Gardner Murphy's, in *The Basis of Ascendancy*, p. 29. See also *Fourth Conference for Education in the South, Proceedings* (Winston-Salem, 1901), pp. 5-6.

14. Booker T. Washington, as Negro agent of the Board, met frequently with the Northerners and spoke on the same platforms with the Southerners in the North and South, but did not attend the Board meetings or Conferences for Education in the South. Ogden failed in an effort to get Washington on the Conference programs. Negroes were never invited to the conferences. Ogden to Baldwin, May 27, 1903, Ogden to Oswald Garrison Villard, March 11, 1905, Ogden to Rev. Samuel H. Bishop of New York City, March 27, 1906, Ogden Papers, Library of Congress—University of North Carolina. Washington com-

were prostitutes consulted when New York City's vice problem was being solved by members of the chamber of commerce?

If race prejudice was due to ignorance and economic competition, the philanthropists reasoned, then through public schools the whites might learn racial tolerance along with skills which would widen their opportunities. An educational movement of constructive character, moving in a path parallel to the destructive White Supremacy movement, could harbor strength by avoiding direct clashes and thus outdistance and check the rival force.

The regional approach was at the center of the Board's plan of action. A single, pervasive institution, the public school, was the lever by which it hoped to move the region, to solve all of the other complex problems arising from Southern poverty, ignorance, and racial tension. To translate into more recent terms, the Board viewed the South as an underdeveloped region, for which its task was to furnish technical assistance and a little money if the South would supply the educational enthusiasm and local leadership. Massive economic aid for Southern education would have had to be federal aid because of the sheer size of the school systems, and that was apparently out of the question after the Blair education bill was defeated in the eighties.[15]

The Southern Education movement began in 1901 with a Pullman-train journey of influential and philanthropic Northerners to North Carolina, the first of a series of annual Southward excursions at Ogden's expense, and a public meeting with Governor Charles B. Aycock and the leaders of Southern white education. Just elected on a platform coupling Negro disfranchisement with universal education, Aycock represented the conservative wing of

---

plained about this to Baldwin, January 22, 1904, Washington Papers, Library of Congress.

15. There was an increase of philanthropic spending in the South after 1900, led by Rockefeller and Carnegie agencies with which members of the Southern Education Board were connected. And there was a considerable increase in Northern capital investment in Southern industry, with which these men had no apparent, direct connection. See note 2 above. Page was at one time a stockholder of the Baltimore *Manufacturers' Record*, and was part-owner of the family lumber estate, a short-line railroad, and a "two-horse" farm in the North Carolina sandhills. H. V. Poor and H. W. Poor, *Poor's Manual of Railroads, 1901* (New York, 1901), p. 392; Henry A. Page MS statement, November 14, 1906, Henry A. Page to Page, September 30, December 13, 31, 1912, Page Papers, Houghton Library, Harvard University.

the White Supremacy movement. A tacit bargain with him underlay the whole educational movement and dictated its tactical methods. The philanthropists acquiesced in disfranchisement and Jim Crow laws and undertook to promote acquiescence in the North, while Aycock pledged publicly that the schools of the disfranchised Negroes would have protection from hostile state legislation through the power and prestige of his high office.[16] The educational leaders at this Conference for Education in the South persuaded the philanthropists to subsidize a region-wide public school campaign through the Southern Education Board.[17]

Ogden's guests, on their return to the North, indicated a complete surrender to White Supremacy. "We have to get rid of our more or less vague idea that all men are created free and equal," announced Editor Lyman Abbott of *The Outlook*.[18] The Reverend Charles H. Parkhurst preached at the Madison Square Presbyterian Church that "we learned to look upon matters more in the way in which the Southern mind regards them." Good Southerners advised the Negro to "keep quiet," said Parkhurst, who had been convinced that "the less the negro talks about his civic rights under the Constitution, particularly the right of suf-

16. Raleigh *News and Observer*, May 21, 1901, January 9, 1903; Connor and Poe, *Charles Brantley Aycock*, pp. 132-35. The philanthropists may have assumed that Southern conservatives such as Aycock would consolidate their victory over Populists and Negroes by making concessions. Curti, *Social Ideas of American Educators*, p. 281. Actually, Aycock did little to protect Negro school funds at county and district levels, and considerably less was spent on Negro rural schools in 1905 than in 1895, according to the North Carolina state superintendent, quoted in Jones, *Negro Education*, I, 29.

17. An annual Conference for Christian Education in the South had been meeting in a West Virginia resort since 1898. It was captured by Ogden's friends, who dropped "Christian" from its title, elected Ogden president, shifted its meetings to leading Southern cities, and brought into it the Southerners representing white schools. Out of a resolution passed at the fourth conference in 1901 grew the Southern Education Board, selected by Ogden with the advice of Southerners McIver, Alderman, and Dabney. The origins of the Conference and Board are discussed at length in Dabney, *Universal Education in the South*, II, 3-73. See also Wickliffe Rose, "The Educational Movement in the South," in *Report of the Commissioner of Education, 1903*, I, 377-78; *Fourth Conference for Education in the South, Proceedings* (Winston-Salem, 1901), *passim;* Malone, *Edwin A. Alderman*, pp. 133-34; Alderman to Marcus C. S. Noble, March 25, 1929, in Malone MS notes, Alderman to Dabney, September 30, 1901, Alderman Papers, Alderman Library, University of Virginia.

18. New York *World*, April 28, 1901; clipping from New York *Journal*, May 24, 1901, in Dickerman clipping books, S.H.C., University of North Carolina.

The Southern Education Board: A Regional Approach 81

frage . . . the sooner he will attain to all the rights that justly belong to him."[19] Walter Hines Page of the *World's Work* admitted that race friction was getting worse, but thought it could not be "allayed . . . by anything whatsoever except the training of the inefficient and the ignorant." Page emphasized a positive approach to Southern problems. "The statesman-schoolmaster," he said, "is the man to build our hopes on."[20] These spokesmen for the philanthropic capitalist did not so much change Northern opinion as indicate its final capitulation to racism. Others had already taken the same path to reunion,[21] and racial discrimination was spreading in the North.

The Board met for a week every winter at Ogden's office, the evenings being filled with Carnegie Hall addresses and millionaire banquets. Every summer the Southern campaigners shook off the dust of the hustings at Abenia, Peabody's country estate on Lake George. Murphy epitomized the spirit of these meetings in verse:

> Again, Abenia, at thy gracious call
> We come to share thy largesse, and to build
> As partners of some grave imperious guild,
> Our plots of far-off ends, our dream of all
> That out of ampler Knowledge may befall
> To make the bound go free;—and, as we willed,
> Our own faith's waiting stature was fulfilled,
> Our life sprang, leaping sunward, out of thrall.[22]

The Board had no money to give away; all of its funds went to the salary of agents[23] and to the propaganda bureau directed by

19. New York *World*, April 29, 1901.
20. "The Only Way to Allay Race-Friction," editorial in *World's Work*, VI (August, 1903), 3720-21. Albert Shaw, also a Board member, viewed with complacency "Disfranchisement in Several States," editorial in *American Monthly Review of Reviews*, XXIII (June, 1901), 643-44.
21. Charles Francis Adams, the capitalist as historian, told a Charleston audience in 1902 that in the secession crisis, "Everybody, in short, was right; no one, wrong." Charles F. Adams, *Studies Military and Diplomatic 1775-1865* (New York, 1911), p. 208, and for his view of the Negro, pp. 230-31. Also illuminating is "Reconstruction and Disfranchisement," editorial in *Atlantic Monthly*, LXXXVIII (October, 1901), 433-37.
22. Edgar Gardner Murphy, "Sonnet at Lake George—August, 1907," MS, Dabney Papers, S.H.C., University of North Carolina.
23. McIver, Alderman, Dabney, Murphy, Washington, George S. Dickerman, Wickliffe Rose, and Albert P. Bourland were paid, though the first three did not appear on the salary list. Dabney MS memoirs, Dabney Papers, S.H.C., Uni-

Dabney at Knoxville for the first two years. Rockefeller's almoner, the Baptist clergyman Wallace Buttrick, and several other Northerners were admitted to membership, as were a number of Southern educational campaigners from time to time.[24]

"My own relation to the whole affair is much like that of a conductor to a street car," Robert C. Ogden told Curry, "my duty being to ring the bell for the starting and stopping and so much intent upon the progress of the vehicle that I cannot take in very clearly what the passengers are talking about."[25] A physical giant well over six feet tall, with a splendid white beard and pince-nez glasses, Ogden cut a fine figure as chairman of educational gatherings. The Yankee shrewdness of his mouth, the sternness of his brow, were belied by the kindly twinkle of his eye. He had considerable business acumen and a flair for advertising and the retailer's "good will" which he could turn to educational propaganda and intersectional compromise. Ogden's friendship for Southerners was transparently sincere, and as a trustee of Hampton Institute for over forty years he supported the type of Negro edu-

---

versity of North Carolina; Ogden to Murphy, October 14, 1904, Ogden Papers, Library of Congress—University of North Carolina.

24. The full membership was: Ogden 1901-13, Curry 1901-03, McIver 1901-06, Alderman 1901-14, Dabney 1901-14, Peabody 1901-14, Buttrick 1901-14, Baldwin 1901-05, Page 1901-14, Hollis B. Frissell 1901-14, Hugh H. Hanna 1901-12, Albert Shaw 1901-14, Murphy 1902-13, Walter B. Hill 1904-06, Frank R. Chambers 1905-14, David F. Houston 1906-14, George S. Dickerman 1906-14, Samuel C. Mitchell 1906-14, Henry E. Fries 1906-14, Philander P. Claxton 1906-14, Sidney J. Bowie 1906-14, James H. Dillard 1908-14, James H. Kirkland 1908-14, Wickliffe Rose 1908-14, John M. Glenn 1909-14, Albert P. Bourland 1913-14, Bruce R. Payne 1914. Hoke Smith was rejected because of his political affiliations.—Ogden to McIver, June 7, 1901, Peabody to Ogden, February 21, 1907, Ogden Papers, Library of Congress; Ogden to Dabney, June 10, 1901, Ogden to Dickerman, June 18, 1901, Dabney Papers, S.H.C., University of North Carolina. Kirkland was blackballed by Page until 1908, though Murphy insisted that "Kirkland is *not* a 'preacher.'" After Kirkland used Andrew Carnegie's philanthropy to emancipate Vanderbilt University from the Southern Methodist bishops, he was welcomed into the Board.—Page to Ogden, December 17, 1903, Murphy to Page, December 10, 20, 1903, Page to Edwin Mims, January 5, 1911, Page Papers, Houghton Library, Harvard University; Edwin Mims, *Chancellor Kirkland of Vanderbilt* (Nashville, 1940), pp. 13, 45, 128-59; Hunter D. Farish, *The Circuit Rider Dismounts: A Social History of Southern Methodism 1865-1900* (Richmond, 1938), pp. 295-96; Kirkland, "Recent History of Vanderbilt University," in *Methodist Review* (Nashville), LIX (April, 1910), 343-58.

25. Ogden to Curry, June 6, 1902, in Jabez L. M. Curry Papers, Library of Congress.

cation which had the endorsement of white Southerners. Edgar Gardner Murphy did not exaggerate Ogden's influence when he said that, "more than any living man, he has changed the attitude of the North toward the vexed problem of negro education, and has brought the aid of the North ... to that kind of education which increases the practical value of the negro not only to himself but to the South."[26]

As a retail merchant, Ogden preached a "business idealism" which he sometimes confused with current corporation practices. He brought to the Southern Education movement the philosophy of the churchman and bourgeois charity-organizer. "Intellectually he measures up to the Sunday School type," said John Spencer Bassett. Free pews and broad views were the extent of Ogden's leadership of Presbyterian laymen, but his charity knew no limit. Before he turned to the absorbing work of uplifting the South, Ogden spent his energies freely and widely in alleviating distress. Southerners were linked in his mind with the others he had helped, the Johnstown and Mississippi flood victims, down-and-outers of New York's Henry Street settlement, the Philadelphia Negroes studied by Du Bois, the struggling sculptor George Gray Barnard, the ravenous Indians, the oppressed Armenians and Russians, Cuban orphans, even Admiral Dewey, for the perpetuation of whose triumphal arch Ogden was chairman of the fund-raising sub-committee for "dry goods (retail)." Southerners of the period seemed to Ogden to fit in with this assortment of derelicts of progress.[27] "My sympathy with the Southern people, who have never had a chance in our democracy, is great," he wrote his fellow millionaire Andrew Carnegie.[28]

26. Letter of Murphy to the editor, in Montgomery *Advertiser*, April 30, 1901, clipping in Dickerman clipping books, S.H.C., University of North Carolina.

27. There are many notices of Ogden's charities in Dickerman clipping books, S.H.C., University of North Carolina, and in the Ogden Papers, Library of Congress. See also the memorial biography, Philip W. Wilson, *An Unofficial Statesman—Robert C. Ogden* (New York, 1924); Curti, *Social Ideas of American Educators*, p. 283; for Bassett's remark, Woodward, *Origins of the New South*, p. 401, n. 15. Ogden was the first of three contributors to the expenses of W. E. Burghardt Du Bois's sociological study of the Philadelphia Negro in 1900. Ogden to William Jay Schieffelin, May 10, 1906, Ogden Papers, Library of Congress—University of North Carolina.

28. Ogden to Carnegie, April 17, 1906, Ogden Papers, Library of Congress—University of North Carolina.

The Southern members of the Board, mostly young men in their thirties and early forties, were only superficially like those of the New South on whom had fallen the mantle of Henry Grady. The educators too were "instinct with nervous energy" and "constantly rushing off, full of business," to New York. They too had "irresistible statistics" to show men of millions and, like the Southern promoters, magnified the virtues of the dominant Northeast, but the essential difference was that their statistics dealt, not with cheap resources, cheap manpower, and "paradisiacal climates," but with poor schools in poor rural areas.[29] In speaking to the philanthropists, Dabney made no compromise with the booster spirit; "blinking nothing of the truth, however unpleasant," he buttressed with statistics his conclusion that "The southern people are poor—many of them extremely poor. Their schools are poor because they are poor; but the converse is equally true—the people are poor because the schools are poor . . . we can measure the wealth-earning power of a people by the school privileges which they enjoy." Agrarians of the preceding decade would have argued that Dabney was confusing cart and horse, but philanthropists were not disposed to do so, and he smoothed over causes of Southern poverty which implicated the Northern capitalist.[30]

"I must place myself in the position in which I can do this work free from the misunderstandings that so often attend the efforts of the clergyman," Murphy wrote to his bishop to explain his resignation from the ministry. "My decision thus springs from a sense of duty."[31] This sense was shared by the others. "My first day's work in this world was for the public schools," Alderman reminded Dabney, "and I have never known a day unconnected with service of some sort for them." As for McIver, he simply thought that

29. The businessman of the New South is sketched from life in "The Atlanta Exposition," editorial in *Scribner's Magazine*, XIX (January, 1896), p. 132.

30. Dabney's speech is in *Fourth Conference for Education in the South, Proceedings* (Winston-Salem, 1901), pp. 47-62. The other Southern school men helped him write it. "I read and reread your speech at Winston," Alderman wrote him, September 30, 1901. "We gave you good advice, I think, concerning the reference to the suffrage and the 'Majors' story did the rest." Alderman Papers, Alderman Library, University of Virginia.

31. Murphy to Episcopal Bishop Charles M. Beckwith of Alabama, February 2, 1903, Southern Education Board circular for private use, Dabney Papers, S.H.C., University of North Carolina.

mass education was what "makes democracy possible. It is the salt that saves the world."[32]

Besides an optimism which was the glow of action, the movement had a progressive philosophy which, said Alderman, "differs fundamentally from the old philosophy which perceived government as a sort of nearsighted and benevolent policeman, and society as a group of units to be protected from violence, to be helped not at all." He hesitantly called the new philosophy "collectivism," but "anything will do."[33] Murphy believed that one of the main tasks of Southern leadership was to bring the region into conformity with the spirit of the times. "It will have all the old faith and pride in the South, but it will possess 'a decent respect for the opinion of mankind,' knowing that no people can ever wisely stand outside of the context of its century and civilization."[34]

The Southern Education Board was interwoven with all of the leading endowed philanthropic boards active in Southern education. Northern members were trustees of the other boards, and several of the Southern members were their salaried agents. At the first meeting of the Southern Education Board a "community of interest" was arranged with the Peabody Fund and the Slater Fund.[35] And when Rockefeller's General Education Board was established in 1902 as the instrument of the oil king's benefactions, it quickly became "a sort of clearing-house for Southern education" and "a permanent 'steering committee' for Northern sentiment interested in the educational advancement of the South." Eleven members of the Southern Board were also members of the General Education Board in its first decade, Baldwin and Ogden being

32. Alderman to Dabney, September 30, 1901, quoted in Malone, *Edwin A. Alderman*, p. 131; McIver, quoted in Charles L. Coon, "Charles Duncan McIver and his Educational Services, 1886-1906," in *Report of the Commissioner of Education, 1907*, I, 335.
33. Edwin A. Alderman, *The National Spirit: An Address before the Washington Association of New Jersey, February 22, 1911* (n.p., 1911?), pp. 21-22.
34. Edgar Gardner Murphy, "The Task of the Leader: A Discussion of the Conditions of Public Leadership in Our Southern States," in *Sewanee Review*, XV (January, 1907), 3, 28-30.
35. Curry to Gilman, August 30, 1901, Gilman Papers, The Johns Hopkins University; minutes of meeting of Southern Education Board and attached memoranda, November 4-9, 1901, Curry Papers, Library of Congress; Gilman to Samuel A. Green, November 2, 1901, Peabody Education Fund Papers, George ePabody College for Teachers.

successive presidents of the latter board and Peabody treasurer of both. "This is a kind of Trust which will appeal to everyone," said the *Nation*.[36] Besides this interlocking directorate, "the Peabody and Slater Boards are now acting very largely through the General Education Board," according to Frissell.[37] The concept of the philanthropic trust became increasingly important as Rockefeller supplemented his initial grant of $1,000,000 by others amounting to $53,000,000 by 1909. A succession of members of the Southern Education Board served as general agents of the Peabody, Slater, and General Education Boards. They continued Curry's policy in regard to Negro education, aiding the industrial schools and giving a cold reception to appeals from Negro colleges designed on the standard American pattern of higher education.[38]

The establishment of the Anna T. Jeanes Foundation in 1907 with a donation of $1,000,000 to aid Southern Negro elementary schools gave recognition to a Negro school problem distinct from that of general Southern educational expansion.[39] Seven of the original trustees—a majority—were members of the Southern Education Board. The president and field agent was the Virginian James H. Dillard, member of the Southern Board and later agent

36. Editorial in *Nation*, LXXIV (March 13, 1902), 202.
37. Frissell to Archer M. Huntington, February 17, 1903, Frissell Papers, Hampton Institute; Rockefeller's letters of gift, in *The General Education Board: An Account of Its Activities 1902-1914*, pp. 216-23.
38. Until his death in 1903, Curry was agent or member of all four funds. Buttrick, a member of the Southern Education Board, was executive secretary of the General Education Board until 1917, when he became president, and acted as agent of the Slater Fund from 1903 to 1910. Dickerman was field director of the Slater Fund from 1907 to 1910, and Dillard field director from 1910 to 1917. Wickliffe Rose of the Southern Education Board was agent of the Peabody Fund 1907-15, trustee of the Slater Fund 1909-23, member of the General Education Board 1911-28, administrative secretary of the Rockefeller Sanitary Commission 1910-15, member of the Rockefeller Foundation and its subsidiary International Health Board 1913-28 and of the International Education Board 1923-28.
39. There is no adequate history of the Jeanes Foundation. See Arthur D. Wright and Edward E. Redcay, *The Negro Rural School Fund, Inc. (Anna T. Jeanes Foundation) 1907-1933* (Washington, 1933); Benjamin Brawley, *Doctor Dillard of the Jeanes Fund* (New York and Chicago, 1930); Lance G. E. Jones, *The Jeanes Teacher in the United States, 1908-1933: An Account of Twenty-Five Years' Experience in the Supervision of Negro Rural Schools* (Chapel Hill, 1937); Myrdal, *An American Dilemma*, II, 890-93, 1417-18; Ullin W. Leavell, *Philanthropy in Negro Education*: George Peabody College for Teachers, Contribution to Education, No. 100 (Nashville, 1930), pp. 71-76, 106-09, 135-37, 156-64.

of the Slater Fund. Ogden himself was at once president of the Southern and General Education Boards, trustee of the Jeanes Fund, president of the Hampton Institute trustees, and a trustee of Tuskegee. Julius Rosenwald aided construction of Negro school buildings through Tuskegee from 1912 to 1920, and only the Phelps-Stokes Fund of 1910, free of the interlocking directorate, brought new personnel and a fresh approach to the problems of Negro education.[40] Virtual monopolistic control of educational philanthropy for the South and the Negro placed on the Rockefeller boards a special responsibility for wise judgment and action. In their early years their work seems to have suffered more from excessive caution than from any abuse of power.[41]

Most of the Southerners of the educational movement were connected with state colleges, while most foundation grants went to private colleges. Nevertheless, proximity to millions was a source of prestige to the campaigners. The philanthropists were assessed and consulted when Alderman was chosen president of the University of Virginia.[42] He persuaded Rockefeller to endow his school of education and was the impulsive Andrew Carnegie's "pioneer in giving to colleges."[43] He became the first Southerner

40. Edwin R. Embree and Julia Waxman, *Investment in People: The Story of the Rosenwald Fund* (New York, 1944), pp. 26-29. On the early years of the Phelps-Stokes Fund, besides the annual reports, see Thomas Jesse Jones, *Educational Adaptations: Report of Ten Years' Work of the Phelps-Stokes Fund, 1910-1920* (New York, 1920?); Anson Phelps-Stokes et al., *Progress in Negro Status and Race Relations 1911-1946: The Thirty-Five Year Report of the Phelps-Stokes Fund* (New York, 1948); there were also twenty-year and twenty-five-year reports.

41. The General Education Board published no report for the first twelve years; its early work is summarized in *The General Education Board: An Account of Its Activities 1902-1914*. After the deaths of Wallace Buttrick and Frederick T. Gates, the Rockefeller agencies changed their policies in the twenties on Negro education. Insight into the early years may be found in Abraham Flexner, *I Remember* (New York, 1940); idem in collaboration with Esther S. Bailey, *Funds and Foundations: Their Policies Past and Present* (New York, 1952); Raymond B. Fosdick, *The Story of the Rockefeller Foundation* (New York, 1952); Allan Nevins, *John D. Rockefeller: The Heroic Age of American Enterprise* (2 vols., New York, 1940); and his *Study in Power: John D. Rockefeller, Industrialist and Philanthropist* (2 vols., New York, 1953).

42. Ogden to Thomas Nelson Page, July 1, 1904, Thomas Nelson Page Papers, Duke University; Malone, *Edwin A. Alderman*, pp. 167-68.

43. The steel magnate's tardy discovery that the University of Virginia was a state institution "proved a lion in his path," and he cut his gift from one million to a half-million dollars. In approaching Carnegie, Alderman had the help of Ogden, Buttrick, and Peabody.—Ogden to Carnegie, February 6, 1905,

on the General Education Board in 1907 in order, "in some way, [to] give the picture of southern conditions."[44] While such gifts and prestige smoothed the rugged path of reform, they were subordinate to the main work of the Southern Board. "In one sense the Southern Education Board has the advantage of any other philanthropic board," said McIver. "It has nothing to give but advice, and has no work except to persuade the judgments and inspire the hearts and consciences of men."[45] Like the Point Four pioneers of a later period, the Southern educators knew that there was a limit to the generosity of the wealthy area, and that most of the funds must come from the Southern people themselves. The educational movement had begun in the equalitarian climate of Populism in North Carolina, and its objective was not charity but self-taxation. "The big point," said Alderman, "is that we . . . probably suggested the great beneficent undertakings of large wealth to *assist* the State, *not* to *take* its place, in the South, in overcoming its fearful difficulties in placing the whole idea of public education in full strength upon the basis needed by modern democracy."[46] There were three steps in the work at hand, as it took form in Alderman's mind:

1. The development of an irresistible public opinion for popular education by popular effort.
2. The crystallization of this sentiment into money, largely through local taxation.
3. The birth of a larger and finer conception of the duties and responsibilities of school-teachers and school-officers. . . .[47]

Ogden to Peabody, February 6, 1905, Ogden Papers, Library of Congress—University of North Carolina; Henry St. George Tucker to Charles W. Kent, February 18, 1905, Henry St. George Tucker Papers, S.H.C., University of North Carolina; Alderman to Thomas Nelson Page, February 16, 1905, Thomas Nelson Page Papers, Duke University. After two interviews in a vain effort to persuade Carnegie to give the other half-million, Alderman thought Thomas Fortune Ryan "ought to give a half million as a *Virginian*, for he can afford it." —*Ibid*.

44. Alderman to George H. Denny, December 17, 1907, quoted in Malone, *Edwin A. Alderman*, p. 260.

45. McIver, in *Seventh Conference for Education in the South, Proceedings* (Birmingham, 1904), p. 61.

46. Alderman to Marcus C. S. Noble, March 25, 1929, Malone MS notes, University of Virginia.

47. Alderman, in *Seventh Conference for Education in the South, Proceedings* (Birmingham, 1904), p. 75.

The Southern Education Board: A Regional Approach 89

Primarily, then, the Southern Education Board was a propaganda agency both in the South and in the North. In the South its message was positive, and in the North negative. The Southern campaigners urged their people to build schools, while their Northern partners urged concession, conciliation, and quiescence.

Within a few weeks after the Board was formed, Dabney began to flood the South with educational propaganda—press handouts, circulars, and thick bulletins filled with statistics.[48] He attracted about 11,000 teachers by 1907 to "the biggest summer school in the world" at Knoxville. Tuition was free, instruction nominal, transportation rates half-fare. "Its object," said Dabney, was "to fill them with our gospel and make them missionaries for the cause."[49] But the primary method of arousing educational sentiment was the state campaign. Beginning in the Southern seaboard, every Southern state except Mississippi had an educational campaign by 1909. The movement gained momentum and lost restraint as it swept westward. In Tennessee it was recognized as "the voice of the people"; the Whirlwind Campaign in Kentucky was "a continuous cyclone bombardment against illiteracy"; in Texas it was "time for the parent to get on the firing line"; and "only one preacher in the entire state" of Arkansas refused to contribute a sermon to the public school cause.[50]

---

48. Dabney, *Universal Education in the South*, II, 74-81; Lewis, *Philander Priestley Claxton*, pp. 112-16; Dabney's report in *Sixth Conference for Education in the South, Proceedings* (Richmond, 1903), p. 45; Augustus W. Long, *Son of Carolina* (Durham, 1939), p. 188; Dabney MS memoirs, Dabney to Ogden, March 3, 1902, Charles L. Coon to Dabney, December 30, 1903, Joseph D. Eggleston to Page, March 17, 1902, Dabney Papers, S.H.C., University of North Carolina; and for a sample of the propaganda, *Southern Education* (Knoxville, biweekly), I, No. 6 (April 16, 1903), 58-59.

49. John Dewey taught one session for a considerable fee. "They sit with their mouths open and catch and swallow what they can," Dabney reported to Dickerman, April 5, 1902, Dabney Papers, S.H.C., University of North Carolina. See also Dabney, *Universal Education in the South*, II, 105-14; Alexander J. McKelway, "The Summer School of the South," in *Outlook*, LXXI (August 2, 1902), 894-96; Dabney MS memoirs, Dabney Papers, S.H.C., University of North Carolina.

50. Words of "a rather cold-blooded" legislator, in Lewis, *Philander Priestley Claxton*, p. 159; Andrew D. Holt, *The Struggle for a State System of Public Schools in Tennessee 1903-1936:* Teachers College, Columbia University, Contributions to Education, No. 753 (New York, 1938), pp. 164-84, 209-64; Louisville *Evening Post*, December 1, 1908, June 28, 1909; Frank L. McVey, *The Gates Open Slowly: A History of Education in Kentucky* (Lexington, 1949), p. 208; *Proceedings of the First Annual Conference for Education in Texas* . . .

Oratory was the chief means of popular persuasion. As Philander P. Claxton said, "people have not yet outgrown, certainly in . . . the Southern states, appeals through the mouth and through the ear, the appeal of the great mass meeting."[51] This was quite necessary in a sparsely settled region with more than three million illiterates. And "for one man who is technically illiterate there is always another who can meet the technical test, but who, to all practical purposes, is illiterate also, illiterate because . . . he is seldom called upon to read or write."[52] Southerners who were "raised on camp meetings" and brought dinner with them would be offended by a half-hour speech, said Claxton. "A man who has come twenty miles to hear a speaking wants to hear a good deal of it, and they have the power to sit and hear it, so that you can appeal to them morning and afternoon and they will remain."[53] At a typical all-day rally in a mountain county, twenty-five miles from a railroad: "The people came in great numbers from the surrounding country. Many walked, some rode in good buggies and surreys; but many families of from three to twelve persons came in plain farm wagons with straw-covered beds, chairs from the fireside as seats, drawn by a yoke of oxen. Many of them were clad in home-woven jeans and cotton; most of them wore shoes, but some, even adults, were barefooted."[54]

The educational orator sought his quarry at schools, camp meetings, churches, church conventions, good-roads meetings, farmers' meetings, political rallies, wherever he smelled human flesh. In North Carolina one could "hardly get off or on a train without meeting an educational campaign orator."[55] Crowds were larger at educational than at political rallies.[56] "Our first thought,"

1907 (Austin? 1907?), pp. 35-36; Little Rock *Arkansas Gazette*, September 29, 1910.

51. Quoted in Woodward, *Origins of the New South*, pp. 404-05.

52. Edgar Gardner Murphy, "Shall the Fourteenth Amendment Be Enforced?" in *North American Review*, CLXX (January, 1905), 125-26.

53. Claxton, "The Methods of an Educational Campaign," in *Eleventh Conference for Education in the South, Proceedings* (Memphis, 1908), p. 79.

54. Joseph B. Graham, "Current Problems in Alabama," in *Annals* of the American Academy of Political and Social Science, XXII (September, 1903), 37.

55. Philander P. Claxton in *Atlantic Educational Journal*, September, 1902, quoted in Lewis, *Philander Priestley Claxton*, p. 116.

56. This was alleged to be true at least in North Carolina and Tennessee. Charles D. McIver, "Current Problems in North Carolina," in *Annals* of the American Academy of Political and Social Science, XXII (September, 1903), 52.

noticed the president of the Farmers' Union, "with the young man, with the old man, is education."[57] It was "wellnigh the universal shibboleth in the South."[58]

Campaigners stressed from the stump the handicaps of ignorance and the economic rewards of education. "The savage pays no tax," McIver told rustic crowds. "Ideas are worth more than acres, and the possessors of ideas will always hold in financial bondage those whose chief possession is acres of land."[59] Debt-ridden farmers were told that "the time is here that to be without a Public School education, is to be a SLAVE."[60]

Adopting a Jeffersonian motto, "Preach a Crusade against Ignorance," the Southern Education Board stressed that "taxation —especially district taxation—for primary schools is pure Jeffersonian democracy."[61] But local taxation, like state-rights particularism, confused Jeffersonian means and ends. Extreme localism of taxation made the Jeffersonian ideal of equal opportunity impossible. Ironically enough, "Every Southern governor is to-day preaching a local tax on the hustings, and urging a local tax in messages to the legislature."[62] There was something to be said in favor of local taxation from the viewpoint of local white taxpayers, and it aroused local interest in the schools. But it was an

57. Barrett, *Mission, History and Times of the Farmers' Union*, p. 26, and for the role of the Farmers' Union in the educational movement, *ibid.*, pp. 88, 247, 263, 277.

58. Editorial in Greenville *News*, quoted in Columbia (South Carolina) *State*, January 1, 1909.

59. Quoted in Coon, "Charles Duncan McIver and His Educational Services, 1886-1906," *Report of the Commissioner of Education, 1907*, pp. 335-36. This argument struck home to the Carolina farmer who said that "people who are educated will not be cheated out of their hard earnings; they will have sense enough to make their own calculations, or, in other words, they will take care of self."—H. A. Gilleland, farmer of Lowesville, in *Fourteenth Annual Report of the Bureau of Labor and Printing of the State of North Carolina, 1900* (Raleigh, 1901), p. 267.

60. Superintendent Y. D. Moore, Caldwell County, North Carolina, circular letter dated October 21, 1905, in Nathan W. Walker clipping books, North Carolina Room, Wilson Library, University of North Carolina.

61. Walter B. Hill, "Local Taxation in Georgia," in *Seventh Conference for Education in the South, Proceedings* (Birmingham, 1904), p. 119; *idem*, "Public Aid to Education in the South," in Southern Educational Association, *Journal of Proceedings and Addresses of the Fourteenth Annual Meeting Held at Atlanta, Georgia, December 30th and 31st, 1903, and January 1st, 1904* (Asheville? 1904), p. 84.

62. Gustavus R. Glenn, in *Sixth Conference for Education in the South, Proceedings* (Richmond, 1903), p. 202.

Achilles' heel of educational reform, because cities and other wealthy districts could wall off their property from taxation for rural schools. Large taxpayers knew that the smaller the tax unit was, the lower the tax rate in a wealthy unit necessary to provide good schools.[63]

The original purpose of the philanthropists was to cushion the Negro against the shock of racism and to keep public education open as an avenue of Negro advancement. They offered the Negro charity rather than full-fledged philanthropy, for in the Negro's behalf they were willing to renounce some of his claims to equal status and opportunity. Not being Negroes themselves, they may not have been fully aware how disappointing such a compromise was to many Negroes, nor how vulnerable the complete loss of political power made the Negroes. And they fatally miscalculated in assuming that the upper-class wing of Southern racism, because it spoke the language of conservatism, would be their effective partner in protecting Negroes. People who were disturbed by the collapse of the Reconstruction settlement undoubtedly sighed with relief that the Negro was keeping education as a solace and hope, and that all they needed to do to further Negro progress was to ride on Ogden's train to hear Southerners speak at educational conferences. But they were misled in this facile optimism.

The Southern Education Board members agreed that for the first two years, at least, "we would not emphasize the *negro* too much," according to Dabney, who ran the Board's propaganda bureau. "In the excited state of public sentiment, this was considered wisest."[64] The Southern campaigners preached in general terms the education of all the people and fairness to Negroes. But as Alderman stated their position in a Northern magazine, the education "of one untaught white man to the point that knowledge and not prejudice will guide his conduct . . . is worth more to the

---

63. S. H. Edmunds (Superintendent of Sumter, South Carolina), "Local Tax, the Hope of the School," in Southern Educational Association, *Journal of Proceedings and Addresses of the Thirteenth Annual Meeting Held at Asheville, North Carolina, June 30-July 3, 1903* (Raleigh? 1903), pp. 49-50; C. S. Maddox (Superintendent of Butts County), in *Georgia School Report, 1908*, pp. 98-100.

64. Dabney to Charles L. Coon, August 27, 1903, Dabney Papers, S.H.C., University of North Carolina.

black man himself than the education of ten Negroes."[65] As Charles B. Aycock simplified the doctrine, "Education of the whites will provide education for the negroes."[66] Exactly how this magic would work was never clear, but the Southern campaigners insisted that education for Negroes was also essential.[67] They said nothing about desegregation,[68] and as little as possible about "separate but equal" education, a doctrine then popular only among constitutional lawyers.

The Northerners took Dabney to task in 1903 for ignoring the Negro entirely in the propaganda he spread over the South. In the Mississippi propaganda, for example, Negro education was not mentioned at a time when James K. Vardaman was trying to destroy the state's Negro school fund. "When I reminded them that a year ago all of them . . . were proclaiming the same principles and policies, I was greeted with silence or explanations," Dabney wrote home. "Recent events have re-excited them about the negro's interests and put them to thinking how they can help to maintain them against the white aggressors."[69] Dabney considered resigning, but the other Southerners patched up the intersectional compromise again.

Spokesmen for Negro schools watched from the sidelines with attitudes fluctuating between suspicion and hope. "The fact that it is controlled by Mr. Ogden & Peabody will make it necessary to

65. Quoted in Malone, *Edwin A. Alderman*, pp. 145-46. Cf. Charles W. Dabney, in a speech at Carnegie Hall, quoted in Raleigh *News and Observer*, January 11, 1903.
66. Charles B. Aycock interview, clipping from Charlotte *Observer*, April 26, 1901, in Dickerman clipping books, S.H.C., University of North Carolina.
67. Edgar Gardner Murphy's report of his remarks at Southern Education Board meeting, August 7, 1907, Ogden Papers, Library of Congress—University of North Carolina. Aycock argued that Negroes needed to be trained like fox hounds and bird dogs. For an example of his technique of folk persuasion, with stage directions, see Vance, "Aycock of North Carolina," *Southwest Review*, XVIII, 296.
68. The Southerners' stand on school segregation was rigid. "A double system of public education is, with all its burdens and with its varied difficulties, an inevitable and unchangeable issue of our problem of population at the South."— Edgar Gardner Murphy, *Problems of the Present South* (New York, 1904, 2nd ed., 1916), p. 37. Ogden told the editor of the Richmond *Times-Dispatch* that he opposed desegregation, Ogden to W. Scott Copeland, February 24, 1905, Ogden Papers, Library of Congress—University of North Carolina.
69. Dabney to Coon, August 27, 1903, Peabody to Dabney, October 7, 1903, Dabney Papers, S.H.C., University of North Carolina.

devote much thought to Negro as well as white education," Principal Hollis B. Frissell of Hampton assured Booker T. Washington in the first year.[70] But Negro college graduates and some Northern liberals were alienated by the fact that the Northern members, who sat on all of the leading philanthropic boards interested in the South, channeled these funds into Negro industrial institutes and white colleges.[71] And Washington himself wrote privately that the Southern educational campaign meant "almost nothing so far as the Negro schools are concerned." He charged that "the Southern members . . . do not put themselves on record in a straight and frank manner as much as they should."[72]

The General Education Board with its millions, prestige, and relative independence might have been expected to balance the caution of the Southern campaigners with its own boldness. But Wallace Buttrick, its executive secretary, was equally cautious and perhaps a bit frightened by the emotional timbre of Southern racism. After a grass-roots conference in the South with North Carolina county superintendents, Buttrick decided that even equal philanthropy for Negroes would make whites cold toward philanthropy. "As a matter of absolute justice they ought to participate proportionately with the whites," he said in a confidential report, "But we are confronted 'with a condition and not a theory.' . . . We shall err and invite defeat, if, in the present state of public sentiment, we demand too much from the white people of the South."[73]

Ogden restrained his own sincere impulse to speak up for

70. Frissell to Washington, November 9, 1901, Washington Papers, Library of Congress.
71. [Flexner and Bachman], *The General Education Board: An Account of Its Activities 1902-1914*, pp. 155-57, 203, 209, has tables showing that that board expended in its first twelve years $3,052,625 to Southern white colleges, $555,781.13 to Negro industrial institutes, and $140,000 to Negro colleges. See also Willard Range, *The Rise and Progress of Negro Colleges in Georgia 1865-1949* (Athens, 1951), pp. 101-02, 164-68; Kelly Miller, "The Education of the Negro," in *Report of the Commissioner of Education, 1900-01*, I, 819-23; Edward T. Ware (chaplain of Atlanta University) to Dickerman, May 9, 1902, Dickerman Papers, S.H.C., University of North Carolina.
72. Washington to Ogden, July 18, 1906, with copies also to Peabody, Buttrick, and Frissell, Washington Papers, Library of Congress.
73. Wallace Buttrick, "Educational Conditions and Needs of North Carolina," confidential report to the General Education Board, January 27, 1904, in Southern Education Board Miscellaneous Papers, S.H.C., University of North Carolina.

Negro education partly from loyalty to his vulnerable Southern allies. He was constantly aware of the danger that the whites might divide the educational tax funds so that Negro schools would receive only the returns from Negro direct taxes, and his Southern friends convinced him that if this question were submitted to Southern voters, the demagogues would win. "For these men to openly attack you," warned Murphy, "would not only be 'unpleasant' but would 'drive to cover' men . . . on whom we—and the negro—*must* depend for fairness and patriotism." "I feel 'like a dog' to have to say these things," Murphy protested, "but I *know* our people."[74] The philanthropists assumed that Southern sensitivity would permit discussion of racial issues only by Southerners. But they might well have risked their timid millions and the added capital of good will so painstakingly accumulated by intersectional conciliation in bold entrepreneurship on the Negro's behalf, in ventures their Southern colleagues could not risk. They decided instead to intensify their original efforts for general popular education.[75] Such action had much to be said for it, but as far as Negro education was concerned it was simply evasion. The real dilemma of the public school campaigns was that white educational sentiment, as it grew, increased the temptation to take the Negro's share of school funds. Educational campaigners were tempted to promise taxpayers a fiscal saving through racial discrimination.[76] The philanthropists, seeking allies

---

74. Murphy to Ogden, April 8, 1904, Ogden Papers, Library of Congress—University of North Carolina. "So many of the officials of the Southern Education Board are identified with state institutions that it has been difficult to do much without embarrassing them (even the University of Virginia is almost absolutely at the mercy of every passing Legislature). . . ."—Murphy to Washington, March 29, 1906, Washington Papers, Library of Congress.

75. Ogden to Page, March 31, 1906, Dickerman Papers, S.H.C., University of North Carolina. "I have an impression that the vigorous prosecution of our general policies of educational progress will constitute a flank movement of considerable power, and . . . would be the wisest plan for the present."—Ogden to Peabody, March 23, 1906, Ogden Papers, Library of Congress—University of North Carolina.

76. After a tour of black Robeson County, campaigner R. F. Beasley of Monroe, North Carolina, reported of the town of Moriah (also called Branchville): "After the speech a majority stood up and said they'd vote the tax—but they won't divide with the negro." He advised the state campaign secretary to write to the young county superintendent, who "hasn't quite caught on to the local tax ideas," and *"tell him* to *push* the tax in that district right now. He can devise some plan for leaving the negro out and the people are anxious but

against the demagogues who exploited lower-class prejudices, actually joined forces with the upper-class conservatives who quietly administered school discrimination.

"Within the saving limits of established principles," said Ogden, "I strive to be, in this Southern Education matter, all things to all men that peace may in the future reign throughout the length and breadth of our land."[77] He sometimes went to great lengths to promote intersectional harmony. He appeared at the New York Union League Club to scotch a proposal to reduce Southern congressional representation as a reprisal for disfranchisement.[78] Avoiding visits to Negro colleges[79] and warning friends against accepting professorships there,[80] he advised Negro leaders to employ "concession, moderation and patience."[81] The editors and public figures who accompanied him southward were counseled to be as "wise as serpents" and as "gentle as doves."[82] "I pursue my own course quietly," he wrote a liberal Southerner,

---

are dependent upon some one outside."—R. F. Beasley to Eugene C. Brooks, September 9, 1903, in James Yadkin Joyner Papers, S.H.C., University of North Carolina.

77. Ogden to Reverend Theodore L. Cuyler, March 30, 1904, copy in Dabney Papers, S.H.C., University of North Carolina.

78. Ogden was denounced for this action by Negro leaders, and explained his motives at length in Ogden to Peabody, April 10, 1903, Ogden to Thomas Wentworth Higginson, June 25, 1904, Ogden Papers, Library of Congress—University of North Carolina.

79. Ogden was particularly careful to avoid contact with Berea College, which was desegregated until a Kentucky law forbade it. William G. Frost to Dickerman, April 7, 1906, in miscellaneous Ogden Papers, University of North Carolina; Ogden to Buttrick, April 13, 1906, Ogden to Baldwin, April 12, 1904, Baldwin to Ogden, April 11, 1904, Ogden Papers, Library of Congress—University of North Carolina. Baldwin disagreed with Ogden's cautious policy of refusing invitations to visit Negro colleges en route to his annual Conferences. A recent study of Berea College is Elizabeth S. Peck, *Berea's First Century* (Lexington, 1956).

80. Ogden to Julius D. Dreher (Selwood, South Carolina), March 26, 1906, Ogden Papers, Library of Congress—University of North Carolina. Dreher, a Southern white, formerly a professor at Roanoke College in Virginia, asked Ogden's advice about teaching at Howard University in Washington, a Negro school. Ogden advised against it.

81. Ogden to Reverend Teunis S. Hamilton (Howard University), March 23, 1903, Ogden Papers, Library of Congress—University of North Carolina; Ogden to Helen M. Ludlow (Hampton Institute), June 15, 1905, Ogden Papers, Library of Congress.

82. Ogden to James E. Russell (Dean of Teachers College, Columbia University), March 26, 1906, Ogden to McIver, January 27, 1903, Ogden Papers, Library of Congress.

"always, however, adapting myself to the standards of the environment in which I may be found."[83] But adaptation to the environment of Southern racism weakened the philanthropists' position as guardians of Negro interests.

It was clear by 1906, the year of the Georgia disfranchisement campaign and the Atlanta race riot, that racism continued to dominate Southern affairs. The Northerners and Murphy held a caucus,[84] and at the next Board meeting Peabody broached the topic of a special campaign for Negro education. The Southern members tried to delay action. "We should avoid anything like a crusade," said Alderman; "guard against going into it with heat." When Peabody replied that it was "about time for a crusade of the right kind," Alderman rejoined: "Southern men have shied from this subject. It has been touching a sore tooth.... We want now to influence public sentiment: stop being silent, but be wise; go forward, but with forethought, not so spectacularly as to set back the movement."[85] This discussion made clear the Board's dilemma, that a crusade for Negro education would jeopardize the crusade for white education. Yielding reluctantly to the superior power of the White Supremacy movement, the Board continued its massive propaganda for schools. Taking a middle path between equalitarianism and racism, it resigned itself by default to the growth of separate and unequal schools.

Pressed from the South by an opposition led by the *Manufacturers' Record,* organ of industry in the South, Page told a Southern newspaper reporter: "You will find when the wood pile is turned over not a nigger, but an uneducated white boy." "There is a man, and it is the man we want to reach."[86] Ogden himself yielded to the temptation to describe his movement as "almost exclusively in white interest."[87] Believing that com-

---

83. Ogden to Dreher, March 27, 1906, Ogden Papers, Library of Congress—University of North Carolina.
84. Minutes of informal conference at the Union League Club, New York, April 25, 1906, in Albert P. Bourland Papers, S.H.C., University of North Carolina.
85. Minutes of Southern Education Board meeting, August 6-8, 1906, Ogden Papers, Library of Congress—University of North Carolina.
86. Quoted in Columbia *State,* April 24, 1903.
87. Ogden to George W. Boyd (passenger agent, Pennsylvania Railroad), February 27, 1904, Ogden Papers, Library of Congress—University of North Carolina.

merce and education could go hand in hand, Ogden was sincerely puzzled by the attacks from the New South. His guests were being called "picturesque junketers," "Pullman car philanthropists," and "the swell-belly parade."[88] The conciliatory methods may have won over some moderate Southerners,[89] but the language of the opposition press could hardly have been stronger if the movement had been bolder.

The *Manufacturers' Record* and about a dozen Southern dailies under its influence constantly attacked the "Ogden movement" for standing "for the same training for the blacks as for the whites."[90] The *Record* went so far as to scatter circulars through Virginia, Kentucky, and South Carolina on the eve of their state educational campaigns,[91] and aroused so many conservatives in Nashville that the philanthropists were forced to retreat from a planned Conference there.[92] Ogden believed that the *Record's* opposition stemmed from the fact that the child-labor crusader, Edgar Gardner Murphy, was a Board agent and had incurred the wrath of child-employing mill men and machinery manufacturers.[93]

88. Editorial in Charleston *News and Courier*, March 13, 1905.
89. The editor of the Richmond *News-Leader* wrote: "The Manufacturers' Record booms the South in the most extravagant terms, regardless of the verities, and bootlicks every Northerner who looks Southward and from whom there is hope of securing a dollar for investment and then turns to blackguard and slander Northern men who are showing sincere benevolence but none of whose money goes through its advertising columns. These things are disgusting to a man who tries to take manly, honest and wholesome views of conditions."—Alfred B. Williams to Ogden, May 9, 1904, Ogden Papers, Library of Congress—University of North Carolina.
90. Richard H. Edmonds (editor of *Manufacturers' Record*, Baltimore) to Dabney, July 14, 1902, Dabney Papers, S.H.C., University of North Carolina.
91. Robert Frazer, report on Virginia to Southern Education Board, December 15, 1904, Dabney Papers, S.H.C., University of North Carolina; Dickerman to Wickliffe Rose, December 13, 1906, Dickerman Papers, S.H.C., University of North Carolina.
92. Nashville *Banner*, November 22, 23, 1906, January 15, 1907; Rose to Dickerman, December 11, 1906, Dickerman to Rose, December 13, 1906, Dickerman Papers, S.H.C., University of North Carolina; Murphy to James H. Kirkland, December 3, 1907, James Hampton Kirkland Papers, Vanderbilt University; Dickerman to Alderman, December 31, 1906, in files of the president, University of Virginia. "It is the part of wisdom," counseled Samuel C. Mitchell, abetted by Murphy and Claxton, "not to be intimidated by some do-nothing politicians and a few reactionaries."—Mitchell to Dickerman, January 6, 1907, Ogden Papers, Library of Congress—University of North Carolina. But other counsels prevailed.—Ogden to Murphy, January 4, 1907, in *ibid*.
93. Ogden to Alexander J. McKelway, April 15, 1903, Ogden Papers, Library of Congress—University of North Carolina; Alderman to Thomas Nelson Page,

The Southern attacks did not conceal the movement's conservatism from the more doctrinaire liberals. Ogden's characteristic methods seemed to Oswald Garrison Villard of the *Nation* "too complacent and too conciliatory; as if there was some lack of the fiery indignation of the reformer."[94] Negro leaders who shared Villard's distrust of the philanthropists and their allies formed in 1906 the militant Niagara Movement, out of which grew the National Association for the Advancement of Colored People, a protest group with a long-range objective of full democratic equality with whites.[95] Warned by Hollis B. Frissell that the new movement stressed "the rights rather than the duties of the colored people,"[96] the philanthropists received it with cold silence and expressed private disapproval.[97] Washington, whose leadership as well as philosophy was challenged, went further. Maintaining a diplomatic public silence,[98] he privately ordered his as-

---

November 16, 1904, Thomas Nelson Page Papers, Duke University. For samples of attacks, see *Manufacturers' Record* (Baltimore, weekly), XLII (August 28, 1902), 93-94; XLV (March 17, 1904), 175; XLV (May 19, 1904), 392; XLV (July 14, 1904), 583; XLVI (December 8, 1904), 495; XLIX (April 19, 1906), 371; LI (February 28, 1907), 177-78; LI (April 11, 1907), 364. Edward Ingle, a former historian and employee of the magazine, wrote an inflammatory pamphlet. See Ingle, *The Ogden Movement: An Educational Monopoly in the Making* (Baltimore, 1908), pp. 6, 9; Ingle to Herbert B. Adams, February 26, 1901, in Herbert Baxter Adams Papers, The Johns Hopkins University.

94. Editorial in *Nation*, XCVII (August 14, 1913), 139; editorial in New York *Evening Post*, August 7, 1913.

95. Jack Abramowitz, "Origins of the NAACP," in *Social Education*, XV (January, 1951), 21-23. See also Eric F. Goldman, *Rendezvous with Destiny: A History of Modern American Reform* (New York, 1953), pp. 176-83; W. E. Burghardt Du Bois, *Dusk of Dawn: An Essay toward an Autobiography of a Race Concept* (New York, 1940), pp. 89-92; Helen M. Chesnutt, *Charles Waddell Chesnutt: Pioneer of the Color Line* (Chapel Hill, 1952), p. 206; Myrdal, *An American Dilemma*, II, 819-36. An early and eloquent statement of the differences between Negro intellectuals and Washington is Du Bois, *The Souls of Black Folk*, pp. 41-59, 88-109.

96. Frissell to Peabody, October 9, 24, 1906, in Hollis B. Frissell letterbooks, Hampton Institute, Virginia.

97. Peabody to W. E. B. Du Bois, August 26, 1911, Du Bois to Peabody, August 28, 1911, in Ogden Miscellaneous Papers, Library of Congress; Ogden to Peabody, January 5, 1904, Ogden to Kelly Miller (Howard University), September 28, 1903, Ogden Papers, Library of Congress—University of North Carolina; Peabody to Ogden, September 1, 1911 (in Samuel C. Mitchell MS biography of Ogden), Ogden Papers, Library of Congress; Du Bois to Peabody, December 28, 1905, quoted in Herbert Aptheker (ed.), *A Documentary History of the Negro People in the United States* (New York, 1951), pp. 881-83.

98. Washington's frame of reference perhaps was exposed by his public re-

sistant to "Telegraph ... newspaper men you can absolutely trust to ignore [the] Niagra [*sic*] movement."[99] His efforts at suppression extended to buying up hostile Negro newspapers.[100]

Washington's own race policy was failing tragically at the time he was trying to prevent alternative policies. His own school and his Southern supporters were under attack.[101] Southern officials were giving Negro schools a smaller and smaller proportion of tax funds.[102] The General Education Board refused to aid Negro high schools,[103] and the Peabody Fund was dissolved without giving Negro schools a proportionate share of the principal.[104] Even in education, the traditional touchstone of Negro advancement, the conservative Negro leader found that he had little to conserve.

The movement was criticized also from another quarter. The Southern liberal William E. Dodd noticed that, with two excep-

---

mark that "a hungry race cannot live upon 'principles,' " though in this case he was referring to liberal arts education rather than public affairs. E. Davidson Washington (ed.), *Selected Speeches of Booker T. Washington* (Garden City, New York, 1932), p. 203. His narrow vocationalism was modified in Booker T. Washington, "A University Education for Negroes," in *Independent* (New York, weekly), LXVIII (March 24, 1910), 613-18. He said privately of this article: "This matter of defending and explaining these so-called higher institutions makes me tired."—Washington to Robert R. Moton, March 24, 1910, Washington Papers, Library of Congress.

99. Washington to Emmett J. Scott, telegram from New York, July 17, [1905 or 1906?], Washington Papers, Library of Congress. The spelling error may have been that of a Southern white telegrapher.

100. August Meier, "Booker T. Washington and the Negro Press: With Special Reference to the *Colored American Magazine*," in *Journal of Negro History*, XXXVIII (January, 1953), 67-90; Abramowitz, "Origins of the NAACP," *Social Education*, XV, 23.

101. A Florida state superintendent who invited Washington to speak at Gainesville was driven out of office by what he called "forgery, perjury, and liberal use of money of certain Book Companies." Washington to Dabney, February 10, 1903, W. N. Sheats to Buttrick, May 25, 1904, Washington Papers, Library of Congress. See also Washington to Peabody, July 18, 27, 1907, *ibid.*; Ogden to Frederic L. Moore (Washington, D. C.), February 9, 1903, Ogden Papers, Library of Congress.

102. This will be discussed in detail in the chapters which follow, but see Washington to Ogden, October 18, 1909, Washington Papers, Library of Congress.

103. Washington to Buttrick, July 23, 1909, Buttrick to Washington, June 18, 1910, Washington Papers, Library of Congress; Walter H. Page to Buttrick, February 23, 1910, Buttrick to Page, February 26, 1910, Page Papers, Houghton Library, Harvard University.

104. Washington to Samuel A. Green, January 21, 1904, January 21, 1913, September 15, 1914, in Peabody Education Fund Papers, George Peabody College for Teachers; Leavell, *Philanthropy in Negro Education*, p. 93.

tions, none of the members "have ever found it possible to condemn publicly the methods of Mr. Rockefeller, their great benefactor." The General Education Board's lack of interest in a request for funds to promote collegiate discussion of momentous political and economic questions seemed to threaten freedom of speech. "If one great theme is tabooed, why not the others?"[105] The conservatism and even timidity of philanthropic foundations of that period was, however, probably not so much a conspiracy as a reflection of the natural attitudes of board members selected by the donors. The young executive agents, many of them trained in the Southern Education Board campaigns, gained greater power after the elders died or retired, and began to support the controversial undertakings that guard the precious diversities of a democratic society.[106] A congressional investigation in 1953-1954 has demonstrated the sort of criticisms leveled at the more intrepid foundations when the projects they support embarrass powerful minorities. Yet by their relative independence and the nature of their organization, "foundations are especially fitted to be the creative minority to spur society on."[107]

105. William E. Dodd, "Freedom of Speech in the South," letter to the editor, in *Nation*, LXXXIV (April 25, 1907), 383-84. Dodd tested his hypothesis by requesting an appropriation from the General Education Board to his college for collegiate discussion of "political and economic questions of moment," and received a noncommittal reply. Dodd to John W. [should be Frederick T.] Gates, October 3, 1905, Buttrick to Dodd, October 11, 1905, Dodd Papers, Library of Congress. Ogden rejected his suggestions for Conference programs, and Page refused to publish his manuscript article on "The Status of History in Southern Colleges." Ogden to Dodd, March 3, 1903, Ogden Papers, Library of Congress—University of North Carolina; Page to Dodd, May 23, 1902, Dodd Papers, Library of Congress.

106. For an analysis of membership in philanthropic boards, see Eduard C. Lindeman, *Wealth and Culture* (New York, 1936), pp. 33-42; on caution and traditionalism, Edwin R. Embree, "Timid Billions: Are the Foundations Doing Their Job?" in *Harper's Magazine*, CXCVIII (March, 1949), 27-37.

107. *Ibid.*, p. 37.

CHAPTER IV

North Carolina: A Schoolhouse a Day— for Whites

NORTH CAROLINA was a proving ground for one of the basic assumptions of the Southern Education movement, that when conservative White Supremacy leaders like Charles B. Aycock promised "universal education," they meant the term to include schools for black children as well as white. Aycock himself insisted that his campaign pledge in 1900 was four months of schooling in every district in the state, "and this, of course, includes the negro districts."[1] "If the whites are educated the negroes will be also," he told the North Carolina Society of New York.[2] By the end of his four-year term, however, it was clear that "universal education" did not mean equal education. Notwithstanding his rhetoric, Aycock presided over the first great unbalancing of school funds in favor of whites.

Aycock's own county convention in 1900 resolved, over his protest, that funds for Negro schools be drawn only from Negro taxes, and there is no doubt that the proposal struck many responsive chords. "We are tired of educating negroes to 'sass' us," said a small farmer.[3] A saw mill owner found "the uneducated negro to be the best we have for drudgery."[4] A bill by Senator Henry A. London, editor of the *Chatham Record*, to effect this

---

1. Connor and Poe, *Charles Brantley Aycock*, pp. 132-35.
2. Raleigh *News and Observer*, May 21, 1901.
3. R. N. Privott, farmer of Rocky Hock, in *Fourteenth Annual Report of the North Carolina Bureau of Labor and Printing, 1900*, p. 41.
4. L. W. Evans, manufacturer of Cisco, Chowan County, in *Fifteenth Annual Report of the North Carolina Bureau of Labor and Printing, 1901*, p. 161.

proposal by constitutional amendment appeared on the floor of the legislature in 1901 with the unanimous approval of the senate judiciary committee. "This struck many of us favorably," Josiah W. Bailey said frankly, "as the most practicable solution of the free-school question."[5] "I believe that it makes Senator London the logical Democratic candidate for Governor in 1904," cried out a legislator from the coastal swamps. "The amendment will be received with enthusiasm in the east and Senator London will have supporters by the thousands." Josephus Daniels of the *News and Observer* took a more cautious, though not entirely noncommittal stand: "It will be better to await the decision of the courts on the suffrage amendment before proposing any more Constitutional amendments, good or bad."[6] London's was only one of a number of such bills, three being submitted in the House on the first day of the session. Another, submitted by a black-county senator and more suited to the interest of eastern whites, proposed to apportion the state fund to counties as in the past, without regard to race, but to divide local tax funds by race. Aycock is said to have threatened to resign if any of these bills were passed. At any rate, he put his brother, a senator from Wayne County, quietly to work against them behind the scenes, and they were defeated. Aycock would need all of the moral force he could muster, Henry G. Connor wrote privately, "and surely he will need even more, than moral force—with some of the men buzzing around him he will need the Armor of the Lord and the Sword of Gideon," for "the struggle for 'White Supremacy' has not brought forth an overabundant supply of political saintliness."[7]

In support of London's proposal, the Charlotte *Observer* argued that it was necessary to release white enthusiasm for their own children's education, that "the white people will pay no more, except in rare cases, than they are now paying for negro education." The Windsor *Ledger* stated its prejudice more aggressively:

5. Bailey, "Popular Education and the Race Problem in North Carolina," *Outlook*, LXVIII, 115.
6. Raleigh *News and Observer*, March 2, 3, 1901.
7. Connor to George Howard, January 15, 1901, Connor Papers, S.H.C., University of North Carolina.

Education has but one tendency: to give higher hopes and aspirations. There can be but one result in educating the negro. . . . We want the negro to remain here, just about as he is—with mighty little change. We want them to become better cooks, better servants, better wash women, better workmen in farm and field and shop. We will cheerfully pay taxes to give him that sort of schooling. But that is not what the negro wants. . . . We pay for a thing we want to get the sort of thing we are willing to pay for. . . . Of course if the negro don't like this he can leave. If he is let alone he will be content.[8]

Governor Aycock, by his message of 1903, blasted the hopes of a number of county conventions. He tried to glorify White Supremacy into a sort of trusteeship. "While universal suffrage is a failure," he quoted from his speech accepting the gubernatorial nomination, "universal justice is the perpetual decree of Almighty God, and we are entrusted with power not for our good alone, but for the negro as well." He resorted to the code of chivalry. "Let us not seek to be the first State in the Union to make the weak men helpless. This would be a leadership which could bring us no honor, but much shame." In his actual stand on Negro education, however, Aycock stepped down somewhat from that moral eminence. After quoting from the Democratic platform of 1900, he commented: "There is in that platform declaration no suggestion of any purpose to take from the negro any part of the school fund *which he was then enjoying*." He did insist that Negro schools should have four-month terms, that under the proposed system of division they would have little more than a month a year, and that education as a governmental function was based on the duty of the state to educate its citizens equally. He did not commit himself to support of Negro education beyond four months, however. He expressed the fear that "the proposed amendment would be declared unconstitutional and the suffrage amendment which we have adopted and which promises so much to the State would undoubtedly follow in its wake."[9] The governor did not bear the full brunt of opposition to division of school funds. Gustavus R.

---

8. Charlotte *Observer*, March 2, 1902, Windsor *Ledger*, August 28, 1902, clippings in McIver clipping books, Woman's College of the University of North Carolina. It hardly needed to be said that "This paper feels kindly to the negro and would have him remain at peace here."

9. Text of the message in Raleigh *News and Observer*, January 9, 1903. Italics mine.

Glenn, former Georgia superintendent and acting agent of the Peabody Fund, told a joint session with unconscious irony that "the colored man will only be a danger to us when we leave him to be educated by outside philanthropists. You need not be afraid of the negro boy. It will take him a thousand years to get where your boy is." White Supremacy, like Hitler's new order of a later day, was intended to endure for a millennium.[10] The school tax division bill of 1903 was defeated, and Furnifold M. Simmons could tell expatriate North Carolinians in New York that "wherever you see there a white school house, somewhere nearby you will find a negro school house, nearly, if not quite, as good." He was not closely in touch with the trends of school expenditure. At the annual Negro fair in Raleigh the following November, Booker T. Washington spoke against division of school funds. The keynote of his whole address, according to the local report, was: "The negro must be trained to make a good workman." On the day following the report of this speech, Daniels began to hound John Spencer Bassett of Trinity College for praising Washington, and eventually made it so uncomfortable for the historian that Bassett left the South.[11]

The defeat of such bills did not mean that Negroes had been receiving or would receive equal per capita share of school funds. It meant only that unequal apportionments would be made through subterfuge by men with uneasy consciences. The legislature placed no *legal* barriers to Negro educational opportunity. The state courts took care of the legal barriers. Though the state supreme court declared in 1902 that Negro children must have the same per capita share as white children, this was soon modified in 1905 to the vaguer requirement that equal facilities must be provided. And a year later the court defined "equal facilities" by the minimum requirement that "the school term shall be of the same length during the school year, and that a sufficient number of teachers competent to teach the children in each building or section, shall be employed at such prices as the board may deem proper." In much the way that a story passed by word of mouth changes its character in the telling, the legal fiction of "separate but equal"

10. Raleigh *News and Observer*, January 14, 1903.
11. *Ibid.*, May 31, October 31, November 1, 1903.

was altered beyond recognition within a decade after 1896. County and district officials were required by law only to have a school of some sort for Negro children and any teacher they could employ.[12] Aycock, who had once been school superintendent of a black county and a school board member, must have known that, behind his bland protection of the Negro school fund at the state level, flagrant racial discrimination occurred daily at the county and district levels.

There is no indication that Aycock's work to prevent racial division of school funds according to taxes at the *state* level helped to advance the local Negro schools in any positive way. Indeed the trend was quite in the opposite direction. State superintendent James Y. Joyner reported: "It will be observed that considerably more was spent on rural Negro schools in 1895 than in 1905. Suppose our white schools showed the same results for the past twenty years, would we not be necessarily alarmed at that evidence of lack of progress?"[13]

"I have never sent one of my children to a public school in North Carolina in my life," said George Henry White, Negro congressman from Tarboro, in 1901. He described most of the Negro schools of the state as really private: "You understand me, when I speak of the whites and colored running these private schools, that is altogether in the cities, and the private school in the rural district is only supplemental to the public school .... conducted in the same building and by the same teacher after the funds are exhausted."[14]

Alexander J. McKelway, like many others, even some Negroes, thought that the educational requirement of the suffrage amendment "would be a stimulus to negro education." Perhaps that was a conscious or unconscious apology for White Supremacy. McKelway wrote in the *Outlook* six years later: "It surely ought to have been. But my latest information is that I was mistaken. There has been no increased interest in education, nor desire for

---

12. Charles S. Mangum, Jr., *The Legal Status of the Negro* (Chapel Hill, 1940), pp. 127-28.
13. Quoted in Jones, *Negro Education*, I, 29.
14. *Report of the* [United States] *Industrial Commission*, X, 425-27. The public records and Southern press reveal hardly a trace of this Negro support of schools after public funds were "exhausted."

North Carolina: A Schoolhouse a Day—for Whites 107

more than the merest smattering of learning, by the negroes of that State. This, also, is an indication of the essential difference between the two races which it is idle to ignore."[15] McKelway did not explain how he measured the Negro's interest in education. The harsh fact was that the sovereign whites, through their administration of the public schools, determined the limits to Negro educational development. Negroes had to take what they were given.

The Aycock administration neither added to Negro education nor quieted the clash of color, and his successors were not restrained by pledges to Negroes. On the first day of the session of 1905 a bill was introduced to amend the constitution so as to give the legislature the sweeping privilege of dividing the school fund as it "may deem just and equitable." Governor Robert B. Glenn publicly opposed this measure, but as he read one of his messages to the effect that "the education of the negro has in many instances been most disappointing," he interjected in the spoken text "and a flat failure."[16] And he flatly stated, as Aycock had not, that he disagreed with those who demanded equal per capita distribution as well as those who demanded division. A bill for racial division of local tax funds was introduced by Representative Winborne, of Hertford County in the eastern section, who told the house judiciary committee that "Governor Glenn heartily approved the bill and had received assurances the Supreme Court considered it constitutional." Somehow the bill got on the floor without a favorable report of the judiciary committee, which Winborne explained by the statement that the committee favored it but remembered the Dortch Law decision. "The bill would greatly relieve the people of the East," he pleaded, "who under the present law were not able to supplement their regular school taxes by special tax, without having to divide it between both races."[17] Winborne claimed that federal court decisions had so changed since the day of the Dortch Law that the court would follow federal precedent in upholding his act. But Alexander W. Graham of Granville County managed

15. Alexander J. McKelway, "The Suffrage in Georgia," in *Outlook*, LXXXVII (September 14, 1907), 65.
16. Raleigh *News and Observer*, January 10, 1905, January 11, 1907.
17. Quoted from the paraphrased report in *ibid.*, February 9, 23, 1905.

to kill the bill by warning that federal authorities might deny the state full congressional apportionment if, after disfranchising Negroes, they openly attacked the Negro school fund. As usual, it was ignored that Negroes were already deprived at the county level.

Superintendent James Y. Joyner believed that most of those who demanded racial division of school tax funds were misinformed. Negroes constituted about one-third of the school population and received about one-sixth of the school fund, he estimated. Negro property and poll taxes paid half of the amount allotted to Negro schools, while the Negro share of other taxes accounted for all or nearly all of the rest. He insisted that "if any part of the taxes actually paid by individual white men actually reaches the negro for school purposes, the amount is so small that the man who could begrudge it or complain about it ought to be ashamed of himself." With apportionment "practically placed absolutely under the control of the County Board of Education," with approximately equal length of term as the only required measurement of equal facilities, there was "no danger of giving the negroes more than they are entitled to." The superintendent warned that if Negro education were not directed by Southern whites, "others that do not understand our social structure" would take charge of it.[18]

North Carolina has often been cited as one of the more liberal Southern states in its policy of Negro public education, and some of the things said about its practices in race relations are justified.[19] Yet wide discrepancies existed between its provisions for white and for Negro education. White schools in black counties profited from Negro numbers on their school rolls, just as in other states. The

18. *North Carolina School Report, 1906-08*, Part I, pp. 42-47. This statement on Negro public education, which appeared in several successive reports with only a revision of the statistics, may have been written by Charles L. Coon. Minutes of Southern Education Board meeting, August 6-8, 1906, Ogden Papers, Library of Congress—University of North Carolina.

19. For example, it was the first state to receive a white agent for Negro schools through the aid of the Peabody Fund and the General Education Board. Nat C. Newbold, on assuming this office in 1913, began the policy of addressing Negro teachers by the courtesy titles (Mr., Mrs., Miss) commonly used in the case of white people. This policy has since been followed by North Carolina state superintendents. Anson Phelps-Stokes et al., *Progress in Negro Status and Race Relations 1911-1946*, p. 74.

extent of black-county discrepancies in school support is indicated by their expenditures for teachers' salaries, though it should be kept in mind that in this basic expense there was less discrimination than in buildings, equipment, and higher schools. In 1907-08 Negroes represented 60.4 per cent of the school population of eight black counties in the coastal plain, had only 43.2 per cent of the number of teachers, and received only 29.3 per cent of the expenditures for the item of teachers' salaries. Table 1 will illustrate the circumstances:[20]

TABLE 1

TEACHERS' SALARIES IN NORTH CAROLINA BLACK COUNTIES, 1907-08

	WHITE			BLACK		
	School Population	Number of Teachers	Salaries	School Population	Number of Teachers	Salaries
Edgecombe	3,249	52	$ 13,001.20	5,467	43	$ 5,804.62
Halifax	3,938	80	19,967.32	7,619	72	9,451.24
Vance	3,051	59	14,660.48	4,000	32	4,218.24
Craven	3,236	72	15,787.31	4,402	41	4,229.00
Robeson	7,606	113	24,260.55	9,136	89	11,234.35
Warren	2,240	47	7,780.00	4,968	41	3,905.00
Hertford	1,975	37	5,490.45	3,168	35	3,082.65
Bertie	3,117	80	10,901.40	4,516	58	4,495.66
Total	28,412	540	$111,848.71	43,276	411	$46,420.76
Per cent	39.6	56.8	70.7	60.4	43.2	29.3

These counties expended for instruction of each Negro child only $1.07 a year, while spending $3.94 for each white child. To have equalized salaries alone would have cost these counties $124,086.68 a year in expenditures to Negro teachers, and this sum may properly be described as their vested interest in the maintenance of a separate and unequal salary schedule. In North Carolina little of the school fund came from the state, but these figures help to explain the interest of black counties in the increase of state appropriations per capita without regard to color, and also the reluctance of white counties to enlarge the state fund except in

20. *North Carolina School Report, 1906-08*, Part II, pp. 184-200. Figures for percentages were computed.

specific items clearly earmarked for white children. One state fund not earmarked for whites was the rural school library fund; yet the Negroes, who were one-third of the school population, had received by 1908 only 71 of 1,892 such libraries and only 5 of the 352 supplemental libraries. During the year 1907-08 the value of white school property was increased twenty-nine times as fast as the year's increase of Negro school property.[21] The average value of colored schoolhouses was actually decreasing, while that of white schoolhouses was considerably increasing. From the state schoolhouse loan fund Negro schools received from 1903 through 1908 only 38 of the 871 grants, and the amount to Negro schools was one-fiftieth of the total.[22] Despite its rhetoric, the Aycock era was one of rapid deterioration in the concept of universal education, and of retrogression in the actual facilities provided for Negro schoolchildren. Even at the state level there seems to have been no sense of obligation to improve the Negro schools, much less to provide equal facilities.

The white schools fared somewhat better in the era of good feeling ushered in by Aycock's victory at the polls. The Educational Legislature of 1901 was "pledged by the most sacred promises to . . . give a four months school to every district," at a time when only one-fourth of the counties had such a term in all schools.[23] As it convened, the whole state was tingling with educational sentiment, and small towns, strung like beads along J. Pierpont Morgan's railroad lines, were securing the necessary petitions for local tax elections. A jubilant educational lobby of school men set up headquarters at a leading Raleigh hotel to draft their ultimata.[24] Their chief strategist was James Y. Joyner, a professor at McIver's normal college at Greensboro, formerly

21. *Ibid.*, Part II, p. 201, Part III, pp. 98-161.
22. *Ibid.*, Part III, pp. 70-97.
23. Raleigh *News and Observer*, December 28, 1900, March 1, 1901.
24. *Ibid.*, December 28, 1900, January 29, 30, 1901. The North Carolina Association of Academies joined in urging liberal appropriations to common schools and state colleges, though Josiah W. Bailey saw ahead the shadow of the public high school and warned the headmasters that "this universal free education has a tendency to crush out the other schools." In Bailey's view, the "inherent defect" of public schools was that "so great a mass" submerged the individuals, the few. "Jesus Himself chose only twelve apostles," he remarked. *Ibid.*, December 28, 1900.

North Carolina: A Schoolhouse a Day—for Whites

superintendent of Aycock's county, and soon to become General Toon's successor as state superintendent.[25]

An "Act to Carry Out the Constitutional Requirements in Regard to the Public Schools," that is, to provide for a four-month term, was passed, thirty years after the constitution was written, with a single dissenting vote. A "Second Hundred Thousand" was appropriated to level up all terms to four months. Each school receiving less than $100 a year from the county was to receive from this fund enough to equal $100. All of the state aid had to go toward the salary of the teacher.[26] The act also fixed a minimum county school tax rate, but relatively wealthy counties found that they could hold down property assessments and receive from the state funds intended for the poorer counties. There was never enough to go around, and the equalitarian features of the act were vitiated also by holding down Negro teachers' salaries in a separate and unequal schedule, so that Negro schools would get a smaller share of the benefits.[27]

The hand of the school lobby was strengthened for the future by the success of the state colleges in getting appropriations. The bargain of 1898 between Furnifold Simmons and the denominational colleges was terminated in 1901. "My heart was filled with pleasure and pride at the increase in the University appropriation," wrote Alderman from Tulane University. "If I had known or dreamed you would take that action I would probably not be so well known in the Southwest but this is confidential."[28]

"This is an educational legislature," the *News and Observer* declared in its resumé of the session of 1901. "If the folks at home do as well as the legislature has done, the needed educational

---

25. Toon was ill when he entered office, and pulling in harness with an "educational governor" was a great strain on the old soldier. He died of pneumonia after an educational speech with Aycock in a drafty hall. On Joyner, see Joyner to Stephen Eure, December 10, 1907, Joyner Papers, S.H.C., University of North Carolina; *Annual of the Baptist State Convention, 1905* (Raleigh, 1905), pp. 40, 70-71; Elmer D. Johnson, "James Yadkin Joyner, Educational Statesman," in *North Carolina Historical Review*, XXXIII, No. 3 (July, 1956), 359-83.

26. Raleigh *News and Observer*, February 26, March 6, 10, 1901.

27. Fred W. Morrison, *Equalization of the Financial Burden of Education among Counties in North Carolina* (New York, 1925), pp. 12, 20-21.

28. Raleigh *News and Observer*, February 22, 24, 27, 28, March 6, 12, 13, 14, 1901; Alderman to Connor, March 25, 1901, Connor Papers, S.H.C., University of North Carolina.

revival will revolutionize the State for good." In the hilarious last hours of the session, after the clock had been stopped, Senator Benjamin F. Aycock was elected "an Educational Agitator for the State of North Carolina," with full power and duty to agitate. "He shall continue to agitate until the entire State is fully agitated from the mountains to the sea." All common carriers must haul him free of charge, all hotels and public eating houses give him free room and board. He must give at least five agitations a week and "open each meeting by singing as loud as he can the Old North State." And "Should he at any time become luke-warm or cease to agitate with full force and effect he shall be arrested, brought before the State Board of Education and there be dealt with as they may direct." The White Supremacy leaders were in fine fettle. "We pledged to the people that no *white man* should be deprived of an education," said John Wilber Jenkins of Granville County, "and we have done our duty."[29]

While the agitation did not become lukewarm or cease, it immediately devolved upon the educators. The state machine through the legislature made no further substantial improvements in the school system for over a decade. Political leaders sang lustily "The Old North State," but with a certain complacency they "took pride" in the four-month term as a party achievement. "Although deeply interested and cooperating from a distance, I did not come to the State to advocate the reform," Senator Simmons later recalled. The disfranchisement amendment was his "educational" contribution.[30]

Not only was the "Second Hundred Thousand" too small a fund for its purpose, but the Educational Legislature failed to provide funds to pay it. The railroads had refused to pay their taxes in 1899 and 1900, and the state corporation commission took the matter to court. Early in January, 1901, Aycock and the corporation commission met with railroad representatives, who had been substantial contributors to the party chest, and worked out a compromise. The terms were that the railroads would pay their back taxes, while the state would assess railroads, like other property,

---

29. Raleigh *News and Observer*, March 16, 1901, my italics. Cf. the actual pledge above, Chapter II.
30. Rippy (ed.), *F. M. Simmons*, p. 32.

North Carolina: A Schoolhouse a Day—for Whites 113

every four years instead of every year. The joker was that the railroad assessments made in 1899 and 1900 were nullified, and the old, low assessment rate of the railroads could not be changed until 1903, thus giving the railroads two more years of respite from reassessment.[31] "It required right much tact and courage to settle the R. Rd. Tax case," thought Henry G. Connor, but Clark and Josephus Daniels believed there was a surrender to "tax-dodging corporations."[32]

The problem was more complex than simply taxation of railroads. The new appropriations for education were passed in the face of a looming treasury shortage, which full taxation of the railroads would have relieved. All through the session Daniels sent out warnings that the "sacred pledge" of a four-month term would be violated by an empty treasury. "Property that cannot be seen will continue to escape until its owners are forbidden to enforce payment unless it is listed," he reminded the public. "Let no tax dodger escape!"[33] Aycock, Daniels, and others proposed various ways to increase taxes.[34] But the legislature adjourned without actually providing funds for the four-month term, and Aycock refused to call an extra session. The schools did receive the "Second Hundred Thousand" for the school session of 1901-02, though it was inadequate for four months in every district. Then the treasury was dry on the eve of the legislative session of 1903, when rural schools that had opened in October began to close in December. The four-month term seemed a hoax, and by that time in truth the people were "educationally awakened."

Superintendent Joyner had to announce in February, 1903, that the money for the "Second Hundred Thousand" for 1902-03 was "neither in hand nor in sight."[35] There was "already . . . a stir in the rural districts," a county superintendent reported. "Why must schools close?" patrons were asking. "You promised us a

---

31. Raleigh *News and Observer*, January 29, 1901.
32. Connor to George Howard, February 9, 1901, Connor Papers, S.H.C., University of North Carolina.
33. Editorials in Raleigh *News and Observer*, January 12, February 20, 22, 1901.
34. *Ibid.*, January 27, March 15, 1901; Connor and Poe, *Charles Brantley Aycock*, pp. 91, 185; Walter Clark to A. W. Graham, June 19, 1902, in Brooks and Lefler (eds.), *The Papers of Walter Clark*, II, 38.
35. Circular letter reprinted in Raleigh *News and Observer*, February 7, 1903.

four-months term." As hopes "vanished just as the schools are finishing up the available fund," the rural press demanded: "Where lies the fault? Who is to blame?" This was embarrassing to Democrats who, in their most recent party platform, had taken pride in the fact that, "for the first time in the history of the State, every school district has been able to maintain a public free school for four months, as required by the Constitution."[36]

The political leaders managed to get out of their predicament without increasing the railroad taxes. Dissolving the ante-bellum Literary Fund, they borrowed one-half of it to end the treasury deficit. The other half they set up as a schoolhouse loan fund for replacing "ramshackle houses all over the state." Representative Thomas W. Blount denounced this "cold-blooded proposition to take $100,000 of the school money," but was assured by its sponsors that the borrowed funds would be repaid by 1906.[37]

For a decade after Aycock entered office, the only increases in state aid to schools, other than the Second Hundred Thousand, were $45,000 in 1907 for high schools and an addition of $25,000 to the First Hundred Thousand in 1909. Of course many bills sponsored by the school lobby, if they contained no appropriation, were passed, often unanimously. For its white schools, at least, North Carolina developed an up-to-date school code.[38] Yet, as Josephus Daniels would say, "It's money runs the mare." The state political machine did not bring about a new era in public education, universal or otherwise.

It was through local taxation that the school men achieved their only solid success in the Aycock era. In the wake of the Conference for Education in the South at Winston-Salem in 1901, they

36. Raleigh *News and Observer*, February 15, 22, 23, 24, June 2, 1903.
37. The sponsors were Representatives Theo Davidson of Buncombe County and L. L. Smith of Gates County. *Ibid.*, February 26, March 4, 7, 8, 10, 20, 1903; *Biennial Report of the Treasurer of the State of North Carolina, 1903-1904* (Raleigh, 1904), pp. 12, 43; *Eighth Conference for Education in the South, Proceedings* (Columbia, 1905), pp. 46-50. By 1915 the loan fund had lent over one million dollars. *North Carolina School Reports, 1902-04*, Part I, p. 17, Part II, p. 176; *1914-16*, Part I, p. 12.
38. Raleigh *News and Observer*, March 4, 10, 1903, June 24, 1904, March 4, 7, 19, 1905, February 9, March 13, 1907, June 30, 1908; Thompson, "The Legislative Development of Public School Support in North Carolina" (unpublished doctoral dissertation, University of North Carolina), pp. 390-93; *Public School Law of North Carolina, 1911* (Raleigh, 1911), pp. 31-32 *et passim.*

began educational rallies to carry the approaching bond elections. "The eyes of the state are on Goldsboro," said the *News and Observer*. "As Goldsboro votes . . . so will vote many towns in North Carolina." Governor Aycock led off the speaking at a rally three days before the election. The biblical prophecy, "A little child shall lead them," was literally demonstrated on election day, when "the boys and girls of our public schools went out upon the streets, in homes, offices and workshops and plead with the indifferent ones to go vote for an approval of the bond issue, which means better schools." Even so, the school forces at Goldsboro won by only sixty-two votes. But this began a series of successful elections during the next two months. Oxford, Kinston, Rockingham, Thomasville, Lexington, and Gastonia voted for graded schools by local taxation on May 8. After Aycock outdid himself at Oxford, the long-delayed final returns showed that local taxation had carried there by four votes. "May, 1901, is a great month for the local taxation idea, for education, and for North Carolina," announced McIver. He noted that all of the towns along the line of the Southern Railway now had good schools, and he was more concerned thereafter about schools for the rural areas.[39] "Everyone is discussing questions of education," said a teacher that summer. "It is the talk on the cars, the theme of discussion on the streets, the gosip [*sic*] of the corner grocery. Our editors are pushing the interests of education. In every town of importance there are graded schools in construction or already constructed." But he was forced to ask, "what is being done in the rural districts? I am sorry to say the educational enterprise is not so active there."[40] Negro schools were rarely mentioned in the local tax elections, except by opponents of higher taxation. A temporary hush, as though in the wake of battle, had fallen over the whole discussion of the Negro in North Carolina.

After a series of conferences in 1901 between Curry, McIver, and Aycock, forty leading educators were called by McIver to meet in Aycock's office at the capital to organize the "Central Campaign Committee," which directed the educational campaigns for the

39. Raleigh *News and Observer*, April 7, 9, 10, 28, May 4, 8, 9, 10, 1901.
40. Letter of W. F. Evans of Greenville to the editor, Raleigh *News and Observer*, June 8, 1901.

next twelve years. Joyner was made chairman of a committee on distribution of literature through the newspapers, and an educational sermon committee included walking delegates of the larger denominations. But the dominating figure of the conference was McIver himself, "full of resources, a trousered steam engine, guiding, cheering, stimulating." The conference ended with a unanimous Declaration against Illiteracy and Resolutions on Local Taxation.[41] The participation of leading denominational educators was designed to mollify them, for Bailey and Kilgo were chagrined that their bargain of 1898 with the state machine had terminated in 1901 with increased appropriations to state higher schools, and the president of Wake Forest College felt impelled to prick the bubble of optimism. "I am not sanguine as to any very large results within the next few months," he wrote Curry.[42] The Raleigh conference was followed by regional ones at Greensboro, Charlotte, and Hickory, each including some fifteen or twenty counties. School superintendents attended at the expense of the Southern Education Board, and each conference was made the occasion of a local rally.[43]

An undercurrent of the whole educational campaign was opposition to Negro schools. "I have heard from Gov. Aycock and Dr. McIver," wrote Henry G. Connor's son, superintendent of one of the new graded schools, "and have been doing some of the work they want, finding out if there are any communities in this county where there is an interest in local taxation for schools." He had found two or three such sections, "but the opinion seems to be that the fact that the taxes will have to support negro schools

---

41. Raleigh *News and Observer*, February 8, 16, 1902; clipping from Raleigh *Morning Post*, dated February 15, 1902, McIver clipping books, Woman's College of the University of North Carolina; McIver, "The Work in North Carolina," in *Fifth Conference for Education in the South, Proceedings* (Athens, Georgia, 1902), pp. 20-26.

42. Charles E. Taylor to Curry, February 22, 1902, Curry Papers, Library of Congress. See also address of J. B. Carlyle to the state teachers' assembly, in Raleigh *News and Observer*, June 10, 1902.

43. The Greensboro conference is described in detail in McIver, "The Work in North Carolina," in *Fifth Conference for Education in the South, Proceedings* (Athens, Georgia, 1902), p. 24; Raleigh *News and Observer*, March 20, 1902; clipping from Greensboro *Record*, dated April 5, 1902, McIver clipping books, Woman's College of the University of North Carolina; Page to Baldwin, April 7, 1902, Page Papers, Houghton Library, Harvard University.

will prevent the people's levying the tax."[44] The sentiment was not overcome, but circumvented, by neglect of Negro schools, as was made clear when "the most largely attended conference of County Superintendents ever held in North Carolina" advised Wallace Buttrick in 1902 to spend Rockefeller's first million-dollar grant mostly on white schools. Walter Hines Page also came down to help the Southern campaigners by a speech to the teachers at Wrightsville, "to roast alive certain old preachers that have been scaring the life out of these teachers—an old Praise-God-Barebones crowd." But he was gone again in a day or so, leaving the tactical problems to the groundlings and day-laborers of educational work.[45]

McIver directed the campaigns until his death in 1906, when James Y. Joyner took his place. The state campaign committee kept on tap the best-known men in the state, such as the manufacturer Julian S. Carr, Governor Aycock, Congressman John H. Small, and President George T. Winston of the State College of Agriculture and Engineering, for rallies in such places as Rich Square and Flea Hill Township. And where no rallies developed spontaneously, they were drummed up. In North Carolina, more exclusively than in any other Southern state, educational campaigners concentrated on local taxation. McIver set the mold, and after his death the policy was continued, even long after it was time to renew pressure on the state political machine. At least for the first five years the policy was realistic, since the legislature had been pushed to the limit of its generosity and resources in 1901, and the bills for racial division of taxation were signs that the political leaders were disgruntled by the educators' pressure.

Local tax elections all over the state had to be held on the same day, the first Monday in June, under the law of 1899. This not only scattered the efforts of campaigners at the critical time, but

44. Robert D. W. Connor to Henry G. Connor, March 13, 1902, Connor Papers, S.H.C., University of North Carolina. The younger Connor later succeeded Brooks as secretary of the campaign committee, and was followed by Charles H. Mebane.
45. Page to Buttrick, April 11, 1902, in Burton J. Hendrick, *The Training of an American: The Earlier Life and Letters of Walter H. Page, 1855-1913* (Boston, 1928), p. 407. Page was also present at the Charlotte conference. Clippings from Charlotte *Observer*, May 1, 2, 3, 1902, McIver clipping books, Woman's College of the University of North Carolina. On Buttrick's conference, see above, n. 73 of Chapter III.

also fixed elections at a time when farmers dreaded bad weather and crop damage and were consequently less likely to vote for taxes to be collected after the ensuing harvest. Educational campaigners were forced to run a "seed-sowing campaign" in July, August, and September, and to reap their victories in a "harvest campaign" during March, April, and May. Though this cycle went against nature, the efforts of campaigners bore fruit. McIver could speak accurately of "the constant campaign," for speakers were sent out from headquarters whenever a community was moved by the educational spirit. The Central Campaign Committee warned its spokesmen that educational campaigning had "largely passed away from the stage of oratory" and that they were wanted "not for the purpose of delivering eloquent dissertations 'in well-turned sentences and rumbling sounds' on the great 'blessings of education,' but for the purpose of discussing in a plain practical way a certain definite problem, to explain its operations and its advantages, to encourage friends, to answer opponents and to clear away the doubts of neutrals."[46] Whether or not the florid style declined, the speakers were convincing. Local tax districts, only seven in number in 1899, rose to 402 in 1906, the year of McIver's death. By 1913, one-fourth of the districts of the state, 1,534, levied local taxes.[47]

Rural districts undertook local taxation on a wider scale in North Carolina than in any other Southern state. In 1906 only one-eighth of the local tax districts were in towns of 1,000 or larger. The Piedmont section, with its high density and proportion of white population and taxable wealth, had six of the ten counties with largest numbers of local tax districts in 1906. Below the fall line, it was white counties such as Dare and Columbus which ranked high in local taxation. The only exception was Robeson County, definitely a black county, with a school population of 9,166 Negroes and 7,416 whites. The Robeson County

46. Robert D. W. Connor, report of the Secretary of the North Carolina Campaign Committee, October, 1904, to November, 1905, Joyner Papers, S.H.C., University of North Carolina.
47. Reports of the Secretary, North Carolina Campaign Committee, August 1, 1906, July 10, 1909, June 23, 1910, July 7, 1911, July 11, 1912, Joyner to McIver, January 18, 1906, Joyner to Albert P. Bourland, September 26, 1913, *ibid.*

North Carolina: A Schoolhouse a Day—for Whites 119

local tax districts simply spent two-thirds or more of their local receipts on white schools.[48] Local tax campaigns were concretely successful in every part of the state, and in 1911 only two mountain counties completely lacked local tax districts. Revenue from local taxation rose from $3,067.79 in 1900 to $1,452,070.77 in 1915, and its proportion of the total school fund increased from 0.3 per cent in 1900 to 30.7 per cent in 1915.[49]

Though the educational stump speakers worked in a sympathetic climate of opinion, there was personal opposition from several directions. Alexander J. McKelway, editor of the *Presbyterian Standard*, informed Dabney that Josiah W. Bailey was attacking the motives and personnel of the Southern Education Board. "He hates McIver and Alderman, and wrote a very sneering article about the new movement, making Frissell, Alderman, McIver and Booker Washington the committee. Every now and then I have to lay him across my knee and give him a good spanking, which his brethren of the Baptist denomination seem to enjoy."[50] The innuendo involving Frissell and Washington, of course, was that they were engaged in educating Negroes.

Bailey's main charge against the Board's Southern agents was that they were "not in sympathy with free schools" and were really only "looking after schools of their own—higher schools." He denounced so freely the Baptist college representatives who attended the Raleigh Conference, "in spite of our warning," that Wake Forest professors forced him to apologize. "We hail the movement with joy," Bailey sang when the General Education Board was formed: "It is a final effort of the American Democracy —not North nor South—to straighten its line for the twentieth century's triumphant march."[51] He may have assumed that

---

48. Robert D. W. Connor to McIver, August 1, 1906, *ibid.*; *North Carolina School Report, 1906-08*, Part II, pp. 32, 40, 57, 130. Robeson County received $2,278.70 from the state per capita fund (First Hundred Thousand) and nothing from the state equalization fund (Second Hundred Thousand). It spent five times as much on white as on Negro schoolhouses, twice as much on white salaries as on Negro salaries.

49. Mebane to Rose, July 7, 1911, Joyner Papers, S.H.C., University of North Carolina; Dabney, *Universal Education in the South*, II, 343; *North Carolina School Reports, 1898-1900*, p. 154; *1914-16*, Part II, p. 2.

50. McKelway to Dabney, December 13, 1901, Dabney Papers, S.H.C., University of North Carolina.

51. *Biblical Recorder*, November 12, 1902.

Rockefeller's board would be a Baptist agency, but two months later he was attacking again. "They blundered," he said of denominational educators who took part in the Raleigh Conference. "Have they been called 'Leading Educators' since? . . . Has the General Education Board said aught to them since?" The propaganda work, said Bailey, was "wholly in the hands of a clique, a very small clique," and its local campaign committee "a mere base of operations for Messrs. McIver and Dabney."[52] During the period of the awkward school fund deficit in 1902, Bailey favored a bond issue rather than to "lay such a tax on industries as will set back our enterprises which are giving the State new life." This harmony of views with the manufacturing interests was eventually to aid Bailey's career as United States senator. "Communism in education is driving out denominationalism," he feared. As a member of the state child labor committee he promoted harmony between reformers and mill owners. This activity and his efforts to wipe out "hell broth centres" in the prohibition crusade soon distracted his attention from the public school campaigns.[53]

The Charlotte *Observer*, one of the larger dailies which spoke for the state's manufacturing interests, sporadically attacked "the Ogden educational mission for the benighted South." Though it echoed "the thunderous belchings from Baltimore,"[54] and supported efforts for racial division of the school fund, the *Observer* had no feud with the local school men and sometimes even gave publicity to their rallies. Among other critics were white mountain Republicans, who denounced Negro education with vigor, possibly because black-county funds ostensibly for Negro education actually went to white schools, and accused Democrats of developing a political machine through the school system. Partisan friction between patrons and teachers was chronic. Some Republicans tried to burn out a Democratic teacher at Job's Cabin, near Wilkesboro, in 1901. When they burned down his schoolhouse, he moved into

---

52. *Ibid.*, January 21, 1903.
53. Editorial in *Biblical Recorder*, August 13, 1902; Raleigh *News and Observer*, December 13, 1902; *Minutes of the Baptist State Convention of North Carolina, Held at Durham, N. C., December 9-14, 1902* (Raleigh, 1902), pp. 45-46; Henderson, *North Carolina*, II, 431, 448-50, 503.
54. Spartanburg (South Carolina) *Herald*, quoted in Charlotte *Observer*, May 4, 1904, clipping in McIver clipping books, Woman's College of the University of North Carolina. The reference was to the *Manufacturers' Record*.

an insured house; they tried to cut off his pay but were unsuccessful.[55] Democrats could argue with some conviction that "unprogressive" Republican superintendents of mountain schools would fail to prepare white boys for the expiration of the grandfather clause in 1908.[56]

Partisan charges and editorial roasts aside, the chief bone of contention over schools was the property tax, and with all the static power of the closed fist, property owners resisted the prying fingers of taxation. "Many of our most progressive towns, commercially, stood solidly against voting any taxes for schools," recalled Eugene C. Brooks in later years. One town, after trying out the public schools for a year or two, voted out the tax and, with glee, "celebrated the event with bonfires and brass bands."[57] McIver reported to Walter Hines Page that "local tax was defeated in two or three places in this State by the opposition of the railroad influences, and different representatives of the roads have complained once or twice about having their taxes increased by our local tax elections." He added that, though there were exceptions, "quite a number of the manufacturers are not inclined to have taxes voted upon their property."[58] Thomas J. Jarvis, reminding the Democratic party in 1902 that it was pledged to universal education, remarked:

> The only adverse criticism I have ever heard of Governor Aycock ... is about what those who criticise him are pleased to call his extreme views on education. And I notice that those who criticise him hide behind the negro. They say they are opposed to taxing the white man's property to educate the negro. This, in my judgment, in most cases, is a mere pretext. If you will get close to one of these enemies of universal education and scratch him deep enough you will be more than likely to find a fellow who is, at heart, opposed to having his property taxed to educate anybody's children.[59]

55. Raleigh *News and Observer*, February 1, 1901. See also *ibid.*, January 8, 13, 1905.
56. *Ibid.*, February 1, 1903, February 11, 1909; legislative debate on a Republican bill for popular election of "certain officers," in *ibid.*, February 16, 1913. The grandfather clause was declared unconstitutional in 1912.
57. Quoted in Henderson, *North Carolina*, II, 437.
58. McIver to Page, April 16, 1904, copy in Dabney Papers, S.H.C., University of North Carolina.
59. Quoted in Raleigh *News and Observer*, March 20, 1902.

Miss Viola Boddie of Nash County believed that times had changed somewhat since her grandfather had committed political suicide by building the courthouse out of brick.[60] But "Why do honest (?) men and members of churches resort to all sorts of tricks and subterfuges in order to evade taxation?"[61] asked the *Chatham Record*. A dangerous stress developed between the pillars of many a church, and relations became "a little strained among some of the good people of Kinston over the graded school question." After a close election at Hendersonville in 1901 provided a local tax but failed to provide a schoolhouse, "desks were improvised out of goods boxes or any other material that came to hand." It was "the day of small things," and "Some aggrieved taxpayers, to make matters worse, applied for an order from the courts restraining the city commissioners from operating the school, alleging that the tax levy had been defeated in the special election." After a year-long court battle, the state supreme court decided in favor of the Hendersonville school forces.[62] Sometimes local school supporters mixed self-interest with their altruism, and the official instructions for local tax elections warned:

It is wise to have the metes and bounds of the special-tax district set forth in plain language in the petition, so that no one can say that he was misled or deceived as to what territory was included in the proposed district.

It is not wise to gerrymander the district simply to win an election. . . .

It is not wise to make a district include part of a farm and exclude a part.

It is not wise or equitable to form a shoe-string district without regard to the needs of the school population, so as to get selfish advantage by including the largest amount of property for the smallest number of children.[63]

60. Clipping labeled *The Graphic* (Nash County, North Carolina), August 21, 1902, in McIver clipping books, Woman's College of the University of North Carolina. Miss Boddie was a teacher in the Woman's College.
61. *Chatham Record* in Raleigh *News and Observer*, June 9, 1903.
62. Raleigh *News and Observer*, September 26, 1901; Sadie S. Patton, *The Story of Henderson County* (Asheville, 1947), p. 159.
63. "Official Instructions as to Forming Special-Tax Districts, Holding Elections, Registration and Qualifications of Voters Therein, Etc." (pamphlet issued by Department of Public Instruction, Raleigh, 1910), p. 2.

The eastern counties were the dark and bloody ground of educational campaigns. By discrimination against its Negroes and gerrymandering of districts, New Hanover County led the state in the length of term of its white schools without a local tax. Local philanthropy provided the white children of Wilmington with a three-story brick high school, and liquor taxes paid the expenses of the city schools until 1909, when, after "a hard fight against the liquor element," the campaigners got a majority for local taxation. Beaufort, also in the East, was the last town of any size to fall into line. "We carried it this year in spite of more unfavorable conditions than I have ever known in any school fight in North Carolina," said Joyner.[64] As the state per capita fund grew from $100,000 in 1899 to $250,000 by 1915, it assumed an increasing importance in the school finance of the eastern counties. Receiving funds for Negro as well as white pupils enrolled in the county, they gave the Negro schools a small portion and used the remainder to provide adequate white schools. The state fund became as important as the county fund, while local funds remained insignificant. After the state "equal facilities" cases of 1905 and 1906 there was no threat of legal restraint on discrimination.

In 1907, after five years of local tax campaigning, the educators felt strong enough to challenge the Barksdale decision of 1886, which restricted public support of the schools. In view of "the changed demands of civilization," Joyner wrote Alderman, "I cannot help believing that the present enlightened Court . . . will over-rule the old decision." Instructing all superintendents to ask their commissioners to levy taxes above the constitutional maximum, he selected Franklin County for the test case. "We were surprised to find that public sentiment was so strongly in favor of the levying of the tax that it was almost impossible to get any man to enjoin its collection," Joyner reported. "We finally induced one man to sue out an injunction, in order to help us to get the settlement of the principle for the entire State. Of course, I had to agree to bear all the expenses of the suit." Drawing funds from the Southern Education Board, Joyner carried the case to the

64. Raleigh *News and Observer*, February 8, May 2, 1901; Joyner to Wickliffe Rose, May 27, 1909, Joyner Papers, S.H.C., University of North Carolina. Cf. the account of white and Negro schools in John A. Oates, *The Story of Fayetteville and the Upper Cape Fear* (Fayetteville, 1950), p. 296.

supreme court.[65] The decision in *J. R. Collie v. Commissioners of Franklin County* in 1907 was frankly sociological. "The doctrine of *stare decisis* is worthy of all respect," acknowledged Justice George H. Brown for the majority, but "The construction placed upon the Constitution by the Barksdale decision has been found to be an especial handicap upon the country schools," while in towns and cities the constitutional requirement of four months was "more than complied with." He pointed out:

Very many country schools cannot continue open for four months unless the tax prescribed by the act is levied. The country school is the nursery of the larger part of the bone and sinew of this land. It carries a greater responsibility than the city schools in proportion to its advantages, for, as is well said by a recent writer, "It is charged not only with its country problems, but with the training of many persons who swell the population of cities. . . ."

Chief Justice Clark, in a concurring opinion, said the maintenance of schools for four months was "imperatively demanded" and that whatever tax was necessary to bring that about was within the legitimate power of the people.[66] The school men properly regarded this as a notable victory and the high-water mark of their educational campaign.[67]

Another reform proposal taken up by the school men was compulsory school attendance. Efforts by the state labor commissioner during the nineties to arouse interest in such a law had had little success, but in the new century the suffrage amendment, local tax agitation, and growing opposition to child labor drew attention to the matter.[68] Nearly all of the educational campaigners assisted in the child labor reform movement.[69]

65. Raleigh *News and Observer*, June 8, 1907; Joyner to Alderman, July 17, 1907, Joyner to Henry E. Fries, July 23, 1907, "The Franklin County Suit" (undated MS), Joyner Papers, S.H.C., University of North Carolina.
66. *North Carolina Reports*, CXLV (Fall Term, 1907), 170-87.
67. There was another test case involving the poll tax for schools, *Perry v. Commissioners of Franklin County*. For a summary and interpretation, see *North Carolina School Report, 1906-08*, Part I, p. 10.
68. Raleigh *News and Observer*, January 11, February 8, 14, 1901; R. L. Madison of Cullowhee High School, in *ibid.*, June 18, 1901; Reverend W. G. Clements, Superintendent of Wake County, in *ibid.*, October 9, 1901; debate at meeting of state Association of Academies, in *ibid.*, December 30, 1902.
69. Among these were Alexander J. McKelway, Josephus Daniels, Charles L. Coon, Josiah W. Bailey, James Y. Joyner, and Charles B. Aycock. Elizabeth H. Davidson, *Child Labor Legislation in the Southern Textile States* (Chapel Hill,

But farmers, from Speedwell to Scuppernong, opposed compulsory attendance so vigorously that it had no chance of success in an overwhelmingly rural state. "It might do in a level country," said a mountaineer. But from the East was heard his echo:

> If school-houses were regulated, then it might do, but in Eastern North Carolina the roads are very crooked, very swampy, and many good people live more than a mile from the road, and sometimes two or three miles from the school-house, and this, in common with the crooked roads, wet swamps, muddy paths in winter, and yellow flies, ticks, mosquitoes, and hot sun in the summer, would be only murder for children to force them to school all the spare time, and we can not hire all our labor and board our children, when they only get perhaps two or three lessons per day, with four words for their share in the class. This is my experience less than two years past. The system might do in the higher parts of the State, where the people are more thickly settled, but with us, in the low east, it would not do.[70]

As for Negro education, "I find the best thing for the colored race is work, and keep him at it until he is tired enough to go home and go to bed."[71] That was the kind of compulsion some North Carolinians wanted. Raising cotton and tobacco was impossible with a compulsory attendance law, some farmers swore; they would not have Negro families as tenants if their children went to school. "So if we have the compulsory law, we do not want any negro farmers, or poor white people."[72] "It looks quite plain to me," said mill owner James A. Call of Coleridge, "that it is necessary to have educated people to fill higher positions, and . . . a large number of illiterate people who perform the labors of the country. I believe that this was ordained from the beginning."[73]

1939), pp. 114-19, 149, 160-61; *North Carolina School Report, 1900-02*, pp. 1-11; Raleigh *News and Observer*, January 6, 1905.

70. *Fourteenth Annual Report of the North Carolina Bureau of Labor and Printing, 1900*, pp. 281-83, letters from J. M. Brown, Sands, North Carolina, Z. V. Watson, Speedwell, North Carolina, and J. H. Snell, Scuppernong, North Carolina, all farmers.

71. D. T. King, Leaksville, Rockingham County, North Carolina, tobacco manufacturer, in *Thirteenth Annual Report of the North Carolina Bureau of Labor and Printing, 1899*, p. 301.

72. F. W. Brown, Huntersville, North Carolina, in *Fourteenth Annual Report of the North Carolina Bureau of Labor and Printing, 1900*, p. 263; W. G. Long, Farmville, North Carolina, in *Sixteenth Annual Report of the North Carolina Bureau of Labor and Printing, 1902*, p. 49.

73. *Fifteenth Annual Report of the North Carolina Bureau of Labor and Printing, 1901*, p. 209.

After child labor reformers had failed in 1903 and 1905 to forbid the practice by legislation, Daniel A. Tompkins of Charlotte, a leading mill owner, announced his support of a compulsory attendance law. This aroused great hope at the Southern Education Board meeting in 1906. Walter Hines Page had a romantic faith in "men of the type of Tompkins of Charlotte—he is offish—some organizations might win him and get his help." Even Murphy, who had been in the heat of the Alabama child labor battle, had hopes of cooperation with Tompkins.[74] But McKelway, the clergyman who led the North Carolina child labor movement, had no illusions about mill men. "It has been generally found that the compulsory education alternative was a dodge," he said, "to prevent needed legislation because it was recognized that the time was not ripe for compulsory education."[75]

Joyner and other school men, without help from Governor Glenn,[76] pushed through the legislature in 1907 a "wise and conservative" local option law for compulsory attendance, described by Joyner as "elastic" or "flexible." Requiring attendance for only sixteen weeks a year between the ages of eight and twelve, it could be applied in a county only by petition or vote and was to be administered at the discretion of the county board of education. A white district could enforce the law "safely . . . by reason of the population," while in the same county it need not be applied to a district where "the temper of the better element of the people is not such as to look with favor upon a law which would operate to force the majority of the children of the colored race in the schools." Eight eastern counties and three others were exempted.[77]

74. Minutes of Southern Education Board meetings, August 6-8, 1906, Ogden Papers, Library of Congress–University of North Carolina; Davidson, *Child Labor Legislation in the Southern Textile States*, pp. 152, 156-57.

75. Raleigh *News and Observer*, January 19, 1905, letter from McKelway. McKelway had been principal of a graded school in a factory town, and was much interested in promoting education, but he would not be sidetracked by pretended interest in compulsory attendance. *Ibid.*, January 29, 1905. Men like McKelway who professed the social gospel were rare in the South in this period. "Trying to give me a vision of a ragged Chinaman when I am looking for a crucified Christ" was Bishop John C. Kilgo's summing-up of the missionary movement. Sermon at Edenton Street Methodist Church, reported in *ibid.*, January 18, 1915.

76. "While it may not be expedient or wise to have compulsory education," said Glenn in 1905, "still in every way possible, let us encourage all to attend school."—Raleigh *News and Observer*, January 12, 1905.

77. The bill was supported by the state teachers' assembly, the North Carolina

Establishment of graded schools in the towns after 1900 led almost immediately to demands for white public high schools. Even the capital, Raleigh, had only seven grades of public education. The legislature in 1905 permitted establishment of high schools, without state aid, but prohibited instruction in high school subjects in the elementary schools. In the same year the University of North Carolina, by contract with the General Education Board, received Nathan W. Walker as "Professor of School Organization," whose salary was paid in part by the Rockefeller agency. Walker's main duties were to advise and organize high schools, and only incidentally to lecture at the state university.[78]

The high school act of 1905 permitted only townships to establish public high schools, and this limited their development to the towns. Over the active resistance of Governor Glenn, the school men under Walker's leadership secured in 1907 a state high school appropriation of $45,000 and an act permitting county boards of education to establish high schools.[79] Denominational preparatory schools, formerly the narrow bridge between common schools and colleges, found in Josiah W. Bailey their only champion against public secondary education. Professor Walker was described in the *Biblical Recorder* as "agent of the State institutions of higher learning in these State high schools." This meant to Bailey, "We must federate and fight, or surrender." But instead of fighting, most denominational leaders surrendered. Trustees sold or gave their preparatory schools to towns, and there was at least one case of a denominational college becoming a public graded school.[80] As late as 1908 there were only two four-year

---

Child Labor Committee, and representatives of the mill owners. Raleigh *News and Observer*, January 11, 22, 25, 26, 27, 29, February 6, 9, 16, March 5, 8, 16, 1907; *North Carolina School Report, 1904-06*, pp. 27-33.

78. University of North Carolina, *University Record*, No. 39 (October, 1905), pp. 15-16.

79. Raleigh *News and Observer*, January 11, March 8, 1907; Thompson, "The Legislative Development of Public School Support in North Carolina" (unpublished doctoral dissertation, University of North Carolina), pp. 477-81.

80. Swain, "Editorial Views of the Religious Press on Education in North Carolina" (unpublished M.A. thesis, University of North Carolina, 1942), pp. 101-09; C. M. Beach, "The Baptist School Problem in North Carolina," in *Biblical Recorder*, July 29, 1908, clipping in Nathan Wilson Walker clipping books, University of North Carolina; Raleigh *News and Observer*, December 13, 1902, September 5, 1903.

public high schools in the state; by 1915 the number had risen to eighty-nine, and 214 schools taught some high school subjects.[81]

A second brief "educational awakening"[82] in 1913 was led not by the old campaigners but by Clarence Poe. A Farmers' Union leader, editor of the *Progressive Farmer,* and Aycock's son-in-law, Poe was better known for his proposal of complete residential segregation of Negroes even in rural areas. Poe's educational movement was inspired by the publication of the unvarnished figures of the 1910 federal census, showing North Carolina at the top in white illiteracy and the bottom state in expenditure per child. Poe did not spare the feelings of the school men. "Our town schools are fairly well supported," he pointed out, "but our country schools, having no lobbyists to plead for them before legislative committees . . . . have been neglected, shamefully neglected, year after year." The reanimated school lobby under his leadership demanded a six-month term and a state-wide "modern and flexible compulsory attendance law," pretty exclusively for white children. Of compulsory education Poe said: "The negro question can also be adjusted in this matter as it has been adjusted in many forms more puzzling than this."[83]

The Farmers' Union, 35,000 strong, endorsed the six-month term and compulsory attendance by nearly one hundred to one and with great enthusiasm, as did 31,000 members of the Junior Order of United American Mechanics, and thousands of club women. Joyner used the Southern Education Board campaign fund "to organize the forces and bring public sentiment to bear upon the General Assembly in behalf of these measures."[84] Soon Governor Locke Craig heard the "command to educate our country children" that "thundered from the conscience of the age." "If we

---

81. Knight, *Public School Education in North Carolina,* p. 355.
82. For evidence of educational doldrums after Aycock left office, see Democratic platform of 1908, in Raleigh *News and Observer,* June 30, 1908; Governor William W. Kitchin's speech in *ibid.*, January 13, 1909; Joyner to Philander P. Claxton, December 22, 1909, Joyner Papers, S.H.C., University of North Carolina.
83. Clarence H. Poe, "What North Carolina Farmers Expect of the Legislature," in Raleigh *News and Observer,* January 19, 1913.
84. Rose to Dickerman, March 31, 1913, Dickerman Papers, S.H.C., University of North Carolina, quoting without date a letter of Joyner to Henry E. Fries; *North Carolina School Report, 1914-16,* Part I, p. 70.

grind the seed corn there will be a failure in the crop of man," said Craig.[85]

The farmers and teachers expected opposition, but the Six Months Term Act was passed with only three negative votes in the house and one in the senate. "We Go Forward," cheered Daniels, a crusader again after several years' lapse.[86] The Six Months Term Act actually raised the term to only five months by an "equalization" fund, and was replaced by a more genuine act in 1919.[87]

Compulsory school attendance had harder sledding. The Baptist State Convention placed its 238,000 members behind the six-month term but not behind compulsory education. "Let's not get the two confused," advised one Baptist.[88] There was no confusion in the mind of A. F. Johnson, chairman of the board of education of Sampson County. Compulsory education "might be acceptable in imperial Germany, but not in a free, liberty-loving State." Particularly not in its eastern part, as he explained: "Again, this compulsory law . . . may be fatal to the cotton crop, which more and more depends upon the labor of children for pickers. The board of education of Sampson County delayed the opening of schools last fall until November 11 on account of necessity of children in the cotton fields, and found it wise to do so."[89]

The compulsory education act, after considerable amendment, required a term of four months for most children between eight and twelve, with enough exemptions and loopholes to make it almost a dead letter.[90]

85. Text of inaugural address, in Raleigh *News and Observer*, January 16, 1913.
86. *Ibid.*, February 19, 20, 21, 22, 1913. The amendment by Senator Victor S. Bryant of Durham allowing counties to increase their taxation by five cents on $100 eased the doubts of many senators. It was quite clear from the debate that senators were resentful of the pressure "gotten up by three organizations" and "sent out from one headquarters" which had caused the furor.
87. The term "equalization" was also misleading, as any Negro teacher could testify. Thompson, "The Legislative Development of Public School Support in North Carolina" (unpublished doctoral dissertation, University of North Carolina), pp. 395-401. A brief general history of state "equalization" funds after 1901 is in Morrison, *Equalization of the Financial Burden of Education among Counties in North Carolina*, pp. 10-25.
88. Letter of Livingston Johnson, Raleigh, North Carolina, to the editor, in Raleigh *News and Observer*, January 26, 1913.
89. Letter to the editor, in Raleigh *News and Observer*, January 26, 1913.
90. Raleigh *News and Observer*, January 19, February 27, March 4, 1914;

North Carolina's educational seed fell upon stony ground, and the state in 1915, as in 1900, illustrated "how far the inhabitants of the United States are from being a democracy enlightened through and through." Lord Bryce had noted, "If one part of the [American] people is as educated and capable as that of Switzerland, another is as ignorant and politically untrained as that of Russia."[91] North Carolinians measured their education and other social institutions by comparing them with those of their fathers rather than with those of wealthy industrial peoples. On such a basis, the growth was remarkable. Total revenues of public schools increased by almost five times between 1900 and 1915. This was about twice as great as the increase of wealth in the same period, and it indicates that the enthusiasm generated by the educational campaigns reached fruition. The extent of the change is indicated in Table 2.[92]

TABLE 2

REVENUE OF PUBLIC EDUCATION IN NORTH CAROLINA, 1900-1915

Source	1899-1900	1904-1905	1909-1910	1914-1915
State funds (appropriation)	$ 90,379.73	$ 200,556.68	$ 289,981.46	$ 769,358.40
County funds	885,952.90	1,341,529.47	1,991,908.57	2,419,729.32
District funds (local tax)	3,067.79	338,414.33	877,799.91	1,452,070.77
Balance and other sources	38,743.19	289,697.45	334,553.94	84,801.13
Total	$1,018,143.61	$2,170,197.93	$3,494,243.88	$4,725,959.62

Local tax funds, which were negligible in 1900, amounted in 1915 to more than the total school fund had been fifteen years earlier. The average length of the school term almost doubled, as did average attendance. While expenditures for schools quin-

Knight, *Public School Education in North Carolina*, p. 347; Turner and Bridgers, *History of Edgecombe County, North Carolina*, p. 384.
91. James Bryce, *The American Commonwealth* (3rd ed., 2 vols., New York and London, 1895-96), II, 316.
92. Figures do not include bonds and loans. *North Carolina School Reports, 1898-1900*, p. 154 (but cf. p. 157); *1904-06*, pp. 65, 89; *1908-10*, Part II, pp. 130, 138; *1914-16*, Part II, p. 2.

North Carolina: A Schoolhouse a Day—for Whites 131

tupled in fifteen years, the value of school property increased ten times. This was mushroom growth, such as no other state could match. The only suitable comparisons would be the mass literacy programs of Soviet Russia and Mexico of a later date, and in North Carolina the movement overcame the handicap of considerable passive resistance from political leaders.[93]

While public support of education in North Carolina was greatly improved, expenditure of the increased funds was unfair. What may properly be described as the rape of the Negro school fund occurred every day and under the process of law. Whereas in 1900 the discrimination in favor of the white child was about 50 per cent, in 1915 it was about 300 per cent. In 1900 the Negro school population was 34.7 per cent of the total, and Negro schools received 28.3 per cent of the school funds. In 1915 the Negro school population was 32.6 per cent of the total, and Negro schools received 13.0 per cent of the expenditures itemized separately by race, which represented 75.1 per cent of all expenditures. Table 3, for the year 1914-15, suggests the line of division of school funds.[94]

In the items for which a separate accounting was made, $7.40 was expended for each white child of school age and $2.30 for each Negro child. Viewed from another angle, for $1.00 expended on a Negro child of school age, $3.22 was expended on the education of a white child of school age. As for the items not separately accounted, it is unlikely that these accrued to the benefit of Negro schools. A supervision and administration which discriminated 3.22 to 1 against Negroes was hardly beneficial to Negroes; Negro school furniture and apparatus were very inferior;[95] Negro schools had little to do with repayments of loans, interest, bonds, and sinking funds, most of which were for building of school-

---

93. *North Carolina School Reports, 1898-1900*, pp. 154-57; *1914-16*, Part II, pp. 76, 91-92.

94. *North Carolina School Report, 1914-16*, Part II, pp. 35, 42, 54, 61, 68, 76. Figures of the report are inconsistent, those on p. 75 not being the same as on p. 23, but the errors are negligible.

95. Of the white schools, 63.3 per cent had patent desks, 30.2 per cent home-made desks, 6.5 per cent benches; of Negro schools, 20.2 per cent had patent desks, 54.0 per cent home-made desks, 25.8 per cent benches. *Ibid.*, Part II, p. 282.

TABLE 3

NORTH CAROLINA PUBLIC SCHOOL EXPENDITURES, WHITE AND NEGRO, 1914-1915

Item of expenditure	White	Negro	Total	Item as per cent of total funds
Teachers' salaries	$2,994,722.01	$492,532.04	$3,487,254.05	57.0
Supervision			245,405.37	4.0
Administration			200,169.46	3.2
Operation and maintenance of school plants			282,349.40	4.6
New buildings, repairs and sites	988,311.10	105,878.95	1,094,190.05	17.8
Furniture and apparatus			122,546.21	2.0
Libraries	17,153.20	577.02	17,730.22	0.3
Repayments, interest, bonds, sinking funds			682,632.21	11.1
Total	$4,000,186.31	$598,988.01	$6,132,276.97	100.0
Per cent of items by race	87.0	13.0		
School population, number	540,410	260,987	801,397	
School population, per cent	67.4	32.6	100.0	

houses; the value of Negro school property was one-eighth that of white school property.[96]

There were other obvious disadvantages of Negro children. Negro rural schools were less than half as numerous, and so Negro children had to walk over twice as far. Few white children as yet, but no Negroes, had public transportation to school. Three-fifths of white rural schools and four-fifths of Negro schools had a single teacher. Of the white teachers employed by the state 2,443 had college degrees, while only 594 Negro teachers were so trained—and their diplomas often represented lower educational attainments.[97]

Teachers complained that they did not make a living wage, and little of the new expenditures went to salary increases. Negro

---

96. Negro school property value was $1,163,533.15; white school property value was $9,270,583.71. This amounted to $4.46 per Negro child, $17.15 per white child. *Ibid.*, Part II, p. 99.

97. *Ibid.*, Part II, pp. 252, 255, 266, 274.

North Carolina: A Schoolhouse a Day—for Whites

TABLE 4
ANNUAL SALARIES OF TEACHERS IN NORTH CAROLINA, 1905-1915

Year	White, city	Negro, city	White, rural	Negro, rural
1904-05	$341.57	$248.85	$125.21	$ 89.08
1909-10	374.12	252.45	159.49	95.91
1914-15	448.61	256.60	247.42	127.78
Increase, per cent.	31.3	3.1	99.2	43.4

salaries remained markedly below those for whites, and increased much more slowly. In Table 4, the more significant figures are those for rural schools. While the "city" schools were actually in small towns, these were few, and nearly all schools were in distinctly rural districts. Note that the salaries are for the year, not month.[98]

High schools, mostly for whites, were growing faster in 1915 than elementary schools. There were 285 public high schools, of which 134 reported four-year courses. Enrollment was 16,783. Besides these, nineteen "farm-life" or agricultural high schools enrolled 1,143. These were all white children; the state recognized no Negro secondary education, though apparently there was some secretive instruction on the secondary level.[99] In the following year the federal commissioner reported one Negro high school in the state with 19 pupils out of a state total of 15,469 secondary students.[100] In fact, local white hostility to the idea was so strong that when the Rosenwald Fund began about this time to aid the establishment of a few Negro secondary schools to train Negro teachers, it called them "training schools" rather than high

98. *North Carolina School Reports, 1904-06*, p. 133; *1908-10*, Part II, p. 192; *1914-16*, Part II, pp. 85-91. Because of errors in the record, salaries for 1914-15 were computed from total expenditure for salaries and total number of teachers. The extremes were much greater. In 1914-15 ten Negro teachers in Burke County received an average of $65.05 a year, ten in Ashe County an average of $56.26 a year, eighty-three in rural Pitt County an average of $71.00 a year, two in the town of Southern Pines $27.50 a year, sixteen in the town of Laurinburg $44.44 a year. Negro salaries were about as low in black counties as in white counties. White rural salaries were higher in the black counties, and the average ranged from $409.16 a year in black Martin County to $120.28 in white Burke County.
99. Report of the state inspector of public high schools, in *North Carolina School Report, 1914-16*, Part III, pp. 15, 19.
100. *Report of the Commissioner of Education, 1917*, II, 513, 612.

schools. The three state Negro normal schools received the modest combined appropriation of $21,553.75 from the state.[101] The Negro Agricultural and Technical College at Greensboro received $19,000 in 1915-16, one-thirteenth of the total state appropriation for colleges and universities. Public higher education for Negroes was almost nonexistent.[102]

Nearly all of the new funds went to white rural children, partly because they were the most numerous class of children. The disparity widened between Negro and white and between town and country. Yet the rural school received considerably larger amounts than in 1900. Even Negro schools were improved in the period, except in the all-important matter of relative status. More children attended more schools, equipped as never before with books, maps, and blackboards.

101. *North Carolina School Report, 1914-16*, Part III, pp. 145-49.
102. *Report of the Commissioner of Education, 1917*, II, 303, 398.

CHAPTER V

Virginia: The Machine and the Schools

"ALL THE STATES but our own are sensible that knowledge is power," wrote Thomas Jefferson toward the end of his unsuccessful struggle for public schools in Virginia, disappointment dulling his usual precision. But the free school idea, supported by a strong minority in the ante-bellum period, remained vigorous enough to give the state system begun during Reconstruction a considerable support among native whites. The public schools survived under a dedicated Redeemer superintendent, William H. Ruffner, and the Readjuster movement of the eighties increased the state fund by 50 per cent. But after a public school famine in the nineties, the expenditure per school child in 1900 was only $9.70 a year, the average annual salary of teachers only $168.19. The school term was 119 days, about one-third of the children attending each day.[1]

---

[1] Jefferson to Joseph C. Cabell, January 20, 1820, quoted in Adrienne Koch, *The Philosophy of Thomas Jefferson* (New York, 1943), p. 168; James A. Quarles (Washington and Lee University), "Our Rural Schools a Makeshift," in Richmond *Times-Dispatch*, January 6, 1907. Useful works on the struggle for public schools in the nineteenth century include James L. Blair Buck, *The Development of Public Schools in Virginia, 1607-1952* (Richmond, 1952); William A. Maddox, *The Free School Idea in Virginia before the Civil War: A Phase of Political and Social Evolution:* Teachers College, Columbia University, Contributions to Education, No. 93 (New York, 1918); Cornelius J. Heatwole, *A History of Education in Virginia* (New York, 1916); Alfred J. Morrison, *The Beginnings of Education in Virginia, 1776-1860: A Study of Secondary Schools in Relation to the State Literary Fund* (Richmond, 1917); William T. Alderson, "The Freedmen's Bureau and Negro Education in Virginia," in *North Carolina Historical Review*, XXIX (January, 1952), 64-90; Amory D. Mayo, "The Final Establishment of the American Common School System in West

The expenditure per pupil in attendance actually declined between 1872 and 1900; although the total amount for education doubled, it lagged behind increasing attendance. Only one-third of the white children attended in 1900, and one-fourth of the Negro children, and the idea of compulsory education still raised nightmares in the minds of some Virginians. "Invade my house and drag my child away to have its memory stuffed. It makes the blood run cold."[2]

For years the state superintendency was a sinecure given for political services. John E. Massey, superintendent from 1890 to 1898, was an apostate Readjuster who declared in the Democratic convention of 1889 that he was "tired of seeing white men taxed to educate negroes, who show their ingratitude by arraying themselves against us at every election."[3] His successor, the physician Joseph W. Southall, had shown moderation as a state senator and made no pressing demands on the legislature during his term from 1898 to 1906. Educational reformers at the turn of the century got little encouragement from Dr. Southall. As far as he could see, "no facts have been brought to light and no suggestions have been made as a result of this agitation that have not been fully considered time and again by the Department of Public Instruction." Distrusting Northern philanthropy, he cautioned Virginians not to "rely too much on help from without."[4]

The chief hindrance to educational reform was the state political machine. The term "machine" usually calls to mind industry and the city, but the Virginia machine in a rural state was powerful

---

Virginia, Maryland, Virginia, and Delaware, 1863-1900," in United States Bureau of Education, *Report of the Commissioner of Education for the Year 1903* (2 vols., Washington, 1905), I, 424-53.

2. W. N. Reed, Long Glade, Augusta County, letter to the editor, in Richmond *Times-Dispatch*, January 22, 1906. Unless existing facilities were increased, compulsory attendance would have meant fifty pupils per white teacher and over a hundred per Negro teacher.

3. Elizabeth H. Hancock (ed.), *Autobiography of John E. Massey* (New York, 1909), p. 274.

4. Lyon G. Tyler (ed.), *Encyclopedia of Virginia Biography* (5 vols., New York, 1915), III, 182-83; Southall to the editor in Richmond *Dispatch*, June 1, 1902. Part of his hostility to the Southern Education Board agents in Virginia was personal. Frissell to Curry, September 20, 1902, Henry St. George Tucker to Frissell, October 12, 1902, copies in Southern Education Board Papers, S.H.C., University of North Carolina.

and thoroughly organized.[5] Because of its peculiar dependence on railroads and other outside corporations for campaign funds, the machine stressed low taxation and therefore neglected welfare legislation and fought against appropriations for public schools.[6] The boss was United States Senator Thomas S. Martin, an unobtrusive Charlottesville lawyer and railroad director, and the whole thing was similar to a holding company, with subsidiaries in every county courthouse.[7]

The machine grasped the schools at two places: in the legislature, which elected the state superintendent and held down school appropriations, and at the county level. The county school trustee electoral board, which had the real power over school administration, was securely controlled by local officeholders chosen by county conventions. This board appointed the three trustees of each school district, who were also members of the county board of education. The county superintendent was also chosen by the machine: nominated at the county Democratic convention, appointed by a state board of education composed of statehouse officials, and confirmed by the senate, so that the machine controlled the office even in Republican counties.[8]

A constitutional convention which met in Richmond in 1901-02, on the eve of Virginia's educational campaign, profoundly affected the relations between white and Negro schools and revealed the social attitudes of the state leaders. Disfranchisement of Negroes was the main business of the convention, but the anti-Negro movement pervaded all of its deliberations, and the changes made in the

5. See Allen W. Moger, *The Rebuilding of the Old Dominion . . . 1880 to 1902* (Ann Arbor, 1940?), and *idem*, "The Origin of the Democratic Machine in Virginia," in *Journal of Southern History*, VIII (May, 1942), 183-209. Its connection with the later Byrd machine is traced by the journalist William Manchester, "The Byrd Machine," in *Harper's Magazine*, CCV (November, 1952), 80-87.

6. "Virginia is as much railroad-ridden as Pennsylvania, only the people don't know it."—William A. Jones, congressman of Warsaw, Virginia, to Henry St. George Tucker, September 4, 1906, Henry St. George Tucker Papers, S.H.C., University of North Carolina.

7. On Martin, see William D. Sheldon, *Populism in the Old Dominion: Virginia Farm Politics 1885-1900* (Princeton, 1935), pp. 105-14, 121-23; Josephus Daniels, *The Wilson Era: Years of Peace, 1910-1917* (Chapel Hill, 1944), pp. 520-25.

8. *Virginia School Report, 1903-05*, pp. 28-31; Robert Frazer in Richmond *Times-Dispatch*, June 17, 1906; Porter, *County Government in Virginia*, pp. 259-60, 294, 335-37.

education clause legalized racial discrimination in the school system.[9]

A fundamental question debated by the convention was Negro education and its relation to suffrage, taxation, and apportionment of school funds. This discussion reflected the general trend, accelerated by the prospect of disfranchisement, toward stripping Negroes of many of the gains they had made since emancipation. Amherst County was opposed to the constitutional convention until a mass rally was called at the county seat, and a certain gentleman "made one of those oratorical flights, in which he dwelt upon a separation of the school tax"; then "the little mass-meeting was carried by three districts out of four."[10] Such sentiments, moreover, found encouragement in high academic places. Professor Richard Heath Dabney of the University of Virginia declared it foolish for the state to tax itself for the education of the colored people it sought to disfranchise. State Superintendent Joseph W. Southall was reported to have said that "negro education is a failure."[11] Paul B. Barringer, chairman of the faculty of the University of Virginia and owner of 1,600 acres of agricultural land, said "the public-school training of this people should be primarily a Sunday-school training." He put the question frankly to a meeting of Southern educators at Richmond six months before the Virginia convention: "Shall we, having by a great effort gotten rid of the negro as a political menace, deliberately proceed to equip the negro of the future as an economic menace?" Barringer warned of the temptation to use industrially trained Negroes as

9. On the subject of disfranchisement in the convention, see Ralph C. McDanel, *The Virginia Constitutional Convention of 1901-02:* The Johns Hopkins University Studies in Historical and Political Science, Series XLVI (Baltimore, 1928); Robert E. Martin, "Negro Disfranchisement in Virginia," in Howard University *Studies in the Social Sciences*, I (Washington, 1938), 49-188; Richard L. Morton, *The Negro in Virginia Politics, 1865-1902:* University of Virginia, Phelps-Stokes Fellowship Papers, No. 4 (Charlottesville, 1919), pp. 148-61; Richard McIlwaine, *Memories of Three Score Years and Ten* (New York, 1908), pp. 368-76 *et passim.*

10. Clarence J. Campbell, delegate of Amherst County, in *Report of the Proceedings and Debates of the Constitutional Convention, State of Virginia, Held in the City of Richmond June 12, 1901, to June 26, 1902* (2 vols., Richmond, 1906), I, 257, hereafter referred to as *Proceedings of Virginia Constitutional Convention.*

11. Frissell to William H. Baldwin, November 2, 1901, copy in Dabney Papers; *Harper's Weekly*, XLIV (February 10, 1900), 120.

strike-breakers, and thought that Negroes should be kept on the farms, where white men could "help him and make him help us." "Their moral training should be supplemented by the three R's, and such simple training in agriculture and the domestic arts as all will need."[12] The accuracy of Barringer's statistics was challenged, but he expressed so clearly the prejudices of the white debtor classes and the interests of landowners and employers that few wished to challenge his attitude toward Negro education.

A Black-Belt conservative was chairman of the education committee of the convention. He was President Richard McIlwaine of Hampden-Sidney College, an elderly gentleman who lectured delegates as though they were his students. McIlwaine's view of Negro education, in harmony with his old-fashioned ideas on suffrage, combined the traditions of paternalism and Christian ethics. Negroes, he said, "have a right—I do not mean in law, but in morals—in their relations to you and me, as Christian men, to learn to read the Bible."[13] A more prevalent black-county attitude was expressed by Walter A. Watson, committee member from Nottoway and Amelia. He was horrified to think that there were 2,500 Negro schoolhouses "turning out your voters by the thousands to meet you, and to meet me at the ballot-box."[14]

Discrimination against Negro schools was certainly no innovation. It was "a well-known fact that in many portions of Eastern Virginia an illegal discrimination is made in favor of the white

12. Barringer, "Negro Education in the South," in *Southern Educational Association, Journal of Proceedings and Addresses of the Tenth Annual Meeting, Held at Richmond, Va., December 27-29, 1900*, pp. 127-37. Julius D. Dreher of Roanoke College, Virginia, and Hollis B. Frissell of Hampton Institute made dignified rebuttals. *Ibid.*, pp. 138-50. But Curry, who was present, wrote to Frissell: "I left R. [Richmond] exasperated and hot with mortification and anger. The paper of the chairman of our great University was pessimistic, untrue and mischievous in the highest degree. Fortunately, you put in effectively an antidote—still, what one, holding such a high position, said will be taken by some 'bloody shirt' sheets, as *ex cathedra* & authoritative. . . . I must take early occasion to blow off my excitement and resentment."—Curry to Frissell, December 31, 1900, copy in Southern Education Board Papers, S.H.C., University of North Carolina. Barringer's paper and the replies were republished in the *Report of the Commissioner of Education, 1901*, I, 517-30.

13. *Proceedings of Virginia Constitutional Convention*, I, 1668. McIlwaine thought a poll tax, property tax, and written registration would "give us a clean-cut franchise law, which will, at one stroke, lop off a large mass of the incompetent and corrupt voting population of the State, and put its government in the hands of the intelligent, tax-paying portion of its citizens."—*Ibid.*, II, 3002.

14. *Ibid.*, II, 3068.

schools under the present law," declared a delegate who wanted discrimination legalized. He insisted that "it is not within the power of this Convention or of the General Assembly of Virginia to prevent that discrimination any more than it has been within the power of either one to prevent irregularities at the polls."[15] His remarks were confirmed by official reports to the convention showing an expenditure of $3.78 per white child and $1.89 per Negro child of school age, or twice as much for whites as for Negroes.[16] The gap of discrimination was already wide.

Racial division of school funds was proposed by both white and black counties,[17] but was rejected by the education committee on the ground of "doubtful constitutionality . . . because the people of the North do not understand the position in which we are situated." The task of the convention, therefore, was to make the school clause "sufficiently flexible to conform to the necessity of the case." Delegate John W. Daniel announced before the convention that he opposed division, and Carter Glass warned that it would "provoke a furious and relentless crusade against our constitutional barriers to an ignorant and venal negro franchise in the South." Furthermore, "If we do not give them a plain schooling best adapted to their needs and useful to them, outside dreamers and fanatics will give them an education that will not be useful to them, but dangerous to the peace of Virginia."[18] Such dire warnings frightened away demands for tax division.

The economic interest of white residents of black counties simply overcame their opposition to Negro education. The white schools of black counties benefited more than those of white

15. *Ibid.*, I, 1665.
16. Communication from the Superintendent of Public Instruction, September 12, 1901, Document No. XIV, appendix of *Journal of the Constitutional Convention of Virginia Held in the City of Richmond Beginning June 12, 1901* (Richmond, 1901); *Report of the Commissioner of Education, 1902*, II, 2064. These figures do not include salaries of superintendents or the state department of public instruction, nor presumably high schools or colleges.
17. Resolution by T. L. Gwyn of Grayson County, in *Journal of the Constitutional Convention of Virginia, 1901-02*, p. 80; statement of Robert Turnbull of Brunswick County, in *Proceedings of Virginia Constitutional Convention*, I, 1671-72. Cf. Bond, *Education of the Negro in the American Social Order*, pp. 87-88.
18. *Proceedings of the Virginia Constitutional Convention*, I, 1220; editorial in Richmond *Times*, April 18, 1901, clipping in Dickerman clipping books, S.H.C., University of North Carolina.

counties from the state school fund apportioned to the counties and thence to the districts on a basis of school population. The education committee recommended, and the convention approved, a provision that the state fund, derived almost entirely from a property tax and poll tax, was "for the equal benefit of all of the people of the State to be apportioned on a basis of school population; the number of children ... in each school district being the basis of such apportionment." The joker was that local taxes legally and state taxes by subterfuge were to be "apportioned and expended by the local school authorities ... in establishing and maintaining such schools as in their judgment the public welfare may require: provided, that such primary schools as may be established in any school year, shall be maintained at least four months of that school year, before any part of the [local tax] fund assessed and collected may be devoted to the establishment of schools of higher grade."[19] Disregarding for the moment the provision for local taxation, one finds that local authorities, "for the equal benefit of all of the people of the State," needed only to maintain such Negro schools as they saw fit for four months, or 1.97 months less than the current state average term, spend only what was necessary to keep a Negro teacher in the school, and use the remainder for white schools. "In other words," commented a white-county Democrat, "you will tax the people in Frederick County to educate the negro children in the Black Belt, and then you will not apply it to the education of the negro children in the Black Belt."[20]

A vigorous dispute of the convention revolved about the local tax paragraph of the education committee's report. Walter A. Watson of black Nottoway County proposed in the committee an optional local tax to be expended by the local school authorities for "such schools as in their judgment the public welfare may require." The committee approved this and also Carter Glass's

19. Constitution of Virginia, 1902, Article IX, Sections 135-36; Report of the Committee on Education and Public Instruction, Section 7, appendix of *Journal of the Constitutional Convention of Virginia, 1901-02.*
20. Thomas W. Harrison of Frederick County and the city of Winchester, in *Proceedings of Virginia Constitutional Convention,* I, 1078. His county had over 94 per cent white population. White-county delegates did not renew the debate, presumably because they could not decide how, constitutionally, to deprive white schools of black counties of their special privileges without enforcing equal facilities for Negroes.

proviso that all primary schools must be maintained at least four months before any part of the fund could be devoted to higher schools. Watson agreed to sign the committee report, but he considered the Glass proviso an outrage.[21]

As Watson explained his local tax clause on the convention floor, "the legal change contemplated here is that in the distribution of county and local school money, instead of population being the basis of division, the public welfare within that community, as determined by the judgment of the local authorities, shall constitute that basis." Immediately D. Q. Eggleston of the black county of Charlotte moved to strike out the four-month proviso, pretending that the only question at issue was whether a few rural communities were to be allowed to maintain high schools.[22] Hal D. Flood, delegate of black Appomattox County, soon cleared the air. "I do not think this fund will all be expended in high schools," he said; "a great deal of it will be spent in white primary schools. But what we ask here is that the local school boards be allowed to expend it in such schools as they see fit, high schools or primary schools. If they want to expend it for the benefit of the white people, let them expend every cent they are willing to tax themselves for the benefit of their own children." This was "not taking anything away from the darkies," said Flood, because there would be no local tax whatever unless whites had a free hand. "You are just prohibiting, you are putting a clog, you are stopping the white people of the black sections from imposing a tax for the benefit of their white children, because they cannot afford to impose that tax and raise it from their taxpayers and then have it divided," spluttered Flood. George B. Keezell, of the Valley white county of Rockingham, answered Flood's argument by citing the educational statistics of Flood's county:

I find that there are in the county of Appomattox 2,073 white children and 1,593 colored children. Last year the county of Appomattox ex-

21. This dispute within the committee was revealed on the floor, after considerable debate on the section. *Ibid.*, I, 1194, 1665. Principal Frissell of Hampton Institute wrote privately that, notwithstanding the four-month proviso, "The effect of this measure will be practically the division of the money for the support of the schools of the two races, and will also tend to shorten the school term."—Frissell to Baldwin, November 2, 1901, copy in Dabney Papers, S.H.C., University of North Carolina.

22. *Proceedings of Virginia Constitutional Convention*, I, 1194-1204.

pended for white schools $5,230.66 and $960 for colored schools. In other words, the State of Virginia sent to the county of Appomattox on account of her colored population $2,277.99, and there was expended for colored education in that county $960. If he can accomplish the end to which he is referring any more successfully than the people of Appomattox now accomplish it, I should like to know the recipe.[23]

McIlwaine pointed out that black counties, through special privileges in apportionment, had almost wiped out white illiteracy, there being only twenty-four white illiterates in Nottoway County, sixty-seven in Appomattox, thirty-one in Amelia. In the course of debate the "intolerable burden" on whites of black counties seemed to grow smaller and smaller. Carter Glass reassured the delegates:

To speak without disguise, Mr. Chairman, the local school fund, assessed alike against blacks and whites, may, by constitutional sanction, be devoted to the maintenance exclusively of white schools, provided the primary schools of a city, county, or school district have been maintained for a period of four months.

Eggleston's amendment would "deprive the negro children . . . of any facilities worthy the name," and its patent unconstitutionality was dangerous.[24] If maintenance of Negro schools for four months proved expensive, some Negro schools might simply be closed. McIlwaine had already in the committee compromised the principle of universal education, but he made a long plea on the floor for limiting discrimination. "I am not talking about negroes or white people; I am talking about the children of this State, and the imperative duty that devolves upon us, as a sovereign convention, to see that the organic law of the State is such that children shall have the benefit, as far as possible, of at least the primary grade of education."[25]

The city men were split on the Eggleston amendment. Certainly they did not support equal opportunity, which they denied to rural whites, but they considered literacy, like publicly built roads and bridges, useful to everybody. "Who wants servants or employees that cannot read and write to conduct their business?"

23. *Ibid.*, I, 1205, 1212.
24. *Ibid.*, I, 1210, 1219.
25. *Ibid.*, I, 1667-69. McIlwaine said that all references to high schools referred to those for whites. "We certainly do not need any high schools for our colored people in these counties."—*Ibid.*, I, 1670.

But Charles V. Meredith of Richmond supported the black counties' opposition to equal education. "Suppose the gentleman had $150 to expend in education and it took $150 to educate his child, would he be willing to divide his means with the child of his colored cook? He knows that he would not. Now, that is a personal application."[26]

In the end the convention agreed with S. P. Waddill of Henrico County that they should not "depart from a system that is fixed, certain and easy of determination and to adopt a plan that no man can define." After his address, the convention hastily rejected the Eggleston amendment by 36 to 15 and approved the section.[27] Notwithstanding the four-month minimum term, the convention surrendered to the hundreds of local authorities its obligation to protect the Negro school fund, clearly understanding that the obligation would be ignored.

Yet the policy of racial discrimination went deeper than legal formalities; it was derived from the people themselves. "The cry of 'Good enough for the Negroes' is heard from the mountains to the sea," said a Richmond Negro weekly. Negroes complained that even the state superintendent, "sworn to recognize the 'civil and political equality of all men before the law' has made a powerful plea in favor of curtailing the educational privileges of the colored children of the commonwealth." They decided he was "an official of the whites and not of all the people of Virginia," and declared: "If we are ignorant, you made us so."[28] But Negro defiance and plain speech were waning. The rate of discrimination, moving almost unchecked, was much higher by 1907-08. In that year, in the least discriminatory feature of education, the salaries of teachers, five selected black counties reported 4.8 times as much per white child of school age as per Negro child, five selected white counties 2.2 times as much,[29] and the city of Richmond 2.2 times

26. *Ibid.*, I, 1213-14, 1680-81.
27. *Ibid.*, I, 1682-86. Waddill remarked that the existing system "largely inures to the benefit of the white children of the State; and against it the colored people are raising no protest or objection." In all the debate, the "separate but equal" doctrine was not mentioned.
28. Editorial in Richmond *Planet*, February 3, 1900, microfilm, The Johns Hopkins University.
29. This was computed from *Virginia School Report, 1907-09*, pp. 128-50, 194-208, by adding the amounts of Negro and white salaries, dividing this by

Virginia: The Machine and the Schools 145

as much. Two Richmond Negro schools in that year were dangerous fire hazards, condemned unqualifiedly by a committee appointed by the mayor. In one of them the children were "being taught in immediate contact with the sights and sounds of our jail."[30]

The dilemma of a school reformer at the county level is revealed by the private correspondence of Joseph D. Eggleston, who returned home from Dabney's Bureau of Information at Knoxville to become Prince Edward County superintendent. "I don't despair—not at all," he wrote his friend Dabney, "—but such a problem! How completely fossilized the system in the State. Really I believe some of the people around here think I am mentally 'cracked' over this school question." With the impatience of ambitious youth, Eggleston tried to transform the whole county:

A school superintendent in the South must be omniscient and omnipresent—and gradually work toward omnipotence. [But how could one consolidate schools] where there is no large town to help any raise of tax; where the population is so sparse that after placing the schoolhouses five or six miles apart, there can be mustered only ten to twenty children to patronize them; where an assessed valuation of property (nearer the real value than anywhere else in the state) for, say, 12,000 people is about $750,000; where the roads are practically impassable in four months of the year; where there are two races and therefore two schools to maintain; and where one race has to pay 80 to 95% of the school tax though the other race stands in numbers as 2½ to one with the whites[?][31]

Eggleston had more success with his teachers than with his white taxpayers,[32] and soon decided that there were limits to reform in the counties. He made plans to oust the incorrigible Joseph W. Southall from the office of state superintendent.

Probably not even a political leader of the La Follette type

---

the proportions of Negro and white school population, and dividing the quotients. See also p. 17, above.

30. *Eighth Annual Report of the Richmond Education Association, 1907-08* (Richmond, 1908), pp. 8-9.

31. Eggleston to Dabney, December 10, 1903, Dabney Papers, S.H.C., University of North Carolina.

32. Eggleston to George J. Ramsey, March 28, 1904, George J. Ramsey Papers, Duke University.

could have challenged the machine after the reduction of the electorate. Disfranchisement was not followed by the emergence of an organized opposition, and the new constituency was inclined to be content with a *status quo* machine, while most discontented elements such as Negroes, white tenant farmers, and mountaineers were denied, by disfranchisement, a political redress of grievances. The nearest thing to La Follette that Virginia reformers could muster was the Richmond lawyer Andrew Jackson Montague, the governor from 1902 to 1906. Montague was non-machine rather than anti-machine, but probably earned the title of Educational Governor by the atmosphere of friendliness toward school reformers during his brief term of office.

In his inaugural address, Montague called Virginia to the machine age by means of industrial education to increase "the wealth producing power of the people; for the material advancement of a State is measured by the school privileges of its people."[33] In his first message to the legislature, Montague insisted that education of both races was "a task for patriotic statesmanship."

Though Montague probably antagonized many Virginians by refusing to exploit race prejudice or to put his shoulder to the wheel of discrimination, his program was too moderate to push Negro education forward. "I would not shut the door of hope," he told a mixed audience at Hampton in a widely quoted speech, "but I would teach that we must begin on a sound basis." In his first message to the legislature he proposed only that in the title of the state Negro school the word "Industrial" be substituted for "Collegiate."[34] Like Aycock in North Carolina, Montague contributed little besides speeches to the advancement of Negro education. Though he probably did more than the North Carolina governor to cushion the downtrend of race relations, he was less effective in leading the white public educational movement. In Virginia the leadership of school reform was held by the Southern Education Board and its local agencies.

The Southern Education Board entered Virginia early in 1902. Since the only member of the Board resident in Virginia was the

33. *Proceedings of Virginia Constitutional Convention*, II, 1710.
34. Virginia General Assembly, *House Journal, 1901-1902* (Richmond, 1902), pp. 139-40; clipping from New York *Sun*, dated April 21, 1904, Ogden Papers, Library of Congress.

Northern-born Hollis B. Frissell, two salaried agents were employed, Henry St. George Tucker and Robert Frazer. Tucker had served four terms in Congress and taught law at Washington and Lee. His family name was familiar to most Virginians, and he was a prominent Baptist, a fact which outweighed some Presbyterian opposition to him arising from his connection with Washington and Lee.[35] Frazer was president of the State Female Normal School. Though lacking the prestige and oratorical gifts of Tucker, he had more realistic knowledge of educational conditions. Frazer carried about with him photographs of the worst-looking schoolhouses in the state; even fellow agitators called him "pessimistic," but it was hard for the city folk to ignore his evidence.[36] William T. B. Williams, Negro graduate of Hampton and Harvard, was an agent of the Board briefly until the General Education Board employed him.[37]

The Board agents immediately sought the cooperation of Superintendent Southall. Curry, Dabney, and others representing "large money influences from outside of the State to be invested in education in the South" arrived at the capitol one day late in 1901. They "came into my office," Southall later recalled, "and conversed with me on the subject of educational schemes and enterprises, which, though not definitely explained or outlined to me at the time, I felt sure would be explained in the near future."[38] But the Board decided instead to work independently of the machine.

35. Frissell to Tucker, November 23, 28, 30, December 18, 31, 1901, Curry to Tucker, December 10, 1901, Tucker to Dabney, December 3, 1901, Tucker Papers, S.H.C., University of North Carolina; Ogden to Dabney, November 26, 1901, Dabney Papers, S.H.C., University of North Carolina; Dickerman, "The Conference for Education in the South and the Southern Education Board," *Report of the Commissioner of Education, 1907*, I, 304. On Tucker's controversy with the majority of the Washington and Lee board of trustees, see Tucker to Rev. George B. Strickler, January 1, 1902, Tucker Papers, S.H.C., University of North Carolina; Frissell to Curry, December 14, 1901, copy in Southern Education Board Papers, S.H.C., University of North Carolina.

36. Frazer to Frissell, November 30, 1901, copy in Southern Education Board Papers, S.H.C., University of North Carolina; Charles E. Burrell, *A History of Prince Edward County, Virginia, from its Formation in 1753 to the Present* (Richmond, 1922), p. 322; Frissell to Ogden, March 6, 1905, Dabney Papers, S.H.C., University of North Carolina. The two agents were employed for two years, and Frazer continued until 1905, when the Cooperative Education Commission employed him.

37. Frissell to Curry, January 10, 1902, Curry to Frissell, April 15, 1902, copies in Southern Education Board Papers, S.H.C., University of North Carolina.

38. Interview in Richmond *Times*, February 13, 1902.

Frissell's advice was that "we have to go to the people, and by dealing with the people we can control the officials." Recalling that the North Carolina campaign had been "like an old-time revival of religion," Tucker sought out the exhorters to find out how it was accomplished. McIver obligingly journeyed to Richmond to give technical assistance.[39]

Meanwhile Frazer took the low road, bringing Editor W. Scott Copeland of the Richmond *Times* to Farmville to see his photograph file of wretched Virginia rural schoolhouses. Copeland agreed to turn on the heat. Some were "mere hovels," he reported, without plastering, with large cracks in the floor, with the unsanitary common bucket and common dipper, and unmentionable outhouses. "Dr. Frazer knows of one case where a man secured a position at $45 a month, hired a girl at $15 a month to do the work and pocketed the difference."[40] The *Times* installed an "Educational Department" of two columns on its editorial page, and Copeland made a tour of the rural state, gathering notes for a rather sensational exposé. *Times* reporters found human-interest stories everywhere. The Richmond Education Association, alleging that the "people of Richmond never had the faintest idea that conditions existed in the rural districts as painted by Dr. Frazer," invited him to a rally in the capital. All this was done before Superintendent Southall knew what was happening, and a storm of *Times* reporters broke over his head. He had "heard nothing authoritatively," said Southall, but he had hoped "that this company of philanthropists would in some efficient way become co-workers with the State organization for the promotion of education in the rising generation." Southall took the educational propaganda as a personal attack on him, and was thrown on the defensive. Go to Chesterfield, he told reporters; there the buildings were "neat, comfortable structures of ample size and pleasing to look at."[41]

---

39. Frissell to Eggleston, April 16, 1902, copy in Southern Education Board Papers, S.H.C., University of North Carolina; Tucker to Alderman, January 9, 1902, Tucker Papers, S.H.C., University of North Carolina.

40. Editorial in Richmond *Times*, February 2, 1902; Copeland's later recollections of the interview, in Richmond *Times-Dispatch*, May 21, 1906.

41. Frank P. Brent, secretary of the Board of Education, said that schoolhouses were usually better than the dwellings of patrons, who did not complain of them. Richmond *Times*, February 13, 14, 1902.

The Board agents found a responsive audience among a people starved for diversion. Tucker spoke to as many as 5,000 at Baptist conventions; on court days at the county seats, stores closed to hear him, courts were suspended, and farmers rode in from twenty-five miles away. Frazer visited sixty of the hundred counties in his first year. He and R. C. Stearnes increased the membership of the state teachers' association by over 2,000.[42]

An important ally of the Ogden movement in Virginia was the Richmond Education Association. A spirit of *richesse oblige* toward the backward countryside induced its members to agitate for better rural schools. Not merely a prestige organization, it was filled with energetic local citizens. Joseph Bryan and W. Scott Copeland of the Richmond *Times-Dispatch* adopted this as one of a number of crusades. Samuel C. Mitchell, professor at Richmond College, was first president of the state Anti-Saloon League. Mary C. B. Munford was a member of the National Child Labor Committee, Lila Meade Valentine the first president of the Virginia Equal Suffrage League (for women, not Negroes). Financial backers included the banker John P. Branch, food manufacturer Ben B. Valentine, and John Stewart Bryan, chairman of the Joint Committee of Progress for a Greater Richmond.[43]

Though the editor of the Richmond *Times-Dispatch* insisted, in one editorial after another, that public education was "socialistic, and it will not do to push too far the principle upon which it rests," he recognized the necessity for mass education. Free textbooks would be pushing the principle too far and might lead to "free lunch and free clothes" and produce "driveling dependents."

---

42. Dickerman, "A Journey in Virginia and the Carolinas, November 6th to December 6th, 1902," manuscript in Southern Education Board Papers, S.H.C., University of North Carolina; Frissell, "Educational Progress in Virginia," in *South Atlantic Quarterly*, II (July, 1903), 204. In a ninety-day period, Frazer made thirty-nine speeches, of which twenty-one were at county courthouses, ten at schools, six at teachers' meetings, one before a Baptist district association, and one before the joint committee on education of the legislature. See copies of his quarterly report as field agent of the Southern Education Board, July 31, 1903, Frissell to Alderman, January 10, 1902, Dabney Papers, S.H.C., University of North Carolina.

43. Samuel C. Mitchell, "The Part of the Citizen in Aiding the Cause of Public Education," in *Sixth Conference for Education in the South, Proceedings* (Richmond, 1903), pp. 190-93; W. Asbury Christian, *Richmond, Her Past and Present* (Richmond, 1912), pp. 494, 497, 519; Robert C. Glass and Carter Glass, Jr., *Virginia Democracy* (3 vols., Richmond, 1937), II, 13, 32.

Compulsory education was acceptable only on a local option basis.[44] While conservative even in its reforms, the *Times-Dispatch* welcomed and assisted the Ogden movement, defending it against critics and giving it essential publicity. The Conference at Richmond in 1903 had front-page headlines for a week, and other papers followed the lead of the *Times-Dispatch*.[45]

College administrators and teachers proved the backbone of the public school movement. Among the most active were Samuel C. Mitchell of Richmond College, Bruce R. Payne of William and Mary, Charles W. Kent of the University of Virginia, George H. Denny of Washington and Lee, William W. Smith of Randolph-Macon, Reverend James Cannon, principal of Blackstone Female Institute, and Charles E. Vawter of the Miller Manual Training School.[46] This sort of support for public education reached its climax after Edwin A. Alderman's arrival in Virginia in 1904.

The University of Virginia, abandoning Jefferson's plan of a rotating chairmanship of the faculty, found in Alderman a president who could get money from millionaires. Alderman brought endowments in his train, but foremost in his own mind was the hope of linking that university, "with all its traditions and its powerful influence on southern thought, with the movement for the democratization of education." Paul B. Barringer, chairman of the faculty before Alderman's arrival, had described the Ogdenites complacently as "whoopers-up of the educational millennium," and, said Ogden, "the whole university was as cold as Greenland's icy mountains" before Alderman's day.[47] Alderman

44. Editorials in Richmond *Times-Dispatch*, January 10, 23, 1904, August 27, 1905, January 16, 18, 1906.
45. *Ibid.*, April 19-26, 1903, and editorial, "R. C. Ogden Stood By Us," on April 12, 1903.
46. Frazer to Frissell, February 10, 1902, copy in Southern Education Board Papers, S.H.C., University of North Carolina; William W. Smith to Alderman, August 4, 1904, Alderman Papers, Alderman Library, University of Virginia; George H. Denny, "What Our Institutions of Higher Learning May Do for the Public Schools," in University of Virginia *Alumni Bulletin*, New Series, V (March, 1906), 320-26; Samuel C. Mitchell, in Richmond *Times-Dispatch*, February 21, 1904; James Cannon, Jr., in Richmond *Christian Advocate*, quoted in Richmond *Times-Dispatch*, February 3, 1904.
47. Barringer to Tucker, May 3, 1902, Tucker Papers, S.H.C., University of North Carolina; *Sixth Conference for Education in the South, Proceedings* (Richmond, 1903), p. 231; Charles P. Jones to Thomas Nelson Page, June 30, 1904, Thomas Nelson Page Papers, Duke University; Malone, *Edwin A. Alderman*, pp. 180-81, quoting from undated clipping of New York *Tribune*;

himself was to be hampered by his school's dependence on the legislature and by machine leaders on its board of visitors.

On a rainy evening in December, 1904, a large conference of "school men" gathered in the basement of a Baptist church in Norfolk. They were members of the Cooperative Education Association of Virginia, formed earlier in the same year to unify all educational pressure groups. Ormond Stone of Charlottesville suggested amid cheers that Montague and Alderman lead a crusade of one hundred speakers the following year in a month-long May Campaign that would set the tone of the political campaign which followed. Alderman, who was busy raising university endowments, was reluctant to assume the leadership of the May Campaign and should have refused. But before the meeting broke up, he agreed to give the movement two weeks of his eloquence.[48]

The connection of this plan with Montague and the implications of a large tax increase did not long escape the attention of the Martin machine. Thomas S. Martin himself, Alderman's next-door neighbor and a member of the university board of visitors, wrote to Alderman in February that "When the arrangement made at Norfolk for an educational canvass of the State, to be made by Gov. Montague and yourself, in the month of May, was announced I confess that the conclusion on my mind was very distinct that the hands of a political schemer had been at work.... I do not even now feel entirely satisfied as to the wisdom of the proposed canvass of the State." Martin went on:

> It will give me great pleasure to see you as soon as I can get to Charlottesville to talk the matter over. Above all things I am anxious to see the interests of the University [of Virginia] advanced, and I will say very frankly that I have grave doubt as to the wisdom of what is proposed when it is viewed from the standpoint of the University. Our schools can not be improved very materially without enlarged ap-

---

Ogden to Dickerman, March 1, 1906, Dickerman Papers, S.H.C., University of North Carolina.

48. Norfolk *Virginian-Pilot*, December 6, 7, 8, 1904; [Samuel C. Mitchell], "May Campaign, 1905," undated MS, Dabney Papers, S.H.C., University of North Carolina; Frazer to Frissell, December 23, 1904, copy in Southern Education Board Papers, S.H.C., University of North Carolina; John A. McGilvray to Alderman, November 29, 1904, Alderman's report to the Southern Education Board, undated MS, between November 22 and December 3, 1906, files of the president, University of Virginia.

propriations, and these can come only from increased taxation, either general or local. To use a common expression, a great deal of "hot air" has been passing round for some years in relation to the betterment of the schools. I have failed to see from any of those leading in this agitation any practical and tangible suggestion whereby the schools may be bettered with the funds now available or whereby additional funds may be provided. During the past thirty years there has been more difficulty to secure the annual appropriation for the University of Virginia than in the case of any other important public appropriation. Since this agitation has been started I have on more than one occasion heard the idea advanced by prominent men that the proposed canvass if it accomplished anything would lead to a discussion of increased taxation for common school education, and that suggestions of that sort were not likely to prove beneficial to the University of Virginia. I can hardly think that there is any occasion for a canvass to inculcate in the minds of the Virginia people the importance of education or the desirability of better school facilities.

As stated above, I do not understand what plan for the betterment of the schools is to be advanced. I throw out these suggestions for your consideration, and hope to have the opportunity very soon to talk them over with you in person.[49]

As Alderman reported to the Southern Education Board, "throat trouble caused me to cancel the entire engagement." He made up for this failure by speaking at strategic locations the following fall. During May he spent a week recuperating at Newport News, while Charles W. Kent, J. Taylor Ellyson, Charles E. Vawter, and others filled his engagements.[50]

Other Board representatives also took back seats on the bandwagon. "The movement seems to [be] attracting the attention of our friends the politicians," Frazer informed Frissell, "and it seems to be important that we should proceed with the utmost circumspection." Ogden was well enough satisfied that the campaign was being undertaken. "Although the inspiration comes from our Board," he wrote to scattered members, "and the ex-

[49] Thomas S. Martin to Alderman, February 15, 1905, files of the president, University of Virginia.

[50] Alderman, undated MS report to Southern Education Board as a member of the campaign committee, around December, 1906, or January, 1907, Alderman Papers, Alderman Library, University of Virginia; Richmond *Times-Dispatch*, May 9, 11, 13, 1905; Samuel C. Mitchell to Alderman, May 24, 1905, files of the president, University of Virginia.

penses [are] paid out of the treasury, it is yet uplifting for the people to feel the responsibility that creates local initiative."[51]

A highlight of the May Campaign was the contest of Joseph D. Eggleston, formerly Dabney's propaganda bureau assistant, for state superintendent. After Southall decided not to run for re-election, John A. McGilvray, clerk in the state department of education, was Eggleston's leading opponent. Eggleston had the same sort of difficulty as Alderman, but his tactics were bolder. He wrote to a friend early in 1905 that he would make the education department "look like a battered ten cent piece before I get through with it."

> This promises to be one of the bitterest fights on record. The Trust is fighting me with all the force possible. I hear that they will spend any amount in reason to defeat me. It's anything to be at me! ... They are supporting McGilvray. That crowd must be hard up for some ammunition; they are circulating all sorts of dirty rumors about me —that I am an "infidel"; that my work under Dabney was unsatisfactory, and hence my resignation; that the [B. F.] Johnson Company [Richmond, Virginia, textbook house] is backing me, etc. ....[52]

At the height of the May Campaign, Eggleston sprang the surprise charge that the state board of education had been "tricked" in the cost of printing the state school register, in which teachers recorded the statistics of enrollment, attendance, and other data required by state law. At a special investigation by the state board, Eggleston presented sensational facts to substantiate his charge and pin guilt upon his opponent McGilvray. The price of the register had risen from 18 to 75 cents after the Richmond high school principal took over the contract, and McGilvray was shown to be his silent business partner. McGilvray did not confess guilt until after the state primary, but Eggleston had his campaign issue. With his leading opponent out of the race, Eggleston won the Democratic nomination, tantamount to election, by ten

---

51. Frazer to Frissell, December 23, 1904, copy in Southern Education Board Papers, S.H.C., University of North Carolina; Ogden to Dabney, March 26, 1905, Ogden Papers, Library of Congress—University of North Carolina.

52. Eggleston to Ramsey, February 27, 1905, Ramsey Papers, Duke University. Eggleston had once been employed by B. F. Johnson Company. Richmond *Times-Dispatch*, June 13, 1903.

to one. During the May Campaign he stumped the state in company with candidates of the Martin machine.[53]

Aware that educational enthusiasm must focus on definite objectives, directors of the May Campaign devised an eight-point program. These points, "the ten commandments of the movement, were dwelt upon at every rally and thus hammered into the minds of the people."[54] The platform included a nine-month term for every child in Virginia, white or black, rural high schools, industrial education, improved teacher training, school consolidation and transportation, rural school libraries, and "an efficient and ramified organization" of local school improvement leagues. Adequate provision for Negro education had no explicit place in the platform, nor did compulsory attendance laws. These were implicit, however, in the plans of the reformers who led the movement. The program was comprehensive enough to keep Virginia school forces busy for a decade.

During the month of May, 1905, a hundred speakers toured the state, making 300-odd speeches, with some 1,500 others from local dignitaries. The May Campaign became a real mass movement, and audiences were estimated to have run into the hundred thousands. Probably few voters were left untouched, and everywhere enthusiasm was reported. Out of the deep country districts, over sand and red clay roads, swarmed "large concourses of the country people" to take part in this "combination of a crusade and a glorified picnic."[55] Even the pressing demands of spring work did not keep them away. "So it is easy to believe that something is going to happen in Old Virginia," reported Frazer.[56] At a

53. Richmond *Times-Dispatch*, May 3, 24, 25, 26, 27, June 23, 24, August 24, 1905; Magruder, *Recent Administration in Virginia*, pp. 26-27. McGilvray at the beginning of the campaign was drawing a salary of $250 from the Southern Education Board for work in the May Campaign. This may partly explain the later embarrassing position of the Board in Virginia. Frissell to Ogden, March 6, 1905, Dabney Papers, S.H.C., University of North Carolina.

54. Samuel C. Mitchell in minutes of Southern Education Board meeting, December 3-5, 1906, Dickerman Papers, S.H.C., University of North Carolina; Mitchell to Ogden, April 4, 1904, Ogden Papers, Library of Congress—University of North Carolina.

55. Frazer to Ogden, July 21, 1905, quoted in Mitchell, MS biography of Ogden, pp. 223-24, Ogden Papers, Library of Congress; Walter R. Bowie, *Sunrise in the South: The Life of Mary-Cooke Branch Munford* (Richmond, 1942), p. 75.

56. Frazer to Ogden, July 21, 1905, quoted in Mitchell, MS biography of Ogden, pp. 223-24, Ogden Papers, Library of Congress.

school rally near Etna Mills in King William County, a local preacher followed the politicians and professors with a good talk about "the shabby school houses in the county, with cracks in the floors, a part of the time no wood, and looked like they had not been painted or whitewashed since Noah was a little boy."[57]

Bruce R. Payne as publicity director poured some 200,000 pages of promotional literature through the country press as well as the Richmond dailies. Preachers were induced to deliver educational sermons during the month, and over 300 School Improvement Leagues were organized to sponsor the rallies.[58] The Richmond *Times-Dispatch*, which considered itself a state newspaper, gave almost daily news coverage to the school rallies.[59]

The politicians who began to campaign for the Democratic primary at the same time found their audiences deserted if an educational rally were near by. As Eggleston, then a candidate for state superintendent, later recalled:

Some of the politicians rather resented the idea of their campaign being interfered with, and coolly stated that the people of Virginia would take no interest in a campaign for public education, when so much stirred up over the political campaign. But the politicians did not know the real heart-hunger of the people for better schools. . . . In a week after our campaign started, the people were flocking to our meetings, and neglecting the political meetings. . . . They now became fervid in behalf of schools. I think that most of them believed that the interest would soon die down and that things would settle back in the old rut.[60]

Even Senator Martin met the educational campaigners about halfway. He was reported as saying on May 9 at West Appomattox that "nine months was too long, but five months was too

---

57. Richmond *Times-Dispatch*, May 16, 1905.

58. Frazer, annual report to the Southern Education Board, December 12, 1905, in Albert P. Bourland Papers, S.H.C., University of North Carolina; Bruce R. Payne, "Report from Virginia," in *Ninth Conference for Education in the South, Proceedings* (Lexington, Kentucky, 1906), pp. 34-36; Samuel C. Mitchell, "The Task of the Neighborhood," in *Tenth Conference for Education in the South, Proceedings* (Pinehurst, North Carolina, 1907), pp. 12-13; Mary C. B. Munford, "Report upon Women's Educational Work in Virginia," in *Ninth Conference for Education in the South, Proceedings*, pp. 40-41.

59. Richmond *Times-Dispatch*, news articles on May 9, 10, 11, 12, 13, 16, 20, 26, 27, editorials on April 29, May 14, 23, 24, 25, June 1, 1905.

60. Eggleston, memorandum in letter to Dabney, October 17, 1933, quoted in Dabney, *Universal Education in the South*, II, 327.

short. Get a boy to the common schools, to church and to public speaking and to reading his county papers, and he will be an educated man at thirty-five years or a fool."[61]

By mid-May, the politicians were proving a "drawback" to the May Campaign in another sense. They crowded the stands at educational rallies and insisted on speaking to the crowds when the educators had finished with them. The editor of the Richmond *Times-Dispatch* complained that the politicians diverted the attention of the audiences, and requested politely: "Let us have a genuine campaign for education, 'unmixed with baser matter.' "[62]

In the primary which followed the May Campaign, an aroused public forced candidates for the legislature to take the pledge, in a manner reminiscent of the recent anti-saloon campaign. Claude A. Swanson, the new governor, was thoroughly committed to better schools. But he was also a swashbuckling lieutenant of the Martin machine; there was resentment in his ranks at the way educational gadflies had pinned them to a platform. President Alderman reported to the Southern Education Board that the new administration was "not wholly sympathetic" and that, although Swanson's men intended to improve the school system, they knew that a certain capital could be made by claiming that it was being done solely by local forces. He explained:

The unfortunate fact [is] that the whole situation has gotten involved with the political contests of Senator Martin and Ex-Governor Montague. The present regime [is] perfectly aware that much of the intense educational enthusiasm was due to the work of this [Cooperative Education] Association, backed by this Board and fostered and encouraged by Montague. Their idea is that they will excel Montague and his regime in devotion to the work proper, but they will not do it in the same way and in a way that makes a certain appeal to one of the rooted characteristics of our people, namely, local pride.[63]

Faced by machine hostility and local pride, Ogden called a retreat but claimed the real battle had been won. He informed his colleagues:

61. Richmond *Times-Dispatch*, May 10, 1905.
62. *Ibid.*, editorial, May 14, 1905.
63. Alderman, report to the Southern Education Board, undated, between November 22 and December 3, 1906, Southern Education Board Box 2, files of the president, University of Virginia. See also Alderman to Page, December 27, 1907, Page Papers, Harvard University.

I think that Virginia is at present a sort of storm centre. The powers that have come into control of the State are entirely under the domination of Senator Martin, who is an absolute machine State boss. It has been made public that many of us in the Board were personal sympathizers with Governor Montague in his contest for the Senate, and it is now thrown back upon the Board that it has been in politics as the friend of Governor Montague. This is, of course, unreasonable. It, however, has the foundation in fact that we were personally friendly to Montague. We could not have been otherwise; he was so much more than a politician in his cooperation with the work of the Board.[64]

With "a certain amount of odium now attached to the Board," Ogden decided that "it would be better to retire from the ordinary popular publicity for a single year." The Virginia campaigners, however, thought that in order to consolidate their gains they must continue the May Campaign, "merely dropping the designation 'May.'" The campaigners and educators held a new series of rallies and organized a central office with a full-time secretary. Though dizzy with success, they realized that propaganda must continue as long as some people were "more interested in a coal mine than in an immortal mind."[65]

"During the recent primaries and election we all pledged ourselves for better schools," Governor Swanson reminded the legislators of 1906. "I, for one, am prepared to approve substantial appropriations for the fulfillment of this promise."[66] During the first week of the session five times as many bills on education were introduced as on any other subject. Fifty-two bills and half of the debate touched childhood at some angle. "This means," said Alderman, "that States are beginning to understand the A, B, C of the causes of their greatness." The Richmond *Times-Dispatch* began a Sunday educational supplement. The school men held a big rally near the capitol. Alderman pleaded so eloquently for more money for his university that the joint committee on educa-

64. Ogden to Murphy, January 4, 1907, Ogden Papers, Library of Congress—University of North Carolina. Similar letters went to other Board members, and the Board pulled in its horns in all of the Southern states about this time.

65. Frazer, annual report to the Southern Education Board, December 12, 1905, Bourland Papers, S.H.C., University of North Carolina; Lynchburg *News*, November 30, December 1, 2, 1905, clippings in Dickerman clipping books, S.H.C., University of North Carolina.

66. Richmond *Times-Dispatch*, February 2, 1906.

tion rattled the window-frames with applause, in "an outburst of rare and genuine enthusiasm uncommon in matter-of-fact legislative halls."[67]

Probably more was done for public schools in this session than in the previous decade. The appropriation to common schools was doubled. Bonds were authorized for schoolhouses, and the old Literary Fund became a schoolhouse loan fund at 4 per cent interest. The Mann High School Act, drafted by Bruce R. Payne and sponsored by a future governor, "brought into active being the dream of Jefferson, by creating a State system of high schools." It appropriated $50,000 to public high schools as "an infant industry."[68] Increasing state aid to the university for the first time in twenty-six years, the legislature went, in Alderman's words, "a long way toward putting the University of Virginia for this Century where it was for the middle Nineteenth."[69]

"The tide has turned," the Richmond *Times-Dispatch* announced. "Where there were many found to belittle or openly withstand the cause of education six years ago there are none who raise their voice against it now; but let us not be mistaken by this apparent unanimity. Like every other liberty, education may only be gained and kept by eternal vigilance...." Frazer reported with less restraint to the Board: "To one who saw conditions four years ago it is akin to the marvelous. And as for the significance of it all—who can measure that? It is the rallying cry of the Virginians to the Republic: 'We are coming.' 'We are coming.' "[70]

Bills for racial division of school funds were voted down with a public show of rectitude in 1906, while a bill serving the same purpose was unobtrusively passed. Introduced by Senator A. F.

67. *Ibid.*, January 15, 31, February 4, 1906; Alderman, "The Opportunity in Southern Education," address at the Conference for Education in the South, Lexington, Kentucky, in Richmond *Times-Dispatch*, May 13, 1906.

68. Richmond *Times-Dispatch*, May 6, 23, 1905, January 30, 31, February 4, March 12, 1906, January 9, 1908; University of Virginia *Alumni Bulletin*, New Series, V (March, 1906), 321, 359; *Virginia Journal of Education*, I (February, 1908), 23.

69. Alderman to Page, March 12, 1906, quoted in Malone, *Edwin A. Alderman*, pp. 205-06.

70. Richmond *Times-Dispatch*, editorial, April 26, 1906; Frazer to Alderman, July 23, 1906, files of the president, University of Virginia. George Foster Peabody wrote Booker T. Washington, January 19, 1907, of the new Alabama governor: "I trust that he may turn out to be as effective an instrument as the new Governor of Virginia."—Washington Papers, Library of Congress.

Virginia: The Machine and the Schools

Thomas of Lynchburg, it gave county and city school boards specific power to apportion funds among the districts according to their best judgment. There was no legal rein on discrimination against Negro schools.[71]

As the dust of the May Campaign settled and a treasury deficit loomed ahead, there was a sharp decline about 1907 in official enthusiasm for public education. "The treasury got low," Superintendent Eggleston later recalled: "A candidate for high office made an attack on the former administration, and painted a very dark picture of the actual conditions. . . . And every little political rat in the Capitol and elsewhere began to throw the blame on every one else. . . . 'Cut down the revenues for schools' is a cry that becomes bolder when it is remembered that children cannot vote!"[72] The Educational Legislature itself had altered the state tax law in 1906, "increasing the burden on the individual and small corporation and incidentally diminishing the necessity for full taxation on Railroads." The machine was driven to choose between the railroads and the schools.[73] In his campaign for the speakership of the lower house, Richard E. Byrd of the "organization" charged that the state board of education was guilty of spendthrift favoritism in the state-wide adoption of textbooks. As chairman of a well-publicized committee to investigate his own charges, Byrd brought leading educators to the witness stand and cast doubt on their cause. Unable to uncover a textbook scandal, Byrd found his scapegoat in the state librarian, who was harried out of office as Byrd went into office.[74]

Expecting a political reaction, the school forces gathered in such full strength that a legislator later remarked bitterly: "The State Board pulls the string and the teachers jump."[75] A mass

---

71. Richmond *Times-Dispatch*, January 28, 1906; Magruder, *Recent Administration in Virginia*, p. 59.

72. Eggleston to Bourland, July 12, 1911, Bourland Papers, S.H.C., University of North Carolina.

73. A. F. Thomas (legislator, Lynchburg, Virginia) to William E. Dodd, March 4, August 30, September 4, 1907, Dodd Papers, Library of Congress.

74. Richmond *Times-Dispatch*, March 1, 7, 8, 11, 1906, January 11, February 5, 7, 10, 15, March 11, 12, 13, 15, 16, April 9, June 30, July 4, 7, 21, November 10, 1907.

75. Representative Love, in Richmond *Times-Dispatch*, February 17, 1910. But cf. Eggleston to Bourland, July 12, 1911, Bourland Papers, S.H.C., University of North Carolina.

rally of school men packed the auditorium of the Jefferson Hotel. All during the session of 1908, but particularly in the closing days, the capitol corridors were crowded with school men and other lobbyists who desired "that their interests shall not suffer in the general shake-up, when the [general appropriation] bill has its final handling in the joint Committee of Conference."[76]

In 1908 the triumph of the school lobby was complete. Forty of their forty-three bills were passed. There was strong pressure to divert school funds to other state functions, but the school men pointed out that for years the state had been giving the schools, by rule of thumb, two-sevenths of the gross revenue and that this would call for an increase of $143,000 to education. The legislature "took no chances, but at once devoted $145,000.00 to the augmentation of the high and common school appropriations." Other reforms included $15,000 for rural high schools, $5,000 for rural school libraries, and a uniform textbook list. On the act establishing minimum salaries for division superintendents, it is true, the legislature neglected to appropriate the money.[77]

Prospects for further educational reform reached a new ebb in 1909, when the "organization" made a clean sweep of offices without any commitments to the school men. Henry St. George Tucker lost in the race for governor to William Hodges Mann of black Nottoway County, a former railway attorney backed by the machine. Swanson, the heir apparent, moved to the senate beside Martin. The alliance of the machine with the educational campaigners, never more than a marriage of convenience, was dissolved.[78]

"I am not an educator," said Governor Mann, "but passing along the roads in the country and the streets in the cities it seems to me that the children going to school have too many books." His only educational recommendation, which carried no appropriation, was that "it would be better not to tax the children with so

76. *Virginia Journal of Education*, II (November, 1908), 25; Richmond *Times-Dispatch*, January 18, February 25, 1908.
77. R. C. Stearnes, "Recent School Legislation," in *Virginia Journal of Education*, I (May, 1908), 1-6; Joseph D. Eggleston, "Appointment of Division Superintendents under the New Law—a Plea for Co-operation," in *ibid.*, II (February, 1909), 9-10; Richmond *Times-Dispatch*, January 3, 10, 11, March 10, 13, 1908.
78. Richmond *Times-Dispatch*, March 29, July 21, 1907, September 21, 1909.

many studies, which, after all, cause confusion and result in a smattering of many things and a clear understanding of nothing, but to teach them in a few branches thoroughly."[79] The change of climate was indicated by the education section being replaced by a comic sheet in the Richmond *Times-Dispatch* after James C. Hemphill of the Charleston *News and Courier* replaced W. Scott Copeland as editor.

One delegate compared the state superintendent with the Czar of Russia, while another swore that the board of education was "a greater menace to the State than negro rule ever was."[80] As Superintendent Eggleston later described the situation: "The terrific political fight made on me on the school progress in the assembly of 1910 took every ounce of strength I had. Since then the fight has continued; and it is a fight of ignorance in partnership with political knavery—a determination on the part of the 'little Englander' and the ringster to get possession of the schools."[81]

The objective of the machine legislators became clear during the last week of the session. "Subtraction, not addition," was the keynote of the general appropriation bills reported by the finance committees of both houses. Senator George B. Keezell announced that the treasury was empty and that all appropriations must be cut. The newly established Corporation Commission had assessed steam and electric railways at only one-fifth of their capitalization. The appropriation bill, he said, "will not permit increases, as the boat is loaded to the water's edge."[82] Part of the jetsam that lightened the ship of state came from the school fund.[83]

To panic the school lobby in 1912 and 1914, legislators threatened to investigate the exclusive contract with the Virginia School Furniture Company, the "architect monopoly," textbook policy, and the teachers' pension system. Increases for public schools were retracted in the final shuffle of each session, and schools were

79. *Ibid.*, February 2, 1910.
80. *Ibid.*, January 12, 28, February 9, 16, 1910.
81. *Ibid.*, February 9, 1910; Eggleston to Bourland, July 12, 1911, Bourland Papers, S.H.C., University of North Carolina.
82. Richmond *Times-Dispatch*, March 9, 11, 1910.
83. *Ibid.*, March 11, 12, 1910. The loss, at first estimated as high as $100,000, amounted in the end to about $12,000. *Virginia School Report, 1909-11*, p. 13.

"given the language but not the money," as a legislator remarked.[84] The state's political leaders could not halt the growth of the school fund, as property values and assessments rose, but kept its portion of the state revenues fixed roughly at two-sevenths.[85] A great increase might come through equalization of property assessment throughout the state, but county treasurers who headed the courthouse rings camped at the capital every session and prevented action.[86]

Despite the mounting resistance of the political machine, there was tremendous increase in the decade and a half after 1900, in expenditure and physical plant. The form of the Virginia reports was such as to obscure many important details, particularly those relating to Negro schools, but the available figures indicate general growth (Table 5).[87]

In the fifteen years after 1900, total school revenue was over 50 per cent greater than in the preceding thirty years. School revenues, by fifteen-year periods, were:[88]

1871-1885	$15,398,881.29
1886-1900	$26,002,566.13
1901-1915	$60,287,934.08

School revenue tripled in the decade following the May Campaign, and many of the other planks of its eight-point platform either were achieved or showed promise of realization: (1) Industrial education, "the cry of the periodicals and the captains of industry," was represented, for whites, by ten county agricultural schools.[89]

84. Richmond *Times-Dispatch*, January 11, 14, February 9, 10, 21, 25, March 7, 9, 1912; *Virginia School Report, 1912-13*, p. 32.

85. See campaign speech by William Hodges Mann in Richmond *Times-Dispatch*, September 21, 1909. If higher education be included, the schools represented 35.4 per cent of the total state disbursements in 1914-15. *Annual Report of the Auditor of Public Accounts, Fiscal Year Ending September 30, 1915* (Richmond, 1916), pp. 5, 11-12.

86. See Richmond *Times-Dispatch*, February 11, 14, 1906, February 17, December 19, 1907, January 27, 28, 30, 31, February 5, March 13, 1910, January 12, March 2, 3, 4, 6, 1912; *Virginia School Report, 1905-07*, p. 24; Magruder, *Recent Administration in Virginia*, pp. 169-70, 176-77. Magruder estimated that the small landowner was paying in proportion to his ability six or seven times as much as wealthy corporate and individual owners of property.

87. *Virginia School Reports, 1899-1901*, pp. xiii-xv, xxi, 9, 27, 35, 37, 164, 169, 177; *1903-05*, p. xxvi; *1905-07*, p. 21; *1909-11*, pp. 13, 30; *1914-15*, pp. 64, 74, 76-79.

88. Computed from figures in *Virginia School Report, 1914-15*, p. 79.

89. Richmond *Times-Dispatch*, March 7, 1908.

TABLE 5
EXPANSION OF EDUCATION IN VIRGINIA, 1900-1915

	1899-1900	1904-1905	1909-1910	1914-1915
Total Revenue of Public Schools	$2,012,734.78	$2,432,102.45	$4,537,676.59	$7,215,602.57
Expenditure for Higher Education	$143,500.00	$353,250.00	$523,017.50	$851,657.50
Value of School Property	$3,536,293.14	$4,297,625.96	$8,555,343.60	$15,206,721.12
Average Salary of Men Teachers (monthly)	$32.47	$36.86	$51.42	$64.71
Average Salary of Women Teachers (monthly)	$26.18	$28.11	$38.39	$43.26
Average Length of Term (months)	6.0	6.4	6.56	7.10
Cost per Month per Child in Attendance	$1.37	$1.51	$2.67	$3.09
Number of Pupils Attending Daily	216,464	215,205	259,394	317,141

(2) The ten high schools and hundred "so-called high schools" had grown by 1915 to 572, of which 196 had a four-year curriculum. High schools enrolled 23,184 whites and 1,761 Negroes (mostly in Richmond), or thirteen whites for each Negro, though their proportions of the school population were only two to one.[90] (3) Improved teacher training was provided for whites by five normal schools and a plethora of summer schools, while Negroes had two normal schools and six summer schools.[91] (4) Consolidation was almost entirely for whites, and (5) public transportation of pupils exclusively so. Almost one-half of the rural white pupils, and one-tenth of rural Negro pupils, attended schools of three or more rooms.[92] (6) School libraries contained 317,867 volumes in 1915, of which 262,099 were rural. Presumably they were almost entirely in white schools.[93] (7) The "efficient and ramified organi-

90. Bruce R. Payne, "A Cursory View of High School Conditions in Virginia, September 15, 1906," MS enclosed in Payne to Alderman, October 18, 1906, files of the president, University of Virginia; Magruder, *Recent Administration in Virginia*, pp. 38-40; *Virginia School Report, 1914-15*, pp. 42-45, 308.

91. *Ibid.*, pp. 12-14; Richmond *Times-Dispatch*, February 16, 18, March 11, 1914; Richard L. Morton, *History of Virginia* (6 vols., Chicago, 1924), III, 273-75.

92. *Virginia School Report, 1914-15*, pp. 314, 445.

93. *Ibid.*, p. 422.

zation" called forth by the May Campaign was by 1915, for whites only, "like a great army well organized, well officered, full of confidence and enthusiasm, an army, indeed, which is advancing every hour of the day." The white teachers' association was flanked by 30,640 laymen of the Co-operative Education Association.[94] (8) The nine-month term for every child was still over the horizon in 1915. The city term was eight and one-half months, the rural white term seven months, the rural Negro term less than six months. Even in length of term, the Negro rural school had stood still as white progress streamed by.[95]

Educational progress in Virginia, though considerable, at least so far as white schools were concerned, did not equal that in other Southern seaboard states. Nor was it equal to New Jersey, the state in the North Atlantic division nearest to it in population. New Jersey had undergone no May Campaign but had nearly three times as much wealth, much of it locally owned. Virginia school expenditures tripled, while those of New Jersey nearly doubled, but in 1915 New Jersey spent over twice as much per capita for public schools and nearly four times as much for higher education. Table 6 compares expenditures of the two states:[96]

TABLE 6

TAXABLE PROPERTY AND EXPENDITURES, VIRGINIA AND NEW JERSEY, 1900-1915

Item	Virginia	New Jersey
True valuation of all property, 1900........	$1,102,309,696.00	$2,733,593,134.00
Expenditure for public education, 1899-1900.	2,012,734.78	11,721,266.63
Expenditure for public schools, 1914-15.....	7,047,713.71	17,158,750.58
Expenditure, including higher education, 1914-1915............................	7,899,371.21	28,102,610.37

The Southern educational campaigners were realistic enough to know the disadvantages, financial, political, and social, under which they labored. But as Alderman said at the beginning of the

94. *Ibid.*, pp. 26, 137.
95. *Ibid.*, p. 275.
96. United States Bureau of the Census, *Statistical Abstract of the United States, 1910* (Washington, 1911), pp. 590-91; *Virginia School Reports, 1899-1901*, p. xxiv; *1914-15*, pp. 66, 74; New Jersey, *Annual Reports of the Board of Education, 1900*, pp. 39, 43; *1915*, p. 107.

May Campaign, "Progress is measured by the distance travelled as well as by the point reached."[97] What, then, had been the distance travelled? Ignoring for the moment the geographic and ethnic differences, it will be recalled that school revenue increased three-fold from 1900 to 1915. This gain came almost entirely from county and district taxation, while the machine legislature kept the state school tax at one mill, the minimum allowed by the constitution.[98] Campaigners might rally at the crossroads without much organized opposition from the Martin machine, but it refused to be a party to educational taxation at the state level. One reason that local taxation grew while state taxation remained fixed was that a strict construction of the state constitution would require whites to share equally with Negro children the funds from the state, whereas there was not even a theoretical check on racial discrimination in the use of local tax funds. But this racial factor was only part of the story. The machine used the racial argument in braking the urge to increase state taxation and thus scattering the efforts of school men over the whole state.

"We are like a great army," Superintendent R. C. Stearnes told white educators, "but we know we are short in 'high explosives,' if I may be pardoned for adopting and adapting the thought contained in the old saying: 'It's money that makes the mare go.' We want to remedy this defect before the enemy finds it out and we now have little fear that the taxpayers will give vent to much of that other kind of high explosive which used to feature their conversation when they were asked for an increase of school rates." If one pardons an old educational warhorse such a mixture of metaphors, here was an interesting insight into the educational movement. The "high explosive" of taxpayers had been hurled against "white men's taxes for negro schools," and such arguments seemed to be losing their force as the federal courts ignored open evidence of racial discrimination.[99]

So completely did the Virginia school reports disguise financial discrimination against Negroes that an ingenuous reader might find hardly a hint of it. In the financial tables, only teachers' salaries

97. Norfolk *Virginian-Pilot*, December 7, 1904.
98. *Virginia School Report*, 1914-15, pp. 30, 213.
99. *Ibid.*, p. 26.

were reported separately by race, and these only by county, not by the districts in which the money was apportioned. Possibly a vague fear of court action against the racially discriminating officer dictated this practice. On the one count of teachers' salaries, Virginia expended $2.45 per Negro child of school age and $9.60, four times as much, per white child.[100]

There were many non-financial indices of the status of the Negro schools. Negroes were more than half as numerous as whites, representing 35.3 per cent of the school population in the state, and approximately the same proportion in the county and city systems, 35.3 per cent and 35.5 per cent respectively. Keeping these proportions in mind, one finds that Negroes had 27.5 per cent of the enrollment in counties and 28.4 per cent in cities; 26.0 per cent of the average daily attendance in counties and 27.5 per cent in cities. Negro schools in the counties had 21.4 per cent of the schoolrooms, 21.3 per cent of the number of teachers, and 23.3 per cent of the classroom seating capacity; and in the cities 24.7 per cent of the schoolrooms, 21.4 per cent of the number of teachers, and 26.4 per cent of the seating capacity. Whereas white schools had seats for over 95 per cent of the whites of school age, there were seats for barely half of the Negro children. Negroes had 1.9 per cent of the high schools and 7.1 per cent of the high school pupils. Of the ten state-aided colleges and other institutions of higher education, the one Negro school received 4.9 per cent of the state aid. On only two counts were Negro schools more blessed. In the city schools, but not in county schools, Negro children received barely more than their proportionate share of the free textbooks for indigent pupils. In the county schools, but not in the city schools, a larger proportion of Negro teachers were graduates of the state-affiliated higher schools.[101]

Discrimination against Negro children, as in other states, promoted discrimination between white schools. Black counties re-

---

100. The amounts were $533,193.45 for 217,760 Negro children, and $3,621,595.12 for 398,408 white children. There was little difference in rate between cities and counties. In the county systems, Negroes were 35.3 per cent of the school population and received 12.2 per cent of the expenditures for teachers' salaries; in the city systems, 35.5 per cent of the school population and 14.2 per cent of the salaries. *Ibid.*, pp. 275, 311.

101. Computed from *ibid.*, pp. 275, 308, 311, 362, 402, 442, 445, 486, 522, 542, 544-45, 551, 558, 570, 574, 579, 596, 606, 618.

ceived from the per capita state fund a considerable amount, on account of Negro children, which was spent on white children and gave them an advantage over those of white counties. This is easily demonstrated. In 1915 there were seven counties in Virginia in which Negroes were over two-thirds of the school population. These counties received from the state $68,449.23, and their total revenue was $189,751.17. Table 7 indicates a discrimination of nearly nine to one in favor of whites in the matter of teachers' salaries, over twice as great as in the state as a whole.[102]

TABLE 7

RACIAL DISCRIMINATION IN TEACHERS' SALARIES IN VIRGINIA BLACK COUNTIES, 1915

County	School Population White	School Population Negro	Salary Expenditures White	Salary Expenditures Negro	Amount per Child White	Amount per Child Negro	Discrimination Rate
Amelia	1,055	2,536	$12,264.62	$2,385.00	$11.63	$.94	12.37
Charles City	337	1,238	4,948.83	3,023.94	14.69	2.44	6.02
Cumberland	912	2,203	12,298.43	3,391.07	13.49	1.54	8.76
Powhatan	723	1,647	5,466.50	2,956.80	7.56	1.80	4.20
Surry	959	1,969	14,515.72	3,023.61	15.14	1.54	9.83
Sussex	1,337	2,689	23,313.85	4,028.25	17.44	1.50	11.63
Warwick	517	1,180	5,807.76	2,043.49	11.23	1.73	6.49
Total	5,840	13,462	$78,615.71	$20,852.16	$13.46	$1.55	8.68

For every dollar spent on instruction of a Negro child in Amelia County, $12.37 went to the schooling of a white child. Educational discrimination against Negroes was greatest in counties with greatest numbers of Negroes. The legend of paternalism was itself exploited to gloss over this practice of the black counties and to take funds from other whites.

Something may be gleaned from the state reports by comparing the black county of Prince Edward, home of Superintendent Eggleston, with mountain white Bland County full of "hillbilly" Republicans, and with the city of Richmond with its valuable property and its average proportion of Negroes. It should be kept in mind that for most children in Bland County the figures are nearly typical of all children, while in Prince Edward and Rich-

102. *Ibid.*, pp. 194-213, 256-75, 309-11.

168   *Separate and Unequal*

mond the statistics represent a middle point between disparate figures for Negroes and whites. The record indicates that schools were improved even in penurious Bland County, and that the growth was most rapid in the city. Richmond was far wealthier, with $875.34 true value per capita of real property and improvements in 1900, as compared with $409.64 in Bland County and $184.62 in Prince Edward. Negroes were 70.9 per cent of the school population in Prince Edward County, 37.1 per cent in Richmond, and 4.1 per cent in Bland County (Table 8).[103]

TABLE 8

EDUCATION IN A BLACK COUNTY, A WHITE COUNTY, AND A CITY IN VIRGINIA

	Prince Edward County	Bland County	Richmond
School Year 1899-1900			
Length of term, months	6.35	3.75	9.05
Percentage of whites of school age in average daily attendance	35.92	43.94	37.41
Percentage of Negroes of school age in average daily attendance	25.02	15.91	40.69
Expenditure per child of school age	$3.06	$2.44	$6.57
Value of school property per child of school age	$2.31	$4.20	$17.74
Monthly salary of men teachers	$28.17	$22.63	$119.37
Monthly salary of women teachers	$22.98	$20.81	$49.60
Number of volumes in school libraries	none	none	1,200
School Year 1914-1915			
Length of term, months, white	7.70	6.15	7.80
Length of term, months, Negro	6.05	6.00	7.80
Percentage of whites of school age in average daily attendance	52.28	52.24	78.03
Percentage of Negroes of school age in average daily attendance	33.21	60.78	63.15
Expenditure per child of school age	$10.10	$7.81	$30.38
Value of school property per child of school age	$11.25	$8.44	$89.07
Monthly salary of white teachers	$59.86	$37.03	$91.10
Monthly salary of Negro teachers	$27.52	$34.07	$58.90
Number of volumes in school libraries	7,462	1,400	17,000

If the Virginia machine, like those of Eastern cities, had been based upon the corrupted vote of the masses, it might have been

103. *Virginia School Report, 1899-1901*, pp. xiii, 104-10, 114-17, 122, 124, 260, 262; United States Census Office, *Wealth, Debt, and Taxation*, Part I, Table 19, pp. 82-83; *Virginia School Report, 1914-15*, pp. 217, 233, 239, 258, 269, 275, 309-11, 340, 353, 359, 405, 417, 422.

more amenable to demands for adequate education. Instead, its bulwarks were corporations and other large taxpayers; its acts were subject to review by a narrow electorate; its watchword was economy in governmental services; and its cry, when provoked, was White Supremacy. When educational funds were demanded, Virginia taxpayers protested that they would be used to educate Negroes. When appropriations were made, however, economy was provided for the taxpayer by racial discrimination.

CHAPTER VI

South Carolina: Inequality as a Higher Law

"Is it too much to hope," asked John E. Swearingen, South Carolina superintendent of education, in 1915, "for a minimum of $25 per white child and $5 per negro child?"[1] It is not that other Southern states were vastly less discriminatory against Negroes, only somewhat less so and less frank about it. But the candor with which South Carolinians discussed their practice of civil inequality does suggest that their attitude was different in kind, and not merely in emphasis, from that of other Southerners. What people believe in is an important part of what they are. The white majority in South Carolina, with some exceptions, ignored the democratic principles which troubled the sleep of some other Southerners who discriminated against Negroes. The educational movement in that state, therefore, was exclusively and openly in white interest, and the main issues were which whites should be aided and how.

The state system of schools stemmed from the Reconstruction constitution of 1868 and the school act of 1870,[2] but much of its

1. *South Carolina School Report*, *1915*, p. 19. In fact this was too much to expect in 1915. The average expenditure that year was $16.22 for each white child enrolled, and $1.93 for each Negro child enrolled, a discrimination amounting to 8.4 to 1. The ratio was even more disproportionate on the basis of population of school age. According to the federal commissioner's estimate of population five to eighteen years of age, the amount for each white child was $13.98, for each Negro child $1.13, a discrimination of 12.37 to 1. *Ibid.*, pp. 20, 215-18; United States Bureau of Education, *Report of the Commissioner of Education*, *1917*, II, 17.

2. John F. Thomason, *The Foundations of the Public Schools of South Carolina* (Columbia, 1925), and Henry T. Thompson, *The Establishment of the*

élan vital evaporated under Wade Hampton and his conservative successors.³ Ten towns with graded school systems and thirty-four local tax districts were the restricted areas of educational progress in the eighties.

The public school movement in South Carolina, just as in North Carolina, began in the agrarian nineties with Ben Tillman's constitution of 1895. Never quite a Populist, Tillman was the leader of the up-country faction called Reformers which controlled the state all through the nineties. The primary purpose of the constitutional convention of 1895 was disfranchisement of Negroes. And efforts were also made to strengthen counties at the expense of the state government, for fear the Conservatives would regain control of the state. County home rule in education, however, meant a weak state school system.

The pre-convention campaign revealed considerable disagreement among Tillmanites on the subject of education. State Superintendent W. D. Mayfield proposed a one-mill state property tax to be spent in counties low in taxable wealth. On the other hand, Tillman's protégé John Gary Evans, state governor and chairman of the convention, had campaigned since 1894 to remove even the two-mill tax provision from the constitution.⁴ Evans complained of the education of Negroes, and suggested a clause merely stating "that a public school system should be provided for by the Legislature and liberally supported, with the right given to the taxpayer to direct to which school his tax should be given." This would

---

Public School System of South Carolina (Columbia, 1927), are the state histories of education for the early years. Works useful on the Reconstruction period include Luther P. Jackson, "The Educational Efforts of the Freedmen's Bureau and the Freedmen's Aid Societies in South Carolina, 1862-1872," in *Journal of Negro History*, VIII (January, 1923), 1-40; Francis B. Simkins and Robert H. Woody, *South Carolina during Reconstruction* (Chapel Hill, 1932), pp. 100, 416-43; Edgar W. Knight, "Reconstruction and Education in South Carolina," in *South Atlantic Quarterly*, XVIII (October, 1919), 350-64, XIX (January, 1920), 55-71; Mayo, "The Final Establishment of the American Common School System in North Carolina, South Carolina, and Georgia, 1863-1900," *Report of the Commissioner of Education for the Year Ending June 30, 1904*, I, 1023-34.

3. Tindall, *South Carolina Negroes, 1877-1900*, pp. 209-14, argues plausibly that Hampton, at least, provided equal school facilities for both races. But Tindall's figures from the state school reports are enrollment figures, rather than those for population of school age. And ten years after the end of Reconstruction, the total school fund exceeded that of the peak Reconstruction year by only $3,000.

4. *Ibid.*, p. 221.

mean, of course, that white property-owners would designate white schools as recipients of their taxes. During the campaign for election of convention delegates, Evans explained that this, along with the educational qualification for suffrage, would certainly exclude Negroes from the ballot box. He aroused the fear that "if our enemy gained control of the Government they could stop every white child to-morrow and devote the entire fund to the education of the negro."[5]

Tillman answered Evans three days later on the issue of constitutional provision for school taxation, though ignoring the race issue involved. In his native Edgefield he spoke frankly to his "wool hats":

If we take the two mill tax out of the Constitution and leave it to the Legislature to make the appropriation there is great danger. When there is a general depression and 4 cents cotton there will be a clamor for lower taxes, and the schools are likely to suffer. The provision will protect you against yourselves and your clamor for lower taxes. If you could get Legislators who would pay no attention to such clamors it would be different.[6]

In the education committee of the convention, Conservatives joined with townsmen from Tillman territory to outvote the delegates of the small farmers. A Charleston lawyer, two Columbia lawyers, and five county seat lawyers—men from the towns with graded schools—stood against two farmers and a country preacher, and the chairman was Charleston lawyer Julian Mitchell, a banker, husband of a Pinckney, and member of the Charleston school board.[7]

Mitchell's majority report to the convention recommended a three-mill school tax to be collected and disbursed within the county, a poll tax to be expended within the district, and the profits of the state liquor dispensary. This extreme localization of expenditure would favor the wealthy counties and districts, but for

---

5. Address at Tirzah, South Carolina, July 25, 1895, in Charleston *News and Courier*, July 29, 1895; *Journal of the* [South Carolina] *Constitutional Convention of . . . 1895* (Columbia, 1895), p. 12.

6. Charleston *News and Courier*, July 29, 1895. See also Tindall, *South Carolina Negroes, 1877-1900*, p. 222.

7. Charleston *News and Courier*, September 12, 1895; *Journal of the Constitutional Convention of 1895*, pp. 305-10, 735-41; Yates Snowden (ed.), *History of South Carolina* (5 vols., Chicago, 1920), V, 76.

the next three years a state tax would be levied for deficient counties whenever any county should fall below a fund of $3 per child enrolled. After three years, this state tax was to be levied only to keep all schools open for a minimum time to be prescribed by the legislature. Such a school system would protect the property of cities from taxation for rural schools and conform to the farmers' unenlightened spirit of independence.[8]

Chairman Mitchell explained on the floor that, though he had favored distribution of school funds on the basis of average daily attendance rather than enrollment, which would favor cities with paved streets and compact population, he had gracefully given way in the committee. A minority report by E. J. Kennedy, a Chesterfield County farmer, however, demanded state aid on an enrollment basis. "You have half a dozen millionaires there who can pay the additional tax and not feel it," he said to the Charlestonian. "The News and Courier shows Charleston's banks have millions on deposit. Chesterfield, though in need of an education, has a large white population." The up-country whites, who helped to control the Negro majority, asked in return state aid to rural schools through state-wide taxation. "It is essentially communistic," a Winnsboro lawyer hastily interposed. Mitchell flew to Charleston's defense with a zeal that thrilled the *News and Courier*. "Those who think Charleston is a fat goose will be mistaken when they go to pluck the goose," he warned. "Charleston is impoverished" and "there are expenses not incurred in other places." Perhaps he referred to the brick buildings and patent desks. "But this political rancor permeates the State until we begin to have an up-country and low-country. The people are liable to forget we are one."[9]

The convention agreed to make the county the unit in distributing school funds. Definition of the term "enrollment" was left to the legislature.

Tillman took an active interest in the education clause. He managed to get a provision that school districts might not be larger than thirty-six square miles. Though many children would have to walk four miles under such an arrangement, Tillman had to

8. *Journal of the Constitutional Convention of 1895*, pp. 308-10.
9. *Ibid.*, pp. 305-07; Charleston *News and Courier*, November 14, 1895.

argue against proposals for larger districts. He battered down all protests against the three-mill tax and the supplementary state tax for weak counties. "We want no wet weather schools," he replied to one landlord, "but all schools to run for five months."[10] Tillman's constitution provided a poll tax, three-mill county tax, dispensary profits, and a potential state tax for public schools, but wealthy districts could levy local taxes without special legislation, and loopholes in the wording would allow circumvention.[11]

A general school bill passed in 1896 put into effect the provisions of the new constitution. Rural legislators saw to it that enrollment was so defined as to include all children who attended ten days. Efforts to divide the school funds so as to give Negro schools only the pittance of Negro taxes were unsuccessful. But Negro trustees were excluded from school administration, even in the rice sections of Beaufort and Georgetown where some districts had scarcely three white men to serve as trustees, by the legislature selecting the county board of education, which in turn appointed the district trustees. A Negro superintendent, elected rather than appointed, served in Georgetown County as late as 1899, but was flanked by two whites on the county board.[12]

10. In the fight over the school tax, a disabled Confederate veteran helped Tillman carry the day. Robert B. Watson, an Edgefield peach grower, recalled a dying comrade on a Virginia battlefield whose children were now illiterate. "Public education is the cheapest of all systems," he insisted. "We are only asking for three mills." South Carolina was paying less than any other state for education; Kansas, a sod-hut frontier when his friend had died, was now paying $18 per school child. Charleston *News and Courier*, November 14, 15, 1895; *Journal of the Constitutional Convention of 1895*, pp. 362, 547-50; Snowden, *History of South Carolina*, III, 231-32. Though present on that day, Tillman did not vote on an amendment by E. J. Kennedy to make the three-mill tax a state tax.

11. Reports and votes on educational provisions are in the *Journal of the Constitutional Convention of 1895*, pp. 305-10, 554-69, 572-84, 603, 677-85; debates in Charleston *News and Courier*, September 21, 24, October 3, November 14-16, 20, 26, 1895. In David D. Wallace, "The South Carolina Constitutional Convention of 1895," in *Sewanee Review*, IV (May, 1896), 356-57, is a succinct summary of the educational clause. The new constitution did not bring about automatic progress. As soon as it increased the county tax by one mill, the city of Columbia reduced its local tax from three mills to two mills, and refused to raise it again for over a decade. Burney L. Parkinson, *A History of the Administration of the City Public Schools of Columbia, South Carolina, Bulletin* of the University of South Carolina, No. 155 (Columbia, January 15, 1925), p. 65.

12. Charleston *News and Courier*, January 15, February 1, 28, 29, March 3, 5, 7, 1896; *South Carolina School Report, 1899*, p. 113. John J. McMahan, letter to the editor, in Columbia *State*, February 2, 1914, is a candid account of the effect of the constitution of 1895 on the South Carolina schools by a man well

District school trustees were empowered by the constitution of 1895 to disburse their share of the county three-mill tax "as the general assembly may prescribe." The assembly in 1896 prescribed that the funds of each district be "distributed and expended by the board of trustees, for the best interests of the school district, according to the judgment of the board of trustees." These mild words gave considerable latitude to district trustees, and the "judgment" of the white trustees of black counties—those with Negro majorities—was not color-blind. Acting "for the best interests of the school district," they gave the white schools a large and increasing proportion of the district's share of the county school fund. The same "judgment" prompted them to use their Negro numbers to get for their district a large and increasing proportion of the school fund of the county. The towns made meager enough provisions for Negro education, but in the countryside the salaries of Negro teachers were little more than bribes. One frank county superintendent stated in the presence of Wallace Buttrick, "In my county the trustees find out how much taxes the colored people pay, and then give them that much education. Let us not be hypocrites about it."[13] Negro teachers were hired at $10 to $20 a month for terms usually less than three months. Sometimes they were given "an extra $5 for twenty-five pupils enrolled above a stated minimum and another $5 as a reward for a further addition of fifteen."[14]

School officials seem to have been as reluctant as election officials to go "behind the returns." It is possible that many white South Carolinians were unaware that whites in black districts were pirating away the funds of districts without Negroes. Perhaps the most frequent argument advanced for the compulsory education of

---

qualified to interpret it. A member of the education committee of the constitutional convention, he was also state superintendent from 1899 until 1903, and a member of the state house of representatives and of its education committee from 1905 until the date of the letter. His letter will be used without further citation for the next few pages.

13. Confidential report to members of the General Education Board, manuscript dated September, 1904, Southern Education Board miscellaneous papers, S.H.C., University of North Carolina.

14. This statement of McMahan's is confirmed by William K. Tate, "A Statement of the Rural School Problem in South Carolina," *Bulletin* of the University of South Carolina, No. 24, Part II (January, 1911), p. 16. Tate was the state rural school supervisor.

whites was that, as the records showed, more Negroes than whites were taking advantage of the public schools. The rotten-borough legislators from below the fall line must have snickered up their sleeves at this type of argument. "The struggle is to get a big roll of negro children," wrote John J. McMahan, "even though usually running wild in the swamps, as each head counts one unit of school funds from the county at large for that district to apply to its schools for white children." District trustees must, of course, "preserve the form" and "operate such negro schools as may be necessary to obtain the entire possible enrollment."

Even on the basis of strictly legal enrollments, black districts could show "the banner white schools of the State" within a few miles of the shacks of a white district. All white schools observed the lines of caste by a thumping superiority to the nearest Negro schools. But white district schools and Negro schools were almost equally destitute of maps, blackboards, window-panes, or patent desks. When the white schools of black districts added the sum cheated from sister districts to that taken from Negro schools "for the best interests of the district," they had as much as $50 or $60 for each white child enrolled, while the Negro schools received about $1 per capita and the schools of white districts about $5 per capita. State school officials recognized some of the inequities, while ignoring others. The state superintendent found in 1906 that "in our State the inequalities are appalling." His clinching illustration, however, was that "in one county the negro schools run twenty-six weeks. In an adjoining county the white schools run twenty-one weeks." Cherokee County, the one cited with the long Negro term, was a most unusual one; it reported only 1,000—and exactly 1,000—Negroes on its school roll. More typical counties reported Negro terms of seven, eight, and nine weeks; and the average white term of the state was ten weeks longer than the Negro term.[15] Inequality indeed!

In some counties school officials yielded to the demands of white districts and spread the Negro school funds more evenly among whites. In Georgetown County there were some districts with only fifteen white children to 500 Negro children, and in one all-Negro district where the tax collections amounted to only

15. *South Carolina School Report, 1906*, pp. 13, 185-86.

South Carolina: Inequality as a Higher Law 177

$200 there were 700 Negro children enrolled. County Superintendent Joshua W. Doar reported without reticence that the law was "impracticable" and was "not complied with." "My remedy," he explained, "is to let the County Board of Education apportion the school funds in each district as they deem proper. . . . Some may argue that partiality would be shown. There is nothing in this argument."[16]

Inequalities between counties were considerable, though not as great as those between districts. Ninety-six per cent of the school funds in 1909 came from sources within the counties, and only four per cent from the state at large. In that year each pupil in Saluda County received $1.09 from the three-mill county tax, in Horry County $1.31, in Richland County almost $10. But in Richland County, favored though it was by a high ratio of taxable property to its population and a relatively high rate of assessment, Negro schools were "taught in unceiled buildings in which one teacher has as many as 80 to 100 pupils for a short term." It was "a matter of common knowledge that the larger part of this money is spent on the white schools." The fall line passed through Richland County, and the cleavage between coastal plain and Piedmont is illustrated there in miniature. Negroes predominated in the districts of the lower section of the county, while there were large white majorities in the Sand Hills and cotton mill districts. The following will illustrate conditions in two school districts of Richland County:

	District A	District B
White pupils	63	617
Negro pupils	647	90
Total pupils	710	707
District revenue	$7,000	$7,000

After maintaining the Negro pupils in the manner to which they were accustomed, the trustees of district A had "at least six times" as much to spend on each white pupil as did district B. "We must bear in mind that the bulk of this money was not raised from either

---

16. Annual report to the department of education, in *South Carolina School Report, 1912*, p. 64.

district," commented the state superintendent who presented these facts, "but was derived from the railroad, the cotton mills, and the industrial and commercial enterprises located in the city of Columbia." The moral he drew was thrown slightly out of focus by the color line: "The white children in the Sand Hill and Cotton Mill sections of the County should receive the same advantages as the white schools in the lower part of the County. The negroes in one section should receive the same treatment as the negroes in the other section."[17]

The leading exponents of neighborhood sovereignty in school matters were the taxpayers of the cities and towns. City superintendents not only guarded the walls around the taxable property of the cities, they also denounced the "inequitable" distribution of the county three-mill tax by the "10-day plan." In the interest of "the greatest good to the greatest number," they demanded its apportionment according to the length of session, which would favor the cities and towns. County authorities did not ask, "How did you pile up your enrollment?" complained City Superintendent N. M. Salley of Greenwood, but simply, "Have you piled up your enrollment?" And if the answer was affirmative, money was forthwith apportioned. As cities turned to local taxation, district tax funds increased six-fold between 1900 and 1915, rising from 11.4 per cent to 27.5 per cent of the total school fund.[18]

"The constitutional convention made a monumental blunder when it provided that the 3-mill tax should be a county tax and not a State tax," said Superintendent Oscar B. Martin. "It tried to remedy the matter by making the dispensary fund a State school fund."[19] Tillman shocked the respectable by having the state's palmetto emblem literally blown into the whiskey bottles, but after he left for Washington the dispensary fell into real disgrace. Its managers began to divert the schools' share of the profits into further production of whiskey, until in 1902 the state superin-

17. *South Carolina School Report, 1911,* pp. 94-95.
18. N. M. Salley, "Equitable Distribution of the 3-Mill Tax," an address before the Association of Town and City Superintendents (a semi-independent branch of the state teachers' association), quoted in Columbia *State,* January 2, 1909; *South Carolina School Reports, 1900,* p. 253; *1915,* pp. 310-11.
19. Letter of Oscar B. Martin to the editor, in Columbia *State,* August 27, 1906.

tendent of education took action to recover some of the diverted funds.[20]

County option, after bitter political struggles which culminated in 1906, took the place of the state dispensary. The state school fund literally dried up for some of the poorer counties, which under the spell of the prohibition preachers were among the first to close their dispensaries. Bishop Warren A. Candler came over from Georgia to tell them that the dispensary "pours liquor down the people to come out in two streams—one negro education, the other white ignorance."[21]

It was natural for South Carolina educators, poorly supported by the political leaders, to welcome the outside leadership of the Southern Education Board. President Robert P. Pell of the Presbyterian College for Women urged Dabney to bring the state's case before the Board on the ground that "no people are more provincial, and, therefore, less in touch with the great educational movement of our country, than South Carolinians." President David B. Johnson of Winthrop College wrote in a similar vein to Peabody. "There is no State in the south which is riper ... and none which needs encouragement more. It is staggering under the burdens which an old, worn out, sandy soil, an overwhelming negro population, and an illiterate white population have imposed upon it."[22]

The Southern Education Board made no campaign in South Carolina during its first year. This was perhaps a tactical error,

20. *Ibid.; South Carolina School Report, 1900*, pp. 30-31; Atlanta *Constitution*, January 11, 1903.

21. Speech in Columbia, in Ellen H. Hendricks, "The South Carolina Dispensary System," in *North Carolina Historical Review*, XXII (July, 1945), 336, quoted from Columbia *State*, July 14, 1905. Actually the dispensary fund yielded school revenue until after 1915. For statistics on this source of revenue, see *South Carolina School Reports, 1902*, p. 320; *1903*, p. 197; *1904*, p. 208; *1905*, p. 242; *1906*, p. 188; *1907*, p. 172; *1908*, p. 180; *1909*, p. 174; *1910*, p. 230; *1911*, p. 662; *1912*, p. 228; *1913*, p. 482; *1914*, p. 218; *1915*, p. 210. Methods of accounting varied. *Ibid.*, *1911*, p. 19.

22. Pell to Dabney, December 5, 1901, Dabney Papers, S.H.C., University of North Carolina; Johnson to Peabody, February 7, 1902, enclosed in a letter to the editor under the heading "South Carolina Is Not Sleeping," in Columbia *State*, April 23, 1902. Johnson claimed in his public letter that the state was "striving to do its full duty to white and black alike in the matter of education." Untruth on that subject had become habitual.

because it gave opponents of child labor legislation, Negro education, and Northern philanthropy time to create an atmosphere of suspicion. When a full dress delegation of twenty South Carolina leaders attended the Athens Conference in 1902, John J. McMahan, the state superintendent, was disturbed to find "Southern mendicants" who had heard that money was "on tap" crowding around Wallace Buttrick of the General Education Board and edging out representatives of the country schools. "Must there always be Judases to intercept the offerings intended for the poor?" he asked. He must have known that the Judases too were poor, but he continued:

To me the Athens meeting was sublime in its sentiment, but I cannot forget my sensations of horror at the sordid public references or still more patently self-seeking private enquiries of those whose sole interest in the movement, and in the inspiring meeting, was "How can I get hold of some money?" The pleasure and uplift of it were almost destroyed when I was forced to reflect that were it still as it began a conference purely for the spirit and the truth there would not have been this large and representative attendance.[23]

It was probably fortunate that leadership in the state campaign passed to Oscar B. Martin, state superintendent in the Conservative administrations of D. Clinch Heyward and Martin F. Ansel. Martin was an energetic man of thirty-two, smooth-shaven and prematurely bald. A teacher since the age of sixteen, when he worked his way through high school by teaching in the rural elementary school from which he had recently graduated, Martin brought to his task a broad practical experience and the attitudes of a modern public administrator.[24] He welcomed the advent of educational reform.

Under Martin's leadership, the "largest body of teachers ever assembled" in South Carolina gathered at Columbia on April 11, 1903, to form the South Carolina Educational Campaign Com-

---

23. John J. McMahan to Dickerman, November 6, 1902, Ogden Papers, S.H.C., University of North Carolina. See also W. Zach McGhee to Dickerman, December 9, 22, 1903, Dickerman Papers, S.H.C., University of North Carolina.

24. Martin later became Southern supervisor of the federal farm demonstration program. Columbia *State*, January 22, 26, April 12, 1903; Oscar B. Martin to Dickerman, February 6, 1904, Dickerman Papers, S.H.C., University of North Carolina.

mittee. "Don't quarrel; don't bushwhack," advised McIver, who came down from North Carolina to the meeting. "Talk of the things upon which all are agreed" was his cardinal rule for propaganda campaigns. Farmers would take care of good roads, he pointed out, and lawyers and doctors would take care of themselves. Educational campaigners should concentrate on schools. McIver answered such critics of philanthropy as the Charleston *News and Courier* by remarking, "If a local man should bring a million dollars here to invest in a cotton mill, he would be looked upon as a benefactor." The same attitude should apply to "the man who goes north and gets a million to be put into the brains of the children."[25]

The conference published an eight-point Declaration of Principles. The educators could not reach agreement on compulsory school attendance and equalization of school funds, but they did declare it high time to redeem a pledge of universal education made by the South Carolina assembly in 1710. The Columbia *State* called on "every circuit rider, every preacher who comes in contact with the humbler and more ignorant elements" to preach an earthly salvation through public schools. County superintendents went on to Rock Hill for a three-day conference with Buttrick, David B. Johnson of Winthrop College, and Governor Heyward. "The first thing we need is money," said the governor. "We must raise it ourselves and there is but one way—taxation. There is no use to wait."[26]

Ogden and his associates made plans about this time to hold their 1905 conference at Columbia. After receiving assurances that Negro education would not be emphasized, James A. Hoyt and Editor William E. Gonzales of the *State* began a series of editorials to educate the public, with the help of the leading Baptist journal, the Spartanburg *Herald*,[27] and some weekly papers.

25. Dabney to Buttrick, May 16, 22, June 14, 1902, David B. Johnson to Dabney, July 8, 1902, Dabney Papers, S.H.C., University of North Carolina; Columbia *State*, April 12, 1903; *South Carolina School Report, 1906*, p. 26.
26. Columbia *State*, April 12, 13, 20, 1903; Charleston *News and Courier*, April 13, 1903; *South Carolina School Report, 1903*, pp. 41-55.
27. After efforts to establish "a kind of tin horn" for the "propaganda, scintillations and so forth" of the Ogden movement, Zach McGhee of the *Herald* became a political reporter for the *State*, and contributed *The Dark Corner* to the

The Board's propaganda bureau sent Charles L. Coon to enlist the rank and file of South Carolina teachers during their summer meeting at a resort hotel. As the teachers arrived, "some tired by a year's hard work, some sick, some who have just secured good positions, some who have just lost a job," Coon tried to interest them in public school reform. He was himself a Tarheel, Coon reassured them, "not a Yankee down here to sell sky to Southerners," but the "talking machine" of practical Southerners working "for southern interests, with no idea of changing southern conditions."[28]

Educational rallies began all over the state in the hot summer of 1903.[29] Martin spent his whole summer at rallies and teachers' institutes, using techniques developed earlier in North Carolina by McIver and Alderman. Others scattered their efforts over too wide a territory, Governor Heyward and other politicians shuttling back and forth between low country and Piedmont. Several Methodist professors from Wofford worked independently of other campaigners. Concentrating on Spartanburg and Greenville counties in the up-country and on Orangeburg and Florence in the low country, so as to saturate them with educational sentiment, they met crowds in country churches and camp grounds as well as country schools, and combined agitation for public schools with recruitment for their denominational colleges.[30]

The South Carolina rallies failed to produce any such ground swell as was then sweeping over North Carolina. Governor Heyward, who dropped out at the height of the educational campaign for a journey on official business in North Carolina, gave an interview to a Charlotte reporter:

---

cause. This novel described the Dark Corner of a hill county, presumably Greenville, from which the hero as county superintendent brushed out the cobwebs. Columbia *State*, editorials, April 25, 27, 28, 29, 1903; Ogden to A. J. S. Thomas, April 3, 1903, Ogden Papers, Library of Congress—University of North Carolina; William Zachariah McGhee to Dickerman, December 9, 22, 1903, Dickerman Papers, S.H.C., University of North Carolina; W. Zachariah McGhee, *The Dark Corner* (New York, 1908), *passim.*

28. Columbia *State*, June 19, 20, 1903.

29. See, for example, the rally at Fork, in Marion County, reported in *ibid.*, July 17, 1903.

30. Reports of rallies in Columbia *State*, July 28, 29, August 3, 7, 9, 13, 17, 21, 1903.

South Carolina: Inequality as a Higher Law 183

"What are you interested in mostly now?" queried the reporter.
"Education."
"In what way? What do you propose to do?"
"Oh—just educate," said the governor with a knowing look in his eyes.
"Education is a dangerous thing?" hazarded the reporter.
"To talk education too much may be a dangerous thing," said the governor thoughtfully.
"What is the most important public question in South Carolina at present?" asked the newspaper man, and Gov. Heyward and General [Attorney General A. W. "Dolph"] Jones both answered at once: "Taxes."[31]

"Although it is very evident that there is an educational awakening in our State," Governor Heyward told the next legislature, "it is equally evident that much remains to be done." The legislature invited the conference to Columbia in 1905, but Heyward's educational reform program failed in the legislature, which had not been committed to concrete reforms. Another campaign was needed, said the Columbia *State*. "A campaign without the demagogue! A campaign in which the aspirants for the legislature will be determined to help the masses, to enlighten the ignorant, to elevate citizenship! Then we will have longer school terms and compulsory education." Meanwhile, for a bad omen, four up-country districts voted in 1904 to end local taxation.[32]

As local arrangements for the conference began at Columbia,[33] a reaction rather naturally issued from Charleston, center both of the true low-country Bourbonism and of a newer denim aristocracy based on investment in up-country cotton mills. Low-country planters were reluctant to educate their swarms of Negro tenants, and cotton mill corporations were equally reluctant to lose their white child labor or to be taxed. Lewis W. Parker, a leading spokesman of the mill men, told his audience at a school rally in Orangeburg: "I wish to tell you gentlemen who live in the country, you farmers, that when you evade taxation and become tax-dodgers,

31. *Ibid.*, August 23, 1903, probably quoting from Charlotte *Observer*.
32. Columbia *State*, January 13, 18, 1904; *South Carolina School Report*, 1905, p. 271.
33. *The Keystone: A Magazine Devoted to Women's Work* (Charleston, South Carolina, monthly), VI (August, 1904), 12.

you provide us who manage the corporations not only with the excuse but with the legal right to become tax-dodgers."[34]

"I look with apprehension at what is said to be going on," wrote elderly William Ashmead Courtenay to Dr. Samuel Green of the Peabody Fund. Courtenay, the owner of a cotton mill at Newry, was a member of the "old guard" of Peabody Fund trustees. He was enraged to hear that its agents were helping to spread the public school propaganda. The Southern states, "who have expended $100,000,000 for education, the larger part for negroes, hardly need *hot air* advice as to their duty in such regard!" he said, and added:

In my opinion we are moving to a sensational status, "hot air speeches," *politico*-educational, and in a few years we will be so mixed up, with utopian schemes—more *political* than educational, that we will lose our identity!

There has never been a more complete *mirage*, than the aim to *educate everybody*, in the sparsely settled south! There is neither money or [*sic*] teachers, and as to the mass of negroes, 40 years of freedom has not advanced them perceptibly. God made them a different race & man cannot change *His* work.[35]

Other mill men wisely allowed the newspapers to speak for them. The Charleston *News and Courier*, possibly influenced by Courtenay, was an incessant opponent of the Ogden movement. It would not be mollified, possibly because Murphy, a child labor crusader, was executive secretary of the Board. The *News and Courier* regarded the Ogdenites with deep suspicion as "an organized body of strangers." "Most of them are Republicans who regret the disfranchisement of a large class of illiterate Republican voters," the editor approvingly quoted from another paper. "The negro ought to be educated, it is felt, enough at least to vote, and his education thus far ought to appeal to powerful interests." The movement was even "the most insidious attack that has ever been made upon the sentiment and civilization of the South." This

---

34. Columbia *State*, August 3, 1909.
35. Courtenay to Green, November 24, 1903, Peabody Education Fund Papers, George Peabody College for Teachers; and see Dabney to Ogden, April 2, 1903, Dabney Papers, S.H.C., University of North Carolina. The words "mirage" and "God" were doubly underlined, and three lines were drawn under "His." Cf. Courtenay to Thomas Nelson Page, August 1, 1904, and Alderman to Page, August 25, 1904, Thomas Nelson Page Papers, Duke University.

South Carolina: Inequality as a Higher Law 185

influential journal, which cheered on the Eastern exploiters of its own region's labor and resources, warned Southern educators to reject "the leadership and label of strangers who offer no compensation of value—not even cash." It advised the Peabody Board to "keep entirely separate from all other enterprises that may be proposed" and to ignore the proposed distribution of its funds in aid of rural public schools, "only a cheap appeal to an ignorant popular fancy." The *News and Courier* seemed instinctively to welcome the harmful and sift out and discard the good in all of the Yankee infiltration of these years. Like the *Manufacturers' Record* it fanned the racial violence of the times, but its main motives seem to have been defense of the textile interests and its editorial rivalry with the Columbia *State*. The latter paper, broadening out from its old Conservative opposition to Tillman, began to crusade a bit and moved in the direction of Wilsonian progressivism.[36]

Colonel James Simons, who published the *News and Courier*, was a member of the Charleston school board and one-time member of the state board of education. He was "a believer in local self-government for schools," which seems to mean that he was unwilling to share the tax wealth of Charleston with the rural schools. The *News and Courier* hoped that its publication of the Census figures on illiteracy would "spur on the people of the counties which are behind hand, to additional effort."[37]

On the eve of the Columbia Conference, the *Manufacturers' Record* sent out from Baltimore marked copies and reprint leaflets opposing the Ogden movement, and some local organizations wavered in their support of the movement.[38] "Candidly, we have

---

36. Editorials in Charleston *News and Courier*, January 26, April 29, 1904, March 27, April 27, 28, 29, 1905. Ogden was told that most South Carolinians read the *State*, which was "as positively our friend as 'The News & Courier' is our opponent," and at Rock Hill in 1904 he was "quietly taken aside frequently that someone might whisper in my ear that I must not be disturbed on account of 'The News and Courier,' as it did not represent the best people in the South."— Ogden to J. E. Chamberlain (correspondent for the New York *Evening Mail*), June 2, 1904, Ogden Papers, Library of Congress—University of North Carolina. A carefully documented account and analysis of South Carolina race relations at about this time is in Tindall, *South Carolina Negroes, 1877-1900*, pp. 233-59.

37. Columbia *State*, January 1, 1910; editorial in Charleston *News and Courier*, February 21, 1904.

38. The official organ of the South Carolina Federation of Women's Clubs at first circulated letters attacking the movement. The president of the federa-

had to combat prejudice in our work for the Conference," reported James A. Hoyt of the *State,* who was in charge of local arrangements.[39] The conference itself ran smoothly. The visitors from the East and South were entertained extravagantly by local dignitaries. Whether by coincidence or design, Andrew Carnegie's gift to the Carnegie Foundation for the Advancement of Teaching appeared on the front pages of the newspapers on the opening day of the conference. The apogee of the conference program was a courageous presentation of the case for compulsory education, regardless of race, by William H. Hand, a local teacher.[40]

Ogden was profoundly disturbed, however, by a disastrous wreck at Greenville after the conference. Several railroad employees were killed; Ogden's private secretary was crippled; several distinguished guests were scarred for life. The *News and Courier* must have considered the event as providential; news of the wreck covered its whole front page the next day. "This ends all excursions of this nature as far as I am concerned," Ogden declared at the time, though he was later persuaded to continue them. The wreck occasioned "serious criticisms . . . concerning the propriety of these trips from the North to the South."[41]

Efforts to win support from the Charleston *News and Courier* met with complete failure. Ex-Mayor Seth Low of New York and the Democratic politician Edward M. Shepard of Brooklyn went to Charleston right after the conference to see James Simons, but their diplomacy failed to reverse the policy of his

---

tion was married to a Philadelphian who managed a Greenville cotton mill. The editor attended some of the educational campaign meetings, however, and was converted into a supporter. *Keystone,* V (January, 1904), 17; V (February, 1904), 9; VI (August, 1904), 12.

39. James A. Hoyt, Jr., to Ogden, April 17, 1905, Ogden Papers, Library of Congress—University of North Carolina.

40. Carnegie had similarly timed his gift of $600,000 to Booker T. Washington of Tuskegee in 1904, when the conference met at Birmingham. Columbia *State,* news articles on April 11, 16, 22-30, 1905, editorials on March 15, 18, 21, April 5, 7, 1905; Richmond *Times-Dispatch,* April 27, 1905; *Eighth Conference for Education in the South, Proceedings* (Columbia, 1905), *passim,* particularly pp. 77-83 for Hand's speech.

41. Printed circular by Ogden "To My Guests on the Special Train that was Wrecked on the Southern Railway about 8 o'clock A.M., April 29, 1905," copy in unsorted Ogden Papers, University of North Carolina; Charleston *News and Courier,* April 30, 1905; Ogden to Dabney, February 27, 1906, Dickerman Papers, S.H.C., University of North Carolina.

paper.[42] The *News and Courier* at this juncture employed Thomas Dixon to write a series of scurrilous articles on race relations in Ogden's New York department store. A retired preacher, Dixon was then living in New York on the profits of his novels of race hate, which were accepted as gospel by a wide public, many of whom had never before read much besides the Bible and school textbooks. His articles were the basis of a whispering campaign that plagued educational reformers for years. Most of Ogden's friends thought Dixon's articles unworthy of reply, but Julius D. Dreher, a native South Carolinian, and the Columbia *State* pronounced them "lie[s] out of whole cloth," and waged a defensive campaign which was probably an ineffective antidote to the ranker prejudices.[43]

The Columbia Conference failed to kindle widespread enthusiasm as earlier conferences had. South Carolina was really not so peculiar as local chauvinists have proclaimed, but its Negro majority and its comparative shortage of other resources than cheap labor gave it a considerable difference even from other Southern seaboard states. A complacent comment of the Laurens *Advertiser* probably reflected the attitude of many South Carolinians. "We have never believed the Ogdenites would do any harm," it said. "When rich Yankees come south in palace cars it generally does good.... If the Ogdenites are merely going to talk it's a disappointment. Our people can talk."[44]

No state school campaign followed the conference, and it was four years before the movement was revived by a visit of Philander P. Claxton of the Southern Board to Columbia. Once again politicians and educators moved systematically to the courthouses, beginning at Spartanburg on August 2, ending at Charleston on September 2. According to a reporter, "The speakers went straight to the point. Not once did the expression 'grand old South Carolina' reverberate; no welkins were split and no time

42. Shepard to Ogden, May 10, 1905, Ogden Papers, Library of Congress—University of North Carolina; Charleston *News and Courier*, April 29, May 4, 7, 15, 1905.
43. *Ibid.*, May 16, 31, 1905; William E. Gonzales to Ogden, May 16, 22, 31, 1905, Julius D. Dreher to Ogden, May 24, June 10, 11, 12, 17, 23, August 24, 1905, Ogden Papers, Library of Congress—University of North Carolina; letter of Dreher to the editor in Columbia *State*, June 23, 1905.
44. Quoted in *ibid.*, April 26, 1905.

was wasted." Like "a body of bank directors," the presidents of colleges and an enlightened despot of half-a-dozen cotton mills described conditions in the schools. There were no "cheap anecdotes or other claptrap." Led by William Knox Tate, Superintendent John E. Swearingen, and William H. Hand, they used the formulas which had been successful in other states; yet measurable results can hardly be traced. Local taxes and state appropriations were only slightly increased.[45] The final attempt by the Southern Education Board was a Conference for the Common Good in 1913, which bore little fruit.[46]

Compulsory school attendance was the overshadowing topic of educational debate among South Carolinians in the years when the constructive program of the Ogden movement was winning successes in other Southern states. This issue absorbed all of the passion for educational reform which built schoolhouses in North Carolina and raised teachers' salaries in Virginia. Though compulsory education was perhaps an implicit obligation of the state under the suffrage clause of the constitution of 1895, it became a political issue in 1900, when young women of Columbia, the King's Daughters, went to the mill districts of the city to teach mill children to read and write. Finding the children at work in the mills, they induced legislators to introduce two bills, one to prohibit child labor, another to compel attendance in public schools. Conditions would seem to warrant passage of both bills, but at each annual session of the legislature they were debated as alternatives, until finally in 1915 advocates of compulsory attendance were so worn down as to accept a weak, local-option law which could not be enforced. These annual jousts, though unproductive, were conducted in high seriousness and sometimes in high dudgeon by legislators pledged in their home districts. Compulsory attendance had many supporters, including every state superintendent of the period and every governor except Cole Blease. Educators pleaded

45. Tillman tried to discourage the movement at the outset by an attack on Claxton. Columbia *State*, January 1, 2, 3, February 2, 8, August 2, 3, 5, 10-15, 21-31, 1909; *South Carolina School Report*, 1909, pp. 35-36, 49-50 *et passim*.
46. Bourland to Ogden, June 16, 1913, Ogden Papers, Library of Congress; clippings from Columbia *State*, dated June 11, August 6, 8, 1913, and circular entitled "Program, Conference for the Common Good, Columbia, S. C., August 6th and 7th, 1913," Southern Education Board Papers, S.H.C., University of North Carolina; *South Carolina School Report*, 1915, p. 133.

for it and clergymen prayed that it might come to pass. The state child labor committee, women's clubs, labor leaders, and politicians worked for compulsory education. Editors demanded it, and cotton manufacturers swore by it.

As soon as a bill to prohibit the employment of mill workers under twelve years of age was proposed, Captain James L. Orr of the Piedmont Mills and other mill spokesmen appeared at the capital to protest this "hostile" and "pure class legislation." They proposed instead the compulsory school attendance of all children eight to twelve. Orr argued that "when the cry is for new mills" there was "no need to pick out textile enterprises" for regulation. "As a rule mills make no money out of children," he claimed. "Cotton mills will not employ such children if it can be avoided. It would be a Godsend if all children could be forced to go to school until 12 years old, at least the white." But idle hands were the devil's workshop. "Don't turn out the children to run wild on the frozen hillsides," pleaded one who called himself "a practical mill man."[47] The mill town illiterate was indeed a problem. It was estimated in 1907 that 50.3 per cent of the mill workers under fourteen were illiterate, while only 14.8 per cent of white children ten to fourteen in the state were illiterate.[48] Thomas F. Parker, owner of one of the model mills, estimated in 1910 that the average mill town teacher, paid and controlled by the mill manager, received a salary of $360 a year, half as much as the average adult mill worker. No South Carolina mill spent as much as one per cent of its capital annually for welfare work, an amount Parker felt to be indispensable to recapture "a true friendliness toward the management" and to "escape the future control of demagogues and labor agitators."[49]

When the child labor law of 1903 forbade employment of children under twelve, cotton manufacturers abandoned their crusade for compulsory education. When the state child labor committee, formed in 1905, began to press for a law raising the

47. Charleston *News and Courier*, January 17, 1900; Columbia *State*, February 2, 1911.
48. Statistics by the United States Department of Commerce and Labor, in Davidson, *Child Labor Legislation in the Southern Textile States*, p. 14.
49. Thomas F. Parker, "The South Carolina Cotton Mill Village—A Manufacturer's View," in *South Atlantic Quarterly*, IX (October, 1910), 351-53.

child labor limit to fourteen years, the mill men returned to the ranks. "Why not be brave enough," they asked, "to give us what we have asked for, and that is a compulsory school law for all children between 8 and 12 years of age in South Carolina?"[50] The South Carolina Cotton Manufacturers' Association passed resolutions in favor of such a law, and over the years mill men such as Thomas F. Parker, Lewis W. Parker, and Ellison A. Smyth presented this as an alternative to a ten-hour day, safeguards of life or limb, and the fourteen-year child labor law.[51] It became a sort of amulet.

The school men, and their editorial patron, the Columbia *State*, publicly accepted at face value the support which the mill men gave to compulsory education, though privately many of them must have viewed the matter with the skepticism which labor leaders openly expressed. Only twenty-two "show mills" reported the condition of their schools when Superintendent McMahan, at the suggestion of William A. Courtenay, sent questionnaires to all mills in 1900. "I was disappointed in receiving so few replies," McMahan remarked dryly. The twenty-two which reported swore honor bright that they worked few children under ten years of age, and one might gather from their answers that most mill schools ran nine or ten months. It required very careful selection of evidence to create this picture of cotton mill utopia, but just such grist was ground out by the Charleston *News and Courier*, which expressed the viewpoint and often the very language of Charleston capitalists interested in up-state mills. The first reaction of *News and Courier* reporters to the compulsory attendance bill of 1900 was a cry against "pure paternalism," and they were later than the cannier mill men in their support of this measure.[52] "The wise plan is to get all the mills we can find room and work for, first, and regulate them afterward," suggested the editor. *News and Courier* correspondents at Columbia, Spartanburg, and other mill towns found evidence that schools there were better than the country schools and that benevolent mill superintendents did all they could

---

50. Quoted from Columbia *State*, January 19, 1906, in Davidson, *Child Labor Legislation in the Southern Textile States*, p. 179.
51. *Ibid.*, pp. 179-81, 184-85, 187; Columbia *State*, June 6, 1906.
52. August Kohn, correspondent at Columbia and leading mill expert, in Charleston *News and Courier*, January 22, 1900.

short of interference with personal rights—rights of parents. One might again infer that these were "representative" mills. Even at Rock Hill, where the mill management had taken the mill school out of the city system and made "special arrangements for the factory settlements alone," the schools might "not be all that could be desired, but such as they are there is still room there. Why provide more room for a patron who will not use what he now has?"[53] Educators took what hope they might from such pronouncements. President George B. Cromer of Newberry College and state high school inspector William H. Hand, as members of the state child labor committee, recommended compulsory education as a means of breaking the deadlock between the demands of reformers and the defenses of vested interests.[54]

The mill men almost undoubtedly knew that effective compulsory attendance would never be enacted. Most of those who had followed Tillman when he stormed the seats of power held by the low-country Conservatives also followed him in his campaign against the powerless Negro. Racial antagonism was sufficient in itself to block the fair distribution of educational opportunity implied in compulsory attendance. But there was opposition also in the mill towns. The widowed mother of a child worker was usually only a residual memory of an earlier, war-destituted generation, but the dinner-toting, whiskey-drinking mill town father was no phantom. He was as real as the company store, and he cast the family vote. Both back-country demagogues and representatives of the white minority in the low country voted down compulsory education bills in the state legislature.

Arguments used by both sides in the fifteen-year debate on compulsory attendance are revelations of the political mind of South Carolina. The shadow of the Negro illiterate was projected across the stage from the wings. Enemies of the common white

53. *Ibid.,* January 22, February 2, 1900, January 21, February 1, 4, 1901; letter of Ellison A. Smyth to the editor, in Columbia *State,* February 6, 1906.

54. "It is interesting to note that South Carolina is the only State where the Child Labor Committee has conferences with the representatives of the mills."— *Keystone,* XII (January, 1911), 4, 9. One of the editors of this magazine, Louisa B. Poppenheim, helped to steer the child labor committee into the channel of compulsory education. See *ibid.,* XI (January, 1910), 3; XI (February, 1910), 5; XII (November, 1911), 6; XIV (January, 1913), 2; George B. Cromer, quoted in Columbia *State,* January 24, 1913.

man called him on stage, while friends of the poor white tried to keep him off. In South Carolina the race question pervaded all others.

"I'm agin' it," said Joshua W. Ashley, an unschooled and rather disreputable legislator. "Citizen Josh" was a "former Reformer" who kept the earthy trappings of the common man, like Davy Crockett, but fought social legislation as an affluent mill town businessman. He had arrived despite his lack of formal education, and therefore children of talent need not be compelled to attend school.[55] But there were more articulate arguments against compulsory education. One class of arguments emphasized the foreign origin and nature of the reform. Though a prohibition leader, Senator J. Steele Brice of York County—"always an advocate of democracy"—thought that when compulsion was applied to school attendance it "smacked of monarchy" and "resembled the hard, German system." He dragged from the dusty historical records of his own state a compulsory attendance bill submitted by a Negro in 1872.[56] Cole Blease as governor charged that sycophantic educators were trying to garner sympathy in the North by advocating compulsory attendance. Blease said that if these men were not "decent enough to resign," they "should be kicked out." Even "if what they say is true," loyal South Carolinians would "not parade it and humiliate our State." The governor had "little patience with, and much contempt for, that man or those men who go around in the State or outside of the State and parade figures to show the percentage of the ignorance of our people."[57]

Compulsory education would also be costly; by forcing on the state 116,000 additional Negro children, it would raise taxes. South Carolina was "paying almost as much for education as any State in the Union," it was claimed. "And we are now in danger of overdoing the thing and making our public education expense a burden"; "the taxes for schools will be doubled, and our people cannot stand it." This viewpoint received official backing. It

---

55. On Ashley's career, see Francis B. Simkins, *Pitchfork Ben Tillman: South Carolinian* (Baton Rouge, 1944), p. 222; Davidson, *Child Labor Legislation in the Southern Textile States*, pp. 90, 178n, 187; Columbia *State*, January 20, 1909; [Oswald G. Villard], "Lynchers Triumphant," editorial in *Nation*, XCIII (October 26, 1911), 386.

56. Columbia *State*, January 25, 1905.

57. Message quoted in *ibid.*, January 18, 1911.

would indeed mean "a great supper," admitted Superintendent O. B. Martin, if the state should "go out into the highways and hedges and compel them to come in." He was more immediately concerned with a larger school fund than with compulsory attendance.[58]

The futility of a compulsory attendance law was a minor theme of opponents. It would cause "division in the school district," "more friction than the dispensary law." No jury would convict a violator. "Let the government of the home be the kingdom and the child its subject," said Senator Brice, erstwhile champion of democracy. Such a law would end "parental authority and the peace of the home," said Blease, and "force orphan children from the factories to the poorhouse." Brice imagined "a widow, poor and practically helpless, who would be arrested because her children would not be in school"; and also a "worthless man who, if his children were sent to school, would try to burn down the schoolhouse, fight the teacher and otherwise institute a spirit of anarchy." Better "a good illiterate than an educated devil," declared one shrewd opponent of plain learning. Some of the worst lawbreakers in the state were white college graduates, with hip-pocket pistols and quite personal responsibilities to the Negro community. "Education is not everything, for virtue is cheap in New England." And, furthermore, "17-cent cotton will do the trick," said John L. McLaurin, the Commercial Democrat; "and then you won't have to go and fine a poor devil because his boy has to plow or work in the mill to help feed the family."[59] There was a certain substance in that last argument, if means were provided.

But the ideas of Ben Tillman tinged the most effective arguments of the opposition. "Compulsory education is a rattlesnake that you can warm into being," said the old chief after years of silence on the subject, "and while it will help some white children, it is fraught with danger." Negroes thus "qualified to vote" would "bring on strife by trying to regain political power."[60] It

58. *Ibid.*, February 1, 1902, February 4, 1910; *South Carolina School Report, 1906*, p. 11.
59. Debates in legislature on compulsory attendance bills, in Columbia *State*, February 1, 1902, January 25, 26, February 13, 1905, January 18, 1911, February 27, 1913; Charleston *News and Courier*, February 8, 1901.
60. Speech reported in Columbia *State*, July 19, 1906.

would "nullify" the suffrage restriction, no less, said a Tillmanite.[61] Aroused lowlanders declared that "if we force the negro into the schools we will be sharpening weapons with which to cut our own throats." It would even seem to be unjust to compel Negro education. "A man will feed a negro family all the winter, and then when the time comes for work on the farm the negro children will all go to school and leave the work undone." The landlord viewpoint was reasserting itself, as farm owners began to get their own carts out of the ditch. "It might be an extreme case," suggested Cole Blease, "but one farmer seeing another prosperous" might indict the latter's Negroes "because they had not sent their children to school." That would never do. A compulsory attendance law might even inspire Northern philanthropists to put up vast sums for Negro public education.[62]

Supporters of compulsory education in South Carolina felt compelled to answer the wild charges that it would put Negroes in school. "There is not so great a fool in South Carolina as to believe white officials will force negro children into school," countercharged the Columbia *State*, anti-Tillman paper, leading press champion of compulsory attendance bills. "And no man knows that better than Ben Tillman."[63] Official guarantees came from school officers, even from the president of the state child labor committee, that Negroes would be excluded from the operation of such a law.[64] There were "no spooks" in these bills, it was urged, no *bêtes noires*, only the "bugaboos" raised up by dema-

61. Captain John G. Richards of Kershaw County, reported in Columbia *State*, February 4, 1910. The term "nullify" would seem to have lost its old sanctity in South Carolina.

62. Debates reported in Columbia *State*, February 1, 1902, January 26, 1905, February 1, 1906, February 4, 1910; Woodward, *Origins of the New South*, p. 408.

63. Editorial, Columbia *State*, July 19, 1906. Though Tillman had the farm owner's contempt for "the damned factory class," his attitude toward them was more humane than his opponents would admit, and more humane than his attitude toward Negroes. Charleston *News and Courier*, August 3, 1895.

64. George B. Cromer quoted in Columbia *State*, January 24, 1913. Superintendent Joshua W. Doar of Georgetown County reported in 1914: "I myself am not in favor of compelling any more negroes to go to school, but I believe if you would make a law, which I term a 'Designated Compulsory Law,' the voters would pass it in this county—that is, pass a law allowing the Board of Education of each county to designate such children in the county as they see fit to attend school. (And let them designate all the white children in the county. Of course this part of the law to be unwritten.)"—*South Carolina School Report, 1914*, p. 79.

gogues. "This is a white man's measure," declared Senator J. W. Barnwell of Charleston. "Why should not the white truant officer look after the interest of the Anglo-Saxon?" asked another old lowlander who could not understand all the fuss. "No one objects to the unequal apportionment of school funds between the races. Would one object to a truant officer neglecting part of his duty?"[65] In the absence of Negro school trustees, if the whites "can't run it to their interest they are a poor set of executives indeed."[66]

The positive arguments for compulsory attendance were more varied. The nature of suffrage restriction obligated the state to educate white boys, for "the time may come when the whites will divide." And what would an illiterate electorate do with initiative, referendum, or recall, asked a troubled city reformer.[67] The state historian, noting that one-fourth of the members of Democratic clubs signed the roll with an X, declared that the Revolutionary generation had been more literate.[68] It did not pass without notice that even the Russian Duma had beaten South Carolina to a compulsory attendance law, leaving the latter commonwealth in a class with "the embattled ignorance of Africa."[69]

Spokesmen of the mill workers, though they charged that mill officials were "covering their rascality under the guise of schools and churches" built with the profits of oppression, and that the "people in these schools teach the operatives that their employers are great benefactors," nevertheless supported compulsory education in order to end the competition of child labor. Night schools were ineffective, they said, because children eager to learn were so tired that they went to sleep in the chairs.[70]

65. Legislative debates in Columbia *State*, February 10, 1901, February 1, 1902; Marshall Moore of Barnwell, South Carolina, letter to the editor in *ibid.*, February 4, 1904.
66. Gaffney *Ledger* editorial, quoted in Columbia *State*, January 26, 1909. Also see *ibid.*, February 6, 1905, February 5, 6, 1906, for an incomplete list of South Carolina newspapers favoring compulsory education. They included the Union *Times*, Newberry *Observer*, Yorkville *New Era*, Winnsboro *News and Herald*, *Southern Christian Advocate*, Easley *Progress*, Fort Mill *Times*, Rock Hill *Herald*.
67. Charleston *News and Courier*, January 22, 1900; Columbia *State*, February 1, 1902; George B. Cromer in *ibid.*, January 24, 1913.
68. Letter of A. S. Salley, Jr., to the editor in *ibid.*, February 3, 1915.
69. *Ibid.*, February 4, 1915.
70. Debate on ten-hour bill, in *ibid.*, February 10, 1905.

As for helping the Negroes, they were said to be already in school.[71] The author of a compulsory attendance bill warned that Negro parents would "make any sacrifice" to send their children to school, "and will do so even if they have to steal from their employers to buy the books and pay contingent expenses." Another testified: "The negro is already using his opportunities. He will take a hunk of corn bread in his pocket, pull up his one 'gallus' and go along to school. Not so with the white child."[72] The *State*, wishing to frighten politicians into supporting compulsory attendance, sent traveling representatives into the countryside. They sounded the alarm:

Thus far this week we have passed two negro school houses, each crowded to the limit, and some of the pupils almost grown, being carefully instructed by competent teachers, who, we were informed, received good salaries from tuition for instructing the negroes in these communities.

In each of these sections we beheld hundreds of acres of cotton being choked out by the grass for lack of labor, which could not be procured at any price, owing to the fact that the labor of these communities was shut up in the school houses, grasping advantages in mid-summer which we learned were neglected by the white children even in mid-winter.[73]

Promises of material prosperity and plenty as an outcome of general literacy accompanied the appeals to humanitarianism and fear of Negro domination. This was firmer ground. Though ignorance was not the only reason the Southerner's denim was rag-

[71]. This line of argument was contradicted by the state school reports, but had an element of truth. The description of a Negro school in 1929 by Thomas J. Woofter, Jr., is applicable to conditions two decades earlier. "And in these schools the pupils are jammed all the way from wall to wall and from the teacher to the door step. There have been times in recent years when a school would become so over-run that the maximum number would be packed in and then the teacher would close the doors and tell the late arrivals they would have to go home."—*Black Yeomanry: Life on St. Helena Island* (New York, 1930), p. 189.

[72]. Thomas M. Raysor in Columbia *State*, January 30, 1903; Senator Knox Livingston of Marlboro County in *ibid.*, February 1, 1902. Raysor was attorney and director of the Bank of Orangeburg and several other financial institutions, and a leader in establishing graded schools in the town of Orangeburg. James C. Hemphill (ed.), *Men of Mark in South Carolina: Ideals of American Life* (4 vols., Washington, 1909), I, 320-22.

[73]. Testing nine white men along the way, the newspaper correspondents found that only four could master "plain readin'."—W. P. E., special report from Clinton, South Carolina, in Columbia *State*, August 3, 1906.

South Carolina: Inequality as a Higher Law 197

ged, it was a major factor. "That is a business proposition," said William E. Gonzales, editor of *The State*. "Can the South afford to carry such a large percentum of the liability of ignorance and permit the other competitor sections so large a percentum of the asset of general intelligence?"[74] Compel education, urged Senator J. W. Barnwell of Charleston, "and you give the poor children the power of becoming rich men." Goods "Made in Germany" flooded the retail stores of South Carolina because Germans enforced education.[75]

Congregations could not read the hymn books, complained a rural preacher.[76] The Cokesbury District Conference of Southern Methodists, which had probably prayed recently for factories, heard in 1906 a moving address from the humanitarian President Henry N. Snyder of Wofford College. In conclusion "he prayed that the day would soon dawn when it could be said not only that every child might go to school but that they had to go. This sentiment met a loud chorus of amens." The conference voted unanimous approval of compulsory education.[77]

The upshot of agitation for compulsory education bills was disappointing. All of the bills failed, in one house or the other, until 1915, when an inadequate, local-option law was passed without providing means of enforcement. After more than a decade of further effort, a stronger, state-wide bill was passed, only to be vetoed by Governor John G. Richards, a veteran opponent of compulsory attendance. The governor held that the older law was sufficient to the state's needs, and that the state had already a public school system "as fine as any in the country." Moreover, "South Carolina has a condition that is peculiarly her own. . . ."[78]

74. Speech at the summer normal school in Columbia, South Carolina, August 12, 1909, quoted in *ibid.*, August 13, 1909.
75. *Ibid.*, February 1, 1902, January 25, 1905.
76. John W. Elkins, Ridgeland, South Carolina, letter to the editor, in *ibid.*, January 22, 1913.
77. *Ibid.*, July 29, 1906. The *State* itself found it wise to use the emotional approach and simplified cartoons. See editorials, January 25, 30, 1905, January 28, 1907; pen sketches, July 15, 24, 27, August 8, 9, 1906, January 31, 1909, February 18, 1910, January 18, 1911.
78. Davidson, *Child Labor Legislation in the Southern Textile States*, pp. 178-93; James K. Coleman, *State Administration in South Carolina*: Columbia University Studies in History, Economics and Public Law, No. 406 (New York, 1935), p. 122. Further information may be found in the legislative journals, and in Charleston *News and Courier*, January 13, 22, 1900, February 10, 11,

An analysis of the voting pattern on compulsory education reveals the Piedmont as the stronghold of opposition. In 1902 when the senate voted 18 to 16 against compulsory education, the up-country senators were 11 to 4 against, the low-country 9 to 6 for, and the middle section 3 to 1 for the measure. When the house voted in 1910 against compulsory attendance by 78 to 20, in the last concerted fight for a state-wide law, the twenty die-hard supporters of such a measure included eleven from the low country, five from the middle section, and only four from the up country. The Piedmont, which had a heavy Negro population, was a center not only of Tillmanism, but of mill villages and racial bitterness.[79]

Money for operation of schools was a problem closer to reality than the vigorous threshing of old straw on the subject of compulsory attendance. The money question hinged upon the obligation of the state under the constitution of 1895 to maintain a school term of adequate length. The battle for sufficient funds was fought and lost in the legislative sessions of 1899 and 1900, and after that time South Carolina slipped below even the other Southern states.

There can be no question of the constitutional obligation of the legislature. After 1898, "the General Assembly shall cause to be levied annually on all the taxable property of the State such a tax ... as may be necessary to keep the schools open throughout the State for such length of time in each scholastic year as the General Assembly may prescribe."[80] But the legislature never made such a levy. To avoid it, legislators by an act of 1899 prescribed as the minimum school term a pitiful three months, a term below which it was believed no school district would fall. This minimum term

---

13, 1901; Columbia *State*, January 15, February 1, 1902; January 30, February 14, 1903; February 3, 16, 1904; January 16, February 3, 1905; February 1, 5, 1906; January 9, 17, 30, 1907; February 8, 19, 1908; April 22, 1909; February 4, 7, 1910; January 18, 1911; January 19, 22, February 3, 13, 26, 1913; January 29, 30, February 1, 10, 13, 28, 1914; January 14, 22, 28, 31, February 4, 6, 9-14, 19, 21, 1915.

79. Records of votes are from Columbia *State*, February 1, 1902, February 4, 1910. The middle-section counties are those through which the fall line passes. See Francis B. Simkins, *The Tillman Movement in South Carolina* (Durham, 1926), map facing p. 10.

80. *Constitution of the State of South Carolina, Ratified in Convention, December 4, 1895* (Columbia, South Carolina, 1895), Article XI, Section 6, p. 51.

South Carolina: Inequality as a Higher Law 199

was still in the school code in 1916.[81] The political leaders, who obeyed the spirit rather than the letter of the suffrage clause of their constitution, complied with the letter rather than the spirit of its educational clause.

February 9, 1900, seemed to a jaded capital reporter "a remarkable day in the South Carolina General Assembly, the day for education—education in the common schools and the higher colleges." In the house that day some of the members "twitted the friends of the colleges" that they were not equally friendly to the schools of the common people, and proposed an appropriation. Ellison D. Smith, a "friend of the common schools" who had voted against the colleges, decided on "a bluff to make the college folks show their hand." He proposed $200,000 for common schools, even $300,000. "He begged for the increase." "The friends of the State colleges said they would support that. There was more anxiety. The friends of the common schools, as they called themselves, thought they might kill the amendment by making it for more than $100,000, although they had taken no test vote." Joshua W. Ashley said that the time had come for the legislature to "show its sympathy for the little bare-footed at home." Protests began to well up on both sides of the sham battle. A friend of the colleges called the proposal "radical and extreme," and an opponent of the colleges thought there was "no use to provide schools and facilities the poor children cannot accept." But the house voted by 77 to 32 for $100,000 for common schools, and then "without the dotting of a letter" approved all appropriations for the state colleges. It seemed that there "ought to be no question now about the college supporters being friends of the common schools." Yet the finance committee of the senate three days later threw out the $100,000 by a vote of nine to three. And when the issue came up on the senate floor, a quick vote was called and the appropriation lost by 18 to 17.[82]

The school forces met defeat at every session. In 1901 the house voted a school appropriation, but the senate rejected it and

81. South Carolina, Department of Education, *General School Law of South Carolina, 1916* (Columbia? 1916?), p. 39.
82. Charleston *News and Courier*, February 10, 13, 14, 1900.

sent the amendment to the house in the closing hours of the session:

> The amendment was read. Mr. Hardin said: "I hope the House will agree." Mr. Stevenson said: "All in favor of the amendment will say 'Aye' and all opposed 'No.'" The viva voce vote was taken and the 'ayes' had it, and in less than a minute the House agreed to the Senate amendment, cutting the $100,000 for public schools. It was done so quickly that scarcely anyone realized that the House had so gracefully receded from its position as to the $100,000 for the public schools.[83]

While the legislature rejected proposals for state appropriations, existing funds were enough to provide only a four-month average term at $25 per month for the teacher. Many rural districts were in worse condition. In that year Gregg District in Edgefield County had terms of ten weeks for whites and eight for Negroes; Dry Branch in Colleton County had thirty weeks for whites, but only eight for Negroes, while Rum Gulley in the same county had twenty-four weeks for whites and only six for Negroes. In Horry County, three white districts ran only nine weeks, four of them eight weeks, and one six weeks, one five weeks, one four weeks, two others two weeks; only a few districts in Horry reported any Negro schools.[84]

South Carolina had no "educational governor," and the only one who claimed the title was D. C. Heyward, who took office in 1903.[85] In his first legislative session the only bill which would give material aid to country schools was killed in the senate. It proposed to use the dispensary school fund for schoolhouses, teachers, and books in the weak districts. But Richard I. Manning declared the plan "radical." Senator Blease saw "paternalism" in it; "negroes would be the principal beneficiaries."[86]

The first state appropriation of any sort, providing $5,000 for rural libraries, was passed in 1904. "Each school would get about enough to give a pupil a smattering of nothing," said one opponent,

83. *Ibid.*, February 8, 14, 1901.
84. Columbia *State*, January 14, 25, 1903; *South Carolina School Report, 1902*, pp. 13, 207, 211, 223.
85. Columbia *State*, January 14, 22, April 11, 1903; editorial in *ibid.*, January 16, 1907.
86. *Ibid.*, February 7, 11, 1903.

and another sneered that this was "like throwing a crumb out on the ocean."[87]

A mild measure to aid in building of schoolhouses was passed in 1905, authorizing the counties to lay aside 5 per cent of their school fund for this purpose, or about $75,000. This added nothing to the total school fund. But as the state superintendent wrote to Charles D. McIver, "We could not pass a law like the N. C. law because we had no loan fund and could not well create one."[88]

The gubernatorial campaign of 1906 indicated that education had small value compared with the dispensary issue in the calculations of South Carolina politicians. One of the weaker candidates, John J. McMahan, did urge longer terms and more schoolhouses. Richard I. Manning, Tillman's protégé, would like to have talked on education, "now regarded as a business matter," but he lacked time. In every speech Cole Blease announced his opposition to public education of Negroes and his desire for racial separation of school tax funds. "He does not dwell on these things," reported Zach McGhee. "He mentions them only to raise a yell from the crowd, and he always gets it." "Let it be the ambition of every mother in this State that her boy shall be as good as every other boy," was the sentence with which A. C. Jones struck the rail of the platform and jarred the perspiration off his face, leading up to a discussion of the "licker" question. Martin F. Ansel, "so polite, so urbane; so desirous that everyone shall have just what he wants," was elected governor. An up-country townsman acceptable to Conservatives, Ansel argued that the constitution had made ample provision for the schools and the responsibility for carrying out its intent rested with the legislators rather than the

[87]. *Ibid.*, February 9, 14, 1904; Snowden (ed.), *History of South Carolina*, V, 110-11; Oscar B. Martin (comp.), *School Law of South Carolina: 1906* (Columbia? 1906?), pp. 36-37. In the first eight months, some 400 libraries were placed in schools, with $12,000 "invested in 30,000 good books." *South Carolina School Report, 1904*, p. 8. A dog tax for schools was also passed in 1904.

[88]. In the first year under the act, about 200 schoolhouses were built. Though not a schoolhouse a day, as in North Carolina, this meant "a revival" and "great things for the public schools in South Carolina." "School Building," a pamphlet reprinted as Chap. III in *South Carolina School Report, 1905*, pp. 51-118; Columbia *State*, January 11, February 2, 1905; circular letter from State Superintendent Oscar B. Martin to county superintendents, February 21, 1905, Martin to McIver, February 2, 1905, Dabney Papers, S.H.C., University of North Carolina.

governor.[89] Governor Ansel did not discourage the educational movement, but he was no crusader.

The South Carolina constitution permitted local taxation for high schools, but jealous localism made units too small except in a few towns. And a social gulf separated college men from the blue-denimed graduates of the elementary public schools.[90] William Hand, the General Education Board agent for high schools,[91] found from a survey that only thirty-three high schools had a four-year course. "Whenever the rural communities have been drained of their best blood and brains," he warned, "and the remaining citizenship is reduced to a kind of peasantry, South Carolina's prosperity is at an end." He drafted three alternative high school bills, with the help of Joseph S. Stewart, pioneer Georgia high school campaigner,[92] but the bill favored by Hand did "not permit a single district, unless it is an incorporated town, to establish one of these high schools." This was intended to encourage consolidation of schools, and it was passed over rural protests. There was only one "objectionable" amendment, Hand reported to the Southern Education Board: "Towns above 1,000 population were cut out from the privileges of the appropriation. We think, however, that a larger town may take advantage of the appropriation by uniting with the township in which it is situated, or by joining in with several adjacent school districts."[93]

89. Columbia *State*, July 10, 11, 18, 21, 31, August 1, 15, 1906; Charleston *News and Courier*, August 1, 1906; Hemphill (ed.), *Men of Mark in South Carolina*, I, 3-4; "A Creditable Result in South Carolina," editorial in *Outlook*, LXXXIV (September 22, 1906), 150-51. For the political background, 1901-06, see Simkins, *Pitchfork Ben Tillman*, pp. 373-92. Manning in at least one speech did favor an appropriation from the state treasury to aid "the least able districts."—Columbia *State*, July 21, 1906.

90. William H. Hand, "The Opportunities and Obligations of the College," in *South Atlantic Quarterly*, IX (October, 1910), 358-63, is a lecture to the white-collar classes about their responsibility for education of the masses and for raising standards.

91. See William H. Hand, "Some Arguments for Compulsory Education," in *Eighth Conference for Education in the South, Proceedings* (Columbia, 1905), pp. 77-83; Dabney, *Universal Education in the South*, II, 417-19; Columbia *State*, January 20, 1906.

92. Columbia *State*, July 12, 1906, January 9, 16, 22, 1907; *South Carolina School Report, 1906*, pp. 51-84; Dabney, *Universal Education in the South*, II, 420-25.

93. *South Carolina School Report, 1907*, pp. 73-95; Columbia *State*, January 23, February 1, 7, 18, 21, 1907; Hand to Dickerman, January 23, February 20, 1907, Dickerman Papers, S.H.C., University of North Carolina.

Hand and city representatives found "absolutely no economy, justice, statesmanship, or patriotism" in giving "a dole from the State treasury to every school which may have a dozen high school pupils one year and but a half dozen the next." He felt that the state had made a "blunder in taxing larger aggregations of wealth and population for the sole benefit of smaller aggregations." Finally, in 1911, towns up to 2,500 were made eligible for state aid.[94]

It became increasingly obvious that rural schools needed special state aid. Fourteen South Carolina counties in 1909 had school terms of less than twelve weeks, and many districts were too poor to provide the needed funds through local taxation. The legislature provided $20,000 in state aid to districts with terms of less than twenty weeks. It was "time to stop considering the negro every time the schools came up," said the sponsor.[95]

William Knox Tate became state rural school supervisor in the same year through a grant by the Peabody Fund. He put all the energy of his six-foot, 225-pound frame for five years into propaganda work in behalf of rural children. He got the rural school act expanded so as to allow schools of less than 100 days' term to receive $60,000 from the state. An appropriation for consolidating and building rural schools rose from a trickle of $15,000 in 1912 to $80,000 in 1915. Tate's mission was not a failure, but he was forced to recognize that "the cities are inclined to view with complacence, or even with opposition, the efforts to improve the general school law under which the country schools must rise or fall." Moreover, the cotton economy kept rural attendance until Christmas down to one-third of the enrollment. Soon after Christmas the rural term was over. Tate had to pin his hopes on crop diversification and the mechanical cotton picker.[96]

As the demand grew for better white schools, educators urged

94. Columbia *State*, February 21, 1907, February 11, 19, 1908, February 3, 1909, January 8, 15, 1910, January 14, February 1, 1911; *South Carolina School Reports*, *1908*, pp. 16-18; *1910*, pp. 132-33.
95. Columbia *State*, January 14, February 4, 15, 25, 28, 1909; Augusta (Georgia) *Chronicle*, April 9, 1909.
96. *South Carolina School Reports*, *1911*, pp. 112, 124; *1915*, pp. 12-13; Dabney, *Universal Education in the South*, II, 224-30; Columbia *State*, February 1, 10, 1910; United States Bureau of Education, *Report of the Commissioner of Education for the Year Ended June 30, 1912* (2 vols., Washington, 1913), I, 207.

a state tax of one mill to provide a permanent source of educational funds and to end "the financial disparities which now prevent us from having any true State school system." Governor Cole Blease endorsed the proposal in 1913, at the same time demanding "THAT YOU PASS AN ACT PROHIBITING ANY WHITE PERSON FROM TEACHING IN NEGRO SCHOOLS OR FROM TEACHING NEGRO CHILDREN."[97] The tax act was passed in amended form, but Blease's opponents in the next legislature repealed it, to the dismay of school reformers, on the ground that it was "taxing the wealthier counties to benefit the poorer," or to benefit "a few old parasites" on the state board of education.[98] Governor Richard I. Manning in 1915 gathered the reins of power in more secure control. By a special message to the legislature, he won a larger appropriation and a mild compulsory attendance law.[99]

In the decade and a half from 1900 to 1915, South Carolina expenditures for education increased four-fold. The amount spent for Negro schools only doubled, while the amounts for white schools quintupled, and Negro schools made no gain for the five years after 1910. In so far as education meant opportunity, the Negro child's chance in relation to the white child dropped from one-fifth to one-twelfth. White schooling in 1915 was still inadequate for the industrial crises and world wars that lay ahead, but the Negro child had the additional handicap of unpreparedness to compete with local whites. Table 9 shows the expansion and racial disparity of the school system over the fifteen-year period.[100]

According to the estimate of the federal commissioner of education, in 1915 there were 209,192 white and 327,473 Negro children in the school population, from five to eighteen years of age. On that basis, $13.98 was expended on South Carolina white

97. He also opposed a central heating plant for the state Negro college: "I see absolutely no use, sense or reason in taxing the white people of this State to pay for a heating plant for negroes to get up and dress by. . . ."—Cole Blease, quoted in Columbia *State*, February 25, 1912. *The State* was unable to cope with most of Blease's messages and ceased publishing them. See *South Carolina Reports and Resolutions*, *1912*, I, 659; *1914*, III, 8, 55, IV, 5-6.
98. Columbia *State*, January 13, February 13, 17, 24, 25, 26, 1914.
99. *Ibid.*, February 11, 14, 19, 20, 21, 1915.
100. *South Carolina School Reports*, *1900*, p. 253; *1901*, p. 263; *1902*, p. 320; *1903*, p. 197; *1904*, p. 208; *1905*, p. 242; *1906*, p. 188; *1907*, p. 174; *1908*, p. 182; *1909*, p. 193; *1910*, p. 247; *1911*, p. 670; *1912*, p. 234; *1913*, p. 523; *1914*, p. 312; *1915*, p. 310.

South Carolina: Inequality as a Higher Law

TABLE 9
EXPANSION AND RACIAL DISPARITY OF THE SOUTH CAROLINA SCHOOL SYSTEM, 1900-1915

Year	White	Negro	Total
1900	$ 588,414.53	$ 171,954.69	$ 827,012.66
1901	744,742.18	217,155.23	962,135.66
1902	743,804.32	206,608.29	950,412.61
1903	820,843.55	225,299.94	1,046,143.49
1904	954,968.25	236,995.11	1,191,963.36
1905	1,060,019.58	244,609.86	1,304,629.44
1906	1,152,093.33	252,380.60	1,404,473.93
1907	1,148,474.11	267,250.18	1,415,724.29
1908	1,321,027.45	274,958.91	1,595,986.36
1909	1,590,732.51	308,153.16	1,898,685.67
1910	1,684,796.85	368,802.64	2,053,599.49
1911	1,818,678.81	349,834.60	2,168,513.41
1912	2,034,169.22	346,544.81	2,380,714.03
1913	2,247,981.05	361,785.56	2,609,766.61
1914	2,619,138.14	378,670.13	2,997,808.27
1915	2,924,859.68	370,646.90	3,295,506.58
Total	$23,454,743.56	$4,583,650.61	$28,103,275.86

schools in 1915 per white child, and only $1.13 in Negro schools per Negro child, a discrimination rate of 12.37 to one. An estimate of the racial proportions of school population in counties, based on the federal census of 1910, reveals the locus of greatest discrimination (Table 10).[101]

101. In Table 10, the Negro percentage of the total population between the ages of 6 and 20 has been estimated by the writer because South Carolina did not have a school census, all state apportionments being on the basis of enrollment. Furthermore, the proportions indicated are computed as of 1910 rather than 1915, from the federal census of 1910. For the individual counties, the population census gives figures by race for ages 6 to 14, and a total number of children from 6 to 20, but for the state as a whole it reports the number of Negroes and whites aged 6 to 20. The figures in the first column were computed, therefore, by simple division to ascertain the percentage of Negroes 6 to 14 in each county and subtracting 1.0 per cent of this percentage as a correction for those in the state as a whole aged 6 to 20. The state-wide figures showed that the proportion of Negroes aged 6 to 20 was more than 0.99 per cent less than the proportion from 6 to 14, and the correction seemed therefore advisable. These proportions are for a year which is five years earlier than that of the money figures, but it is probably as accurate as figures for other states which had a five-year school census, and likely more accurate, since there was less temptation for federal census-takers to pad the returns. The computation was made on the figures in United States Bureau of the Census, *Thirteenth Census of the United States Taken in the Year 1910*, Volume III: Population 1910, Reports by States with Statistics for Counties, Cities and other Civil Divisions (Washington, 1913), 658-65. The money figures in the second and third columns are copied from *South Carolina School Report, 1915*, pp. 215-16. In the fourth column the estimate based on enrollment is taken from the figures of amounts

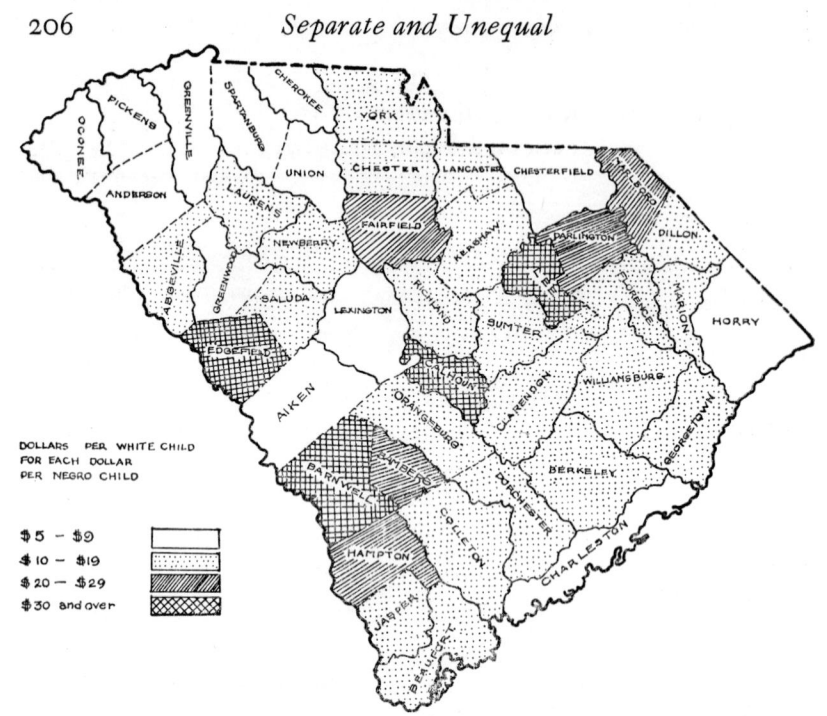

DISCRIMINATION IN SOUTH CAROLINA COUNTIES IN 1915
From *South Carolina School Report*, *1915*, p. 429.

These figures indicate that discrimination in favor of white children was much greater than even the enrollment records indicate, that every county was involved at least to the extent of four to one. The general, though not absolutely consistent, trend was toward far greater discrimination in black counties, whether in the low country like Barnwell or in the up-country like Edgefield. The lowest rate of discrimination was in the swamps and hills, where many Negro schools were necessary to pile up the enrollment. The urban counties of Charleston and Richland indicate a discrimination less than average, but by no means so little as to deserve the encomiums they awarded themselves. The map above of

per white child and Negro child in *ibid.*, p. 20, by simple division of the smaller number (always Negro) into the larger. The estimate for the fifth column was computed by dividing the third column of figures by the first column, dividing the second column of figures by the white percentage complementing that for Negroes in the first column, and dividing the larger quotient (always white) by the smaller quotient. Since Jasper County was created out of Hampton and Beaufort counties between the 1910 census and 1915, the proportions for that county were computed in the only convenient way, by finding the average proportions of Negro and white population for the two counties taken together.

TABLE 10
RATE OF DISCRIMINATION IN SOUTH CAROLINA COUNTIES

Counties, arranged by Negro proportion of total population	Negro per cent of total pop. 6-20 years estimated	Expenditure White	Expenditure Negro	Amount Per White Child For Each Dollar Per Negro Child — On enrollment	Amount Per White Child For Each Dollar Per Negro Child — On pop. aged 6 to 20 years
Beaufort.......	89.05	$ 21,658.45	$ 12,435.79	$ 7.15	$14.16
Calhoun.......	78.99	32,467.41	3,643.70	23.84	33.50
Fairfield.......	78.65	37,421.20	5,106.00	23.33	27.00
Jasper.........	78.32	14,552.19	2,716.87	12.97	19.35
Berkeley.......	77.89	19,090.08	5,162.59	8.62	13.03
Sumter........	77.38	70,102.93	12,054.27	16.90	19.89
Barnwell.......	75.61	104,411.70	7,731.01	27.89	41.87
Clarendon......	75.37	43,377.76	6,929.00	13.82	19.16
Edgefield......	75.23	58,626.22	5,250.50	24.78	33.91
Bamberg.......	73.94	34,212.74	4,190.86	15.23	23.16
Georgetown....	73.60	39,358.95	6,611.36	9.46	16.60
Lee...........	72.66	57,980.94	3,875.26	23.95	39.76
Orangeburg....	69.23	97,642.33	11,697.87	13.74	18.78
Chester........	68.91	53,101.53	6,335.61	14.99	18.58
Newberry......	68.71	59,371.65	7,528.76	13.65	17.32
Abbeville......	68.25	42,628.55	7,677.87	10.12	11.94
Charleston.....	67.26	158,303.06	56,622.95	4.33	5.74
Hampton......	65.80	29,567.23	2,356.21	12.41	24.14
Greenwood.....	65.64	54,051.47	11,653.74	7.18	8.86
Marlboro......	65.36	49,382.46	4,334.69	14.59	21.50
Colleton.......	65.05	34,286.99	3,327.50	9.26	19.18
Dorchester.....	64.97	38,032.42	4,979.30	9.91	14.17
Williamsburg...	64.38	55,360.25	6,185.26	15.03	16.18
Kershaw.......	64.19	42,480.43	6,189.90	8.94	12.30
Darlington.....	63.82	116,631.99	9,524.67	15.04	21.60
Florence.......	60.80	145,806.39	12,808.87	10.99	17.66
Laurens.......	58.44	86,101.67	6,970.40	11.97	17.37
Richland.......	57.86	193,607.83	24,430.07	8.65	10.88
Aiken.........	57.80	63,755.56	13,388.02	6.40	6.52
Marion........	57.64	43,748.82	4,200.62	7.37	14.17
York..........	57.20	95,813.86	8,384.49	14.29	15.27
Union.........	57.11	48,339.37	7,288.20	6.96	8.83
Saluda........	57.07	28,074.90	3,157.95	10.04	11.82
Dillon.........	54.78	54,580.34	4,528.17	12.57	14.60
Lancaster......	51.84	43,685.21	4,116.04	9.25	11.42
Chesterfield....	42.14	64,514.52	5,528.80	6.11	8.50
Lexington......	41.18	52,129.02	3,698.52	7.57	9.87
Anderson......	41.07	130,659.82	13,172.99	5.72	6.91
Cherokee......	36.01	45,708.26	5,379.10	4.46	4.78
Spartanburg....	34.01	163,906.67	16,414.29	5.03	5.15
Greenville.....	33.09	142,453.21	13,433.66	4.23	5.24
Oconee........	27.68	55,697.43	3,647.91	5.97	5.84
Horry.........	26.45	49,135.01	2,821.80	7.33	6.26
Pickens........	23.59	53,040.84	3,155.46	4.28	5.19
South Carolina.	58.74	$2,924,859.68	$370,646.90	$8.40	$11.23

South Carolina counties in 1915 will indicate the location of counties and the geographical pattern of discrimination rate, based on estimated population aged six to twenty years.[102]

It is clear from this map that the discrimination rate followed no rigid geographic pattern, but was based on other factors, of which perhaps personal choice of school officers and density of population were most important. It should not be forgotten, however, that the significant facts were the universality of racial discrimination and the varying amounts of available school funds. Nor should the urban differences be given undue importance. Charleston County, with its wealth and reputation of paternalistic toleration of Negroes, reported in 1909 that it spent $35.70 per white child enrolled, and $2.55 per Negro child. This record, which may be inaccurate, represented a greater inequality than in most of the rural counties. In 1910 the city of Charleston had only two Negroes as teachers and 128 whites, at total salaries of $1,030 and $90,210 respectively.[103]

By other measurements than gross expenditures, it is clear that South Carolina whites were overcoming the reluctance of con-

TABLE 11
SOUTH CAROLINA WHITE AND NEGRO SCHOOLS, 1900 AND 1915

		1900	1915
Length of term, days	White	105	133
	Negro	75	67
Average annual salary of teachers	White	$ 170.73	$ 383.39
	Negro	$ 77.34	$ 112.31
Expenditure per pupil in attendance	White	$ 6.51	$ 23.76
	Negro	$ 1.55	$ 2.91
Expenditure per pupil enrolled	White	$ 4.66	$ 16.22
	Negro	$ 1.11	$ 1.93
Expenditure per child aged 5 to 18 years	White	$ 3.17	$ 13.98
	Negro	$ .55	$ 1.13
Pupils enrolled per teacher	White	38	36
	Negro	65	64
Value of school property per child 5-18	White	No accurate reports until 1911	$ 32.11
	Negro		$ 2.57
High school enrollment	White	3,829	8,229
	Negro	169	668
State college enrollment	White	1,153	2,687
	Negro	644	467
Expenditure for higher education by state	White	(incomplete data)	$456,277.58
	Negro	$12,457.00	$ 23,897.48

102. Discrimination rate is taken from the fifth column of figures in Table 10.
103. *South Carolina School Reports, 1909*, pp. 10-11; *1910*, pp. 245, 269.

South Carolina: Inequality as a Higher Law 209

servative political leaders and the hesitancy of white voters. Efforts at economy were centered on the Negro school, where the length of term actually declined, according to local records. Table 11 indicates some of the growing disparity, as well as the neap tide of white schools.[104]

Wide as were the inequalities in the county averages, Negroes and whites shared even more unequally in many districts. In district 6 of Charleston County, according to reports in 1913 which may be unreliable, six white children each received $465.95 for their education, while the 613 Negro children of the district received only $3.01 each. The value of school property for each child enrolled in the city of Charleston was a little under $60, while only $6.12 in the white district 2C of Greenville County and $2.03 for a typical Negro school at Smith's, in Georgetown County.[105]

Such inequalities persisted and increasingly represented the basis on which which white voters, legislators, and school administrators economized in the provision of greater educational opportunities for white children. The exaggerations of the trend of depriving Negro children, moreover, were persistently in the low country. In the last "prosperity year" before the Great Depression, in 1928-29, South Carolina school funds were so distributed as to give $60.06 to each white enrolled, and $7.89 to each Negro enrolled. In Barnwell County the division was $124.29 per white enrolled and $5.85 per Negro enrolled.[106] Cotton picking time still flushed pupils and teachers out of the rural schools. During another era of prosperity, the state in 1951 authorized a bond issue up to the amount of $75,000,000 for a program to equalize educational facilities for all South Carolinians. This was over twenty times more than the total expenditure of 1915, an index not only of the gap between the separate systems, but of the extent of intervening economic changes.[107]

104. *South Carolina School Reports, 1900*, pp. 213, 254-54, 268; *1915*, pp. 251-55, 310-11; United States Bureau of Education, *Reports of the Commissioner of Education, 1900*, II, 2129, 2503; *1917*, II, 17, 513. Figures for high school enrollment and for ages five to eighteen years are based on federal reports.
105. *South Carolina School Report, 1913*, pp. 203-08, 293, 295, 299.
106. Columbus Andrews, *Administrative County Government in South Carolina* (Chapel Hill, 1933), table on p. 142.
107. Tindall, *South Carolina Negroes, 1877-1900*, p. 307.

CHAPTER VII

Georgia: Public Schools and the Urban-Rural Conflict

GEORGIA had the simplest system of educational finance on the Southern seaboard. The state government was the sole means of public support of the schools, except for independent districts in cities and in four urban counties. Distributed to counties on the basis of population of school age, this state fund would seem on the face of it to be the ideal method of providing equal educational opportunity, for whites at least, throughout the state. Wealthy counties would share their substance with poorer counties far more than in states like South Carolina, where county taxes furnished the bulk of the school fund, or North Carolina and Virginia, where local taxation was emphasized. But actually the independent districts outside of the state system contained much of the state's taxable property, which was separately taxed to provide far superior schools for the cities. And the black counties received large amounts from the state school fund for Negro children and spent this to give their white children superior schools.

Georgia's experience accentuates the fact that simply enlarging the unit of taxation was not a solution of the inequities of Southern school finance, even for whites. There are many indications that school officials were aware of the relation of Negro children on the school census to the amount they received for white schools. Movements for local taxation stemmed from the high country where Negroes were few, while the staunchest defenders of state appropriations were from the coastal plain and lower Piedmont where Negroes were thickly settled. "I am not opposed to local taxation, but I am opposed to any further appropriation for public schools," said a superintendent of a county which was losing money to counties with more Negroes. White-county school officials sometimes joined the large property-holders and cities in insisting that the state school fund would "bankrupt" the state. Superintendent C. S. Maddox jeered at this attitude; in his county Negroes outnumbered whites over three to one. "Tax the people equally from the mountains to the seashore," he advised, "so as to raise a sufficient sum of money to operate the schools eight months."[1]

Nowhere did Georgia rural schools compare with city and town schools, because the Georgia constitution forbade local taxation except by special legislation. Meanwhile the booster section of the Atlanta *Constitution* furnished glowing reports of progress in the towns, in what it called its "campaign of education" for prospective investors and immigrants. The school property of thirty-five towns was twice as great as that of all rural schools, and twenty times greater than the publicly owned rural school property. The school expenditure of those towns was more than one-third of the amount for the whole state.[2] Many of these town school enterprises reflected the hope for rather than the realization of a prosperity that would set them apart from their rural neighbors. But in passing through small towns in that day, as fifty years later, one might see moderate comfort up to the town's edge and desolation in the surrounding country. County superintendents' every-day experience of this contrast influenced their attitude toward local taxation. Meanwhile many rural schools extended their terms by tuition beyond the public term, paying the teacher for another month or more. But only the sons of fortune could pay the extra tuition, and poorer children returned the following year several months behind the wealthier. This part-public, part-private

1. Superintendent W. H. Wooding of Banks County, in *Georgia School Report*, *1901*, p. 90; Superintendent C. S. Maddox of Butts County, in *ibid.*, *1899*, p. 88.
2. One reads that the "grand little town" of Roberta is "moving forward" by erecting a schoolhouse which "is a splendid display of taste," and by a special tax that enables trustees to pay "handsome salaries." At Madison "the city's pride is the public school for whites." At Social Circle, a $10,000 brick school building is going up; at Bibb City, a textile company town on the edge of Columbus, a large frame house is provided for children too young for the mills. Even in the town of Nicholls "a good school building will be added to the list of improvements in the near future."—Atlanta *Constitution*, November 29, 1903; *Georgia School Report*, *1896*, pp. ccccii-cccciii, ccccxiii.

system in the ungraded, one-teacher schools produced baffling complications.

The nature of Georgia state records makes it impossible to determine precisely how Negro school facilities compared with those for whites. According to the report for 1896, Negro children comprised 47.9 per cent of the school population. Yet there were barely half as many Negro teachers, and the amount of their monthly salaries was barely one-third the amount for white teachers, presumably for a shorter term. Only one schoolhouse in twelve was publicly owned, but of these only one-eighth were Negro schoolhouses. The Negro share in the total school fund was not separately accounted for in the report, but the available facts above indicate a wide inequality.[3]

Between Negro urban and rural schools there was no such contrast as that between schools for whites. Conditions were about as bad in the schools of Atlanta's Negro district as in the country, according to Ray Stannard Baker's report:

> Several new schools have been built for white children, but there has been no new school for coloured children in fifteen or twenty years (though one Negro private school has been taken over within the last few years by the city). So crowded are the coloured schools that they have two sessions a day, one squad of children coming in the forenoon, another in the afternoon. The coloured teachers, therefore, do double work, for which they receive about two-thirds as much salary as the white teachers.

Classroom seats were available for less than one-third of the Atlanta Negroes of school age, but for more than two-thirds of the white children.[4] The only secondary education for Atlanta Negroes before 1924 was provided by the private Negro colleges.[5] And,

---

[3] The year 1896 is used because later reports did not include some of the facts about Negro schools. *Georgia School Report, 1896*, pp. 32-34, ccci, cccxxii. The estimate of monthly salaries was computed by multiplying the average salary in each grade by the number of teachers, Negro or white, in that grade, and then adding for each race. By this method, it is found that all white teachers received $146,450.09 per month as salary, all Negro teachers $55,460.44.

[4] Ray Stannard Baker, *Following the Color Line* (New York and London, 1908), pp. 52-54. Some of the private Negro schools were even more primitive than the public ones.

[5] Henry R. Hunter, *The Development of Public Secondary Schools of Atlanta, Georgia:* George Peabody College for Teachers, Abstract of Contribution to Education No. 244 (Nashville, 1939), pp. 5-6.

while rural whites could debate with urban whites about the public school policy of the state, Negroes simply had to accept the dispensation of the whites.

The practice of racial inequality in Georgia education was tested in the federal Supreme Court in 1899, three years after the Plessy case. A Georgia county abandoned its aid to a Negro high school while continuing to contribute to a similar private white high school. The school board argued that, since the fund was not large enough to support two Negro schools, it was therefore in the interest of the community that all Negro funds be given to the elementary school. The federal Court sustained the board, ignoring the fact that the board did manage to find a large enough fund to aid a white high school.[6]

As in the Carolinas, the nineties brought the first wave of Georgia educational reform.[7] In their efforts to counter the attractions of Populism, conservative Democrats raised the state school appropriation from nothing to one million dollars in the five years before 1893, and held it at that level for four more years. The mask was thrown aside in 1898, when Populist strength had collapsed and Allen D. Candler became governor on a platform of economy. With the governor's endorsement, a bill cutting the school fund in half was quietly introduced. It was halfway to passage when outraged school officials stormed in from the county seats, roused the state superintendent, and managed to hold the

6. *Cumming v. Board of Education*, 1899, summarized in Mangum, *Legal Status of the Negro*, p. 95.
7. The Georgia state school system was begun on the eve of the Civil War. The Reconstruction government wrote specific and mandatory provisions for education into the constitution, provided for Negro education, and allowed uniform state school taxation. Conservatives in the two decades after 1872 reduced the educational budget and changed the requirement of equal facilities in the dual system to equal facilities "as far as practicable." Atlanta, Savannah, Augusta, Macon, Columbus, and smaller mill towns walled in their property and with the aid of the Peabody Fund built schools of brick and stone, while Superintendent Gustavus J. Orr pleaded in vain for fifteen years for state appropriations and federal aid. R. R. Hollingsworth, "Education and Reconstruction in Georgia," Part I, in *Georgia Historical Quarterly*, XIX (June, 1935), 124-31, Part II in *ibid.*, XIX (September, 1935), 249; Albert B. Saye, *A Constitutional History of Georgia 1732-1945* (Athens, 1948), pp. 270, 279-83, 288, 307-08; C. Mildred Thompson, *Reconstruction in Georgia, Economic, Social, Political, 1865-1872*: Columbia University Studies in History, Economics and Public Law, LXIV (New York, 1915), 336-37; Dorothy Orr, *A History of Education in Georgia* (Chapel Hill, 1950), pp. 167-207.

fund at the $800,000 mark, where it remained for the next six years.[8] At the turn of the century there was a deadlock between educational reformers and large taxpayers, between white counties and black counties.

The outstanding difficulty of the Georgia school system was its failure to pay teachers on time. This was largely because the legislature, unable to reduce the state appropriation below $800,000, accomplished its purpose circuitously by failing to provide enough taxation to pay out the full amount. Every year thereafter the funds were short, and teachers were forced to wait for their pay until the next annual tax collection. Teachers were given scrip instead of cash for decades, and usually had to discount the scrip for living expenses. As early as 1901 the state was in arrears to teachers by a year and four months. Governor Candler was refused a loan by New York capitalists, and the state treasurer refused to divert to teachers' salaries the half-million surplus in the treasury because of his bonded pledge to apply it to the old funded state debt. Atlanta and Savannah banks made short-term loans in 1901, but the crisis returned the following year when these loans were repaid. Teachers continued to draw scrip.[9]

Teachers who lost 12 to 24 per cent of their salaries through "heavy tithing by banks and loan sharks"[10] viewed with understandable skepticism the official efforts of conservative administrations to improve the schools in other respects. When educational orators declared that "the teachers had more cause to go on strike than any other class," they were "greeted with applause." The class consciousness which had seemingly died among farmers had a recrudescence among teachers. "Demand your rights and

8. *Ibid.*, pp. 226-28, 251; Mayo, "The Final Establishment of the American Common School System in North Carolina, South Carolina, and Georgia, 1863-1900," *Report of the Commissioner of Education for the Year Ending June 30, 1904*, I, 1077, 1083-85. The rural term was reduced by a month or more by the 1898 retrenchment. "The burden of the blow fell upon the country people," observed Superintendent Gustavus R. Glenn, "the very people who were least able to bear it."—*Georgia School Report, 1898*, pp. 7-8.

9. Candler made a trip to New York in an unsuccessful effort to borrow the money. New York *World*, April 12, 1901; Atlanta *Journal*, May 2, 6, 1901.

10. School Commissioner M. B. Dennis of Putnam County, "Hope for Improvement in the Public School System Barely Flickers," article in Atlanta *Journal*, December 10, 1901. The title "school commissioner" was changed in 1911 to the more usual title of "superintendent." For convenience, the latter title will be used throughout.

stand upon your demands," former Governor William J. Northen advised teachers. "I do not like to counsel rebellion, but if there was ever a time when labor should throw down its tools and walk away from the shop and leave the industry untouched that time has come to the teachers of Georgia, if your appeals are not heard and satisfied."[11] The appeals were heard, but not satisfied; no one called a strike, but a whole generation of Georgians was schooled by disgruntled teachers, who considered the state's treatment of them *"nothing less than a legalized outrage!"*[12] Georgia's educational movement was weaker at the base than in other states because of this resentment. "Soured, harassed, embittered teachers are a curse to the children that sit at their feet," warned the state superintendent, "and a source of disgust to all with whom they come in contact."[13]

Georgians generally seemed rather cold to educational reform, as either a Yankee innovation or a cause of taxation, "and then the negro question plays an important part in the matter."[14] Rebecca L. Felton, wife of the state's most hardy Independent, found the state system "a great circumlocution affair," and was shocked to discover "the employment of nearly ten thousand teachers, black and white (the teachers averaging over $20 per month)." This seemed to her wasteful extravagance.[15] The local disputes dealt not so much with how school funds might be increased as with how the existing and available funds were to be spent. There was no group of indigenous educational reformers whom the Southern Education Board could enlist for its outside agency. Even on the county boards of education were men unsympathetic to educational objectives; others "might almost be called illiterate," according to a superintendent's testimony, and therefore incapable of enlightened opinions on the proper scope of public education. "They ought to be men familiar with books," said the superintendent,

---

11. Atlanta *Constitution*, July 10, 18, 1903.
12. Wade H. Wood, Superintendent of Washington County, in *Georgia School Report, 1905*, p. 110.
13. *Ibid.*, *1908*, p. 27.
14. *Ibid.*, *1902*, p. 72.
15. Mrs. William H. Felton, "Shall Every School Have Its Wagon?" in Atlanta *Journal*, November 15, 1900. It is possible that the system of apportionment was at the bottom of Mrs. Felton's complaint, for she was from a mountain white county.

"not . . . textbooks merely, but the books that constitute literature."[16]

The Ogden movement started on its awkward foot in Georgia. When Ogden's party reached Atlanta after the Winston-Salem Conference in 1901, they held a meeting at a Negro church, with Booker T. Washington in attendance. Governor Candler refused an invitation to attend, and was reported to have said in explanation:

I declined because I did not purpose to give official sanction to their schemes. This man Parkhurst, who seems to be one of the leading spirits, is an old crank, as everybody knows who has followed his career. . . .

I don't think much of it. Booker Washington was the best man in that party. Washington is a good negro and is doing pretty good work. It is to his interest to get these Northerners interested in his schools. He gets money out of them and I don't blame him for that at all. Dr. Curry, the Peabody agent, is a good man, but I don't know much about the others.[17]

The Board's entering wedge was a Conference for Education in the South at Athens in 1902, sponsored by Eugene C. Branson, president of the state normal school in that city. Branson had known Page and Dabney in North Carolina, had taken his white students to Hampton, and was in touch with Booker T. Washington.[18] Curry helped to lay the groundwork by a visit to the legislature in 1900. "The state can educate all the children and at half the price that the church or individuals can educate one-fourth of the children," he said.[19] George S. Dickerman, agent of the Board, made a swinging tour through the state and enlisted the leading city superintendents.[20]

16. *Georgia School Report, 1900*, pp. 129-30.
17. Candler also expressed hostility to Negro higher education. Interview, quoted in New York *Herald*, April 25, 1901, clipping in Dickerman clipping books, S.H.C., University of North Carolina. After considerable editorial attack from Northern newspapers and from New South leaders such as Aycock, Candler denied that he had been correctly quoted.
18. Branson to Washington, January 29, 1902, Washington Papers, Library of Congress; Branson to Frissell, November 25, 1901, Southern Education Board Papers, S.H.C., University of North Carolina. Branson was the Georgia state institute conductor in the nineties, though less spectacular than McIver and Alderman in North Carolina.
19. Atlanta *Journal*, November 23, 1900.
20. Dickerman to Ogden, December 11, 1901, Dickerman to Murphy, February 6, 1902, Dickerman Papers, S.H.C., University of North Carolina.

Governor Candler refused to welcome the conference, but Hoke Smith, publisher of the Atlanta *Journal* and a leading anti-corporation lawyer, was there. Though he claimed that Southern whites, after paying 95 per cent of the school taxes, "with equal justice distributed it to black and white," Smith insisted that "the doctrine of human rights" demanded the training of "the children of both colors . . . to their minds' highest possible accomplishment."[21] There was no intimation here that Smith would let slip the dogs of race war four years later. More diffident was the greeting of Clark Howell, railroad director and editor of the Atlanta *Constitution*, the state's leading conservative paper. Howell called for "the biggest and most comprehensive trust yet attempted—an educational trust." But in the part of his speech which did *not* find its way into the *Proceedings*, he expressed some resentment of Northern-educated Negroes and warned that white education must be made a primary goal.[22]

On Confederate Memorial Day, Wallace Buttrick put the General Education Board into partnership with the United Daughters of the Confederacy for furnishing scholarships and a dormitory to the state normal school. The General Education Board, Ogden, and Peabody followed up with other grants in the state.[23]

Walter Barnard Hill, chancellor of the state university, was the Board's Georgia agent until his death in 1905. A man of the world, Hill had been one of the state's leading railroad lawyers until 1899, when his law partner Nathaniel E. Harris and Senator Augustus Octavius Bacon secured for him the chancellorship. "It is certain that he carried both the great denominations of the state, the Baptists and the Methodists," as well as directors of the Central Railroad of Georgia, to the support of the state university. Furthermore, as a former lobbyist, "he reconciled the General

---

21. Hoke Smith, "Popular Education as the Primary Policy of the South," in *Fifth Conference for Education in the South, Proceedings* (Athens, 1902), pp. 48, 51.
22. *Ibid.*, pp. 96-97; Atlanta *Constitution*, April 25, 1902.
23. *Fifth Conference for Education in the South, Proceedings*, pp. 5-6; Edward S. Sell, *History of the State Normal School, Athens, Georgia* (Athens? 1923), pp. 31-38; Atlanta *Journal*, April 26, 30, November 11, 1902; Nancy Telfair, *A History of Columbus, Georgia, 1828-1928* (Columbus, Georgia, 1929), pp. 233-36, 252; Selene Armstrong, "Magnificent Public School System and Industrial Advantages of Columbus, Georgia," in *Georgia School Report, 1906*, pp. 297-309; Ware, *George Foster Peabody*, pp. 107-16.

Assembly to the University."[24] The Georgia campaign needed such diplomatic talents.

The philanthropists could hardly go into partnership with the actively hostile Allen D. Candler, but he was succeeded in 1902 by another conservative governor, Joseph M. Terrell,[25] a man not unfriendly to education and willing to have his name on the state campaign committee. At best, Terrell was a neutral element in the educational movement, while his political faction fought increases in school funds. He was from the black county of Meriwether, where white schools thrived on the Negro two-thirds of the school fund furnished by the state, financial discrimination being about fifteen to one in favor of white children.[26]

The Georgia Educational Campaign Committee was organized by Charles D. McIver at a quiet conference in 1903 in Governor Terrell's office. It included Hill, Terrell, ex-Governor W. J. Northen, State Superintendent William B. Merritt, Hoke Smith, Southern Methodist Bishop Warren A. Candler, and Superintendent Mell L. Duggan of Hancock County.[27] In the customary address "To the People of Georgia," one plank was local in significance and was the key to the state campaign which followed: "We appeal to the people to adopt the Constitutional amendment reclaiming for themselves the right of supplementary local taxation to be exercised in those communities that desire it in accordance with the democratic principle of home rule." As Ogden explained this matter to a New York City friend: "The Constitu-

---

24. Nathaniel E. Harris, "Memorial Sketch," in *Walter Barnard Hill, Chancellor of the University: Bulletin* of the University of Georgia, Memorial Number (May, 1906), pp. 11-15; idem, *Autobiography: The Memories of an Old Man's Life with Reminiscences of Seventy-Five Years* (Macon, 1925), pp. 249-72, 303. In six years, Hill raised more money for the university than in the previous seventy-five years. A recent study of his administration is in Robert P. Brooks, *The University of Georgia under Sixteen Administrations, 1795-1955* (Athens, 1956), pp. 111-35.

25. "The Georgia Governorship," editorial in *American Monthly Review of Reviews*, XXVI (August, 1902), 170-71.

26. According to the school census taken in 1893, Negro children of the county were 64.6 per cent of the school population. In 1906, while Terrell was governor, Negro teachers of the county received 11.5 per cent of the amount spent for salaries. Salaries represented 95 per cent of the county's educational expenditures. *Georgia School Reports, 1896*, p. ccccxix; *1906*, pp. 337-39, 372-73, 378, and note on p. 366 that Meriwether County failed to report the monthly cost of education per white and Negro pupil.

27. *Georgia School Report, 1903*, pp. 30-33.

Georgia: The Urban-Rural Conflict 219

tion of the State of Georgia forbids the levying of a local tax for educational purposes. . . . Until the Constitution of Georgia is amended at that point, progress will be greatly impeded. Therefore, our first objective in that State is to so arouse public opinion as to make a universal popular demand for the needed amendment to the Constitution."[28]

Ogden's analysis was substantially accurate. The constitution did not precisely prohibit local taxation, but no property-owner could complain that the craftsmen of the law had served him poorly. Any petition for a local tax election must first be approved by two successive grand juries, "composed of older men and property-holders, whose children have been educated by the men themselves," and who were "opposed to anything that will touch their individual pockets pretty heavily."[29] If a local tax proposal could get past the grand jury, it had to be approved by the affirmative votes of two-thirds of all qualified voters in the county, including those still on the rolls who had died or had left the county and those cut off from the polls by creeks, impassable roads, or sheer indifference. Thus the constitution required virtual unanimity, such as the Pied Piper had evoked. And the towns, which in nearly every county had already secured local taxation within their own limits by special enactment, had no burning desire to share the returns from their property with the country folk.[30] Thus, if Ogden simplified the matter, he did not exaggerate.

To begin the campaign for the amendment, Jere M. Pound of the Georgia Teachers' Association prepared an effective bill and lobbied for it in Atlanta, with the advice and assistance of other school men.[31] A compromise measure sponsored by a black-county senator passed both houses by more than the requisite two-thirds vote, because it was linked with another amendment limiting state

28. Ogden to Isaac N. Seligman, January 14, 1904, Ogden Papers, Library of Congress—University of North Carolina.
29. Superintendent J. D. Gwaltney of Floyd County, in *Georgia School Report, 1901*, p. 87.
30. Superintendent M. B. Dennis of Putnam County, in *Georgia School Report, 1899*, pp. 155-56. McIver called the Georgia clause "an ironclad protection against taxing property."—McIver, "Current Problems in North Carolina," *Annals* of the American Academy of Political and Social Science, XXII, 58.
31. *Georgia School Report, 1902*, pp. 88, 123, 141-64; Atlanta *Journal*, April 15, 16, 1903; Atlanta *Constitution*, June 26, 1903.

taxation of property to five mills per dollar. The McMichael amendment called for significant changes in the constitution. Local tax elections could be called, without the delay of two successive grand juries, for levying a five-mill property tax if two-thirds of the voters approved.[32]

During the year between passage and submission to the voters, the Educational Campaign Committee conducted a systematic drive for public sentiment in favor of the amendment. About a hundred rallies on Thanksgiving Day in 1903 were followed in the fall and winter by rallies during court week at each county seat, where there was always a crowd during the farmers' slack season. The committee distributed a great variety of literature in the press and in leaflet form.[33]

Some aggressive superintendents overcame the "croakers and enemies to the cause" by "all-day singings, rallies, barbecues, etc." In one county educational fairs displaying the artifacts of the schoolrooms drew large crowds; "and, as the old man described the storm, 'we blowed down trees that never had been blowed down before.' "[34] Superintendent Merritt went out to dozens of rallies as the prophet of "a calamity of great proportions" if the amendment were rejected. No organized opposition developed, possibly because the amendment was linked to the limitation of state taxation; to make sure of success, Chancellor Hill secured the public backing of the chairman of the Democratic state executive committee.[35] And the amendment was ratified, along with the one which limited state taxation, by a comfortable margin.

The legal obstacle was overcome, but subsequent efforts to carry the counties for local taxation met with less success. Incorporated towns with local taxation opposed efforts to include them in the county system. A few counties were able to muster the necessary

32. The vote in the house was 138 to 2. The sponsor, E. H. McMichael, was from Tazewell in Marion County. He and his father-in-law were active in the Democratic machine. Atlanta *Constitution*, August 11, 14, 1903; Orr, *Education in Georgia*, p. 260.

33. Walter B. Hill, "Local Taxation in Georgia," in *Seventh Conference for Education in the South, Proceedings* (Birmingham, 1904), pp. 118-19; Atlanta *Constitution*, October 2, 1904; *Georgia School Report, 1903*, pp. 53-55.

34. County superintendents' reports, quoted from *Georgia School Report, 1902*, pp. 63, 72.

35. Atlanta *Constitution*, October 2, 1904.

votes. Fulton County did so only after three elections, and without benefit from the property of Atlanta.[36] In Pierce County local taxation was defeated by four to one, and its superintendent admitted, in oblique reference to the race issue, that "other questions" were injected into the campaign which "had more to do with its defeat than the question of taxation." In another county the opposition fought back at the polls "by technical irregularities in holding the polls, delivery of returns, etc."[37] The original local tax act was amended in 1905, over the opposition of rural legislators, to allow smaller units, as well as counties, to levy local taxes.[38]

The death in 1905 of Walter B. Hill, state campaign leader, threw the state campaign committee into confusion from which it never quite recovered, though it continued to send out speakers, press releases, and local tax pamphlets.[39] A triumvirate consisting of David C. Barrow, who succeeded Hill at the University of Georgia, Hill's widow, and the state superintendent divided responsibility for the campaigns, but failed to win hearty support from citizens and educators.[40]

The White Supremacy campaign of 1906 and the race riot which followed it startled the philanthropists and shattered their optimism. The progressive Hoke Smith, in his struggle for the governorship, injected the race issue into his campaign. "Everybody knew that the Disfranchisement issue was the cause of our success," his ally Tom Watson later wrote.[41] To prove their

---

36. Marion L. Brittain, in *Georgia School Report, 1905*, p. 74.

37. J. M. Purdom, Blackshear, Georgia, to Ogden, February 26, 1907, Dickerman Papers, S.H.C., University of North Carolina; Superintendent F. L. Florence of Morgan County, in *Georgia School Report, 1908*, pp. 171-72.

38. Atlanta *Constitution*, July 6, 29, August 11, 1905.

39. *Georgia School Report, 1906*, pp. 26-28, 43; William B. Merritt to Alderman, January 14, 1907, Southern Education Board Box 2, files of the president, University of Virginia.

40. Alderman to Ogden, February 2, 1907, files of the president, University of Virginia; Celestia S. Parrish to Ogden, March 25, 1907, Ogden Papers, Library of Congress—University of North Carolina; Parrish to Dickerman, April 1, 1907, unsorted Ogden Papers, S.H.C., University of North Carolina; Henry M. Bullock, *A History of Emory University* (Nashville, 1936), p. 254.

41. Quoted in C. Vann Woodward, *Tom Watson: Agrarian Rebel* (New York, 1938), p. 379; Dewey W. Grantham, Jr., "Georgia Politics and the Disfranchisement of the Negro," in *Georgia Historical Quarterly*, XXXII (March, 1948), 1-11. On Smith's political background, see *idem*, "Hoke Smith: Secretary of the Interior, 1893-1896," in *ibid.*, XXXII (December, 1948), 252-76, and J.

orthodoxy on White Supremacy, the other candidates and leading newspapers outstripped each other in incitement to white aggression. Clark Howell, the conservative candidate, said the educational qualification sponsored by Smith would disfranchise poor whites and give the college Negro "the absolute balance of power." And "whenever the nigger learns his haec, hoc, he right away forgets all about gee-whoa-buck!" Nor were the minor candidates offering a different fare. Colonel James M. Smith, millionaire farmer and convict lessee, argued that his own success with illiterate Negroes proved that Negroes needed no education to be satisfactory farm laborers.[42] Yellow journalism was not confined to Atlanta. "FIVE BLACKS TO ONE WHITE SEEN GOING TO PUBLIC SCHOOLS," reported an Augusta paper; "NEGROES OF RURAL SECTIONS PATRONIZING PUBLIC SYSTEM OF EDUCATION TO SURPRISING IF NOT ALARMING EXTENT."[43]

At placid Lake George, members of the Southern Education Board deplored the Georgia situation. "The Campaign in Georgia now makes a critical situation," said Peabody. "This will soon be over. Then will be the time for action."[44] A month after the election, Atlanta became for four days "An American Kishinev," in which Atlanta University was besieged by armed bands of whites. Before troops ended the pogrom, seventeen were dead. The assassination of two Negro barbers suggests an economic undercurrent of the racial antagonism, and the riot called into question the effectiveness of the philanthropists' approach to Southern problems.[45]

In this crisis of Southern race relations, the Northern philan-

---

Chal Vinson, "Hoke Smith and the 'Battle of the Standards' in Georgia," in *ibid.*, XXVI (September, 1952), 201-19.

42. Grantham, "Georgia Politics and the Disfranchisement of the Negro," *Georgia Historical Quarterly*, XXXII, 7; Peabody to Ogden, March 21, 1906, enclosing clipping from Athens *Banner*, Dickerman Papers, S.H.C., University of North Carolina.

43. Augusta *Chronicle*, February 13, 1906, clipping in Dickerman Papers, S.H.C., University of North Carolina.

44. Minutes of Southern Education Board meeting, August 6-8, 1906, Ogden Papers, Library of Congress—University of North Carolina.

45. "An American Kishinev," editorial in *Outlook*, LXXXIV (September 29, 1906), 243-44. Cf. "A Notable Address," editorial in *ibid.*, LXXXIII (July 14, 1906), 589. Kishinev was the scene of a massacre of Jews at the instigation of Russian officials in 1903.

thropists turned, not to the Negro protest movement then developing at Harper's Ferry, but to closer association with Southern paternalists. They gave their private blessing to a regional race commission organized by ex-Governor William J. Northen.[46] But Northen's benevolent interest in Negroes had a low ceiling. The best Negroes were helped by education of "the right sort," he believed, and Southern whites were willing to provide it. "Indeed, their educational opportunities are in advance of those of the white man, in that the white people pay by far the greater bulk of the taxes while the schools for the races are the same in character and advantages." Northen opposed "would-be friends" who had educated the Negro "entirely out of his place among the people who would be more than glad to use him, with profit to himself, if he were only willing to serve."[47]

Another effort at rapprochement with Southern conservatives was through a Businessmen's Committee, organized by Georgia delegates at the Pinehurst Conference for Education in the South in 1907 to give pith and moment to the state educational campaigns.[48] Educators took on new life, "an electric and quickened attention," even before the businessmen began to take the educational balance sheet. "When men of affairs think it worth while to turn aside for a while to consider educational questions," declared the state superintendent, "the whole world sets greater value on them."[49]

46. Reverend John E. White of Atlanta presented the proposal to Ogden. Memorandum of a conference at Ogden's office, January 24, 1907, Ogden Papers, Library of Congress—University of North Carolina. White was formerly the North Carolina clergyman who, with Kilgo and Bailey, agreed to support White Supremacy in North Carolina in 1898 in return for a promise to curb appropriations to state colleges. See above, Chapter II.

47. Report of a speech by Northen, in Atlanta *Constitution*, July 8, 1907.

48. Samuel M. Inman, the chairman, was a self-made man who had come from East Tennessee to Atlanta just after the Civil War and put his quick profits as a cotton broker into the land which slowly became valuable city real estate. He had a hand in nearly all local business and philanthropic enterprises. Two colleges, for example, were located in the midst of his real-estate subdivisions. And the other members of the committee had similar qualifications. Lucian Lamar Knight, *A Standard History of Georgia and Georgians* (6 vols., Chicago, 1917), IV, 1846-50.

49. Address to the Georgia County School Officials' Association, April 23, 1907, in *Georgia School Report, 1906*, pp. 248-49; Atlanta *Constitution*, April 26, 27, 28, 1907; Orr, *Education in Georgia*, p. 269; Thomas J. Woofter to Dickerman, December 22, 1906, Southern Education Board Papers, S.H.C., University of North Carolina.

The businessmen could hardly call the school system a going concern. Only 40 per cent of the children of school age attended daily, and $3.77 was spent per rural child enrolled, in a term of 103 days, while town systems spent $12.72 per child in a term of 170 days. The businessmen found that, under the constitutional limitation of state taxation on which some of them had insisted, "immediate prospects of sufficient funds from the State" for needed improvements was impossible. The only remedy they could see was local taxation. "The public mind and conscience must be educated and aroused," they resolved, until "so strong that the necessary supplemental local tax is demanded." A businesslike school system called for "living salaries at least" for better-trained teachers.[50]

The most tangible proposal for improving the schools came from Governor-elect Hoke Smith, who sat in on the meeting. Tax the underassessed and undertaxed railroads, said Smith, but his suggestion was omitted from the committee recommendations.[51]

The local tax movement meanwhile was running into difficulties. Complying with an act of 1907, county boards of education laid off districts approximately sixteen miles square, so large that daily attendance dropped about 6,000, mostly among Negroes. The official explanation was that boards of education gerrymandered the districts with "greater regard, as was natural, for the white schools."[52] Whites in favored districts also discriminated against other whites. Superintendent Marion L. Brittain explained in 1911 the effect of the McMichael laws:

> Following the example set by many of the larger towns and cities, many districts with railroad crossings or corporations of some value have availed themselves of the privileges of the McMichael Bill, fenced off the richest portion of the county they could secure, and voted additional school funds by taxation. This once attained, as a rule, they have stood as an impregnable bar in the pathway of educational advancement. In some cases they have by solid vote and influence de-

50. Resolutions of the committee, in *Georgia School Report, 1906*, pp. 270-72.
51. Atlanta *Constitution*, May 25, 1907. Editor James A. Gray urged a state-wide direct tax for schools as the only way to do the job in a businesslike hurry, but his suggestion was also ignored.
52. Superintendent William B. Merritt in *Georgia School Report, 1907*, p. 10.

feated the efforts of the rest of the county to secure additional school facilities through local taxation.[53]

Complexities in the local tax law also discouraged some barely literate school officials.[54]

The state Farmers' Union refused to support local taxation in 1907, and proposed instead that "all taxes coming to the state be made one pot and that the sum for schools be drawn from that fund."[55] Though some optimistic superintendents reported that local taxation was "sweeping over the State," twenty counties in 1907 had no local taxation whatever, not even in the county seats.[56] Superintendent Merritt "allowed the local tax campaign to slow up" several months before he left office, and Mrs. Hill found that arousing interest among the women was "very uphill business." "If the world could be built of 'pie-crust' promises," she reported impatiently, "we could very soon have the milennium [*sic*]."[57]

The Southern Education Board was linked with the conservative faction in the public mind of Georgia, and when Atlanta was selected for the 1909 Ogden conference, Governor Hoke Smith's attitude was found to be lukewarm at most. The Atlanta sponsors of the conference were nearly all conservatives: city boosters, clubwomen, New South editors, and machine politicians, led by Samuel Inman and Clark Howell. But the attendance of many rural teachers and members of the Farmers' Union gave the movement a broader backing.[58]

53. *Georgia School Report, 1910*, p. 26. Others corroborated this at the local level. E. G. Greene of Dooly County, in *ibid., 1908*, p. 126. Railroads went to court to fight rural district taxation. Atlanta *Constitution*, August 22, 1903.
54. Walter B. Hill, "Rural Survey of Clarke County, Georgia, with Special Reference to the Negroes," Phelps-Stokes Fellowship Studies, No. 2, *Bulletin* of the University of Georgia, XV (Athens, March, 1915), 42-43.
55. Atlanta *Constitution*, July 26, 1907; Barrett, *Mission, History and Times of the Farmers' Union*, pp. 215-17, 221.
56. *Georgia School Report, 1906*, pp. 70, 75, 87, 89, 98, 140-41, 165, 180; Atlanta *Constitution*, July 7, 1907.
57. Sallie B. (Mrs. Walter B.) Hill to Dickerman, April 4, 1908, September 28, 1907, Dickerman Papers, S.H.C., University of North Carolina. The spelling out of "millennium" seems to have given unusual trouble to Southerners of this period.
58. Rose to Ogden, January 2, 1909, Ogden Papers, Library of Congress—University of North Carolina; *idem* to *idem*, March 10, 23, 1909, Harry Hodgson (cotton-oil manufacturer, Athens) to Ogden, March 15, 1909, Isma Dooly (reporter, Atlanta *Constitution*) to Ogden, March 30, 1909, Ogden Papers,

Direct opposition to the Atlanta conference was led by Southern Methodist Bishop Warren A. Candler of Atlanta. Candler had formerly encouraged the movement and served on the state campaign committee,[59] but his attitude changed after Andrew Carnegie and the General Education Board went to the aid of Chancellor James H. Kirkland in his struggle with Methodist bishops for control of Vanderbilt University.[60] Ogden's position as president of the General Education Board made his conference fair game as an arm of the "Educational Trust."

Candler published a series of articles in the Atlanta *Journal* and elsewhere which were collected in the pamphlet: *Dangerous Donations and Degrading Doles, or A Vast Scheme for Capturing and Controlling the Colleges and Universities of the Country*, the title of which indicates their main theme. Candler acknowledged his debt to the *Manufacturers' Record*, but in appealing to the general public he avoided the heavy-handed emphasis on the Negro and the child labor crusader in the educational movement which characterized the *Record's* approach.[61] In support of Candler's viewpoint, Len G. Broughton, of Atlanta's Baptist Tabernacle, called the conference "paganistic." Ben J. Davis, vacillating editor of the Atlanta *Independent*, a Negro weekly, joined Candler in saying "Away with your millions." Touching a really weak spot of the philanthropic boards by mentioning that nearly all grants went to white colleges, Davis declared: "We agree with

---

Library of Congress; Atlanta *Constitution*, April 4, 16, 1909; *Georgia School Report, 1908*, pp. 48-49.

59. Candler pleaded prior engagements when asked to speak at Conferences in 1906 and 1907. He once requested a grant for a Methodist college through Ogden. Ogden to Candler, August 17, 1905, Dickerman to Frissell, March 11, 1907, Dickerman to Alderman, March 19, 1907, Dickerman to Candler, March 19, 1907, Ogden Papers, University of North Carolina; Candler to [Dickerman?], March 3, 1906, Dickerman Papers, S.H.C., University of North Carolina.

60. Alfred M. Pierce, *Giant Against the Sky: The Life of Bishop Warren Akin Candler* (New York and Nashville, 1948), deals with the controversy in a light favorable to Candler. Mims, *Kirkland of Vanderbilt;* and *idem, History of Vanderbilt* (Nashville, 1946), pp. 291-318, present the other viewpoint. Though the grants to the university were not made until 1910, philanthropic agents had done the groundwork earlier.

61. Warren A. Candler, *Dangerous Donations and Degrading Doles* (Atlanta, 1909), pp. 3, 15, 27. For a later expression of his views on Northern philanthropy, see Candler, "Mr. Carnegie and the Churches," in Atlanta *Journal*, July 20, 1913.

Bishop Candler, your money is a curse and the South should refuse it. If you are going to use it for the purpose of kindling more racial hate, we do not need it; if you are going to spend it in a way to encourage us to lessen our personal efforts to help ourselves, again, we say away with it."[62] As one of Ogden's local friends warned him before the conference, some Atlantans "would be pleased to see the conference achieve only a half hearted success."[63]

Governor Smith's public greeting to the conference was perfunctory. "It would be strange if in such a gathering as this there were not found diverging views," he said. "None the less I welcome you to Georgia." His own view was that "the negro engaged in the simplest manual labor will find his first inspiration from being taught the pleasure of doing . . . labor with artistic skill." "Mere instruction from books will accomplish almost nothing for him. He must lean upon the direction of the white man and grow by imitation."[64] Smith may have seen the record of expenditures of the General Education Board for 1907 which somehow reached the hands of the *Manufacturers' Record* and appeared in its columns. One item of expenditure was $900 to the conservative Joseph M. Terrell, who as governor had served on the state educational campaign committee. There may also have been other reasons for mutual distrust between Smith and the Ogdenites.[65]

62. Atlanta *Independent*, June 12, 1909, clipping in Ogden Papers, Library of Congress. On Davis, see Meier, "Booker T. Washington and the Negro Press: with Special Reference to the *Colored American Magazine*," *Journal of Negro History*, XXXVIII, 83.
63. Harry Hodgson to Ogden, March 15, 1909, Ogden Papers, Library of Congress.
64. Hoke Smith, "Address of Welcome," in *Twelfth Conference for Education in the South, Proceedings* (Atlanta, 1909), pp. 12-13, 17.
65. Ingle, *The Ogden Movement*, p. 17, citing *Manufacturers' Record*, March 12, 1908. Smith was also a trustee of the Peabody Fund, which made plans in 1905 to expend the principal of the fund and aid Peabody Normal College. The Northern faction of Peabody trustees, connected with Ogden and his friends, secretly planned to submerge this college in Vanderbilt University, while a Southern faction, which included Smith, opposed both the Peabody College grant and the connection with Vanderbilt. Smith to Richard Olney, June 27, 1904, Peabody Education Fund Papers, George Peabody College for Teachers; Smith to Alderman, January 19, 1905, files of the president, University of Virginia; Peabody Education Fund, *Proceedings of the Trustees at their Forty-Sixth Meeting, Washington, 24 January, 1905* (Cambridge, Massachusetts, 1905), pp. 7-9, 13;

228   *Separate and Unequal*

For several years after the conference at Atlanta, educational campaigning was in the doldrums. Apparently the conservative allies in Georgia confined themselves to generalities about education. And in 1911, when Smith was again governor, he requested that the educational campaign funds come from the Peabody Fund. Ogden felt that the Southern Education Board had failed in Georgia, though he was assured that educational legislation during Smith's second term was "the direct outcome" of measures "formulated by the campaign committee about four years ago."[66]

Actions of the legislature were particularly important to Georgia schools because the state appropriation played a major part in school finance. Legislative contests centered around unsuccessful efforts to divide by race the tax funds for schools, successful efforts to allow local taxation and establish public high schools, and efforts which achieved nominal success to establish compulsory attendance.

As an integer in the school census the Negro played a crucial, though passive, role in supporting black-county white schools. In 1900, the year of adoption of the Democratic white primary, agitation for racial division of school tax funds began. "Who is afraid of negro votes?" asked state senator Hiram P. Bell. Negro education had been started by a convention of "field hands, Yankee settlers, bummers and camp followers."[67] Bell's bill for school tax division was tabled, but the next year he had statistics, some of them to the third decimal point, others more vague. Negroes paid only .229 per cent of the property taxes, he argued, and their children should therefore receive about $50,000, instead of the $250,000 which he estimated that they currently received. Bell's proposal, passed in the senate over "Fierce opposition" from black-county representatives, was rejected by the house.[68]

The black counties had their inning in 1903, when Representative Bower of Decatur County proposed a joint resolution

---

J. W. Brouillette, *The Third Phase of the Peabody Education Fund:* Abstract of George Peabody College for Teachers, Contributions to Education, No. 280 (Nashville, 1940), pp. 4-5.

66. Rose to Ogden, August 29, 1911, unsorted Ogden Papers, S.H.C., University of North Carolina; Rose to Ogden, August 24, 1911, Ogden Papers, Library of Congress.

67. Atlanta *Journal*, December 5, 1900.

68. *Ibid.*, November 27, 28, December 2, 5, 1901.

expressing "the wish of the general assembly" that school funds be "separated after receipt by the county authorities so that the part used by the white schools shall be in proportion to the tax paid by the white people." Representative Grice of black Pulaski County said this was "a milk and cider resolution" compared to his own bill. Representative Stovall of Chatham, a black county in which Savannah was located, opposed the resolution, but not on equalitarian grounds. "How can the amount be accurately apportioned between the races?" he asked, since the state treasury kept no separate accounts of special taxes by race. Besides, such action would "put the north on notice that we are about to perpetrate an injustice on the colored race. It would precipitate a series of endowments to colored institutions." John N. Holder, who rallied the votes of white counties to defeat the measure, was assisted by the appearance in Atlanta of Booker T. Washington, who warned a mixed audience, including some legislators: "Destroy the schools in the country districts and the negro will vacate your farm lands and come to the cities, where he is sure of finding a school in session eight or nine months in the year."[69]

Meanwhile Grice's constitutional amendment bill to accomplish the same purpose appeared in the house, and another black-county spokesman threatened to oppose local taxation until it was ratified, because, he alleged, "that would throw the whole burden on ... the so-called black belt." Charles Murphey Candler of DeKalb, a white county, was probably sincere in warning: "If you divide this money among classes as this bill proposes, the time will come when it will be divided among individuals. ... That is the extension of this same principle, and at last it comes to the point where you will use only Jones' money to educate Jones' children. Then what will be the use of collecting any taxes at all? This proposition is a dangerous one and we should let it alone." And Stovall of Chatham, who feared that the Blair bill might be revived, said that "the school fund is not now divided according to population. The county school boards divide it equitably and use it to what they consider the best advantage." It was really absurd for the black counties to propose legislation for what they were already doing, and enough of them realized it to join white-

69. Atlanta *Constitution*, July 7, 10, 14, 1903.

county representatives in defeating the bill. The white counties dropped the issue, probably because they needed black-county votes for the local tax amendment bill passed later in the session.[70] As far as law was concerned, Negroes could still vote, and possibly white-county representatives feared that black counties, if provoked, might once again turn loose on them a controlled Negro vote. At any rate, they hesitated to deprive black counties of their special white school privileges. Later bills to divide the school fund were killed in education committees, while school funds in practice were divided so as to favor whites in black counties.

Education itself, of anybody's children, was denounced in the legislature in 1903 by John Fletcher Hanson of Macon, mill owner, railroad official, publisher. Hanson was a lobbyist against child labor legislation, which he described as "worse than paternalism run mad; it is down right rank socialism." The public schools, which he regarded as merely paternalism run mad, should "require any one who desired to be educated to bring a certificate that they had been at work." Public education was not a panacea for all human ills, he told the legislators; "on the contrary, the experience of the people of the south with reference to this question up to this time should teach us to handle it with the utmost caution."[71] In the same period South Carolina textile manufacturers used compulsory attendance as a foil against child labor laws, but the more candid Georgians howled down child labor legislation as an "entering wedge" for compulsory attendance.[72]

The educational reformers usually subordinated compulsory attendance to local taxation and legislative aid, but the question was thrown into the chaos of Hoke Smith's reform legislative session in 1907 by a group of women's organizations, which joined in a memorial to the legislature urging a literacy test for child workers eight to fourteen.[73] Possibly conservatives encouraged the women in order to impede Smith's reform program, just as they used

70. *Ibid.*, July 15, 1903.
71. *Ibid.*, June 30, 1903. Hanson warned that an educated working class might end the wage differential and wreck the prosperity of Southern textile mills.
72. *Ibid.*, July 8, 1903; Atlanta *Journal*, December 3, 1902; Davidson, *Child Labor Legislation in the Southern Textile States*, pp. 86-88.
73. This was intended to shore up the inoperative educational requirement in the child labor act of 1906. *Ibid.*, pp. 201-02.

a prohibition bill to use up thirty days of the fifty-day session.[74] The lobbyists for compulsory attendance pointed out that one-fifth of the state's children between ten and fourteen, and one-eighth of white voters, were illiterate. This gave cause for alarm to conservatives, though they had neglected the public schools for decades, because the legislature was then wrestling with Smith's disfranchisement amendment, which included a literacy qualification among the safeguards of the pedigreed vote. "There ain't a half a dozen men in this house who could write this paragraph," asserted conservative Representative Joseph Hill Hall of Bibb County after proving that he could at least read aloud Article IV, Section 1, Paragraph 1 of the state constitution, "and I can disfranchise half of you if you tried it." Hall was fighting, however, not for compulsory attendance, which received a quick defeat in the house, but for the "direct reason" for disfranchisement—because a Negro was a Negro—as against the legal refinements of the Smith administration bill. The literacy clause in Georgia did not stir up the fears and educational enthusiasm which accompanied disfranchisement in North Carolina. One may conjecture that by 1907 it was manifest that white registrars listened more sympathetically to the stumbling words of white applicants. There was a grandfather clause in the Georgia amendment, as well as other safeguards of the white voter, and probably Georgia conservatives hesitated to stir up educational enthusiasm by heavy emphasis on the literacy clause. They endorsed the disfranchisement amendment, and were soon able to oust Smith on another issue. The Atlanta *Journal* spoke for most qualified voters in proclaiming, "This is the white man's Georgia from now on."[75]

But compulsory attendance did intrude somewhat into the conservative legislature of 1909, when the lobby led by Emma Garrett Boyd came close to success. The Farmers' Union and labor unions supported the women's clubs, and about twenty local committees were organized, chiefly in cotton mill towns. A

74. Dewey W. Grantham, Jr., "Hoke Smith: Progressive Governor of Georgia, 1907-1909," in *Journal of Southern History*, XV (November, 1949), 428.

75. Atlanta *Constitution*, July 21, August 8, 13, 18, 1907; Atlanta *Journal*, October 11, 1908, quoted in Grantham, "Georgia Politics and the Disfranchisement of the Negro," *Georgia Historical Quarterly*, XXXII, 20.

memorial two hundred feet in length, containing over 5,000 signatures, asked for a moderate but enforceable law. About 20,000 pieces of literature were distributed, and each legislator received at least four official yet personal letters. Propaganda flooded the newspapers, of which about two-thirds supported the reform. The Atlanta *Journal* and *Constitution* vied with one another in zeal, and the *Journal* put its crack cartoonist to work on the issue, while the Atlanta *Georgian* for two weeks gave the first two columns of its editorial page to a dramatic and sometimes sensational support of compulsory education. There was a disillusioning denouement, staged in the smoky committee rooms and corridors of the capitol. Mrs. Boyd, ex-Governor Northen, Mrs. Passie Fenton Ottley, and the state superintendent appeared in behalf of the bill before the committees of education of both houses. The house committee, in what seemed to be an excess of zeal, changed the effective ages from eight to fourteen years to six to eighteen years. It otherwise strengthened the bill, until even the reformers urged moderation. The bill was then favorably reported, and hardly a day passed when Mrs. Boyd was not "in communication with active ushers for the bill among the legislators." As the session droned toward its close she demanded a hearing before the house rules committee. When she appeared every member swore that he personally favored the bill, but that it was "too important a measure to be acted upon without long and deliberate consideration." For this reason Representative Littleton, the sponsor, withdrew the bill from consideration. And so, when the session ended, the bill had not appeared on the floor of either house. "This is in spite of the fact that the petition asking for immediate action was incomparably the longest ever presented to the Georgia legislature," commented the stunned Mrs. Boyd; "that the alliance of organizations is said to be the strongest ever back of a measure in the state"; and that the press was not only "practically unanimous," but gave the bill "more space and more favorable encomiums than have ever been given to any measure" except prohibition and abolition of convict lease. Before the legislators escaped by subterfuge, supporters of the measure had pledged 114 members of the house, a majority, and got less formal promises from enough others to make two-thirds.[76] Mrs. Boyd refused to give up, and added to the "encomiums" a parliamentary skill learned in this hard school. In the next session, the bill was thoroughly debated in the house. But a vote was taken at 1:50 P.M., when some members had gone for their lunches. The vote was favorable but six votes short of a constitutional majority.[77]

The winds of opposition over the years slowly weathered away the demands of the compulsory attendance advocates. The Negro was abandoned as a beneficiary. In 1913 the state superintendent suggested that boards of education be given "power of excuse in cases of peculiar hardship and circumstances affecting the negroes particularly."[78] And the bill finally passed in 1916 "might almost be called a bill to Encourage School Attendance. In its preparation the compulsory laws of the Southern States only—those having like conditions with our own—have been consulted...." This bill provided for compulsory attendance between the ages of eight and fourteen, or else through the fourth grade, for twelve weeks a year, allowing any exemption acceptable to the school boards. Even so, the superintendent felt called upon to explain that it was not "likely that the school boards would deal with the problem of negro education in a way that would cause dissatisfaction to the white people." He would not spell out the loopholes of the bill any more plainly. Besides, he remarked irritably, "Those who favor the sending of missionaries to Africa and other lands to teach the reading of the Bible should be willing to have it taught to all classes of people at home."[79]

Neither the Southern Education Board nor the Georgia campaign leaders gave much direct attention to the problems of the Negro public schools. The General Education Board and the foundations for Negro education were somewhat more active, but their work did not touch the state school fund which was the crux of the problem of poor Negro schools. After 1913, George

---

76. Emma Garrett Boyd's account in Atlanta *Constitution*, August 15, 1909; *ibid.*, July 24, August 9, 1909; *Georgia School Report, 1908*, p. 10.

77. Atlanta *Journal*, July 7, 30, August 2, 1910.

78. *Ibid.*, July 14, 20, 1911, August 11, 1913; Atlanta *Constitution*, August 7, 1911; *Georgia School Report, 1912*, p. 34.

79. *Georgia School Reports, 1914*, pp. 21-22; *1915*, pp. 9-11; Atlanta *Constitution*, July 4, August 7, 1915; Davidson, *Child Labor Legislation in the Southern Textile States*, p. 211.

D. Godard, a white Alabamian, was supported by the General Education Board as state supervisor of Negro schools. The energetic Godard organized teachers' institutes and summer schools, advised Jeanes Fund industrial teachers in twenty-one counties, supervised two county "training schools" (a name for Negro high schools acceptable to local whites) aided by the Slater Fund, helped to build Rosenwald schools in five counties, and directed General Education Board canning and corn clubs.[80] Such brooms, however, could hardly sweep back the tide of white discrimination.

Georgia was one of the first Southern states to organize a state system of white public high schools. George Foster Peabody agreed in 1903 to pay half of the salary of a high school evangelist, Joseph S. Stewart, the forerunner of other such officials supplied by the General Education Board.[81] Stewart found only seven Georgia public high schools of four-year curriculum, their graduates totaling ninety-four.[82] And the constitution allowed state funds to be used for "the elementary branches of an English education only." The state was even forbidden to aid a school which used any other funds to teach students above the elementary level. Stewart circumvented the organic law in 1906 by getting state aid for what were called "district agricultural schools" in each congressional district.[83] His efforts to amend the constitution were sidetracked in 1907 by the press of Smith's reform legislation, but Stewart's bill was passed in 1910 and ratified in 1912. State aid followed, and white secondary education boomed. By 1914-15 there were 11,167 enrolled in 111 public four-year high schools, which were replacing the private schools.[84]

80. *Georgia School Report*, *1915*, pp. 37-44.
81. Dabney, *Universal Education in the South*, II, 410-17, is the most complete account of Stewart's work.
82. Stewart to Dabney, December 8, 1931, Dickerman Papers, S.H.C., University of North Carolina; Orr, *Education in Georgia*, p. 263; *Georgia School Report*, *1915*, p. 241.
83. Sponsored by Dudley M. Hughes, a large employing farmer, these schools were pilot projects for those later established by the Smith-Hughes act, which Hughes and Hoke Smith sponsored in Congress. Hughes liked the idea of the public's training his labor supply. *Georgia School Report*, *1906*, p. 6; *Atlanta Constitution*, July 2, 4, August 14, 1907; Stewart, report as professor of secondary education for June and July, 1906, Southern Education Board miscellaneous papers, S.H.C., University of North Carolina.
84. Marion L. Brittain, *Our Educational Needs: An Address Before the Georgia Educational Association* (pamphlet issued by Georgia Educational Cam-

Georgia: The Urban-Rural Conflict

The state school fund, appropriated per capita to counties, remained the most important source of revenue for most schools and was the subject of the bitterest legislative debates in the period after 1898. It increased strikingly in two periods, the nineties and the Hoke Smith administrations. Table 12 will indicate its fluctuations:[85]

TABLE 12
STATE PUBLIC SCHOOL FUNDS IN GEORGIA, 1871-1915

1871	$174,107	1886	$312,292	1901	$1,505,127
1872	No schools	1887	489,008	1902	1,615,052
1873	250,000	1888	330,113	1903	1,538,955
1874	265,000	1889	490,708	1904	1,591,471
1875	151,304	1890	638,656	1905	1,735,713
1876	149,464	1891	935,611	1906	1,711,844
1877	150,225	1892	951,700	1907	1,786,688
1878	154,378	1893	1,021,512	1908	2,000,000
1879	155,264	1894	937,874	1909	2,250,000
1880	150,789	1895	1,266,707	1910	2,250,000
1881	196,317	1896	1,161,052	1911	2,500,000
1882	272,754	1897	1,169,945	1912	2,550,000
1883	282,221	1898	1,640,361	1913	2,550,000
1884	305,520	1899	1,398,122	1914	2,550,000
1885	502,115	1900	1,440,642	1915	2,550,000

There is no doubt that the distribution per capita of the Georgia state fund, combined with discrimination against Negro schools, produced a discrimination almost as great between white schools. This can be shown by tedious but simple arithmetic. Five black counties and five white counties have been arbitrarily selected. Each black county had, by the federal census of 1910, over two-thirds Negro school population, the average being 79.0 per cent. Each white county had less than one-tenth Negro school population, the average being 5.2 per cent.[86] In 1908 the five

---

paign Committee, 1911), p. 4; Orr, *Education in Georgia*, p. 264; Atlanta *Journal*, July 29, August 4, 5, 1910; *Georgia School Report, 1915*, p. 237.

85. *Ibid.*, p. 507, has the list of figures from which this is taken. Of course the school census had more than doubled during this period, but it was increasing as fast in 1880 or in 1900 as it was in 1895 or in 1907.

86. The black counties were Baker, Burke, Calhoun, Camden, and Chattahoochee; the five white counties, Catoosa, Cherokee, Dade, Dawson, and Fannin. United States Bureau of the Census, *Thirteenth Census of the United States Taken in the Year 1910*, Vol. II, Population 1910 (Washington, 1913), pp. 372-81. The census reported an aggregate of 22,293 persons aged 6 to 20 inclusive in these black counties, and 15,991 persons of these ages in these white counties. There being no ethnic division of these persons, the division of those 6 to 14 inclusive was used to reach the percentages given above. Since these

black counties received from the state by per capita apportionment $49,355.62, or $2.21 per child according to the census of 1910,[87] while the five white counties received from the same source $32,155.13, or $2.01 per child according to the census of 1910. The five black counties in 1908 expended on Negro schools $17,507.85, or 99 cents per Negro child of school age, leaving for white children $31,847.77, or $6.80 per white child *from the state fund alone*, regardless of any local taxation. The white counties in 1908 expended on their widely scattered Negro schools $1,504.40, or $1.81 per Negro child, leaving from the state fund $30,650.13 for white schools, or $2.02 per white child.[88] In brief, these black counties discriminated against Negro children and in favor of white children at the average rate of nearly seven to one, giving these white children a financial advantage greater than three to one over those in white counties.

---

are very nearly the percentages for all of ages 6 to 20 inclusive, they have been used to estimate that in the black counties there were *about* 4,682 whites and 17,611 Negroes of school age, and in the white counties *about* 15,159 whites and 832 Negroes of school age. All of the figures below are therefore necessarily estimates, though the margin of error seems negligible.

87. *Georgia School Report, 1908*, pp. 488-89. The differences in amount per child are so minor that they may be explained by inaccuracy of either the federal census or state school census, probably the latter, because in that census taken by local school officers the temptation would be to pad the census or to fail to count some children in the coves of mountain white counties. The census records, when compared with apportionments, indicate that no tacit compromise between black and white counties was reached at the state superintendent's office. Funds were distributed to the counties per capita, according to law.

88. *Ibid.*, pp. 460-61, 466-67, 494-95. The Georgia counties reported to the state the monthly average cost per white pupil and per Negro pupil, the number of white and Negro pupils enrolled in and in attendance, and the number of days of the public school session (20 school days being a school month by state law). The figures above are computed by reversing the process by which monthly cost per Negro and white pupil was originally computed by the county, that is to say, by multiplying the average monthly cost per white pupil by the number of months of the term and by the number of white pupils enrolled (except in Catoosa and Dawson Counties, where the county obviously used the number in attendance as a divisor). Checking this against the record of total school expenditure for the counties shows less than 5 per cent error, which would be reduced further if the balance at the end of the year were included in the calculation. The amount per child of school age is figured on the basis of the federal census of 1910. While error cannot be eliminated because of the nature of the record, the proportions would not be substantially changed by more precise data. None of these figures takes into account the extension of the term for white schools by private subscription, from one to six months in all of these black counties and in two of the white counties, without any accounting to the state or to the Negroes.

Georgia: The Urban-Rural Conflict

It is not surprising that Negroes, lacking votes and freedom of speech, could neither resist nor protest. But why were the whites of white counties silent? Why did they not shout from the mountain tops and from the floor of the legislature? They had votes, they were in the center of the only stronghold of independent politics in the state. Certainly they were not restrained in speech. And their dislike of the lowland white was proverbial. And yet, far from disputing the distribution of the state school fund, their representatives joined with those of rural whites from Piedmont and plain in demanding an ever larger state school fund. They distrusted the local tax amendments, fearing that they were roundabout attacks on the state school fund.[89] The harmony of white and black counties on the question of the state school fund seems more enigmatic when it is recalled that in other Southern states they struggled openly and bitterly over distribution of the state fund.[90] Reports of the state and county superintendents were almost utterly silent on the subject. Nor was it discussed on the floor of the legislature.[91] Clearly the reason was that the rural white and black counties had common interests which they did not want to jeopardize by a dispute over distribution of the state school fund. They shared a common prejudice against the Negro competitor, in a region of labor surplus and marginal occupations; and possibly whites in white counties feared that, if forced to decide between losing the apportioned state fund and spending more on Negro schools, the black counties would take the latter course and thus arm the Negroes for labor competition. But more important was a common feeling toward the cities, which seems to be the true key to rural agreement in favor of the state school fund. Hatred of the cities was not only rural Georgia's legacy from Populism, but a response to ever-present economic realities.

Most of the Georgians who could be called beneficiaries of the Industrial Revolution lived in five cities—Atlanta, Savannah,

89. See, for example, the remarks of the representative of Miller, a predominantly white county, on the second McMichael local tax amendment, in Atlanta *Constitution*, July 29, 1905.
90. Perhaps the bitterest fight was in Alabama. See Bond, *Social and Economic Influences on the Public Education of Negroes in Alabama*, pp. 148-63, 178-94, 246-54.
91. *Georgia School Report, 1915*, pp. 16-17, the only unmistakable reference found by the writer, avoids specific mention of the Negro.

Augusta, Macon, and Columbus. Here were the factory owners, bankers, dealers, distributors, and employees of outside corporations, and here was concentrated the wealth and economic power of the state. The five counties in which these cities were located held 39.8 per cent of the estimated true value of all real property and improvements, though they contained only 14.6 per cent of the population.[92] Property in these five counties was assessed at even lower rates than in the other 41 counties, being 37.4 per cent of the state total.[93] In these five urban counties there was almost four times as much wealth per person in real estate and improvements as in the rest of the state, $594.75 per capita as compared with $153.48. Both white counties and black counties had so little wealth to be taxed that they could not maintain schools without the state fund from taxation levied on the cities. In fourteen of these, ten of which were white counties, the true value of real property and improvements was less than $100 per person, one-sixth of the amount in the five urban counties.[94]

Nearly all rural counties, which contributed in many ways to urban wealth, needed to tax the plump city man to feed educationally the lean country child. The state school fund was necessary for their schools, and they submerged their disposition to quarrel over its distribution in their common effort to increase its size. Many rural representatives were willing to tax the cities as far as they

92. In the counties of Fulton (Atlanta), Bibb (Macon), Chatham (Savannah), Muscogee (Columbus), and Richmond (Augusta), the estimated true value of real property and improvements was $191,893,966, out of a total of $482,534,050 for the state. Their aggregate population was 322,646 of a state total of 2,216,331. United States Census Office, *Wealth, Debt, and Taxation* (Washington, 1907), pp. 50-51.

93. Turning over a few rotten logs of Georgia's tax structure at the turn of the century, Schmeckebier found that the valuation of real property in Atlanta, Augusta, and Macon on their *city* digests totaled $68,486,866, and on the *county* digests for state taxation totaled $51,780,853, or a difference amounting to $16,706,013 between their assessment for local and state purposes. Laurence F. Schmeckebier, *Taxation in Georgia:* The Johns Hopkins University Studies in Historical and Political Science, Series XVIII (Baltimore, January-April, 1900), p. 231.

94. The urban-rural contrast in personal property was probably even greater. The black counties below $100 per person were Baker, Bryan, and Liberty; Effingham was about evenly divided; the white counties were Charlton, Clinch, Coffee, and Miller with over 25 per cent Negro population, and Forsyth, Gilmer, Pickens, Rabun, Towns, and Union with less than 12 per cent Negro population. These counties averaged $88.66 per capita. United States Census Office, *Wealth, Debt, and Taxation*, pp. 50-51.

were able, though others voted with the machine in favor of urban interests. The county-unit system in the Democratic primary and in legislative apportionment gave rural voters a commanding voice in the selection of governors and legislators.[95] Wealthy city-dwellers continued to rule through rustic demagogues, and the cities protected their schools' superiority through special acts. They could not reduce the state school fund, but could lower their assessment.[96] All property in Georgia, particularly urban property, was grossly undervalued and became increasingly so for decades, until the state eventually turned to other forms of taxation.[97]

The contrast between urban and rural schools, and between white county and black county schools, is shown by the records of Fulton County, with some incomplete figures for Atlanta within the county, the black county of Randolph, and white Cherokee County (Table 13).[98] Fulton, an urban county, had enough taxable wealth to furnish good schools for all. It had good white schools. Randolph County's "burden" of 2,680 enrolled Negro children, who received one-ninth of the amount per capita spent on white children, provided good schools from the state fund for the 1,423 white children enrolled. Randolph County drew from the state about $12,000 on account of Negro children, expended less than $6,000 on them, and turned the remainder over

95. Key, *Southern Politics in State and Nation*, pp. 117-24, is a lucid account of the Georgia county-unit system.

96. Though they had grown tremendously in the meanwhile, these five cities by 1913 lowered their proportion of assessed real property and improvements from 37.4 per cent of the state total to 35.3 per cent. In personal property they reported only 28.0 per cent of the state total. United States Bureau of the Census, *Wealth, Debt, and Taxation, 1913* (2 vols., Washington, 1915), I, 803-04.

97. The aggregate value of Georgia tax returns increased 106.2 per cent between 1900 and 1915, and only 45.3 per cent from 1915 to 1945. After 1915 the state turned to sales taxes and income taxation. Acts in 1926, 1937, and 1942 were designed to approach equalization of educational facilities for whites. Robert P. Brooks, *The Georgia Property Tax: History and Administrative Problems*: Institute for the Study of Georgia Problems, Monograph No. 7, *Bulletin of the University of Georgia*, L (January, 1950), 21; Robert P. Brooks, *The Financial History of Georgia, 1732-1950*: Institute for the Study of Georgia Problems, Monograph No. 9, *Bulletin of the University of Georgia*, LII (Athens, 1952), 62; Melvin C. Hughes, *County Government in Georgia* (Athens, 1944), pp. 119-21.

98. United States Census Office, *Wealth, Debt, and Taxation*, Part I, table 20; *Georgia School Reports, 1903*, pp. 227-29, 248-50, 260-62, 294, 300; *1913*, pp. 167, 190, 325, 328, 335, 361, 364, 371, 397, 400, 407, 471, 491, 511. Figures for true value of property were computed to the nearest dollar, amounts per pupil enrolled or attending to the nearest cent.

to white schools. Its white literacy rate was 99.996 per cent. In Atlanta and Fulton County less than half of the school fund was from the state, whereas in Randolph County and Cherokee County more than half of the school fund came from the state. The rural counties, then, were very dependent on the state fund; urban counties resorted to local tax.

TABLE 13

WEALTH AND SCHOOL FACILITIES IN GEORGIA URBAN AND RURAL COUNTIES

	Atlanta	Fulton County	Randolph County	Cherokee County
True value of real property and improvements per school-age child, 1904	no record	$3,287.00	$516.00	$427.00
Expenditure per pupil in daily attendance, 1903	$18.02	6.01	5.48	5.16
Expenditure per pupil in daily attendance, 1913	27.71	32.40	15.29	10.04
Expenditure per white pupil enrolled, 1913	no record	35.96	19.84	6.63
Expenditure per Negro pupil enrolled, 1913	no record	3.66	2.15	3.02

While most of the state school fund was derived from a state tax,[99] another important source was a half-share of the income from lease of state convicts to business enterprises, amounting to $82,019 in 1902. Convict labor costs had risen slightly since Joseph E. Brown had built his mining and railroad fortune upon them at seven cents a day, but convicts were still cheaper labor than chattel slaves had ever been, and were mistreated by overseers.[100] When exposures of fantastic brutalities were backed up by sober testimony in 1903, philanthropists and good-roads reformers joined forces to try to end the system and employ these

99. In 1901-02 the general tax levy was 3.1 mills and the school tax levy was 2.1 mills. Legislative appropriations in the sessions of 1898, 1900, and 1902 were $800,000 a year, in spite of vigorous efforts to raise the amount. Atlanta *Journal*, December 2, 10, 1902; United States Census Office, *Wealth, Debt, and Taxation*, p. 682.

100. James M. Smith, millionaire farmer and politician, was alleged to have leased convicts at $10 to $11 a year around 1906. A. Elizabeth Taylor, "The Origin and Development of the Convict Lease System in Georgia," in *Georgia Historical Quarterly*, XXVI (June, 1942), 113-28; Woodward, *Origins of the New South*, p. 15; Atlanta *Journal*, August 4, 1906.

unfortunates in chain-gangs on county roads. But Governor Terrell's official investigation committee hastily sustained the lessees. Friends of the schools (and of convict lessees) protested against Thomas S. Felder's proposal to take away one-fifth of the unpaid teachers' salaries, and inquired, "Where will you get the money to educate your children if you strike this quarter of a million from that fund at one blow?" Prominent supporters of public schools were charged with disloyalty to school interests if they opposed convict lease. Abolition was defeated and contracts were made for another five years.[101]

Arguments for a new lease of convicts in 1908 were reinforced by the recent loss by the schools of a quarter of a million dollars through liquor prohibition. The Columbus *Enquirer-Sun* remarked in defense of convict lease, "Some of the legislators are coming to the conclusion that while morality is a very good thing, it don't go very well with a low tax rate." Governor Hoke Smith had to call even the "reform legislature" into special session to end this abuse of sovereignty.[102]

For six years the school appropriations were held down to the level of 1898, while funds for other state agencies rose along with the tax returns. Then, in the flush of their local tax movement, the school forces invaded the legislature of 1904 and managed to raise the state appropriation once again to one million. Representative Joseph Hill Hall of Bibb County, in which the textile center of Macon was located, tried to stem the tide. Hall was a burly giant with matted black hair and beard, who wore a chewing cigar in the corner of his mouth. "You loud-mouthed advocates of the children, where is this leading to?" he cried out. "You will finally get all your convicts on the public roads and then where will your school fund, from convict hire, be?" Despite bitter attacks on the

---

101. To mollify the reformers, rates of lease were increased so as to yield about $200,000 a year. Counties could use it for either roads or schools, and many of them used it for roads. *Georgia School Report, 1906*, p. 62; Atlanta *Journal*, August 25, 1908; Atlanta *Constitution*, July 17, 22, 23, 29, 1903. Thomas S. Felder of Bibb County, John N. Holder, and C. Murphey Candler of DeKalb County were the leading abolitionist legislators.

102. Columbus *Enquirer-Sun*, July 28, 1908, quoted from A. Elizabeth Taylor, "The Abolition of the Convict Lease System in Georgia," in *Georgia Historical Quarterly*, XXVI (September-December, 1942), 278; Atlanta *Journal*, August 25, 1908.

school lobby, the house voted the million and persuaded the senate to agree.[103]

Though Governor Hoke Smith's specific campaign commitments of reform and disfranchisement had a natural priority during his two-year lease of power, he had long been interested in the public schools. His executive intervention brought about an increase of about 30 per cent in the state school fund, and he also called attention to hitherto obscured sources of state revenue for schools.[104] Smith never coupled public education with disfranchisement as had Aycock of North Carolina, nor was he on the other hand pledged as Aycock had been to universality of education. Thus he was freer to channel increased funds into white schools.

Actually relations between school men and reformers, during the first promising session in a decade, were strained by a clash of immediate concerns. Teachers and school administrators wanted more money; progressive political leaders worked primarily for tax reform. Some bitter words were exchanged. "These railroad men whip the school people into line by saying, 'If you don't help us get what we wish, we will prevent you from securing your appropriations,'" declared an administration senator, who concluded that "By these infernal methods" of "one of the dirtiest and most pernicious lobbies that has ever been in the capitol," "our tax acts have been made to suit the railroads."[105]

The reformers proposed two million dollars for schools, which would double the fund in five years and justify higher railroad taxation.[106] Another proposal was to create an independent school fund by an occupation tax on public utilities, from which salaries of teachers could be paid. But both plans were defeated and the reform faction was finally tied in the same Gordian knot which had entangled the easy-going Governor Terrell. Back salary for

103. Atlanta *Constitution*, July 29, 30, August 2, 7, 9, 11, 12, 1904.
104. Grantham, "Hoke Smith: Progressive Governor of Georgia, 1907-1909," *Journal of Southern History*, XV, 432.
105. Atlanta *Constitution*, August 18, 1907. Superintendent Merritt, a conservative opponent of Smith and reputed architect of this lobby, soon afterward resigned. Mrs. Sallie B. Hill to Alderman, November 11, 1907, Southern Education Board Box 1, files of the president, University of Virginia.
106. Atlanta *Constitution*, August 3, 6, 9, 10, 17, 1907. For Alexander J. McKelway's illuminating explanation why the Georgia senate was "the graveyard of all good legislation," see Davidson, *Child Labor Legislation in the Southern Textile States*, p. 201.

teachers continued to be a matter about which governors lectured legislators.[107] At least the reform legislature gave the teachers more scrip than had been the custom. And a number of the reform faction seriously sought to enhance the school system. Though a bachelor, Madison Bell of Atlanta said he would favor any proposed increase for the schools and had a compulsory attendance bill ready as soon as schools could accommodate the children. Hooper Alexander, a reformer angry over the defeat of the tax bills, retorted that he had six children, "and I think there is ample time to make appropriations . . . after we see where the money is to come from." Though he had helped to kill a utilities tax the day before, Joe Hill Hall asked: "Don't you know you have got to tax somebody to get all this money you want to give away?"[108] Though the legislature raised the school appropriation to $2,000,000, it failed to provide additional tax funds, and so the teachers continued to be paid a year late.[109]

Conservatives who returned to power in 1909 under Governor "Little Joe" Brown reduced taxation and tried to trim the school fund. "Rest on your oars," suggested one legislator.[110] The conservative heyday was temporarily interrupted when Hoke Smith returned to the governorship in 1911—only to be lured off in the same year to the United States Senate. Smith's legislative supporters bent their backs against the rising state expenditures as vigorously as had the conservatives, in the hope of ending the treasury deficit. The call to "cut to the bone" was sounded by Hooper Alexander. Conservative stalwart Hall asked: "Ain't you rather late?" He answered his own question: "The gentleman is five or six years late." Hall told a chastened audience of reformers that "it is not Bibb County's duty, nor that of the state, to support these country schools." They "come here for all," he charged, "instead of helping themselves some." After voting down five proposals to increase the school fund, the house yielded to a sixth. Two urgent messages from the governor and several stormy conference committee meetings cut the increase in half. In public finance Smith had always been conservative, a Cleveland

107. Atlanta *Constitution*, August 13, 1907.
108. *Ibid.*, August 11, 1907.
109. *Ibid.*, August 14, 16, 18, 1907.
110. *Ibid.*, July 2, 28, August 4, 12, December 26, 1909.

Democrat, and he wanted to increase the pressure behind reform of tax assessment. He pointed with pride to the five-month average school term and the fact that the schools were already receiving nearly half of the state revenue.[111]

Smith turned over the state, half-reformed, to conservative Acting Governor John M. Slaton, who called a special election and campaigned for Brown. The school forces abandoned efforts to increase state appropriations and concentrated on securing the teachers' back pay.[112] In the era of educational progress, the situation of teachers was actually declining. "For the first time in thirty years the teachers have not been paid by August, one dollar by the state," observed the Atlanta *Journal*. As "Miss Country School Teacher" put it more crudely in a country weekly, "Do you think we can eat your hot air and dress with your gas?"[113]

Governor Nat E. Harris rather understated the case when he declared in 1915, "This state of affairs seems well nigh a public scandal." After columns of newspaper debate and "a series of measures drafted and redrafted," a bill endorsed by the incoming governor provided that state warrants be issued monthly to teachers, payable in the fall when tax returns were in. This plan was cleared by officials of the district federal reserve bank, who believed that these warrants would be taken up at less than 6 per cent discount. About one-third of the counties already had an arrangement with a Michigan bank for loans at 6 per cent (the teachers paying the interest rate).[114] It seemed in 1915, then, that in the future there would be less tithing of teachers by banks and loan sharks.

111. *Ibid.*, August 10, 11, 12, 15, 17, 18, 1911. Actually, the term was barely four months in many rural schools.

112. The annual borrowing power of the state was increased from $200,000 to $500,000 by a constitutional amendment, but this was only a stop-gap measure. A one-mill tax was proposed, and the lease of the state-owned terminals at Atlanta and Chattanooga to the Louisville and Nashville Railroad. An inadequate appropriation of $50,000 was applied to teachers' salaries. The "brave way to do it," Governor Slaton believed, was by an extra tax and equalization of assessment rates, but the legislature would only authorize the governor to borrow the $500,000 for teachers' pay. Atlanta *Journal*, July 23, 24, 1912, July 22, 23, 24, 25, August 1, 7, 8, 9, 13, 1913; *Georgia School Report, 1911*, pp. 7-8, 13.

113. Atlanta *Journal*, August 11, 1913; *Pike County Journal* (Zebulon, Georgia), in *ibid.*, August 3, 1913.

114. Atlanta *Constitution*, July 10, 23, 1915; *Georgia School Report, 1908*, p. 18.

TABLE 14
AVERAGE MONTHLY SALARIES OF TEACHERS, GEORGIA ELEMENTARY SCHOOLS

1901		1915	
White, first grade	$36.90	White men	$60.25
" second grade	28.11	White women	45.70
" third grade	22.33		
Negro, first grade	25.60	Negro men	30.14
" second grade	26.00	Negro women	21.69
" third grade	16.30		

Though severely hampered by their position in the national economy, Georgians advanced public education between 1900 and 1915 to an unprecedented extent. Old restrictive laws were sent to the wastebasket. Enrollment increased by 30 per cent, attendance and number of teachers by over 50 per cent. One-teacher schools were disappearing among whites. Salaries of teachers, though still ridiculously low and paid in scrip, had increased somewhat, particularly for whites. Because of changes in published data, Table 14 can only roughly indicate the change.[115] The total school fund more than quadrupled, from $2,053,657 in 1900 to $8,313,791.54 in 1915. The rise in value of school buildings and grounds was almost as spectacular—from $2,995,808.75 in 1901 to $11,583,744 in 1915.[116]

Discrimination against Negro schools in Georgia followed the general pattern of the Southern seaboard and may be taken as fairly typical, not quite so discriminatory as South Carolina, slightly more so than North Carolina and Virginia. In the state report for 1915, over five-sixths of the total expenditure was accounted for by race. In studying the figures in Table 15, it is well to keep in mind that 46.1 per cent of the estimated population of school age was Negro, nearly one-half, and Negro children might expect about half of the school fund under the "separate but equal" doctrine. High schools and colleges, almost exclusively reserved for whites, are not accounted for, but only common schools for the inculcation of "the elements of an English education only."[117]

115. *Georgia School Reports, 1901*, p. 408; *1915*, p. 5.
116. *Report of the Commissioner of Education, 1900*, I, lxxv; *Georgia School Reports, 1901*, p. 408; *1915*, pp. 5, 449-50.
117. *Georgia School Report, 1915*, pp. 446-49.

Table 15
Georgia Common Schools—Expenditures in 1915

Item	White	Negro	Total
Total cost of supervision......	not reported separately		$ 297,471.47
Teachers' salaries............	$3,689,454.92	$695,803.85	4,385,258.77
Buildings...................	592,044.38	25,308.27	617,352.65
Equipment..................	100,926.50	3,398.18	104,324.68
Supplies....................	82,028.05	7,297.07	89,325.12
Repairs.....................	128,010.04	8,975.34	136,985.38
Libraries....................	not reported separately		16,169.37
Janitors, fuel, water, lights....	not reported separately		110,090.39
Promotion of health.........	not reported separately		6,150.58
Insurance...................	not reported separately		18,198.43
Interest.....................	not reported separately		90,429.90
Transportation...............	28,709.80	"(white only)"	28,709.80
Miscellaneous expenses.......	not reported separately		294,409.26
Total expenditures..........	$4,621,173.69	$740,782.71	$6,194,875.80

In the educational items reported separately, then, the Georgia Negro child received one-sixth as much as the white child; one-twenty-fifth of the amount for buildings and one-fifteenth of the repairs on them, one-twelfth of the supplies, one-thirtieth of the equipment, and none of the transportation, though his schools were 50 per cent more widely scattered.[118] As for the items not reported separately, it is unlikely that Negroes received one-sixth as much as whites. Some of the items are related to buildings—janitors, fuel, water, lights, insurance, and interest. Since Negro schools represented only one-thirteenth of the value of publicly owned school property, it is improbable that they shared heavily in expenditures related to school property.[119] White school libraries in 1915 were valued thirty-two times higher than those for

[118]. There were 4,985 white schools and only 3,378 Negro schools in Georgia in 1915. In North Carolina the average white rural school served an area of 8.9 square miles, the average Negro school 20.8 square miles, and a lone Negro school served Haywood County's 541 square miles. *North Carolina School Report, 1914-16*, Part II, pp. 103, 106. "The multiplication of small one-room schools which has led to the movement for consolidation in the case of white children has not extended to the colored public schools. Colored schools have never multiplied fast enough to be too close together, and it is not uncommon to find pupils who walk 6 or 7 miles to attend school."—Jones, *Negro Education*, I, 33.

[119]. Of the school property owned by counties and municipalities, Negro schools represented $865,321, white schools $10,718,423. *Georgia School Report, 1915*, p. 449.

Negroes.[120] One may conjecture that Negro teachers counted themselves lucky if they were not supervised. And apparently they were not. Negro schools in towns were of course in the segregated Negro district, while in rural areas they might be anywhere or nowhere. Social distance, a feature of all segregation, was probably a reason for the ethical callousness with which white superintendents performed the ritual of discrimination against Negro schools.

Besides the funds for common schools, Georgia reported almost two million dollars, in which Negroes hardly shared, for education above the elementary level. Ninety-two schools and sixty-seven teachers were reported to be training 1,411 Negro secondary students. The record does not explain how sixty-seven teachers could give courses in ninety-two schools. Perhaps the term "secondary" was loosely used.[121] The federal commissioner reported 310 Negroes in public high schools in 1916 and fifty-four times as many whites.[122] At the college level, the only state Negro school received the *pourboire* of $8,000 a year from the state in 1915 for current expenses, about 1.3 per cent of the amount for white state colleges.[123]

120. *Ibid.*, p. 450.
121. *Ibid.*, pp. 445-46.
122. *Report of the Commissioner of Education, 1917*, II, 513.
123. *Ibid.*, II, 394, 398; *Georgia School Report, 1915*, pp. 447-48.

CHAPTER VIII

Educational Expansion and the Context of Racism

"THESE ARE STIRRING TIMES," said educational campaigner James Y. Joyner in 1909. "The forgotten man has been remembered; the forgotten woman has been discovered; the forgotten child shall have his full chance in the South at last, thank God."[1] Edgar Gardner Murphy, a more analytical but not thereby less zealous participant, saw that "the campaign for the development of educational enthusiasm has gained astonishing headway in every state" and that "in helping the movement for 'more money' we have aided the South in assembling the raw materials, the stone and mortar, for the building of an educational system. But the nature of the building, from its very foundations, is still to be determined."[2]

Though Southern Education Board claims were sometimes excessive, there really was a remarkable expansion in Southern public education in the years after 1900. In eleven Southern states where the Board was active, annual expenditures for schools increased by $18,169,848 between 1900 and 1909. The total amount raised in these states between 1903 and 1909 was over $51,000,000.[3] And the expansion continued to accelerate until the Great Depression of the thirties.

1. *Twelfth Conference for Education in the South, Proceedings* (Atlanta, 1909), p. 212.
2. Murphy to Buttrick, November 14, 1907, Southern Education Board Papers, University of North Carolina.
3. [George S. Dickerman and Wickliffe Rose], *Southern Education Board: Activities and Results 1904-1910:* Southern Education Board Publication No. 7 (Washington, 1911), pp. 8-10, 13, 17-21, 25-26.

"The people are taxing themselves for public education as they have never taxed themselves before," Murphy said in 1909.[4] Not only did educational expenditure in the Southern seaboard increase 180 per cent in the period from 1900 to 1912. It also increased faster than the true valuation of all property, which in the same period increased 140 per cent. The amount spent on public education per dollar of property value increased by 14 per cent in the Southern seaboard, and by 31 per cent in North Carolina; only in Georgia was there a decline, by 3 per cent.[5] Thus the educational campaigns succeeded in capturing for the public schools an increasing share of the returns on an increasing wealth. While a slight monetary inflation in the period should be considered to qualify the extent of increase of both true value of property and educational expenditure, that factor has little or no bearing on the relation between the two.

The Southern seaboard school in 1915 was still, predominantly, the rural, ungraded, one-teacher school, but it was greatly improved. The average term was longer than in 1900 by over a month in every state and by over two months in North Carolina, being 145 days in Virginia, 140 days in Georgia, 122.8 days in North Carolina, 110 days in South Carolina.[6] Enrollment had increased, and now almost half of the children of school age attended daily.[7] The average child of school age attended school 51.4 days a year in South Carolina, 65.8 days in Georgia, 66.1 days in North Carolina, and 69.7 days in Virginia. These figures sharply contrast with those of 1900, when the average North Carolina child attended 21.9 days out of 365.[8]

The annual expenditure per pupil in attendance increased between 1900 and 1915 from $9.70 to $21.14 in Virginia, from $6.64 to $14.65 in Georgia, from $4.34 to $13.29 in North Caro-

---

4. Murphy to Ogden, January 9, 1909, Ogden Papers, Library of Congress—University of North Carolina.
5. Computed from figures in United States Census Office, *Wealth, Debt, and Taxation*, p. 36; United States Bureau of the Census, *Wealth, Debt, and Taxation*, *1913*, I, 24; *Report of the Commissioner of Education*, *1900*, I, lxxvii; *ibid.*, *1913*, II, 32.
6. *Ibid.*, *1917*, II, 48. This volume contains school statistics for 1914-15 because Congress failed to appropriate to the Bureau sufficient funds for earlier publication.
7. *Ibid.*, *1917*, II, 41, 46.
8. *Ibid.*, *1917*, II, 48; *ibid.*, *1900*, I, lxix.

lina, from $4.44 to $12.79 in South Carolina. The amount had more than doubled in every state, and more than tripled in North Carolina. The expenditure per school-age child showed, of course, a similar increase, and was now $10.17 a year in Virginia, $6.89 in Georgia, $7.15 in North Carolina, $5.98 in South Carolina.[9] The value of publicly owned school property rose phenomenally in these years; the value per child of school age increased four-fold in Virginia and Georgia and eight-fold in North and South Carolina. In 1915 the average amount in the Southern seaboard was $17.00 per child of school age.[10] Salaries of teachers increased less spectacularly than school buildings and equipment. Yet the longer average term and rise in monthly salary rates combined to triple the annual salary in North Carolina and double it in the others, the average in 1915 being $332.19 in Virginia, $305.97 in Georgia, $282.68 in South Carolina, and $251.34 in North Carolina. The increase in real income was somewhat less than these dollar figures indicate because living costs also rose to a lesser extent in the same period.[11]

High schools (for whites only) likewise multiplied. Between 1901 and 1916 the total number of public high schools increased from 324 to 991, the number of four-year high schools from 123 to 509. In the same period the number of secondary students increased from 16,319 to 63,900. Most of these were white students, who increased twice as fast as Negro secondary students and in 1916 outnumbered the latter twenty-nine to one.[12] More than two-thirds of the high school students were whites in rural areas and towns of less than 8,000 population.[13] There are no reliable records of receipts or expenditures for the new high schools, but they mounted into millions.[14]

9. *Ibid.*, *1917*, II, 55; *ibid.*, *1900*, I, lxxix.
10. *Ibid.*, *1917*, II, 41, 50; *ibid.*, *1900*, I, lxiii, lxxiii.
11. *Ibid.*, *1917*, II, 50. The general trends and problems involved in estimating real income of teachers since 1900 are discussed in George J. Stigler, *Employment and Compensation in Education:* National Bureau of Economic Research, Occasional Paper No. 33 (New York, 1950), pp. 19-22. See also Seymour E. Harris, *How Shall We Pay for Education?* (New York and London, 1948), pp. 72-74.
12. *Report of the Commissioner of Education, 1901*, II, 1915, 1979-83, 2085, 2121-23, 2138-40; *ibid., 1917*, II, 513, 520.
13. *Ibid.*, II, 518-19.
14. In 1916, 534 high schools reported income from all sources as $1,519,811. *Ibid.*, II, 525.

Members of the Southern Education Board were inclined to take major credit for the change. "That this Board alone has wrought the change no man would say: that the change—without this Board—could or would not have been wrought so generally or so soon every man must say who has any adequate personal knowledge of the facts," said the intellectually conscientious Murphy. To Walter Hines Page, with the perspective of New York, Southern educational advance seemed a miracle worked by Ogden:

> What a fine thing to look back over—this Southern Board's work! Here was a fine zealous merchant twenty years ago, then fifty-seven years old, who saw this big job as a modest layman. If he had known more about "Education" or about "the South, bygawd, sir!" he'd never have had the courage to tackle the job. But with the bravery of ignorance, he turned out to be the wisest man on that task in our generation. He has united every real, good force, and he showed what can be done in a democracy even by one zealous man. I've sometimes thought that this is possibly the wisest single piece of work that I have ever seen done—*wisest*, not smartest.[15]

But more detached observers were also impressed. Educational progress was one of the indications to William Garrott Brown that the South was taking a full-fledged place in the nation. The burden of illiteracy and ignorance, though "still heavy enough in all conscience," was "at least perceptibly lightening. Our people are aroused to the shame and the misery of it. There is still, it is true, much fear and dislike of the schoolhouse for negroes. But a healthier sentiment and opinion grow apace."[16]

In the heat of educational campaigns and the flush of victories it was easy to forget that the South pursued a chimera in its efforts to equal national averages in educational facilities, that Southern public education was at least as dependent on the Southern economy as the economic status was dependent on education. The Southern financial bondage to the Northeast tended to perpetuate an edu-

---

15. Murphy to Ogden, January 9, 1909, Ogden Papers, Library of Congress—University of North Carolina; Page to Alderman, January 26, 1913, in Burton J. Hendrick, *The Life and Letters of Walter H. Page* (3 vols., New York, 1922), I, 126.

16. William G. Brown, "The South in National Politics," in *South Atlantic Quarterly*, IX (April, 1910), 14.

cational disparity as the typical Northerner enriched by the South supported the schools of his own region through taxation or philanthropy. Occasionally the Southern educators reminded themselves, as did Alderman in 1907, that there was "no State in the South with enough money at its disposal to have a good school system and keep it open for eight or nine months in the year."[17] Great as were the regional gains in education, the non-South made comparable gains without the stimulus of educational campaigns. The rest of the nation was able to expand education with comparative ease because of a larger surplus of wealth and income above immediate needs for subsistence. For example, Virginia in 1915 spent for public schools less than half, and South Carolina less than one-third, of the amount per capita of population spent in the North Atlantic states or in Massachusetts alone. The expenditure per capita of the school population was less than one-third in Virginia and less than one-fifth in South Carolina of the amount spent in the North Atlantic states or in Massachusetts. In the Southern seaboard the school term was two to three months shorter than in Massachusetts, the average daily attendance 49 per cent as compared with 62 per cent, the average salary of teachers far less than half, the school property per school-age child less than one-sixth.[18]

The South lagged behind the rest of the country even in the amount expended for education from each dollar of property value, and was closing the gap only very slowly. In 1900 the Southern seaboard states expended one dollar for education per $546 true value of property, the whole country one per $406, Massachusetts one per $315. In 1912 the Southern seaboard expended one dollar per $469, an increase of 14 per cent, while the national average was one dollar per $391, an increase of 4 per cent, and Massachusetts expended one dollar per $280, an increase of 8 per cent.[19] Out of each dollar of its property, South Carolina still spent on education only half as much as Massachusetts. In a

17. Minutes of Southern Education Board meeting, August 6, 1907, in unsorted Ogden Papers, S.H.C., University of North Carolina.
18. *Report of the Commissioner of Education*, 1917, II, 41-42, 46, 50-52, 55.
19. United States Census Office, *Wealth, Debt, and Taxation*, p. 36; United States Bureau of the Census, *Wealth, Debt, and Taxation*, 1913, I, 24; *Reports of the Commissioner of Education*, 1900, I, lxxvii; 1913, II, 32.

sense, Southern public schools can be understood only on their own terms, in relation to the impinging regional conditions rather than in comparison with national averages. The task of educating all children in a democracy seemed "simply stupendous" to the Virginian professor Robert E. Blackwell. Though the South could provide a system extending from elementary schools to universities, it was "in no condition to inaugurate this scheme of education in all its fullness" or effectiveness. "With its scattered population, its comparative poverty, and its extra burden of separate schools for whites and blacks, it is handicapped in the race. Yet it is essential that our schools shall be as good as those of any other part of the country. For suddenly the world has grown small, and the change in the method of doing business makes it necessary that our children be able to compete with the children educated in states wealthier and furnishing better educational advantages.... Unless then our Southern young men are to be mere hewers of wood and drawers of water, they must have as good training as young men of any other part of the country."[20]

The Southern educators' hope for public school equality with the Northern states, their "dream of all that out of ampler knowledge may befall," was hardly less impossible of realization in 1915 than in 1900. The climax of the Ogden movement was actually about 1907, though it followed up for another decade the initial impetus it had given to educational campaigns. Created in response to deeper historical forces of economic and social change, it supplied leadership for educational expansion only so far as Southern economic conditions and the prevailing state of race relations permitted. As early as 1906 the General Education Board branched off into farm demonstration work, partly to oppose the boll weevil menace, but also in hope of increasing Southern income on which future educational expansion must be based.[21] In

20. Robert E. Blackwell, "The Necessity for Conservation of Educational Energy in the South," in Association of Colleges and Preparatory Schools of the Southern States, *Proceedings of the Sixteenth Annual Meeting Held at Athens, Georgia, November 3-4, 1910* (Nashville, 1910), pp. 37-38.

21. "The fundamental necessity is greater profits in farming," Wallace Buttrick told the educators; "all things hark back to a surplus." Of course, the surplus itself became a problem with which farm demonstration methods were inadequate to cope. Minutes of Southern Education Board meeting, December 3-5, 1906, Dickerman Papers, S.H.C., University of North Carolina. On the farm demonstration movement, see Joseph C. Bailey, *Seaman A. Knapp: School-*

the same year the initial grant was made to the Anna T. Jeanes Foundation for aid to Negro schools, soon followed by the Phelps-Stokes Fund in 1911 and the Julius Rosenwald aid to Negro schoolhouses in 1912.[22] At the same time that educational campaign organizations in the various states began to supply their own momentum, the philanthropists began to specialize more in certain problems. The Southern Education Board supported a school improvement supervisor in each Southern state and shared with the Peabody Fund support of state rural school supervisors. The General Education Board made contracts with twelve Southern states to support state high school inspectors or "professors of secondary education." The Southern Education Board and the Peabody Board began with Jackson Davis of Virginia the support of a state supervisor of Negro schools, a work soon taken over by the General Education Board. The Southern Education Board itself was rendered obsolescent by the problems and issues growing out of its successful campaigns. It survived only a year after Ogden's death in 1913, and the Conference for Education in the South folded up in 1917. The Southern members continued in their local positions, of course, and many of the agents were absorbed by the philanthropic foundations in neighboring fields.

An assessment of the work of the Southern Education Board, while recognizing its major role in the achievement of fuller educational opportunity for Southern whites, cannot escape the conclusion that it failed in its program of Negro education and also failed to challenge or deflect the anti-Negro movement which it paralleled. "Passionate and rapidly developing enthusiasm for white education is bearing sharply and adversely upon the opportunities of the negro," noted the sensitive Murphy in 1907. "There is not only no chance to help the situation of the negro educationally, but it is steadily growing worse, and their schools, upon every sort of pretext, are being hampered and impoverished where they are not actually abandoned."[23] The demoralizing

---
master of American Agriculture (New York, 1945); *The General Education Board: An Account of Its Activities, 1902-1914*, pp. 18-70; Woodward, *Origins of the New South*, pp. 408-12.

22. A good composite account of the work of the foundations for Negroes is Dabney, *Universal Education in the South*, II, 432-83.

23. Murphy to Buttrick, November 14, 1907, Southern Education Board

realization that their educational campaigns were driving a wider wedge between white and Negro schools may well have been a factor in the decline of the Southern Education Board after 1907.

Disfranchisement and the Jim Crow laws were the most characteristic overt features of white aggression against Negroes in the early years of the twentieth century, whereas education was commonly considered the Negro's solace and hope. Negroes themselves very evidently thought so. The "public schools and the graveyard will ultimately bring things right," said a college-bred Negro who believed that he lived in the *Sturm und Drang* period of the Negro's existence.[24] But the educational laws under which the Negro public schools were operated were themselves Jim Crow laws, and separate education moreover schooled the white and Negro children in the acceptance of segregation. As Woodward has observed, "The Jim Crow laws, unlike feudal laws, did not assign the subordinate group a fixed status in society. They were constantly pushing the Negro farther down."[25] Negro education, however inadequate, aided the Negro rather than pushed him down. But the current of the times, deeper than law and often defiant of law, was expressed in a typical asseveration of a North Carolina farmer that "the negro don't need any education," that "He was never intended for anything but to work in the field," and that "to give him any education at all takes him out of the field and he is not worth anything to the farmer."[26]

The economic disadvantages under which the Negro school child labored made even the regional disadvantages of Southern whites pale into relative insignificance. For example, the average annual expenditure for each South Carolina white child in 1915 was $13.98, or approximately half of the amount, $28.12, expended on

---
Papers, S.H.C., University of North Carolina, written after a tour of the South. Murphy pointed out to his local friends not only "the danger of injustice to the negro, but the danger of establishing our whole educational system on a thoroughly undemocratic basis."

24. Quoted in Du Bois, "The College Bred Negro," Chapter III in *Report of the Commissioner of Education for the Year 1903* (2 vols., Washington, 1903), I, 217-18. This is a condensation of *idem, The College-Bred Negro:* Atlanta University Publications, No. 5 (Atlanta, 1900).

25. Woodward, *The Strange Career of Jim Crow,* p. 93.

26. R. R. Caw of Willow Grove, in *Sixteenth Annual Report of the North Carolina Bureau of Labor and Printing, 1902,* p. 92.

children in the North Central states. For each South Carolina Negro child in the same year, $1.13 was expended, an amount less than one-twelfth of that for the South Carolina white child, about one-twenty-fifth of that for children in the North Central states.[27] South Carolina is selected as an example not because it was unique, but because its reports on Negro school expenditures were more nearly complete and more candid than those of other states. The rate of racial discrimination in school expenditures varied somewhat from state to state, from an amount probably somewhat less than 100 per cent in North Carolina to 1000 per cent in South Carolina, Virginia's pattern being closer to that of North Carolina and Georgia's closer to that of South Carolina. Official reports of the Southern seaboard states other than South Carolina did not divide all expenditures by race, but their records of teachers' salaries and school property gave positive evidence that discrimination was extreme and nearly universal. And the significant differences were not those of states, but of counties—or, more precisely, those of geography and population ratio. These differences have persisted, and are now cardinal factors in the tactics of the desegregation movement.[28]

Above the elementary schools, public education showed a much deeper ethnic gap. The federal commissioner in 1916 reported 310 secondary students in Georgia Negro high schools, 1,133 in Virginia, 668 in South Carolina, 19 in North Carolina, a total of 2,130. Though whites of school age were less than 20 per cent more numerous than Negroes, almost 3,000 per cent more of them attended public high schools. The state Negro colleges in the four states received from their states less than one-eighth of the amount for whites in Virginia alone.[29]

Separation itself for the subordinate race, aside from the financial inequalities which it made easier for white officials, was a hampering and unequalizing feature of Southern education. Educational segregation seemed less incongruous to whites and Negroes

27. See above, Chapter VI; *Report of the Commissioner of Education*, *1917*, II, 55.
28. Charles S. Johnson, "Some Significant Social and Educational Implications of the U. S. Supreme Court's Decision," in *Journal of Negro Education*, XXIII (Summer, 1954), 364-71.
29. *Report of the Commissioner of Education*, *1917*, II, 394, 398, 513; *Virginia School Report*, *1914-15*, pp. 486, 492, 542, 551, 558, 570, 574, 579, 596.

as Jim Crow spread to railroads, residence, public recreation, water fountains, hospitals, elevators, Bibles on witness stands, graveyards, and even cadavers for medical schools.[30] And educational inequality came to seem part of the normal scheme of things when Negroes lacked equality in virtually every phase of opportunity. As George S. Mitchell remarks of desegregation, "it would all be so much easier if Negroes all over the South had good, modern homes, instead of the slum shacks in which pervasively they still live; if Negroes on the land were owners or secure tenants, with years of reputable standing in their part of the countryside; if in commercial and industrial employment there were genuine equality of opportunity; if everybody had a reasonable chance to find personal health."[31]

Though teachers' salaries were perhaps the least discriminatory feature of dual school systems, we can use this as an illustration of minor differences from state to state. In the years 1911-12 and 1912-13, the average white teacher's salary was two and one-half times higher annually than the Negro salary, though low enough itself in all truth. White-Negro salary differentials ranged from less than two to one in North Carolina and Virginia to more than three to one in South Carolina (Table 16).[32]

Other Negro handicaps in education developed out of dis-

TABLE 16
AVERAGE ANNUAL SALARIES OF TEACHERS IN THE
SOUTHERN SEABOARD, 1911-1913

State	Teachers White	Teachers Negro	Salaries White	Salaries Negro	Av. Ann. Salary White	Av. Ann. Salary Negro
Virginia.........	8,576	2,441	$2,767,365	$ 421,381	$322.69	$172.63
North Carolina...	8,716	2,875	1,715,994	340,856	196.83	118.59
South Carolina...	4,363	2,760	1,454,098	305,084	333.28	110.54
Georgia.........	9,053	4,052	2,884,580	483,622	318.63	119.35
Southern Seaboard......	30,708	12,128	$8,822,037	$1,550,943	$287.29	$127.88

30. Segregation laws and the change in folkways which they engendered are summarized in Woodward, *The Strange Career of Jim Crow*, pp. 81-95.
31. George S. Mitchell, "Next Steps in Racial Desegregation in Education in the South," in *Journal of Negro Education*, XXIII (Summer, 1954), 388-89.
32. Jones, *Negro Education*, I, 34. Aggregates and averages for the Southern seaboard were computed by addition and division.

criminatory application of school laws and out of poverty and neglect. "Evidence is plentiful that the compulsory attendance laws of this region are largely inoperative as concerns negro children," remarked Frank A. Ross in a census monograph in 1920, "and it is a hopeful sign that as large proportions attend as the rates indicate."[33] For such reasons as distance from the schoolhouse, lack of seating space in the school, lack of clothes or textbooks, or pressing need to supplement the family income, only 37.7 per cent of the Negro children of school age attended daily in the Southern seaboard in 1915, as compared with 58.2 per cent of white children of school age. There were 95 Negro children to every Negro teacher in the area, as compared with 44.6 white children per white teacher. It would be impossible to measure the extent to which this situation was due to the policies of white superintendents or to the economic position of Negro families which was fixed by their lower-caste status. In the South as a whole there were 315,000 Negroes aged fifteen to twenty enrolled in 1910; of these only about 10 per cent were in high schools and the remainder were adolescents in elementary schools, causing frequent problems for the Negro teacher. Feeble-minded adults were also given asylum in Negro classrooms.[34]

Around 1914, on the eve of the First World War, a certain amount of calm began to settle about the race question. The White Supremacy movement had many of the elements of civil conflict, and white victory took form in Jim Crow laws and customs. Interracial violence subsided when it became superfluous. "Indeed, a certain paralysis of feeling about the whole matter due to exhaustion," Edwin A. Alderman was inclined to think, "seems to have overtaken both sections . . . the Negro has somehow gotten off the Southerner's nerves and out of the Northerner's imagination." His own opinion was that the Southerners had acted "with a great deal of instinctive wisdom" and that "the result of their constructive thought has been acquiesced in by the people of the North with remarkable and commendable faith and confidence." Perhaps Alderman, then under treatment for tuberculosis, was

33. Frank A. Ross, *School Attendance in 1920:* United States Bureau of the Census, Census Monographs, V (Washington, 1924), 57.
34. *Report of the Commissioner of Education, 1917,* II, 17; Jones, *Negro Education,* I, 33; Myrdal, *An American Dilemma,* II, 903.

Educational Expansion and the Context of Racism 259

exhausted by all of the complications that race had made in his life. But at a gathering of Southern professors shortly before his death in 1915, Booker T. Washington laid bare the hopelessness of his own accommodating Negro leadership. "We are trying," he said, "to instil into the Negro mind that if education does not make the Negro humble, simple, and of service to the community, then it will not be encouraged."[35]

The gap between white and Negro school opportunities, already wide in 1915, reached its farthest extent about 1930, when very slowly and slightly the gap began to be narrowed.[36] Segregation made financial discrimination easier, and was therefore one of its contributing causes. More fundamental causes were the relative poverty of the region which tempted white taxpayers and officials to economize on the vulnerable Negro school; the complacent sense of magnanimity with which Southern whites regarded any expenditure, however inadequate, for Negro education; fear of Negro labor competition among whites of the lower economic class; and the distaste with which Southern employers regarded education for Negroes. Negroes suffered harsher indignities in employment, recreation, travel, and other social activities, but unequal educational opportunity was more crippling.

The part played in racial discrimination by poor-white antagonism was less than is commonly supposed, at least in education. It did have an important part because of the Southern economy, and because poor whites more often resorted to violence. But differentials in educational expenditure were most glaring where white landlords and dependent Negroes predominated, rather than

35. [William M. Hunley, secretary], *Minutes of the University Commission on Southern Race Questions* (n.p., n.d.), pp. 17, 29. Alderman's letter was read at the third meeting in 1913.

36. Trends in the fifteen years after 1930 are studied in Alethea H. Washington, "Availability of Education for Negroes in the Elementary School," Walter G. Daniel, "Availability of Education for Negroes in the Secondary School," and Martin D. Jenkins, "The Availability of Higher Education for Negroes in the Southern States," in *The Availability of Education in the Negro Separate School:* Yearbook Number of *Journal of Negro Education*, XVI (Summer, 1947), 439-49; 450-58, 459-73. In each of these studies, the conclusion was that differentials remained very great along all major lines and the decreases of differential pitifully gradual. On the same theme, see Theodore Brameld, "Educational Costs," in R. M. MacIver (ed.), *Discrimination and National Welfare: A Series of Addresses and Discussions* (New York and London, 1949), pp. 41-42.

in "white" counties where dispossessed whites were more numerous. The paternalists who used the Negro "economically" also used him "educationally" to secure larger funds from the state for white schools. Of course everywhere in the South it was wealthier whites who sat on school boards and committees, but this was particularly true in the "black counties." Thomas Jesse Jones of the federal Bureau of Education undertook for the Phelps-Stokes Fund in 1916 the first thorough survey of Negro education. Though his primary task was to evaluate private and higher separate schools for Negroes, Jones reached some significant conclusions about public schools in the states which maintained separate systems. While per capita expenditures for Negroes varied from state to state, he found that the most striking differences were in county expenditures, since it was county officers who divided the funds unequally; whereas the states apportioned them to counties without regard to race. Jones reduced his findings to a neat formula by arranging the Southern counties according to percentage of Negroes in the population and giving the aggregate and per capita expenditures for teachers' salaries, this being not only the largest item but the only one reported in all of the states. The resulting table (Table 17) and his comments upon the evidence are quoted at length because they distill the essence of the Southern educational pattern.

TABLE 17

PER CAPITA EXPENDITURES FOR WHITE AND NEGRO IN SOUTHERN COUNTIES

County groups, percentage of Negroes in the population	White teachers' salaries	Negro teachers' salaries	Per capita, white	Per capita, Negro
Counties under 10%........	$ 7,755,817	$ 325,579	$ 7.96	$ 7.23
Counties 10 to 25%.........	9,633,674	1,196,788	9.55	5.55
Counties 25 to 50%.........	12,572,666	2,265,945	11.11	3.19
Counties 50 to 75%.........	4,574,366	1,167,796	12.53	1.77
Counties 75% and over.....	888,759	359,800	22.22	1.78

According to this table [Table 17] the per capita in the counties 75 per cent Negro was $22.22 for each white child and $1.78 for each colored child. The per capita sums for white children decrease and those for colored children increase with considerable regularity as the proportion of Negroes becomes smaller. The marked inequalities in the counties 75 per cent Negro are partly explained by the necessity of providing relatively more schools for the scattered white population. [The same is true of Negro schools for counties under 10 per cent Negro.] The lower wage scale of colored teachers and the lack of high-school provisions also reduce the expenditures for colored schools. It is evident, however, that these explanations by no means account for the wide divergencies of the "black-belt" counties. These divergencies are further emphasized by the fact that the Southern States appropriate annually $6,429,991 for higher schools for white pupils and only a little over a third of a million for higher schools for colored people. The latter include the agricultural and mechanical schools, largely maintained by Federal funds, and six normal schools of elementary and secondary grade.

A proper appreciation of the significance of these figures requires the consideration of at least two facts. The first is that, although the wealth of the South is at present increasing very rapidly, the South has had to maintain a double system of schools on the comparatively limited resources of a section largely rural and only recently recovered from the burdens of the Civil War. The second fact is that, though the per capita for white pupils in the South is four times that for Negroes, the per capita in most of the Northern States is two and three times that for the white pupils in the South. These facts do not justify the present inequalities between the expenditures for white and colored pupils. They should, however, modify criticism of the situation. When all explanations have been made, the inequalities stand as an emphatic appeal to county, State, and Federal Governments for larger and more definite interest in Negro education.[37]

Certainly some soul-searching was called for when whites already enjoying special advantages deprived Negro children in order to increase their advantage over poorer whites. The vaunted paternalism of the lowlander was fundamentally corrupt. It is not surprising, then, that Negro emigration was first and heaviest from the centers of Negro concentration. There has been a positive relation "between the concentration of Negroes and the unsatisfactory influences under which they live," though neither is entirely explainable as a cause of the other.[38]

37. Jones, *Negro Education*, I, 7-8. The bracketed remark above is the author's, not Jones's.
38. Joseph H. Douglass and Albert N. Whiting, "An Approach to Negro-White Relations," in *Phylon*, X (Second Quarter, 1949), 146-52, contains a brief analysis of the relation between Negro concentration and living conditions.

Much of the variability of school facilities was a derivative of racial discrimination, but not all. The unequal geographical distribution of wealth, most notably between urban and rural districts, was an important factor. This trend was aggravated and extended after 1900 by increasing racial discrimination and urbanization. City schools and black-county white schools were improved, at the expense of good will in other districts. On the average, the urban-rural disparities were not so great as the white-Negro disparities, being much less than two to one in expenditures per pupil in average daily attendance.[39] As in white-Negro disparities, though to a lesser degree, current expenditures per pupil are merely indicative of a much greater disparity in school plant, equipment, instruction, and general educational efficiency. Rural children were handicapped in their increasingly close relationship to America's urban-industrial culture. Rural Negroes were far more handicapped, for they were poorly equipped to compete with whites.

Within the Southern cities discrimination in favor of white schools was hardly less than in the rural areas, but since the cities had more wealth with which to support education, the Negro schools there were far better than the rural schools for Negroes, with facilities at the elementary level about equal to those of rural whites. These city Negro schools were inadequate for an urban environment, particularly because of restriction of high school facilities. Yet it is worthy of note that city Negroes made good use of such opportunities as they were given. In Virginia in 1918-20, city Negroes made slightly higher scores than rural whites on addition, spelling, reading, and writing, and their schools were given a higher "index of efficiency." City whites scored higher than either of these groups, and rural Negroes markedly lower.[40]

39. The annual expenditure per pupil in average daily attendance in cities of 5,000 population and over, and in the state as a whole was in 1915-16 in Virginia $22.46 and $21.53; in North Carolina $20.37 and $12.31; in South Carolina $16.31 and $12.80; in Georgia $25.60 and $13.77. The disparities between urban and rural children of school age would be somewhat greater, but aggregate figures for such a comparison are not available. See the state chapters above for some of the more striking discrepancies. *Report of the Commissioner of Education, 1917*, II, 82, 102.

40. Charles H. Thompson, "The Educational Achievements of Negro Children," in Donald Young (ed.), *The American Negro: Annals* of the American Academy of Political and Social Science, CXL (November, 1928), 207-08.

Educational Expansion and the Context of Racism 263

Doubtless it is true that the very impersonality which heightened the walls of urban segregation carried some small advantages for the Negro city school. In the rural areas, the school board member or district committeeman was usually himself a property-owner paying a large portion of the school tax; he was also frequently an employer of Negro labor who had a direct interest in the cotton picking seasons or other times when unskilled farm work was needed. In the city, on the other hand, the school board member usually had at most an indirect interest in curbing Negro education. In the cities a greater proportion of taxation was indirect, and even where taxation was direct it was usually not his own taxes which the school board member disbursed. Except in cotton mill towns, and even there less frequently after the turn of the century, there was little use of white child labor, and even less of Negro child labor. On the other hand, merchants wanted Negroes to be able to read their advertisements. Crowded city dwellers recognized the school as a moulder of public order or even as a disciplinary institution. The city offered varied entertainments to compete with Negro-baiting. Industries in cities called for more skill in workmanship to be acquired at public expense, and impersonal corporations which paid a larger proportion of the school tax in urban areas were more concerned about taxation than about expenditure of school funds. When all of this is said, however, it is doubtful that conscious white opinion on Negro education was radically different in Southern cities and towns than in rural areas. John Hope, president of Morehouse College in Atlanta, spoke frankly about city schools to a race commission meeting in 1917 at Raleigh:

In nineteen years, he said, Atlanta had gone backward in public school facilities for the Negro. There is no Negro high school in Atlanta, he said, and only about three in the State of Georgia. He stated that in the Atlanta colored schools there was no industrial training at all. He added, however, that the Negroes had voted for school bonds and had been promised additional schools. "The Negroes have complained and have received a respectful hearing from the school board," he said, "but they still believe that it 'won't do no good.' The Negroes are growing restless. When Atlanta was 'cleaned up,' the Negro quarter was ignored. These things are conducive to migration."[41]

41. *Minutes of the University Commission on Southern Race Questions*, p. 42.

Another result of the educational campaigns was inequality of educational facilities for whites in different localities. Usually this inequality was much less extreme than that between whites and Negroes, but it grew in much the same way during the educational expansion and was closely linked with Negro-white inequality. In each of the Southern seaboard states we have seen that cities and other units favored by a relative abundance of taxable wealth used local taxation and special districting to provide superior facilities for themselves. Rural counties favored by a relatively large number of Negro children on the school rolls also used the state per capita school fund in a similar spirit to provide schools superior to those for most rural white counties. And then there were also inactive areas, as Murphy reported to co-workers, "in which lethargy or poverty or other local difficulties are holding back their people, and the opposition—which is being developed by our very progress—is finding their constituency and their leverage in the people of these localities."[42]

Inequality of educational opportunity among whites, besides being less in degree than the white-Negro inequality, was more subject to adjustment by political pressure. Perhaps the major Southern achievement of the period between 1900 and 1915 was that conservatives who dominated Southern life were forced to grant educational opportunities to the white masses. The conservatives were able to curb the growing expense of public schools by appealing to the fear of poor whites that Negroes, if educated, might compete with them and worsen their economic and social status. One might almost speak of a tacit bargain in this matter. Meanwhile, conservatives were able to use the method of distributing school funds at the state and county level to secure special educational advantages for their own children. The disfranchised Negro could only make requests for better schools; these requests could be made only to and through paternalistic and conservative whites whose group interests, in turn, were involved in preservation of inadequate Negro schools so that white schools of "black counties" might be more adequate; and the occasional genuine personal friends of Negroes among the white

---

[42]. Murphy to Buttrick, November 14, 1907, Southern Education Board Papers, S.H.C., University of North Carolina.

upper classes were limited by their social and economic need to remain identified with the white group. The enfranchised white of the lower economic classes, on the other hand, could protest against educational disadvantages on democratic and equalitarian principles, and could vote according to his interests in so far as he understood them. While it is true, as Myrdal has pointed out, that racial discrimination is a dilemma of the democratic creed, whites eager for educational opportunities for their children were able temporarily to ignore the more puzzling aspects of this dilemma and to appeal for equal educational opportunities for whites in voices of genuine conviction.

Demands for equalization of the school funds allotted to whites began almost as soon as the school systems were established. These demands first took the form of legislative bills to divide the school funds between whites and Negroes at the state level according to the amount paid in taxes by each ethnic group. The obvious difficulties in such a procedure caused this to be abandoned in each state well before 1915, though Negroes received through county and district allotments little, if any, more than they might be credited with in an equitable division of tax funds. Around 1915 movements began for reorganization of state taxation systems and for the increase of state appropriations for educational activities reserved to white schools. In 1915 these movements were still in an ineffective stage, however, and the trend over the period 1900-1915 had been in quite the opposite direction. Table 18 will indicate to what extent the Southern seaboard states went into line with the national custom of local taxation for public schools. For the purposes of the table, county and district taxes are termed local.[43] It is clear from the evidence given in the table that, while the total revenue from state taxes in the period increased by about 50 per cent, its proportion of the total school revenue declined from 57.6 per cent to 27.63 per cent. Meanwhile revenue from local taxes increased over 800 per cent and its proportion of the

43. *Report of the Comissioner of Education, 1900*, I, lxxv-lxxvi; *ibid., 1917*, II, 51-52. In the table for 1900, the figures given for North Carolina are those of the school year 1897-98. The last digit in the figures for total revenue of South Carolina in 1915, an obvious miscalculation, has been changed from 3 to 4. Percentages for the Southern seaboard were computed by simple addition and division.

TABLE 18
SOURCES OF SCHOOL REVENUE IN 1900 AND 1915

State	Income from permanent fund, school land rents	From state taxes	From local taxes	From other sources	Total revenue excluding balances, proceeds from bond sales
SOURCES OF SCHOOL REVENUE 1900					
Virginia	$ 47,533	$ 964,282	$ 943,346	$ 55,463	$2,010,624
North Carolina	56,849	760,460	21,522	147,683	986,514
South Carolina	......	533,639	112,254	156,931	802,824
Georgia	212,152	1,111,001	367,815	362,689	2,053,657
Total	$316,534	$3,369,382	$1,444,937	$ 722,766	$5,853,619
Per cent	5.4	57.6	24.7	12.3	100.0
U. S. per cent	4.2	16.1	68.9	10.8	100.0
SOURCES OF SCHOOL REVENUE 1915					
Virginia	$93,128	$2,110,652	$ 4,062,320	$ 664,293	$ 6,930,393
North Carolina	......	722,244	3,871,800	131,915	4,725,959
South Carolina	......	306,934	2,342,194	677,146	3,326,274
Georgia	......	2,608,487	2,387,729	823,654	5,819,870
Total	$93,128	$5,748,317	$12,664,043	$2,297,008	$20,802,496
Per cent	0.45	27.63	60.88	11.04	100.0
U. S. per cent	2.90	15.45	77.50	4.15	100.0

total school revenue increased from 24.7 per cent to 60.88 per cent.

Local taxation by 1915 had replaced the state appropriation as the chief means of financing Southern seaboard education. The state school fund had begun in the seventies, when whites and Negroes shared equally in the distribution of funds. In the eighties and nineties, as discrimination against Negroes deprived them of school funds and enriched the schools of black counties, the state per capita apportionment fell into disrepute among residents of the white counties and contributed to the so-called educational lethargy of the period. As white small farmers of the uplands overthrew the state oligarchies of the lowlands, they turned to local taxation as the method of educational finance for all whites, and the trend was running strong in 1915. Nearly all of the new funds for education came from this source. But local taxation itself carried a disadvantage to the white children of poorer counties. The righteous indignation of white counties was expressed in demands for "equalization" funds. The term "equalized," as Bond has pointed out, "cannot be applied to schools for Negro children save in a farcical sense."[44] The broader meaning of the term was ignored. State funds for consolidation of rural schools, pupil transportation, rural school libraries, encouragement of high schools, and a state-wide minimum term tended to equalize educational opportunities of white children only.

While property taxation remained the backbone of state finance, this system was under re-examination in every state by 1915, as tax rates were raised to meet the new demands on state and local governments. The general property tax was increasingly recognized as inequitable on grounds of ability to pay and of unequal assessment. Twenty-one Virginia non-railroad counties, for example, were trying to educate 50,000 enrolled children with only $412,000, or $8.24 per capita. "Our attempt to provide good schools on such a financial basis is little short of pathetic," commented the state superintendent, "and now that we are able to carry out the plans and wishes of our forefathers, we should do so without delay."[45]

Efforts to correct disparities of assessment through state boards of equalization apparently had little success.[46] On the other hand, state railroad and corporation commissions were successful in raising the assessments of corporation property. In North Carolina, for example, between 1900 and 1915 the assessed valuation of railroads and other corporations with right of eminent domain quadrupled, while land assessment a little more than doubled, town real estate tripled, personal property doubled, bank and building-and-loan stock increased seven-fold.[47] The way was income taxation and indirect taxation in the decade of the twenties. Cities were protesting that their property was assessed at higher rates

44. Bond, *The Education of the Negro in the American Social Order*, p. 253.
45. *Virginia School Report, 1914-15*, p. 34.
46. William K. Tate, *Country School Movements and Ideals in South Carolina: Bulletin* of the University of South Carolina, No. 36, Part II (Columbia, January, 1914), 29-30, a reprint from *South Carolina School Report, 1913;* Charles L. Raper, "North Carolina's Taxation Problem and Its Solution," in *South Atlantic Quarterly*, XIV (January, 1915), 1.
47. North Carolina, *Report of the Corporation Commission as a State Board of Tax Commissioners, 1916* (Raleigh, 1917), p. 376.

than in rural counties, while farmers insisted that in relation to their income they were paying more heavily than anyone else. But the local property owner's interest in keeping assessment localized and more subject to individual pressure was combined with distrust of the state political machines to prevent more uniform levy and assessment.[48] So assessment remained in the hands of a local agent of the machine, usually a member of the courthouse clique.

These arguments over taxation indicated that the Southerner was beginning to feel the strain of increased costs of education. Yet Southern expenditure was destined to quadruple again by 1930, and yet again by 1945. Educational expenditures were a larger proportion of total governmental expenditures in the South than in the rest of the nation. And, though in 1915 the relatively poor Southerner still apparently spent less for education out of every dollar of his income than the Northerner, he was headed toward a reversal of this position by 1950.[49]

By 1915 the educational campaigns had run their course and the Southern Education Board had given full trial to its idea of diverting Southern attention from racism. There really was a Southern educational awakening. Annual expenditures quadrupled, kept well ahead of the rise in property values, and acted as a springboard for further increases in the next decade, though the lag behind non-Southern schools continued.[50] Whites in the cities, finding the main stream of the national economy coursing through them, tapped the stream for educational and other advantages and forgot their country cousins as quickly as had the North.

On the other hand, the Board's efforts seem to have had almost

48. One Virginia senator warned that a state tax commission would become "a political oligarchy as conscienceless as the Czar of Russia," and make "cringing cowards of assessors."—Senator Noel of Lee County, in Richmond *Times-Dispatch*, January 27, 1910.

49. Compare the income figures for 1919 in Leven and King, *Income in the Various States*, p. 256, with per capita expenditures in *Report of the Commissioner of Education*, 1917, II, 52; for later trends, see Harry S. Ashmore, *The Negro and the Schools* (Chapel Hill, 1954), pp. 144-45; Bond, *The Education of the Negro in the American Social Order*, pp. 213-14, 227, 229.

50. The claim that material improvements in the twentieth century schools have been accompanied by improved education of the pupils is subject to such skepticism and alarm as that expressed in Randall Jarrell, "The Schools of Yesteryear," in *New Republic*, CXXXV (November 19, 1956), 13-17.

no effect on the Negro schools. Nor did it brake or deflect the course of racism. The time was out of joint, and the statesman-schoolmaster could not set it right. Massive financial discrimination against the already conveniently segregated Negro schools apparently developed out of a conjunction of motives: increased white desire for education, white racial hostility, and efforts of taxpayers to limit taxation. It is misleading to think of the dual system as a financial burden when the two systems are grossly unequal. Discrimination against Negro schools represented a fiscal saving and was a basis for compromise between taxpayer and tax layer. The educational campaigns themselves drove the wedge of inequality between the two systems. Discrimination varied from place to place, but it was almost universal, flagrant, and increasing. And the fact that it was most excessive in the black counties, where Negroes were economically most useful to paternalistic whites, refuted the basis of Booker T. Washington's "pragmatic compromise."[51]

Educational reform within the context of racism partook of racism, whatever may be the long-range effect of expanded education on white attitudes. Discrimination in education was a cancerous growth that fed on reform. The Southern Education Board's sympathetic and gentle approach to the race issue in Southern public education lacked the moral firmness of such a movement as Gandhi's Soul Force, and was therefore weakened by compromise.

51. It also opens to serious question the equation of the rise of the poor whites with the decline of Negro opportunity and status. Cf. Bond, *Education of the Negro in the American Social Order*, pp. 84-115, and Tindall, *South Carolina Negroes, 1877-1900*, pp. 213-17, 222-23, with Truman H. Pierce *et al.*, *White and Negro Schools in the South: An Analysis of Biracial Education* (Englewood Cliffs, N. J., 1955), pp. 170-72.

Essay on Sources

THE PURPOSE of the following essay is simply to serve as a guide to the more relevant and important primary sources and secondary works for the history of Southern seaboard public education between 1901 and 1915. Those searching for more detailed information are referred to the rather complete bibliographical information in the footnotes. This essay would serve little purpose by any simple repetition of the information already presented. The short pamphlets with long names, the stillborn dissertations based upon questionnaires, have therefore been eliminated, as have many general works on the period and subject which are available in other bibliographical compilations.

I. Manuscripts

The private papers of most of the leading members and agents of the Southern Education Board were available for use in this study, and they were heavily used in treating that aspect of the subject. By contrast, relatively little manuscript material was easily available on the actual workings of public school support or race relations in the Southern seaboard. The manuscript sources are therefore almost entirely confined to those related to the Board and its Southern work.

Largely because of the diligent work of the late Charles W. Dabney, there is a Southern Education Collection of some 21,900 items in the Southern Historical Collection in the Wilson Library of the University of North Carolina. The largest collection of papers directly related to the Board, it is divided into six parts: (1) the Charles William Dabney Papers, including records of the propaganda bureau and summer school at Knoxville, a manuscript autobiography, and typed copies of letters from the Hollis Burke Frissell Papers and Walter Hines Page Papers; (2) the George Sherwood Dickerman Papers, particularly valuable for the period when Dickerman was executive secretary; (3) the James Yadkin Joyner Papers, largely on the North Carolina school campaigns; (4) Robert Curtis Ogden Papers, including only a fragment of his total correspondence for the period after 1901, the remainder being in the Library of Congress; (5) the less significant Albert Pike Bourland Papers, covering the years of the Board's decline; and (6) the Southern Education Board Papers, which are miscellaneous manuscripts and copies made by Dabney from other collections. Supplementing this Southern Education Collection in the same repository are the Charles L. Coon Papers and Henry Groves Connor Papers, which contain some items on education and race relations in North Carolina; the disappointingly slim Edgar Gardner Murphy Papers; and the papers of the Board's Virginia agent, Henry St. George Tucker.

The Library of Congress contains several collections of papers related to the Southern Education Board. The Robert Curtis Ogden Papers include his voluminous correspondence with leaders of Northern opinion, a manuscript biography of Ogden by Samuel C. Mitchell, and many items on his business career. This collection now contains also those papers cited in footnotes as "Ogden Papers, Library of Congress—University of North Carolina" because they were used at both repositories during a period when they were claimed by both. The Jabez Lamar Monroe Curry Papers in the Library of Congress, including microfilm of the additional Curry Papers in the Alabama State Archives, were valuable for insight into the formation of the Southern Education movement, as were the Booker Taliaferro Washington Papers. In the same repository the William E. Dodd Papers, used by permission of Mrs. Martha Dodd Stern, provided insight into Virginia education and politics as well as liberal criticism of the Northern philanthropists.

Other scattered collections of varying usefulness are the Walter Hines Page Papers, Houghton Library, Harvard University; Edwin Anderson Alderman Papers, Alderman Library, University of Virginia, and two useful boxes on the Southern Education Board in the files of the president of the University of Virginia, in the same repository; the Thomas Nelson Page Papers and George J. Ramsey Papers in the manuscript collections of Duke University Library; the files of Principal Hollis Burke Frissell at Hampton Normal and Industrial Institute, Hampton, Virginia; the Daniel Coit Gilman Papers and Herbert Baxter Adams Papers at The Johns Hopkins University; the small collection of James Hampton Kirkland Papers in Vanderbilt University (a larger remainder being in possession of his family); the Peabody Education Fund Papers at the George Peabody College for Teachers; and, in the North Carolina Department of Education, the official correspondence of Superintendents Charles H. Mcbane and Thomas F. Toon.

Manuscript collections are of less value than might be expected because the same piece of writing often appears a dozen times in different forms in the several collections, which are replete with form letters, circulars, and press handouts, not to mention menus of memorial dinners. Furthermore, much of the correspondence and circular literature of the Southern Education Board dealt unrealistically with educational conditions in the South, perhaps because of the Board's propagandistic function and its headquarters location outside of the region. Other primary sources of local origin in the Southern seaboard, then, particularly state documents and newspapers, were needed to bring the study down to earth.

II. Government Publications

Public documents served in this study as a basis for analysis of public educational trends and as a check on crusading propaganda of public school promoters. Of paramount importance among United States government sources were the annual reports of the commissioner of education for the school years 1899-1900 to 1916-1917 (2 vols., annually, Washington, 1901-17). In this series one volume for 1914-15 was never published, but the statistical summaries for that year are found in the 1916-17 report. The commissioner was dependent on state sources for statistical information, and this information was therefore frequently missing or out of date. Nevertheless his reports are valuable because he collected information omitted from some of the official state reports and because of the convenience of aggregate figures collected by a standard procedure. The meager records of the federal commissioner on Negro education may be supplemented by Thomas Jesse Jones in cooperation with the Phelps-Stokes Fund, *Negro Education: A Study of the Private and Higher Schools for Colored People in the United States,* U. S. Bureau of Education, Bulletins, 1916, Nos. 38 and 39 (2 vols., Washington, 1917), which contains, in spite of its title, some information on public schools. Though the Bureau of the Census published periodic reports on the Negro in the United States, probably the most useful Census publications were *Wealth, Debt, and Taxation* (Washington, 1907), and *Wealth, Debt, and Taxation, 1913* (2 vols., Washington, 1915). Another surprisingly rich federal source on Southern public education and attitudes toward it was the *Report of the Industrial Commission* (19 vols., Washington, 1900-02).

It was, however, the annual reports of the Southern seaboard state superintendents of public instruction (biennial reports in North Carolina and in Virginia until 1911) that reflected in full color the local variability, complexity, and racial discrimination of the public schools. These reports were more useful than any other documentary sources, not only for their statistical information but because of the insight into the attitudes of public school administrators furnished by the essay reports of the county and state superintendents. Among the variations from one state or administrator to another it was interesting to note that evidences of racial discrimination surreptitiously concealed by Virginians received blatant emphasis in the South Carolina reports.

Other state documents of considerable value were the journals of proceedings and debates of the constitutional conventions of Virginia in 1901-02 and of South Carolina in 1895, the reports of the superintendent of the Richmond public schools, codifications of school law, handbooks, and pamphlets from the state departments of education.

III. NEWSPAPERS

The Southern seaboard daily newspapers, particularly those published in the state capitals, were valuable sources for public educational history because of their reporting of legislative debates on education, local school conferences and rallies, and school tax elections. The Richmond *Times* and *Dispatch* (combined after 1903 as *Times-Dispatch*), Raleigh *News and Observer*, Columbia *State*, Atlanta *Journal*, and Atlanta *Constitution* were generally sympathetic to the Southern Education Board and its local agencies, while the Charleston *News and Courier* was uniformly hostile. All of these newspapers, without exception, were supporters of racial discrimination in public school facilities and hostile to the Negro. The Raleigh *News and Observer* and the Columbia *State*, both published in small towns, gave a wider coverage of state educational news than the Richmond and Atlanta papers written for a more exclusively urban group of readers.

Other Southern seaboard newspapers of value on occasion were the Norfolk *Virginian-Pilot and Norfolk Landmark;* the Negro weekly Richmond *Planet* (on microfilm in The Johns Hopkins University Library); Charlotte *Observer;* Greensboro (N. C.) *Daily Industrial News; Patron and Gleaner* (Lasker, N. C.); and Augusta *Chronicle.* Denominational attitudes on public education were checked in the Baltimore and Richmond *Christian Advocate* (Southern Methodist) and the Raleigh *Biblical Recorder* (Southern Baptist), both weeklies.

The voluminous clipping books kept by members of the Southern Education Board were useful in surveying Northern opinion on Southern educational and race affairs. Of these clipping books the most extensive group consists of the twenty-six volumes of George S. Dickerman and his successors as agents of the Board, covering the period from 1899 to 1907, in the Southern Historical Collection, University of North Carolina. There are also several clipping books in the Robert Curtis Ogden Papers, Library of Congress, and two compiled by Charles D. McIver on the North Carolina school campaigns in the library of the Woman's College of the University of North Carolina at Greensboro. Only the latter give an adequate picture of local problems of public school

Essay on Sources

support, the others being largely confined to the speeches and doings of Southern Education Board members.

IV. PERIODICALS

The general periodicals of the period, though dealing with Southern educational and race problems in a superficial way, were important outlets for views of the educational reformers. The most helpful Southern periodicals are the *South Atlantic Quarterly*, published at Trinity College, the *Sewanee Review*, a quarterly of the University of the South, and the weekly Baltimore *Manufacturers' Record*, organ of industry in the South and opponent of the public school movement.

Three New York periodicals closely connected with the Southern Education Board are the *World's Work* (monthly) and the *American Monthly Review of Reviews*, both edited by members of the Board, Walter Hines Page and Albert Shaw respectively, and the weekly *Outlook*, edited by Lyman Abbott, a frequent guest of Ogden and a mouthpiece for Booker T. Washington. The New York weekly *Nation* and the *Independent* were the leading outlets of liberal and pro-Negro criticism of the Southern Education movement. For analysis of Negro educational trends the annual Atlanta University *Publications* were useful. The promoters of public education summarized their movement and objectives in the proceedings of the annual Conferences for Education in the South and of the Southern Educational Association.

V. SECONDARY WORKS

1. *Educational Philanthropy in the South*

Probably the clearest expressions of the attitude of the agents of Northern philanthropy in the South at the turn of the century are Walter H. Page, *The Rebuilding of Old Commonwealths* (New York, 1902), more recently published under the title, *The School That Built a Town* (New York, 1952); Edgar Gardner Murphy, *Problems of the Present South* (New York, 1904), and *The Basis of Ascendancy* (New York, 1909).

There are also biographies of the leading Southern Education Board members. Ogden received uncritical treatment from Francis G. Peabody, William H. Taft, Samuel C. Mitchell, and others, *A Life Well Lived* (Hampton, Va., 1914), Henry E. Fries (ed.), *In Memory of Robert Curtis Ogden* (Garden City, N. Y., 1916), and Philip W. Wilson, *An Unofficial Statesman— Robert Curtis Ogden* (Garden City, N. Y., 1924). Other Northern members are treated in Louise Ware, *George Foster Peabody* (Athens, Ga., 1951), John Graham Brooks, *An American Citizen: The Life of William Henry Baldwin, Jr.* (Boston and New York, 1910), and George S. Dickerman's autobiographical *Vistas of Remembrance* (New York, 1928?).

On the Southern members there are several good biographies, such as Dumas Malone, *Edwin A. Alderman* (New York, 1940). See also Clement Eaton, "Edwin A. Alderman—Liberal of the New South," in *North Carolina Historical Review*, XXIII (April, 1946), 206-21. Charles L. Lewis, *Philander Priestley Claxton: Crusader for Public Education* (Knoxville, 1948), probably evokes more than any other book the mood and environment of the educational campaigners. Benjamin Brawley, *Doctor Dillard of the Jeanes Fund* (New York and Chicago, 1930), and Edwin Mims, *Chancellor Kirkland of Vanderbilt* (Nashville, 1940), devote little attention to the Southern Education Board. Allen J. Going has made the most of scattered materials in "The Reverend Edgar Gardner Murphy: His Ideas and Influence," in *Historical Magazine of the Protestant Episcopal Church*, XXV (December, 1956), 391-402. Besides Booker T. Washington's own autobiographical works, the most useful sources are E. Davidson Washington (ed.), *Selected Speeches of Booker T. Washington* (Garden City, N. Y., 1932), Samuel R. Spencer, Jr., *Booker T. Washington and the Negro's Place in American Life* (Boston, 1955), which is based on research in the Washington Papers, and two articles by August Meier, "Booker T. Washington and the Negro Press: With Special Reference to the *Colored American Magazine*," in *Journal of Negro History*, XXXVIII (January, 1953), 67-90, and "Toward a Reinterpretation of Booker T. Washington," in *Journal of Southern History*, XXIII (May, 1957), 220-27. Just off the press is *McIver of North Carolina* (Chapel Hill, 1957), by Rose H. Holder, which is based on the Charles D. McIver Papers.

Jabez L. M. Curry and Walter Hines Page, Southern-born

members resident in the North, have each attracted the attention of several biographers. Edwin A. Alderman and Armistead C. Gordon, *J. L. M. Curry* (New York, 1911), is superseded by Jessie Pearl Rice, *J. L. M. Curry* (New York, 1949), and Suzanne Carson's unpublished thesis on Curry as a philanthropic agent (Johns Hopkins University, May, 1948). Burton J. Hendrick, *The Life and Letters of Walter H. Page* (3 vols., New York, 1922-25), was followed by the same author's *The Training of an American: The Earlier Life and Letters of Walter H. Page, 1855-1913* (Boston, 1928). Somewhat autobiographical is Walter H. Page's anonymous novel, *The Southerner: Being the Autobiography of Nicholas Worth* (New York, 1909). Page's friend Edwin Mims published some of their correspondence in "Walter Hines Page: Friend of the South," in *South Atlantic Quarterly*, XVIII (April, 1919), 97-115, and a recent scholarly study is Charles G. Sellers, Jr., "Walter Hines Page and the Spirit of the New South," in *North Carolina Historical Review*, XXIX (October, 1952), 481-99.

The most complete account of the activities of the Southern Education Board is in the second volume of Charles W. Dabney, *Universal Education in the South* (2 vols., Chapel Hill, 1936). Other useful sources are George S. Dickerman, "The Conference for Education in the South and the Southern Education Board," in *Report of the Commissioner of Education for . . . 1907* (2 vols., Washington, 1908), I, 291-327, Wickliffe Rose, "The Educational Movement in the South," in *Report of the Commissioner of Education for . . . 1903* (2 vols., Washington, 1905), I, 359-90, [Abraham Flexner and Frank P. Bachman], *The General Education Board: An Account of Its Activities 1902-1914* (New York, 1915), and Wallace Buttrick, "The Beginnings and Aims of the General Education Board," in *Journal . . . of the National Education Association . . . 1903* (Winona, Minn., 1903), 116-23.

The large number of official and scholarly histories of the Peabody, Slater, Jeanes, Carnegie, and Rockefeller Foundations will not be listed here. However, two sources of special value for this study were Ullin W. Leavell, *Philanthropy in Negro Education:* George Peabody College for Teachers, Contributions to Education, No. 100 (Nashville, 1930), and William M. Hunley (Secretary), *Minutes of the University Commission on Southern Race Questions* (Lexington, Va., 1917), covering the first eight meetings 1912 to 1917.

2. *Public Education and the Southern Region*

Most of the distinctive problems of Southern public education centered around two themes: the region, with its colonial economy, rural society, and one-party state political machines; and race, or more precisely, the inequality of educational opportunity for Negroes and the attitudes of the dominant white group toward the cultural needs and aspirations of Negroes. Region and race touched each other at many points, of course, but most studies of public education in the South have centered around one or the other. This section will deal with studies in the regional approach, and the next section with those emphasizing race.

Regional studies of Southern schools are really limited to Charles W. Dabney, *Universal Education in the South* (2 vols., Chapel Hill, 1936), and the textbook by Edgar W. Knight, *Public Education in the South* (Boston, 1922). There are useful chapters on Southern schools and educators in Merle E. Curti, *The Social Ideas of American Educators* (New York, 1935), Howard K. Beale, *A History of Freedom of Teaching in American Schools* (New York, 1941), and C. Vann Woodward, *Origins of the New South 1877-1913*, Vol. IX of *A History of the South* (Baton Rouge, 1951). Elizabeth H. Davidson, *Child Labor Legislation in the Southern Textile States* (Chapel Hill, 1939), touches on compulsory school attendance and is a model for writing Southern social history.

Probably because of the institutional pattern of the schools, there are many more studies of state-wide scope. Cornelius J. Heatwole, *A History of Education in Virginia* (New York, 1916), written in the wake of the May Campaign and evoking its tone, has been followed by the more staid and scholarly work by James L. Blair Buck, *The Development of Public Schools in Virginia 1607-1952* (Richmond, 1952). Few of the state and local educational histories are works of scholarship. Edgar W. Knight, *Public School Education in North Carolina* (Boston and New York,

Essay on Sources 279

1916), conforms more to the restraints of scholarly method than Marcus C. S. Noble, *A History of the Public Schools of North Carolina* (Chapel Hill, 1930). Fred W. Morrison, *Equalization of the Financial Burden of Education among Counties in North Carolina* (New York, 1925), was written in a period when white counties were devising ways to gain equality of public school opportunities with other white schools without sharing this equality with Negroes. Charles L. Coon contributed factual information to the educational campaign in three pamphlets, *A Statistical Record of the Progress of Public Education in North Carolina, 1870-1906* (Raleigh, 1907), *Significant Educational Progress in North Carolina, 1900-1906* (Raleigh, 1907), and *Facts about Southern Educational Progress: A Study in Public School Maintenance for Those Who Look Forward* (Durham, 1905). Also useful was his article, "School Support and Our North Carolina Courts, 1868-1926," in *North Carolina Historical Review*, III (July, 1926), 399-438. A most helpful unpublished study was Samuel A. Thompson, "The Legislative Development of Public School Support in North Carolina" (Ph.D. dissertation, Department of Education, University of North Carolina, 1936). Dorothy Orr, *A History of Education in Georgia* (Chapel Hill, 1950), is better than the other state school histories in the Southern seaboard.

The most extensive and effective of the counter-propaganda pieces against the educational movement were Edward Ingle, *The Ogden Movement: An Educational Monopoly in the Making* (Baltimore, 1908), and Warren A. Candler, *Dangerous Donations and Degrading Doles . . .* (n.p. [Atlanta?], 1909).

Among the biographical studies that throw light on the struggles over public schools in the period, the more valuable are Walter R. Bowie, *Sunrise in the South: The Life of Mary-Cooke Branch Munford* (Richmond, 1942), Aubrey L. Brooks and Hugh T. Lefler (eds.), *The Papers of Walter Clark* (2 vols., Chapel Hill, 1948-50), Aubrey L. Brooks, *Walter Clark: Fighting Judge* (Chapel Hill, 1944), Josephus Daniels, *Editor in Politics* (Chapel Hill, 1941), Francis B. Simkins, *Pitchfork Ben Tillman: South Carolinian* (Baton Rouge, 1944), John A. Rice, *I Came Out of the Eighteenth Century* (New York, 1942), Ludwig Lewisohn,

Up Stream: An American Chronicle (New York, 1922), C. Vann Woodward, *Tom Watson: Agrarian Rebel* (New York, 1938), and the fragments already cited in the text of Dewey W. Grantham's biography of Hoke Smith, soon to be published. Biographical references for Charles B. Aycock, the North Carolina White Supremacy leader, include Robert D. W. Connor and Clarence H. Poe, *The Life and Speeches of Charles Brantley Aycock* (New York, 1912), Edwin A. Alderman, "Charles Brantley Aycock: An Appreciation," and other articles in the same number of the *North Carolina Historical Review*, I (July, 1924), 243-50, and the more critical Rupert B. Vance, "Aycock of North Carolina," in *Southwest Review*, XVIII (Spring, 1933), 288-306. Sidelights on Aycock are given by his campaign manager in J. Fred Rippy (ed.), *F. M. Simmons, Statesman of the New South: Memoirs and Addresses* (Durham, 1936), and by his law partner in Robert W. Winston, *It's a Far Cry* (New York, 1937).

3. *The Negro and Public Education*

Studies on the broader subject of Negro status or history include the indispensable Gunnar Myrdal and assistants, *An American Dilemma: The Negro Problem and American Democracy* (2 vols., New York, 1944), C. Vann Woodward, *The Strange Career of Jim Crow* (New York, 1955), Rayford W. Logan, *The Negro in American Life and Thought: The Nadir, 1877-1901* (New York, 1954), E. Franklin Frazier, *The Negro in the United States* (New York, 1949), John Hope Franklin, *From Slavery to Freedom* (New York, 1947), George B. Tindall, *South Carolina Negroes, 1877-1900* (Columbia, 1952), Paul Lewinson, *Race, Class and Party* (New York, 1932), Helen G. Edmonds, *The Negro and Fusion Politics in North Carolina, 1894-1901* (Chapel Hill, 1951), Charles S. Mangum, Jr., *The Legal Status of the Negro* (Chapel Hill, 1940), Guion G. Johnson, "The Ideology of White Supremacy, 1876-1910," in Fletcher M. Green (ed.), *Essays in Southern History Presented to Joseph Gregoire de Roulhac Hamilton*... (Chapel Hill, 1949), 124-56, William E. Burghardt Du Bois, *The Souls of Black Folk* (Chicago, 1903), his *Dusk of Dawn* (New York, 1940), and Ray Stannard Baker, *Following the Color Line* (New York and London, 1908).

Essay on Sources

Two works by Horace M. Bond, *Social and Economic Influences on the Public Education of Negroes in Alabama 1865-1930* (Washington, 1939), and *The Education of the Negro in the American Social Order* (New York, 1934), were very influential in this study because of their departure from the narrowly institutional approach and their clarification of the relationships between Negro and white schools.

Other illuminating studies of Negro education are August Meier, "The Vogue of Industrial Education," in *Midwest Journal* (Jefferson City, Mo., 1949-56), VII (Fall, 1955), 241-66, William E. Burghardt Du Bois (ed.), *The Negro Common School* (Atlanta, 1901), Charles L. Coon, *Public Taxation and Negro Schools* (Cheyney, Pa., 1909), Kelly Miller, "The Education of the Negro," in *Report of the Commissioner of Education for the Year 1900-1901* (2 vols., Washington, 1902), I, 731-859, and Willard Range, *The Rise and Progress of Negro Colleges in Georgia, 1865-1949* (Athens, 1951).

While this study is only indirectly related to the present issues arising out of the school segregation cases decided unconstitutional by the federal Supreme Court in 1954, some of the more important studies of segregation have been helpful. Several articles in *The Availability of Education in the Negro Separate School:* Yearbook Number of the *Journal of Negro Education*, XVI (Summer, 1947), present conclusive evidence of the racial differential. Harry S. Ashmore, *The Negro and the Schools* (Chapel Hill, 1954), is not only a good summary but a point of departure for further research. Ira de A. Reid (ed.), *Racial Desegregation and Integration: Annals* of the American Academy of Political and Social Science, Vol. 304 (Philadelphia, March, 1956), places the educational changes within a broader framework. A timely article by Leslie H. Fishel, Jr., "Can Segregated Schools Be Abolished?" in *Journal of Negro Education*, XXIII (Spring, 1954), 109-16, bases his optimism on sound scholarship. The monthly *Southern School News* has so far, since September 3, 1954, rendered a remarkably objective reporting service on the Southern schools.

Index

Abbott, Lyman, 78n, 80
Adams, Charles Francis, 81n
Adams, Spencer B., 68
Alderman, Edwin Anderson, conductor of N.C. teachers' institutes, 45-46, 48-49; describes N.C. schools, 45-46; professor in State Normal and Industrial School, 48; president of University of North Carolina, 52; eloquence of, 52; lobbies for local tax bill, 52-53; helps local tax campaign, 55; on N.C. legislature, 62, 111; president of Tulane, 62; comments on Aycock, 64-65; commended, 72; member of Southern Education Board, 77, 80n, 81n, 84n; views of on educational movement, 84-85, 88; president of University of Virginia, 87, 95n, 150-51; member of General Education Board, 88; on Negroes, 92-93, 258; aids Va. public school movement, 150-51, 157, 164-65; frustrated by Martin machine, 151-52, 156; gets state aid for university, 157-58; on Southern economic problems, 252; tuberculosis of, 258-59; mentioned, 64, 119, 123, 216n
Alexander, Hooper, 243
Andrews, Alexander B., 71
Anna T. Jeanes Foundation, 86-87, 234, 254
Ansel, Martin F., 180, 201-2
Ansell, H. B., 21n
Ashley, Joshua W., 192, 199

Atlanta *Constitution*, 211, 217, 232
Atlanta *Georgian*, 232
Atlanta *Independent*, 226-27
Atlanta *Journal*, 217, 231, 232, 244
Atlanta race riot, 97, 222
Atlanta University, 222
Aycock, Benjamin F., 103, 112
Aycock, Charles Brantley, supports local tax campaign, 55, 72; links disfranchisement and education, 63, 65, 67-68; gubernatorial campaign of, 64-68; characterized, 64-65, 68; opportunism of, 64-65, 67; tacit bargain with philanthropists, 79-80, 93; educational campaign techniques of, 93n; effect of on Negro education, 102-10, 112; aids white public schools, 110-11, 113, 115, 117, 121; agreement of with railroads hampers schools, 112-14; opposes child labor, 124n; Montague compared with, 146; criticizes A. D. Candler, 216n; Hoke Smith compared with, 242

Bacon, Augustus Octavius, 217
Bailey, Josiah W., editor of *Biblical Recorder*, 53; opposes state aid to higher education, 53, 58, 60; supports local tax law, 53, 55, 72; opposes local tax campaign, 56; bargain with Simmons, 60, 62, 111; comments on Aycock's campaign promises, 67; favors racial division of school tax funds, 70, 103; opposes public high schools, 110n, 127; op-

Index 283

aided public school movement, 116, 119-20; on child labor reform, 120, 124n; mentioned, 223n
Baker, L. T., 22n
Baker, Ray Stannard, 212
Baldwin, William Henry, Jr., 76, 77-78, 82n, 85-86, 96n
Baptists, oppose state aid to higher education, 52-53, 60, 62, 111, 116, 217; and public school movement, 52-53, 55, 56, 65, 67, 70, 110n, 116, 119-20, 149, 226
Barksdale decision, hampers N.C. education, 46-47; overthrown, 123-24
Barnard, George Gray, 83
Barnwell, J. W., 195, 197
Barrett, Charles Simon, 31, 90-91
Barringer, Paul B., 138-39, 150
Barrow, David C., 221
Bassett, John Spencer, 83, 105
Battle, Kemp P., 71n
Beasley, R. F., 95n
Bell, Hiram P., 228
Bell, Madison, 243
Berea College, 96n
B. F. Johnson Company, 153
Biblical Recorder. See Bailey, Josiah W.
Bingham, Robert, 7n, 31-32, 43n
Blackwell, Robert E., 253
Blair, Henry W., 6-7. See also Federal aid to education
Blease, Coleman L., 188, 192-94, 200, 201, 204
Blount, Thomas W., 114
Boddie, Viola, 122
Boone, Thomas D., 53, 57-58
Bourland, Albert P., 81n, 82n
Bower, legislator, of Decatur County, Ga., 228-29
Bowie, Sidney J., 82n
Boyd, Emma Garrett, 231-33
Branch, John P., 149
Branson, Eugene C., 216
Brent, Frank P., 148n
Brice, J. Steele, 192, 193
Brittain, Marion L., 27n, 28n, 224, 232, 234n
Brooks, Eugene C., 96n, 117n, 121
Broughton, Len G., 226
Brown, F. W., 125n
Brown, George H., 124
Brown, Joseph E., 240
Brown, Joseph M., 243, 244

Brown, J. M., 125n
Brown, William Garrott, 251
Bryan, John Stewart, 149
Bryan, Joseph, 149
Bryant, Victor S., 129n
Bryce, James, 130
Busbee, Fabius H., 55
Businessmen's Committee, 223-24
Butler, Marion, 56, 64
Buttrick, Wallace, member of Southern Education Board, 82; employed executive secretary of General Education Board, 86n, 180; opposes equal philanthropy for Negroes, 87n, 94; meets N.C. superintendents, 94, 117; meets S.C. superintendents, 175, 181; aids Ga. normal school, 217; emphasizes need for farm profits, 253n
Byrd, Richard E., 150

Cable, George Washington, 8n, 19
Call, James A., 125
Campbell, Clarence J., 138n
Candler, Allen D., 14n, 26n, 213, 214, 216-17
Candler, Charles Murphey, 229, 241n
Candler, Warren Akin, 179, 218, 226-27
Cannon, Reverend James, 30n, 150
Carlyle, J. B., 116n
Carnegie, Andrews, 76, 79n, 82n, 83, 87, 88n, 186, 226
Carr, Julian S., 55, 117
Caw, R. R., 255n
Central Railroad, of Georgia, 217
Chambers, Frank R., 76n, 82n
Charleston *News and Courier*, 173, 184-87, 190-91
Charlotte *Observer*, 66, 103, 120
Chatham Record, 102, 122
Child labor. See Compulsory attendance and child labor reform
Church-state controversy. See Baptists, Methodists
Clark, Walter, on teachers' pay, 27n; proposes railroad tax for schools, 70-71; denounces Aycock's agreement with railroads, 71, 113; supports schools in crucial court case, 124
Claxton, Philander P., aids local tax campaign, 55; member of Southern Education Board, 82n; on campaign

methods, 90; opposes yielding to reactionaries, 98n; aids S.C. campaign, 187; attacked by Tillman, 188
Clements, Reverend W. G., 124n
Cleveland, Grover, 6-7, 243
Columbia *State*, 181, 183, 185-87, 194, 196-97, 204n
Columbus *Enquirer-Sun*, 241
Compulsory attendance and child labor reform, South not affected by before 1900, 30, 39, 98; in N.C., 124-26; in Va., 136, 149-50; in S.C., 184, 188-98; in Ga., 230-33
Conference for Education in the South, Negroes excluded from, 78n; at Winston-Salem, 79-80, 114; retreat of from Nashville, 98; other annual conferences, 8on, 92, 150, 180-81, 183-87, 216-17, 223, 225-28, 254. *See also* Southern Education Board
Conference for the Common Good, 188
Connor, Henry Groves, 61, 69, 73, 103, 113
Connor, Robert D. W., 116, 117n
Conservative Democrats, 5-6, 8-9, 41, 46-47, 49-51, 60-74 *passim*, 135-37, 145-46, 168-69, 171, 172, 180, 183, 201, 213, 217-31 *passim*, 243-44
Convict lease, 9, 240-41
Coon, Charles L., 15n, 19n, 20-21, 108n, 182
Copeland, W. Scott, 148-49, 161
"Corn Cracker" (M. L. White), on rural teachers, 26, 27, 72; on educational progress, 72
Cornwell, J. L., 58
Courtenay, William A., 184, 190
Craig, Locke, 67n, 128-29
Cromer, George B., 191, 194n, 195n
Cronk, B. W., 22n
Cumming v. Board of Education, 213
Curry, Jabez L. M., advice on philanthropy for Negroes, 7-8, 14, 86; on Southern Education Board, 76, 77n, 82; work in South, 115, 116, 139n, 147, 216

Dabney, Charles William, member of Southern Education Board, 77, 8on, 82n; director of Board's propaganda bureau, 81-82, 89, 92-93; explains Southern conditions to philanthropists, 84; neglects propaganda for Negro education, 92-93; in Va., 147; mentioned, 120, 145, 153, 216
Dabney, Richard Heath, 138
Daniel, John W., 140
Daniels, Josephus, on Southern poverty, 35; opposes local tax campaign, 56-60; injects race issue, 56-57, 60; criticizes Page, 59; comments on Alderman, 62n; supports Mebane, 66; opposes bargain with railroads, 71-72, 113-14; on racial division of school funds, 103; attacks Bassett, 105; on state child labor committee, 124n; for six-month term, 129
Davidson, Theo, 114n
Davidson College, 53
Davis, Ben J., 226-27
Davis, Jackson, 254
DeHay, A. H., 22n
Democrats. *See* Conservative Democrats, Progressives, Reformers
Dennis, M. B., 214n, 219n
Denny, George H., 150
Desegregation, ix-x, 93, 256, 257. *See also* Segregation
Dewey, John, 89n
Dickerman, George Sinclair, 15, 81n, 82n, 86n, 149n, 216
Dillard, James Hardy, 82n, 86-87
Dillingham, Reverend Pitt, 4
Doar, Joshua W., 177, 194n
Dodd, William E., 27n, 38, 60, 68, 71n, 72, 100-1, 159n
Dooley, George L., 39n
Dooly, Isma, 225n
Dortch, William T., act for racial division of school tax funds, 47-48, 107; influence on Aycock, 64
Dreher, Julius D., 96n, 139n, 187
Drinkard, A. W., 27n
Du Bois, William E. Burghardt, criticizes treatment of Negro schools, 13-14, 15n, 18, 19n, 40n; research aided by Ogden, 83; opposes B. T. Washington, 99n
Duggan, Mell L., 218
Duke, Washington, 53n, 60
Dunston, Tom, 52

Eaton, James Y., 69
Economic conditions and schools. *See* Public education
Edmunds, S. H., 92n
Education. *See* Public education

Educational statistics, inaccuracy of, ix, 9, 29n
Eggleston, D. Q., 142-44
Eggleston, Joseph D., 145, 153-55, 159, 161, 167
Elkins, John W., 197n
Ellyson, J. Taylor, 152
Evans, John Gary, 171-72
Evans, L. W., 102
Evans, W. F., 115n

Farmers' Alliance, 37, 48-49, 50. *See also* Fusionists, Populists
Farmers' Union, 31, 91, 128, 225, 231
Federal aid to education, Hoar bill, 6; Blair bill, 6-7, 46, 79, 229; Smith-Hughes Act, 234n
Felder, Thomas S., 241
Felton, Rebecca L., 215
Flood, Hal D., 142-43
Florence, F. L., 221n
Foushee, Howard A., 62n
Franklin County, J. R. Collie v. Commissioners of, 123-24
Frazer, Robert, 137n, 147-49, 152, 154, 158
Fries, Henry E., 82n
Frissell, Hollis Burke, on nepotism in schools, 25; spokesman for Negro schools, 82n, 86, 94, 119; opposed to NAACP, 99; aids educational campaign in Va., 139n, 142n, 147, 148, 152
Fulton, J. G., 10n
Fusionists, in N.C., 50-51, 52, 54. *See also* Farmers' Alliance, Populists

Gandhi, Mohandas K., 269
Gates, Frederick T., 87n, 101n
General Education Board, interlocking membership with Southern Education Board, 76, 85-88, 100-1; activities in Southern seaboard, 94, 108n, 119-20, 127, 147, 180, 202, 217, 226, 227, 223-34, 253-54
George Peabody College for Teachers, 227n
Georgia Educational Campaign Committee, 218-21, 226, 227
Georgia public education, 5, 9-32 *passim,* 210-47 *passim,* 249-57 *passim,* 262n, 266
Gilleland, H. A., 91n
Glass, Carter, 140-43

Glenn, Gustavus R., 104-5, 214n
Glenn, Robert B., 107, 126-27
Godard, George D., 233-34
Godkin, Edwin L., 7
Gonzales, William E., 181, 197
Grady, Henry, 84
Graham, Alexander W., 107-8
Graham, Joseph B., 90n
Graham, William A., 73
Gray, James A., 224n
Green, Samuel, 184
Greene, E. G., 225n
Grice, legislator, of Pulaski County, Ga., 229
Grimsley, George A., 52n, 66n
Guthrie, William A., 66
Gwaltney, J. D., 219n
Gwyn, T. L., 140n

Hall, Joseph Hill, 231, 241, 243
Hammond, Harry, 14
Hampton, Wade, 6, 171
Hampton Institute, 43, 76n, 82, 87, 94, 146, 147, 216
Hand, William H., 27n, 28n, 29n, 186, 188, 191, 202-3
Hanna, Hugh H., 82n
Hanson, John Fletcher, 230
Harris, Nathaniel E., 217, 244
Harrison, Thomas W., 141n
Hemphill, James C., 161
Heyward, Duncan Clinch, 180-83, 200
Hill, Isaac W., 25n
Hill, Walter B., 82n, 91n, 217-18, 220, 221
Hill, Mrs. Walter B., 221, 225
Hill, Walter B., Jr., 225n
Hodgson, Harry, 225n, 227n
Hogg, Alexander, 7n
Holder, John N., 229, 241n
Hope, John, 263
Houston, David F., 82n
Howard, George, 50, 61, 69n
Howell, Clark, 217, 222, 225
Hoyt, James A., 181, 186
Hughes, Dudley M., 234n

Inabinet, John W., 22n
Industrialists and public education, 38-39, 45, 46, 60, 62, 97-98, 121, 126, 137, 178, 183-85, 188-91, 195, 223-24, 230
Ingle, Edward, 99n
Inman, Samuel M., 223n, 225

James, Henry, 31
Jarvis, Thomas J., 55, 60-62, 121
Jeanes Foundation, Anna T., 86-87, 234, 254
Jefferson, Thomas, vii, 6, 135, 150, 158
Jeffersonian ends and means, 91
Jenkins, John Wilber, 112
John F. Slater Fund, 7-8, 14, 77n, 85-86, 234
Johnson, A. F., 129
Johnson, David B., 179, 181
Johnson, Lillian W., 76n
Johnson, Livingston, 129n
Jones, A. C., 201
Jones, Thomas Jesse, 260-61
Jones, William A., 137n
Joyner, James Y., as educational promoter, 26, 72, 110, 116-17, 123, 126, 128, 248; on Negro schools, 106, 108; becomes N.C. state superintendent, 111, 113; for child labor reform, 124n; mentioned, 64
J. R. Collie v. Commissioners of Franklin County, 123-24
Junior Order of United American Mechanics, 128

Keezell, George B., 142, 161
Kennedy, E. J., 173, 174n
Kent, Charles W., 150, 152
Kilgo, John Carlisle, 53, 60, 62, 69-70, 116, 126n
King, D. T., 125n
King's Daughters, 188
Kirkland, James Hampton, 82n, 226
Kohn, August, 190n

Labor unions, 39n, 195, 231
Lane, Joe P., 27n
Laurens *Advertiser*, 187
Littleton, Ga. legislator, 232
Livingston, Knox, 196n
London, Henry A., 102-3
Long, W. G., 125n
Love, Va. legislator, 159n
Lovett, J. A. B., 7n
Low, Seth, 186

McGhee, W. Zachariah, 23n, 181n, 201
McGilvray, John A., 153, 154n
McIlwaine, Richard, 139, 143

McIver, Charles Duncan, conductor of N.C. teachers' institutes, 46, 48-49; president of State Normal and Industrial School, 48; advocates local tax law, 52-53; leads local tax campaign, 55-60; denounces Democratic bargain with church colleges, 62; member of Southern Education Board, 77, 80n, 81n, 88; views of on public education, 84-85, 91; directs N.C. public school campaign, 115-18, 121; attacked by Bailey, 119-20; aids campaigns in other states, 148, 181-82, 201, 218, 219n; mentioned, 64, 216n
McKelway, Alexander Jeffrey, 106-7, 119, 124n, 126, 242n
McLaurin, John L., 193
McMahan, John J., 174n, 175-76, 180, 190, 201
McMichael, E. H., 220, 224-25, 237n
MacRae, James C., 49n
Maddox, C. S., 92n, 211
Madison, R. L., 124n
Mann, William Hodges, 158, 160-61, 162n
Manning, Richard I., 200-1, 202n, 204
Manufacturers' Record, 97-98, 120n, 185, 226, 227
Marble, A. P., 7n
Martin, Oscar B., S.C. state superintendent, 178, 180, 182, 193, 201n
Martin, Thomas S., machine boss, 137, 154, 157, 165; opposes educational reformers, 151-52, 155-56, 165, 168-69
Massey, John E., 136
May Campaign in Va., 151-56
Mayfield, W. D., 171
Mayo, Amory D., 7n, 54
Means, Paul B., 66
Mebane, B. Frank, 52
Mebane, Charles H., Populist state superintendent, 51-52, 56, 60, 72-73; advice to Negroes, 57n; runs for renomination, 66; secretary of N.C. educational campaign committee, 117n
Meredith, Charles V., 144
Merritt, William B., 218, 220, 221, 224n, 225, 242n
Methodists, oppose state aid to higher education, 53, 60, 62, 111, 116, 217,

226; and public schools, 53, 69-70, 182, 197, 218, 226
Mitchell, Julian, 172-73
Mitchell, Samuel Chiles, 82n, 98n, 149-50, 154n
Montague, Andrew J., 146, 151, 156-57
Moore, Marshall, 195n
Moore, Y. D., 91n
Morehouse College, 263
Munford, Mary Cooke-Branch, 149
Murphy, Edgar Gardner, on racism, 76, 85, 95, 254; organizes race conference, 77; member of Southern Education Board, 81, 82n; on Kirkland, 82n; on Ogden, 83; resigns from ministry, 84; on Southern leadership, 85, 95; on Negro schools, 93n, 97, 254, 255n; child labor crusader, 98, 126, 184; on results of educational campaigns, 248, 249, 251, 254, 264

Nance, Mary T., 22n
Nation, The, 6-7, 86
National Association for the Advancement of Colored People, 99-100
Negro, assumptions of this study about, x-xi; attitude of Southern Education Board toward, xi, 75-81, 86-87, 92-100, 254-55, 269; protest movement at Harper's Ferry, 223
Negro disfranchisement, threatens Negro schools, 40; spurs white education, 40-41; diverts agrarians to education, 41; in N.C., 63-70; in Ga., 97, 221-22, 231; in Va., 137, 139n, 146; in S.C., 171-72; effect of, 255
Negro education, compared with white, viii-ix, 8-20 *passim*, 27, 39-40, 43, 55, 94, 100, 105-11, 119, 126, 131-34, 136, 139-46 *passim*, 163-64, 166-68, 170, 175-78, 195, 204-9, 212-13, 224, 235-36, 245-47, 254-64, 269; industrial schools favored by philanthropists, 8, 86, 94, 100n, 186n; Fifteenth Amendment and, 9; in N.C., 47-48, 55-62 *passim*, 67-70, 74, 102-10, 116-28 *passim*, 129n, 131-34; state colleges for, 49, 134, 146, 166, 204n, 247, 256, 261; Southern Education Board on, 75, 78-80, 86, 92-97, 100; educational campaigners neglect, 92-93, 95-96;

in Va., 137-46, 154, 162-69; in S.C., 170-200 *passim*, 204-9; in Ga., 210-13, 217-34 *passim*, 235-37, 239-40, 245-47; in Southern seaboard about 1915, 250, 251, 254-65, 268-69. See also Racism, School tax funds, Segregation
Newbold, Nat C., 108n
New York *Evening Post*, 6-7
Niagara Movement, 99-100
Noel, legislator, of Lee County, Va., 268n
North Carolina Agricultural and Technical College, 49, 134
North Carolina Central Campaign Committee, 115-18
North Carolina public education, 9-32 *passim*, 45-74, 77, 79-80, 88, 90, 91n, 93, 95, 102-34, 246n, 249-57 *passim*, 262n, 266, 267
North Carolina Society of N.Y., 102
(North Carolina) State Normal and Industrial School, founded, 48; becomes a college, 59n; Page speaks at, 59; endangered, 62; Joyner at, 110; Viola Boddie at, 122. *See also* McIver, Charles Duncan
Northen, William J., 215, 218, 223, 232

Ogden, Robert Curtis, on race problems, 75, 77n, 78n, 83, 94-98; leader of Southern Education movement, 75-76, 79-82, 85-87, 93; philosophy and methods of, 78-80, 82-83, 94-99; on segregation, 93n, 96-97; in Va., 150, 152-53, 156-57; in S.C., 181, 185-87; in Ga., 216, 217-19, 227, 228; praised by Page, 251; death, 254
Orr, Gustavus J., 213n
Orr, James L., 189
Otken, Charles H., 24
Ottley, Mrs. Passie Fenton, 232
Outlook, The, 80, 106

Page, Walter Hines, on superintendents, 28-29; on "mummies," 46; on "Forgotten Man," 59; on Southern Education Board, 76, 82n; on Negro, 77n, 78n, 97; investments of, 79n; speech in N.C., 117; on Tompkins, 126; on Ogden, 251; mentioned, 121, 216

Parker, Lewis W., 183, 190
Parker, Thomas F., 189-90
Parker, W. S., 58
Parkhurst, Charles H., 80-81, 216
Parrish, Celestia S., 221n
Payne, Bruce R., 28n, 82n, 150, 155, 158
Peabody, George Foster, member of Southern Education Board, 75-76, 77n, 81, 82n, 86, 87n, 97, 158n; urges aid to Negro schools, 97, 222; aids Ga. schools, 217, 234
Peabody Education Fund, 7-8, 14, 77n, 85-86, 100, 105, 108n, 184, 203, 213n, 216, 227n, 228, 254
Pell, Robert P., 179
Phelps-Stokes Fund, 87, 254, 260
Philanthropy. See individual organizations, Negro education
Pike County Journal, 244n
Plessy v. Ferguson, x, 12, 213
Poe, Clarence H., 128
Polk, Leonidas L., 49
Ponies, used by teachers, 25n
Poppenheim, Louisa B., 186n, 191n
Populists, 9, 37, 41, 42, 50-52, 56, 62, 64, 66, 88, 171, 213, 237. See also Farmers' Alliance, Fusionists
Pound, Jere M., 219
Presbyterian Standard, 119
Pritchard, Jeter C., 66, 69n
Privott, R. N., 102n
Progressive Farmer, 49, 128
Progressives, 37-38, 85, 185, 221. See also Reformers
Pruden, William D., 57
Public education, black counties and white counties compared, viii-ix, 16-18, 108-10, 118-19, 123, 140-44, 166-68, 206-8, 210-11, 235-40, 259-61, 265-67; urban and rural compared, ix, 11-12, 15-16, 24, 110, 115, 118, 128, 133-34, 143, 167-68, 173, 178, 203, 206-9, 211-12, 224, 237-40, 262-65, 268; early developments in, 3-5, 15; contrast with non-Southern schools, 3-4, 9-11, 31-32, 130, 164, 251-53; under Redeemers, 5-6, 8-9; enrollment and attendance, 9-10, 13, 72, 130, 135-36, 163, 203, 208, 224, 245, 249; school term, 9-10, 13-14, 47, 52, 54, 67, 72, 73, 105, 111, 113-14, 124, 128-30, 135, 141, 163-64, 174, 198, 200, 203, 208, 224, 249; teachers, 10, 13, 17-18, 22-28, 58, 72, 89, 109, 111, 132-33, 135, 148, 163-64, 182, 195, 204, 208, 212, 214-15, 224, 242-46, 250, 257-58; schoolhouses, property, and equipment, 10, 13, 18, 20-23, 45, 110, 131-32, 148, 155, 158, 163, 168, 176, 201, 203, 208, 209, 212, 246, 250; school finance, 10, 13, 19, 31-36, 46-48, 52, 54, 62-63, 70-72, 91-92, 106, 111-14, 118, 130-32, 135-36, 141-42, 158, 160, 162-64, 170-79 *passim*, 188, 199-201, 203-9, 210-12, 218-20, 224, 235, 240-45, 248-50, 265-68; effect of economic and social conditions on, 11, 27n, 30-46, 50, 58, 59, 73-74, 84, 90-91, 117-18, 124, 125, 179, 183-84, 188-91, 198, 203, 210-13, 237-40, 251-53; private schools compared with, 23-24; superintendence, 25, 28-30, 131, 136-37, 145, 174, 180, 215, 246; high schools, 28, 110n, 127-28, 133, 142, 158, 160, 163, 202-3, 208, 234, 247, 250, 256; black and white districts in S.C. compared, 175-78, 209; conditions about 1915, 248-69 *passim*. See also Compulsory attendance, Georgia public education, Negro education, North Carolina public education, South Carolina public education, Virginia public education
Purdom, J. M., 221n

Quarles, James A., 135n
Quarles, J. M., 30n

Racism, in Southern seaboard, vii, 8-9, 38, 40-44, 75-76, 79, 93-98, 251, 254-59, 269; in N.C., 40-41, 45, 55-57, 60-62, 63, 67-70, 74, 93, 94, 95n, 102-12 *passim*, 116-17, 120, 121, 125; in Va., 40, 137-45 *passim*, 165, 169; in S.C., 40, 170-73, 178, 184-85, 187, 193-98, 200-1, 204; in Ga., 40, 216, 217, 221-23, 227-31, 233, 247; in the North, 43, 77-81; philanthropists and, 77-81, 92-97
Railroads and public education, 45, 60, 62, 71, 72-73, 76n, 97n, 110, 112-13, 121, 137, 159, 161, 178, 217, 224, 225n, 230, 242, 267

Index

Raleigh *News and Observer*. *See* Daniels, Josephus
Raysor, Thomas M., 196n
Readjusters, 135, 136
Reconstruction, 3, 5, 6, 8, 15, 22, 46, 135, 170, 171n, 192, 213n
Redeemers, 5-6, 8-9, 46, 61, 135
Reed, W. N., 136n
Reformers, 171, 192, 221, 230-31, 241-44. *See also* Progressives
Republicans, 29, 50, 51, 66, 68, 69, 106, 120-21, 137, 167, 184. *See also* Fusionists, Readjusters
Rice, John A., 26
Richards, John G., 194n, 197
Richmond Education Association, 148-49
Richmond *Times*, 148
Richmond *Times-Dispatch*, 149-50, 155, 156, 158, 161
Rockefeller, John D., 82, 85, 86, 87, 101
Roesel, A. V., 30n
Rose, Wickliffe, 81n, 82n, 86n, 228n
Rosenwald, Julius, 87, 254
Rosenwald Foundation, ix, 133, 234
Ross, Frank A., 258
Ruffner, William H., 135
Russell, Daniel L., 66
Russell Sage Foundation, 76n
Ryan, Thomas Fortune, 88n

Salley, A. S., Jr., 195n
Salley, N. M., 178
Schools. *See* Public education
School tax funds, efforts to divide, 19, 47-48, 58, 61-62, 69, 70, 95, 102-8, 140-44, 158-59, 174, 175-78, 228-30
Segregation, x, 5, 8, 15, 38, 39, 44, 78, 93, 204, 247, 255-57, 263, 269. See also *Plessy v. Ferguson*, Racism, "Separate but equal" doctrine
"Separate but equal" doctrine, x, 12, 93, 98, 105-6
Shaw, Albert, 78n, 81n, 82n
Shearer, James B., 53
Sheats, W. N., 100n
Shepard, Edward M., 186
Simmons, Furnifold M., 60, 62, 64, 67n, 105, 111, 112
Simons, James, 185-87
Slater Fund, John F., 7-8, 14, 77n, 85-86, 234
Slaton, John M., 244
Small, John H., 66, 117
Smith, Ellison D., 199
Smith, Hoke, rejected for membership in Southern Education Board, 82n; supports Ga. educational campaign, 217, 218; hostility of to Negroes, 217, 221, 227; gubernatorial campaign of, 221; aids schools, 224, 235, 242-44; hostility of to Ogden movement, 225, 227-28; on Peabody Board, 227n, 228; leader of reform faction, 230, 242-44; disfranchises Negroes, 231; sponsors Smith-Hughes Act, 234n; opposes convict lease, 241; compared with Aycock, 242
Smith, James M., 222, 240n
Smith, L. L., 58, 114n
Smith, William W., 150
Smyth, Ellison A., 190, 191n
Snell, J. H., 125n
Snyder, Henry N., 197
Southall, Joseph W., 136, 138, 144, 145, 147-48, 153
South Carolina constitutional convention, 171-74
South Carolina Cotton Manufacturers' Association, 190
South Carolina Educational Campaign Committee, 180-82
South Carolina public education, 6, 9-32 *passim*, 170-209, 249-57 *passim*, 262n, 266
Southern Education Board, objectives, 75-76, 79, 85, 88-89, 97; attitude toward Negroes, 75-81, 86-87, 92-100; membership and organization, 75-82, 85-88; activities in South, 76n, 102, 115-16, 146-53, 156-58, 179-82, 184-88, 202, 215-22, 225-28, 233; finances, 76n; criticism of, 93-94, 97-101, 119-20, 136n, 156-57, 184-87, 216, 226-28; accomplishments of, 248-51, 254; failure to aid Negroes, 254-55, 258-59, 268-69
Stearnes, Reaumur C., 149, 165
Stewart, Joseph S., 202, 234
Stone, Ormond, 151
Stovall, legislator, of Chatham County, Ga., 229

Summer School of the South, 89
Swanson, Claude A., 156-58, 160
Swearingen, John E., 170, 188
Swindell, W. B., 39n

Tate, William K., 30n, 175n, 188, 203
Tax funds. *See* School tax funds
Taylor, Charles E., 116
Terrell, Joseph M., 218, 227, 241, 242
Thomas, A. F., 158-59
Tillman, Benjamin R., 171-74, 178, 188n, 191, 193-94, 198, 201
Tompkins, Daniel A., 55, 126
Toon, Thomas F., 65-67, 111
Trinity College, 53, 105
Tucker, Henry St. George, 147-49, 160
Turnbull, Robert, 140n
Tuskegee Institute, 42-43, 76n, 87, 186n

Union League Club, N.Y., 96, 97n
Unions, labor, 39n, 195, 231
United Daughters of the Confederacy, 217
United States Industrial Commission, 4, 14, 18n, 61n, 73, 106
University of Georgia, 217-18, 221
University of North Carolina, 49, 52, 55, 62, 64, 71, 111, 127
University of Virginia, 87, 88n, 95n, 138, 150-52, 157-58
Utley, Charles H., 55-56

Valentine, Ben B., 149
Valentine, Lila Meade, 149
Vanderbilt University, 82n, 226, 227n

Vardaman, James K., 93
Vawter, Charles E., 150, 152
Venable, Francis P., 71n
Villard, Oswald Garrison, 99
Virginia constitutional convention, 137-44
Virginia public education, 5, 9-32 *passim*, 135-69, 249-68 *passim*

Waddell, Alfred M., 67n
Waddill, S. P., 144
Walker, Nathan W., 127
Warren, Mortimer A., 23n
Washington, Booker T., conservative Negro leader, 42-43, 78n, 81n, 94, 99-100; activities in South, 105, 119, 186, 216, 229, 259, 269
Watson, Robert B., 174n
Watson, Thomas E., 221
Watson, Walter A., 139, 141-42
Watson, Z. V., 125n
Wharton, W. Carl, 30n
White, George Henry, 61n, 106
White, Reverend John E., 60, 223
White, M. L. *See* "Corn Cracker"
Wiley, Calvin H., 46
Williams, Alfred B., 98n
Williams, William T. B., 147
Winborne, N.C. legislator, 107
Wofford College, 182, 197
Wood, Wade H., 215n
Wooding, W. H., 30n, 211n
Woofter, Thomas J., Jr., 196n

X for signature, Aycock's mother uses, 64; many S.C. white voters use, 195